Military Intelligence and Revolt

This book examines the use and exploitation of intelligence in formulating Britain's strategy for the Arab Revolt in the First World War. It also presents a radical re-examination of the achievements of T.E. Lawrence (Lawrence of Arabia) as an intelligence officer and guerrilla leader. Modern intelligence techniques such as Sigint, Imint and Humint were incorporated into strategic planning with greater expertise and consistency in Arabia than in any other theatre during the war and their deployment as tactical support for the Arab forces was decisive. The unprecedented involvement of intelligence officers in active operations and decision-making on the ground led to important contradictions with official policy in London; it would also stand as a precursor for the famous intelligence accomplishments of the SOE (Special Operations Executive) twenty-five years later in the Second World War.

Using much previously unpublished material, this study shows conclusively how Britain's intelligence community in Arabia influenced the conduct of the Arab campaign, promoted a full-scale guerrilla war and thereby facilitated the Arab armies' march north into Syria and Palestine, and the modern Middle East. The book contributes to an unveiling of another hidden corner of the history of Middle East, and to better understanding of the significance of intelligence in formulating strategic processes in the modern era.

This book will be of much interest to students of intelligence studies, military history, Middle Eastern history, guerrilla warfare and insurgency.

Polly A. Mohs is an historian and holds a Ph.D from the University of Cambridge.

Studies in intelligence series
General editors: Richard J. Aldrich and Christopher Andrew
ISSN: 1368–9916

The growing interest in intelligence activities and the opening of hitherto closed archives since the end of the Cold War has stimulated this series of scholarly monographs, wartime memoirs and edited collections. With contributions from leading academics and prominent members of the intelligence community, this series has quickly become the leading forum for the academic study of intelligence.

British Military Intelligence in the Palestine Campaign 1914–1918
Yigal Sheffy

British Military Intelligence in the Crimean War, 1854–1856
Stephen M. Harris

Signals Intelligence in World War II
Edited by David Alvarez

Knowing Your Friends
Intelligence inside alliances and coalitions from 1914 to the Cold War
Edited by Martin S. Alexander

Eternal Vigilance
50 years of the CIA
Edited by Rhodri Jeffreys-Jones and Christopher Andrew

Nothing Sacred
Nazi espionage against the Vatican, 1939–1945
David Alvarez and Revd Robert A. Graham

Intelligence Investigations
How Ultra changed history
Ralph Bennett

Intelligence Analysis and Assessment
Edited by David Charters, A. Stuart Farson and Glenn P. Hastedt

TET 1968
Understanding the surprise
Ronnie E. Ford

Intelligence and Imperial Defence
British Intelligence and the defence of the Indian Empire 1904–1924
Richard J. Popplewell

Espionage
Past, present, future?
Edited by Wesley K. Wark

The Australian Security Intelligence Organization
An unofficial history
Frank Cain

Policing Politics
Security intelligence and the liberal democratic state
Peter Gill

From Information to Intrigue
Studies in Secret Service based on the Swedish Experience 1939–45
C.G. McKay

Dieppe Revisited
A documentary investigation
John Campbell

More Instructions from the Centre
Christopher and Oleg Gordievsky

Controlling Intelligence
Edited by Glenn P. Hastedt

Spy Fiction, Spy Films and Real Intelligence
Edited by Wesley K. Wark

Security and Intelligence in a Changing World
New perspectives for the 1990s
Edited by A. Stuart Farson, David Stafford and Wesley K. Wark

A Don at War
Sir David Hunt K.C.M.G., O.B.E. (reprint)

Intelligence and Military Operations
Edited by Michael I. Handel

Leaders and Intelligence
Edited by Michael I. Handel

War, Strategy and Intelligence
Michael I. Handel

Strategic and Operational Deception in the Second World War
Edited by Michael I. Handel

Codebreaker in the Far East
Alan Stripp

Intelligence for Peace
Edited by Hesi Carmel

Intelligence Services in the Information Age
Michael Herman

Espionage and the Roots of the Cold War
The conspiratorial heritage
David McKnight

Swedish Signal Intelligence 1900–1945
C.G. McKay and Bengt Beckman

The Norwegian Intelligence Service 1945–1970
Olav Riste

Secret Intelligence in the Twentieth Century
Edited by Heike Bungert, Jan G. Heitmann and Michael Wala

The CIA, the British Left and the Cold War
Calling the tune?
Hugh Wilford

Our Man in Yugoslavia
The story of a Secret Service operative
Sebastian Ritchie

Understanding Intelligence in the Twenty-First Century
Journeys in shadows
Len Scott and Peter Jackson

MI6 and the Machinery of Spying
Philip H.J. Davies

Twenty-First Century Intelligence
Edited by Wesley Wark

Intelligence and Strategy
Selected essays
John Robert Ferris

The US Government, Citizen Groups and the Cold War
The state–private network
Edited by Helen Laville and Hugh Wilford

Peacekeeping Intelligence
New players, extended boundaries
Edited by David Carment and Martin Rudner

Special Operations Executive
A new instrument of war
Edited by Mark Seaman

Mussolini's Propaganda Abroad
Subversion in the Mediterranean and the Middle East, 1935–1940
Manuela A. Williams

The Politics and Strategy of Clandestine War
Special operations executive, 1940–1946
Neville Wylie

Britain's Secret War against Japan, 1937–1945
Douglas Ford

US Covert Operations and Cold War Strategy
Truman, secret warfare and the CIA, 1945–53
Sarah-Jane Corke

Stasi
Shield and sword of the party
John C. Schmeidel

Military Intelligence and the Arab Revolt
The first modern intelligence war
Polly A. Mohs

Military Intelligence and the Arab Revolt

The first modern intelligence war

Polly A. Mohs

LONDON AND NEW YORK

First published 2008
by Routledge
2 Park Square, Milton Park, Abingdon, Oxon, OX14 4RN

Simultaneously published in the USA and Canada
by Routledge
270 Madison Ave, New York NY 10016

Routledge is an imprint of the Taylor & Francis Group, an informa business

Transferred to Digital Printing 2009

Typeset in Times by Wearset Ltd, Boldon, Tyne and Wear

British Library Cataloguing in Publication Data
A catalogue record for this book is available from the British Library

Library of Congress Cataloging in Publication Data
A catalog record for this book has been requested

ISBN10: 0-415-37280-1 (hbk)
ISBN10: 0-415-49331-5 (pbk)
ISBN10: 0-203-94462-3 (ebk)

ISBN13: 978-0-415-37280-0 (hbk)
ISBN13: 978-0-415-49331-4 (pbk)
ISBN13: 978-0-203-94462-2 (ebk)

To my parents, Mary and Fred Mohs

Now the reason the enlightened prince and the wise general conquer the enemy whenever they move and their achievements surpass those of ordinary men is foreknowledge. [...] What is called 'foreknowledge' cannot be elicited from spirits, nor from gods, nor by analogy with past events nor from calculations. It must be obtained from men who know the enemy situation.

Sun Tzu, *The Art of War*

We called ourselves 'Intrusive' as a band; for we meant to break into the accepted halls of English foreign policy, and build a new people in the East, despite the rails laid down for us by our ancestors. Therefore from our hybrid intelligence office in Cairo [...] we began to work upon all chiefs, far and near.

T.E. Lawrence, *Seven Pillars of Wisdom*

Contents

Foreword

Very few British officials stationed in the Middle East have aroused as much interest as T.E. Lawrence. His justly celebrated *Seven Pillars of Wisdom* has remained continuously in print ever since it was first published in 1922. The fact that Polly Mohs has been able to cast so much new and important light on a career which has been so extensively studied for over eighty years is a remarkable achievement. The history of the Arab Revolt has also generated a large literature. Dr Mohs, however, is the first to establish its claims to be 'the first modern intelligence war'.

This is the first book to demonstrate the important role of both signals intelligence (Sigint) and imagery intelligence (Imint), as well as intelligence from human sources (Humint), in the career of Lawrence and in the course of the Arab Revolt. There were few aspects of international relations which twentieth-century historians found more difficult to cope with than Sigint. At the end of the Second World War, GCHQ (the British Sigint agency) wanted to keep Ultra (the intelligence derived from breaking high-grade enemy ciphers) secret indefinitely, but did not expect to be able to do so for more than a few years. The clues, it believed, were simply too obvious for historians to miss: '[T]he comparing of the German and British documents is bound to arouse suspicion in [historians'] minds that we succeeded in reading the enemy ciphers.' For almost thirty years after the war, however, the great majority of historians suspected no such thing. Some of the clues which they overlooked now seem remarkably straightforward. It was common knowledge, for example, that British cryptanalysts had broken German ciphers during the First World War; indeed one well-publicised German decrypt – the Zimmermann telegram – may even have hastened American entry into the war. But, until the revelation of the Ultra secret in 1973, almost no historian even considered the possibility that German ciphers had been extensively broken during the Second World War as well as the First. Even more remarkably, it has taken another thirty years for the importance of Sigint in the Arab Revolt to be demonstrated for the first time by Dr Mohs.

During the First World War Imint played only a marginal role in the trench warfare on the Western Front, where reconnaissance aircraft were unable to penetrate more than a few miles beyond the front line. Polly Mohs shows for the first time that the Imint revolution began not in Europe but in the Middle East during the Arab Revolt, where aerial reconnaissance was usually able to benefit from both clear skies and a lack of enemy aircraft. T.E. Lawrence was probably the first to grasp its full potential, clearing landing grounds for reconnaissance aircraft on his own initiative and coordinating flight plans to meet the Arabs' operational needs, as well as paying detailed attention to the maps required.

Dr Mohs's pioneering work deserves to act as an inspiration to other historians of the twentieth century. Indeed, within the Cambridge University Intelligence Seminar, of which she is a distinguished member, it has already done so. Though the role of Sigint and Imint during the Second World War is now well established, much remains to be discovered about their role in the Cold War. Indeed, most histories of the Cold War make no mention of Sigint at all. Their authors will find much of importance to ponder in this path-breaking book. The combination of Sigint and Imint, whose potential was first demonstrated during the Arab Revolt, later helped to stabilize the Cold War. The arms control and arms limitation agreements of the later Cold War were dependent on verification by Sigint and Imint, euphemistically termed 'national technical means'. Their importance was specifically recognized by the START treaty of 1989, which cut strategic nuclear arsenals by about 30 per cent and required both the United States and the Soviet Union 'not to interfere with the national technical means of verification of the other Party' and 'not to use concealment measures that impede verification by national technical means'.

There is much more to this remarkable, well-rounded book even than its understanding of the role of 'national technical means'. It shows, more broadly, how much the relatively new field of intelligence history can contribute to the political, military and international history of the twentieth century. 'The Arab Revolt', Dr Mohs concludes, 'was one of the British success stories of the Great War'. Her sophisticated grasp of intelligence history enables her to explain why.

Christopher Andrew
Professor of Modern and Contemporary History
University of Cambridge

Acknowledgements

I am deeply grateful to Professor Christopher Andrew for his encouragement and generous support throughout this work. I am most indebted to Dr Zara Steiner for her invaluable time and counsel during the preparation of this manuscript. I am grateful to Dr Martin Thomas for his support and engagement with the material. I extend most eternal thanks to Dr Andrew Webster for his essential review of this work at a key stage.

This research has benefited greatly from personal assistance. I want to thank Christine McCrum and A.J.B. fforde for sharing records pertaining to their grandfather, Arthur Browlow fforde. I am particularly grateful to Patience E. Clayton (Marshall) and Dr. John Clayton for their observations on their father, Brigadier-General Gilbert Clayton; to Mr Martin Dane for his reminiscences of his grandfather, Sir Reginald Wingate; to Mr Oliver D.H. Clauson for his notes on his father, Gerard Clauson. I express warmest appreciation to M.R.D. Foot for his steady support. I am also grateful to John Ferris, Michael Herman, Michael Handel (in memoriam), Alan Stripp, Gaines Post, Martin Alexander and David Reynolds for their helpful observations on this research along the way.

I am indebted to the staffs of the archives, museums and libraries for their assistance in making their collections available for this research. I want to thank the staff at the National Archives, Kew; in particular Hugh Alexander of the Image Department, National Archives. I am most grateful to Jane Hogan and her staff at the Sudan Archive, University of Durhan; Mr Muir and his staff at the India Office Library; Mr Roderick Suddaby and the staff of the Department of Documents, Imperial War Museum; Andrew Riley, Claire Knight and the staff at the Churchill College Archives, Cambridge; and Godfrey Waller and the staff at the Manuscripts Department, Cambridge University Library, Cambridge.

For permission to quote from copyrighted material I am indebted to the following: Mrs Patience Clayton (Marshall) for the papers of Gilbert Clayton; Mr Martin Dane for the papers of Sir Reginald Wingate; Mr Oliver D.H. Clauson for the papers of Gerard Clauson; the Churchill Archives at Churchill College, University of Cambridge for extracts from George Lloyd's papers. Crown copyright material in the National Archives [formerly Public Record Office], Kew, is reproduced by permission of the Controller of Her Majesty's Stationery Office. Every effort has been made to locate and acknowledge copyright holders and for any inadvertent infringement, I apologize. Any errors of fact or judgement appearing in these chapters are, of course, entirely my own.

I was extremely fortunate to have met Roy Barlow, Senior Graphics Designer at Pandls, who designed this book's map of the Hejaz. The clarity and elegance of his design have been the greatest asset in the presentation of this history.

Finally, I would like to thank my family and friends for their unstinting support; without their care and interest, this book could never have been written. In particular I want to acknowledge Kirsten Bramsen, Nicole Herbst, Dr Barbara Metzger, Deirdre Collings, Rafal Rohozinski, Sue Chadwick, Dr Catarina Cardoso, Dr Russell Anderson, Dr Su Dalgleish, Ann Cotton, Dr Eleanor O'Gorman, Dr Shilpa Davé, Kate Knowles, Tommy McGhee and Rafael Kadushin. I give special thanks to Dr Alistair Thomas whose inspiration and confidence has been a mainstay throughout this work. I dedicate this book to my parents, Mary and Fred Mohs, in gratitude for their enthusiasm, interest and love.

Abbreviations

ADM	Archives of the British Admiralty, National Archive
AIR	Archives of the Royal Flying Corps and Royal Air Force, National Archive
Arbur	Telegraphic address of the Arab Bureau, Cairo
BEF	British Expeditionary Force (Western Front)
CAB	Archives of the British Cabinet Office, National Archives
CGS	Chief of General Staff
CID	Committee of Imperial Defence
CIGS	Chief of the Imperial General Staff
CO	Commanding Officer
CPO	Chief Political Officer
CUP	Committee of Union and Progress (Turkey)
Dirmilint	Telegraphic address of the Director of Military Intelligence, London
DMI	Director (Directorate) of Military Intelligence (London)
DMO	Director (Directorate) of Military Operations
DNI	Director of Naval Intelligence
Egyptforce	Telegraphic address for Egyptian Expeditionary Force (British)
FO	British Foreign Office (London)
GHQ	General Headquarters
GLLD	Papers of George A. Lloyd, Churchill Archives Centre, Churchill College, Cambridge
GOC	General Officer Commanding
GOC-in-C	General Officer Commanding-in-Chief
GS	General Staff
Hardinge Papers	Papers of Charles Hardinge, Lord Hardinge of Penshurst, Churchill Archives Centre, Churchill College, Cambridge
HEF	Hejaz Expeditionary Force (Turkish)
HMG	His Majesty's Government
HMS	His Majesty's Ship
Humint	Human intelligence
IEF 'D'	Indian Expeditionary Force 'D'

Imint	Imagery intelligence
IWM	Imperial War Museum
IO	India Office
IOLR	India Office Library Records, London
l.	*lire* (shorthand for Turkish *lire*)
L/P&S	Political and secret papers of the British India Office, India Office Library and Records, London
MEF	Mediterranean Expeditionary Force
MI	A section of the Military Intelligence Directorate, Egypt
MSS	Manuscripts
OC	Officer Commanding
PEF	Palestine Exploration Fund
PID	Political Intelligence Department
PoW	Prisoner-of-War
QF	Quick-firing
RFC	Royal Flying Corps
RR	Railway
Sigint	Signals intelligence
SNO	Senior Naval Officer
SOE	Special Operations Executive
SSI	Secretary of State for India
SSO	Special Service Officer
tel.	Telegram
USS	Under Secretary of State
W/C, W.C.	Wireless communication
WO	British War Office (London)
W/T	Wireless transmission

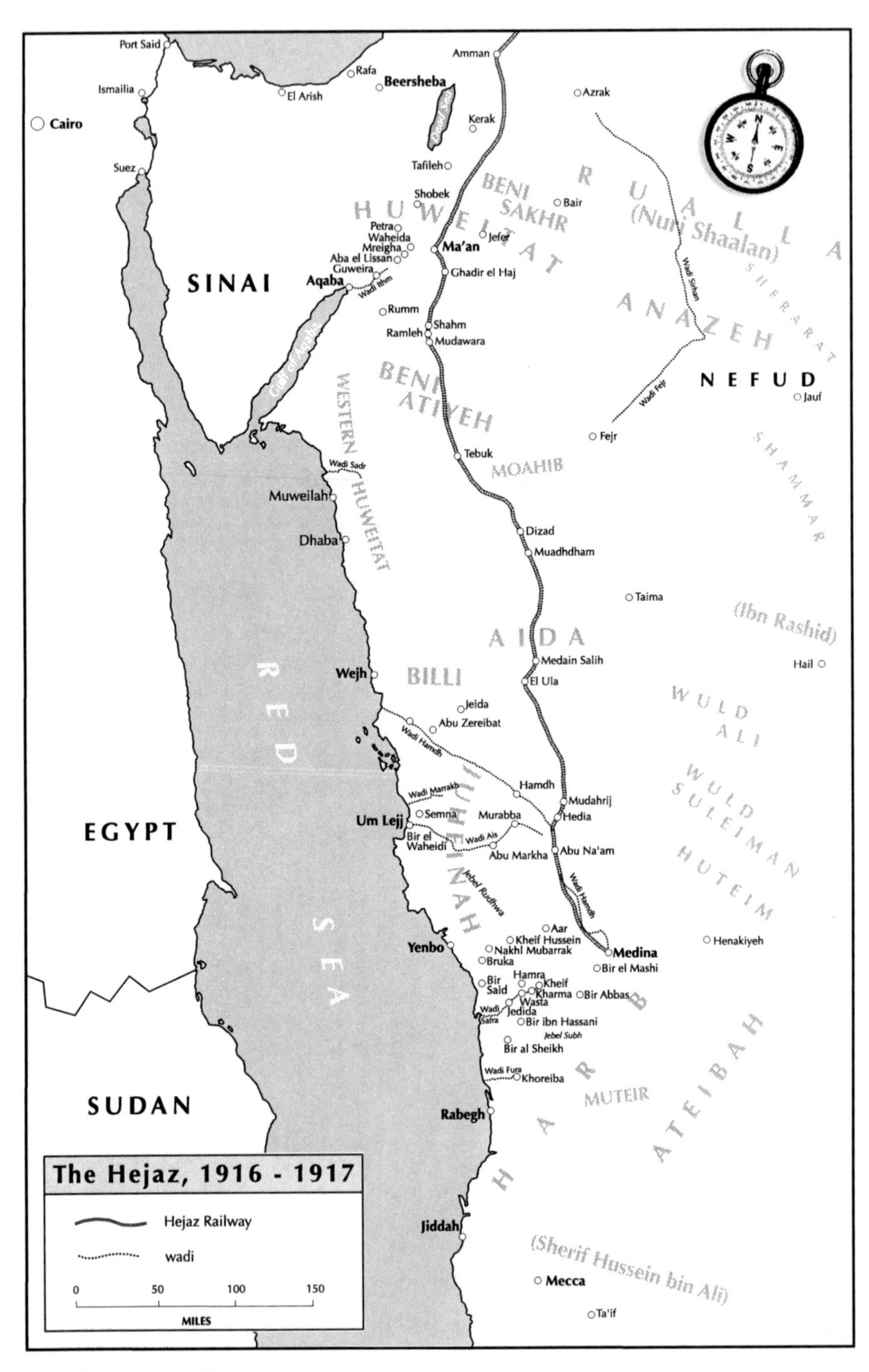

The Hejaz, 1916–17.

Introduction

Although the events discussed in this book occurred nearly a century ago, the portrait of an intelligence community at odds with its government on policy matters resonates with many of the debates on intelligence reform that preoccupy us today. This history focuses on the course of a single military campaign, the Arab Revolt of 1916–17, but in concentrating on the role of British intelligence in that campaign, it also functions as an intelligence case study with application beyond the First World War. The singularly close relationship that developed between British intelligence and the creation of policy in the Hejaz was not only a landmark for intelligence history, it produced one of the most strategically successful military campaigns of the war.

A bright line normally separates intelligence from decisions over political and military policy. Governments institute clear organizational boundaries to ensure that the intelligence analyst's environment of objectivity is protected from the political pressures and calculations weighing on politicians and generals. Yet under extraordinary conditions, intelligence organizations may drift across task boundaries, and complex intelligence judgements that are based on personal experience and expertise will become more subjective. As one intelligence scholar has observed, it will often be this 'inherent ambiguity', the impossibility of sustaining a politically or historically abstract environment for analysts, that renders 'the intelligence process so susceptible to political interference' – from inside, it might be added, as well as out.[1]

During the eighteen months following the Arab Revolt's outbreak in June 1916, the British intelligence community in Egypt exploited its own institutional 'ambiguity' in the service of the British war effort. Senior political and military voices from London to the Red Sea to India expected to lead the formulation of Britain's policy for the crumbling Ottoman territories, but in the end it was a small, elite intelligence group in Cairo that pushed through the most important policy initiatives for the theatre. This book explores the intelligence officers' expansion of their conventional role into one including policy advocacy, operational decision-making and even active duty in the field. This book is a historical case study and does not purport to be prescriptive, but the value of regional expertise and the advantages of maintaining a symbiotic relationship between intelligence and tactical or strategic deliberations tend to be supported, not refuted, by the following historical events. The theatre pressures that motivated the Cairo intelligence community's enlargement of responsibilities may have been unusual but they were not exceptional. The course of the Arab Revolt raises a rare difficulty for intelligence historians in that it was clearly the incorporation, not exclusion, of intelligence experts into policymaking for the Hejaz campaign that brought success.

Legacies of the First World War

The First World War's iconography of needless sacrifice materialized out of a painful contemporary debate. It reflected the war's human cost as the slaughter continued in the French trenches, and expressed a new state of disillusionment. The image of patriotic young men marching to their deaths impugned the military command's obsolete expectations for combat and underscored their psychological isolation from events on the ground. Eloquent testimonies by men such as Wilfred Owen, Siegfried Sassoon and Basil Liddell Hart articulated the horrors of the Western Front firsthand, and condemned the generals' strategy as a failure. The Middle East theatre also saw the loss of thousands of troops to ritualistic military principles. The dismal routs at the Dardanelles and Gallipoli and the shocking massacre of British troops that followed the Turkish siege at Kut in Mesopotamia (Iraq) revealed the lack of imagination plaguing much of the military leadership. For relief, the public turned its attention to the new press image of a diminutive Englishman dressed in Arab robes and mounted on a racing camel, standing in front of a wrecked train carriage or driving in an open armoured car into the city of Damascus. War correspondents and photographers promoted T.E. Lawrence as an adventure hero even before the conflict had ended. The romantic imagery of his desert operations was an antidote to the wastage occurring on the regular European, Balkan and Atlantic fronts, and the desire to see Lawrence as a foil for the British establishment's expediency remains a compelling one. His history has become the subject of books, documentaries, cinema and television films, in various and often contradictory incarnations. Myriad attempts have been made over the past decades to puncture his credibility as a sincere actor, though this argument has become more difficult to make now that most of the primary documents have been declassified. Lawrence's military writings have been revisited more recently in the press and in military circles. They are now being reviewed for their prescience regarding the nationalistic and ethnic political identities then emerging in the Arab territories, but more particularly for their bold examination into the political and military machinery required to sustain an insurgency.

Considering the remarkable degree of attention given to Lawrence's activities over the decades, it is all the more striking that the intelligence dimension behind Lawrence's professional achievements in the Hejaz has never been fully recognized. Lawrence and his colleagues initiated some of the most imaginative experiments with modern intelligence then recorded for the British services. They coordinated multiple intelligence capabilities and developed a proactive, ground-based approach to intelligence assessment in support of the Arabs' operations. The intelligence community's aim was both basic and ambitious: to ensure that fresh, accurate intelligence coupled with regional expertise informed British military planning and the formulation of high policy. The resonance of their activities would shake Britain's colonial trajectory in the Middle East. Their intelligence innovations formalized practical principles for irregular warfare that remain fundamental for the understanding of modern asymmetric conflicts nearly 100 years later.

Britain's political and military interests in the Ottoman Arab territories have been addressed by several significant histories, but there has been little examination of Britain's policy confusion as it affected day-to-day action on the ground. The British government's alliance with the Hashemite dynasty in Mecca has been well explored; several histories of the Arab Revolt have investigated Britain's fair- or double-dealing, the Arabs' conflicts regarding their own self-interest, and any number of individuals' culpability in the larger political fraud. The costly denouement of the Anglo-Arab alliance after 1919 only underscored the historical portrait of tainted wartime relationships. In military terms, the Hashemite uprising is usually dismissed as having been irrelevant to the war's outcome; it could be argued that it was a poor military return for cost and perhaps too often simply a repository for anti-French imperial reflexes. The impression of the Arab Revolt as an anomalous if colourful 'sideshow' of the real war in Europe has been present from the beginning. Granted, it was Prime Minister David Lloyd George's belief that an eastern victory might be Britain's only hope of stanching the haemorrhaging of manpower on the Western Front, when concerns were current that the war was likely to last several more years. Yet, despite Liddell Hart's or Robert Graves' later defence of the Arab Revolt as an ingenious diversion of enemy resources, war historians might well wonder whether the most incontestable value of the Anglo-Arab partnership and Britain's great investment of financial and political capital was the ushering of British interests into the geostrategic oil-rich provinces of Iraq and the Gulf.

This history proposes a new legacy by focusing on the intelligence that guided British policy towards the Arab Revolt and ensured its survival as a successful wartime campaign. Political and military decision-making for the Middle East was never a simple process. According to Sir Mark Sykes at the War Office, the proliferation of individuals, departments, colonial administrations and wartime bodies with an official interest in the region meant that at least eighteen different voices could lobby the British government:

> With the exception of the ancient constitution of Poland, it would be difficult to find a precedent for so complex or unworkable a political arrangement as the British system which has evolved itself in Arabia since the war broke out in August 1914.[2]

In the end, however, it was not the politicians, civil servants in London nor even the local military commanders who exercised the most influence over decisions in the Arabian campaign. The most effective strategy for addressing the Anglo-Turk conflict was delivered by the intelligence officers on the ground. Their commitment to ensuring that accurate political and military information took precedence over cultural myths and institutional ideologies stands as a lesson for decision-makers in any era.

Intelligence: suspended potential

Great Britain entered the war in 1914 armed with modern intelligence techniques that had the potential to transform intelligence collection and operational support. Although the British services, Foreign Office and colonial administrations had been relying on human intelligence (Humint)[3] and open source intelligence for centuries, recent progress in wireless technology, the development of encryption and cryptology, and the acceleration of signals intelligence (Sigint) were already revolutionizing wartime communications. New photographic techniques combined with advances in the aeroplane produced a similar sea-change with the employment of imagery intelligence (Imint) to track enemy movements and map terrain. Aeroplanes fitted with wireless telegraphy equipment could transmit the results of aerial surveillance in real-time.

Many campaigns during the war might have been strengthened by these new techniques, but geographical or military constraints blocked their application. The Western Front, in contrast to the Arabian peninsula, was typical of the difficulties faced by intelligence. Gains from Humint depended upon the penetrability of the environment. The conditions of German-occupied Europe made it impossible for Allied operatives to establish agent networks behind enemy lines. Likewise, worthwhile Sigint depended upon the enemy's communication practices. After 1914 and the solidification of the Western Front, the German army shifted their transmission load to well-protected land lines, a situation that obtained until movement returned to the front in 1918.[4] The scope for employing Imint in Europe was only slightly better. In 1914, the newly established Royal Flying Corps (RFC) used modern photographic techniques to surveil the German army's advance into Belgium and France. After December 1914 and the sinking of trenches from Switzerland to the English Channel, Germany began transporting troops by rail, where they were easily masked, instead of by road, and useful targets for Imint dwindled. By January 1916 the RFC's flights were almost entirely halted by the Fokker monoplane's domination of the airspace. At no point in the history of trench warfare on the Western Front were Imint missions able to penetrate more than a few miles beyond the front line. Finally, the effectiveness of aerial observation was limited by the fact that Intelligence Corps officers were not placed in the planes flying over the western battlefields until the end of 1916.[5]

Another barrier to intelligence deployment in many theatres was the psychological resistance of commanders to any intrusion on their decision-making. Institutional prejudices at the leadership level in the European theatre tended to preclude any serious exploration of intelligence capabilities. Military and intelligence scholars trying to recover what Christopher Andrew has termed 'the missing dimension of intelligence'[6] have focused on theatres involving large regular battle groups, such as the Western Front and the Atlantic maritime campaigns. But these campaigns were usually led by conventionally minded officers whose rigidity towards operational strategy kept intelligence officers outside the planning stages, with no certain access to the commander-in-chief.

The central government's difficulty when confronted with uncoordinated intelligence from far-flung territories was the final obstacle. London faced urgent policy questions regarding the collapse of the Ottoman Empire, and needed political and military guidance from the region in order to devise its strategy. Under the pre-war system, intelligence sections in colonial postings in India, Persia, Egypt, Turkey and the Mediterranean, the armed services and central headquarters sent their intelligence separately to London without inter-regional consultation or coordination. These intelligence summaries tended to reflect the parochial attitudes of the region and could effectively bury the policy-making process in internecine feuds over official priorities, when what was required was an integrated, comprehensive intelligence profile.

Progress to the east

The conditions for intelligence in the Middle East were much more favourable. There were abundant, if uneven, Humint opportunities from the local population, agents, refugees, Prisoners-of-War (PoWs) and deserting Ottoman Arab officers. The latter supplied British intelligence with some of its most valuable information on the enemy's condition and distribution of force. Cairo intelligence also had detailed Sigint on Turkish movements from intercepted communications between the Turkish army garrisons on the peninsula and the military command in Syria, as well as from wider German and Turk military and political traffic. Imint became one of the most influential sources of information in this sphere, assisted by perfect atmospherics and British pilots' almost complete command of the Arabian airspace. The inhospitable climate, dearth of water and lack of landing sites made flying operations difficult but were not prohibitive. Seaplanes from carriers based in the Red Sea led the way, but within months an RFC Flight was assigned for duty inside the Hejaz to give closer assistance to the Arab fighters. Both British and Arab leaders relied heavily on Imint for reconnaissance and operational support.

The attitude towards intelligence amongst military decision-makers in the Arabian sphere was also more sophisticated. The First World War took place at a time when the attitudes inside the empire were shifting; at the outbreak of hostilities the British government declared a Protectorate over Egypt rather than annexing it outright, as India would have done. In small but significant ways, military and imperial outposts were already challenging nineteenth century conventions. Colonial armies in the Near, Middle and Far East had been enduring special humiliations in the field due to cultural over-confidence. Pinned down in remote locations and without the possibility of reinforcements, trained British troops had been besieged and defeated by bands of comparatively small, poorly armed and untrained native fighters. From Morocco to Egypt, Madagascar and Afghanistan, from India to Burma, imperial soldiers had been forced to confront the combat techniques of the prototypical guerrilla force: superior mobility, continuous intelligence-gathering, deception and a rigorous avoidance of casualties. The lessons of these asymmetric colonial campaigns, or 'small wars', as they were termed by Colonel C.E. Callwell at the turn of the twentieth century, altered institutional memory for Britain's eastern armies and administrations in ways that European battle groups could hardly imagine.

The new age of warfare demanded a different approach to intelligence in combat and a new perspective on imperial survival. Modern conventional weaponry and training would never compensate, as Callwell warned, for the risks to life or the 'grave embarrassments due to want of accurate intelligence as to the theatre of war, and as to the movements, the strength and the fighting value of the bodies opposed to it'.[7] The fate of the French army against the Algerian guerrillas or the Chinese, and the British army's defeats at the hands of the Zulus and the Boers were presented as cautionary tales. British colonial garrisons started to revise their notions of European racial and cultural superiority and studied the native enemies' tactics. Intelligence became the chief consideration in preparations for small wars. The possession of basic information on the enemy and terrain was emerging as an essential rather than optional priority. Continuous intelligence on the enemy's condition and a full reconnaissance of ground conditions, as well as facility in the tactics of ambush, evasion and quick dispersal would be seen as new hallmarks of a resourceful military capability.[8]

The organizational ability to assess complicated streams of intelligence from disparate sources was also in place in the Middle East. In early 1916 the War Committee in London sanctioned a special centralizing headquarters for intelligence in Cairo to 'harmonize' all regional political and military intelligence related to Arab affairs for the government. In part, the creation of 'the Arab Bureau' was a natural expression of Britain's nineteenth century confidence in the prowess of the expert, a figure described by one social historian as 'a protean image of authority and rational knowledge'.[9] The British Empire's vast possessions were governed by a comparatively small investment of civil servants and military groups who believed they exerted a natural authority over the colonial territories; their command of local political, economic, scientific, cultural and linguistic information functioned as an 'imperial archive', as one historian described the phenomenon.[10] The Arab Bureau's approach to intelligence would involve a similarly catholic approach to intellectual analysis.[11] But it was, at the same time, a bold departure from any intelligence organization that preceded it for its territorial reach, topical specialization and placement in the theatre itself. The Arab Bureau was invited to process and streamline information on Arab political and military affairs from sources around the Middle East, and allowed to occupy a central office in Cairo, not London, as several figures had originally requested. Moreover, the office was placed under the authority of the High Commissioner in Egypt and the Foreign Office rather than being attached to Egyptforce or any other regional military group, a position that underscored the political emphasis of its outlook. This unusual constitution was only the beginning of the Arab Bureau's singularity as an intelligence section.

The Arab Bureau and British policy

The Arab Bureau's mandate to address the wartime cross-currents of Arab/Turk affairs followed an intelligence investment rooted during the first signs of war in 1914. Many Arab Bureau officers were gleaned by Gilbert Clayton, its chief, from the Arabists who had already been working under him in his capacity as head of military and civil intelligence in Cairo. They hailed from backgrounds as diverse as the Levant Consular service, the Turkish gendarmerie, British politics, journalism, banking, colonial administration, academia and archaeology. They combined abundant regional experience, language fluency in Arabic and Turkish and, most importantly, confidence in modern intelligence techniques.

After Turkey's decision in November 1914 to join Germany and Austria-Hungary in the war against Great Britain, Anglo-Egypt's intelligence community explored several possibilities for allying with secret Ottoman Arab nationalist groups in Syria[12] and Arabia. Representatives of these societies had already approached the British authorities for support. The military benefits of an Arab insurgency appeared straightforward: if an Arab uprising led to substantial desertions from the Ottoman army, it could cripple the enemy forces facing the British on the Suez Canal and in Mesopotamia, and the Russians in the Caucasus. Such a loss might even compel the Turks to withdraw from the war, in which case, as one German commentator observed in early 1916, 'English world-power is saved. If not, even tolerably favourable terms of peace elsewhere will hardly compensate.'[13] The political effect of an Arab rebellion was also potentially significant, if more complicated, as a war aim. Cairo believed that an Arab rebellion, even a simple commitment of neutrality, would undermine the Turkish Sultan-Caliph's call for an Islamic *jihad* against the European Allies. The threat of an even modestly successful *jihad* in Britain's colonial territories haunted every review of regional security from Egypt to Aden to British India.

In many ways, contemplating an Arab uprising raised awkward and unfamiliar questions for British policy. The Hejaz theatre was surrounded by the planning catastrophes of the Dardanelles, Gallipoli and Kut; none of these operations had been distinguished by the active sympathy of local minority groups, military or civilian, behind Turkish lines. More importantly, the region was already secretly earmarked by post-war planners for partition into European spheres of control. The powerful Government of India strongly objected to forging alliances with Arab minority groups in the targeted territories. Cairo's interest in stirring up an Arab nationalist movement would raise complications for Indian authorities moving into Mesopotamia (eastern Iraq), who intended to administer the territory after the war. France was also opposed to encouraging Arab nationalist sentiments, having claimed Syria and the Lebanon as its own desiderata.

But Cairo's views were represented with enthusiasm to the War Cabinet by the former Consul-General of Egypt, now Secretary of War, Lord Kitchener. Kitchener convinced the War Committee and the Foreign Office to authorize negotiations for an alliance with the named Arab leader, Sherif Hussein bin Ali, the Emir of Mecca, Guardian of the Holy Places of Mecca and Medina.

The significance of the Arab Bureau's new profile as an intelligence office became clear after active operations began in the Hejaz, a theatre under its responsibility. In June 1916, the Sherif launched a revolt of tribal fighters against the Turkish troops occupying Mecca and the port of Jiddah. It was a stunning coup that took the British authorities and the Turkish government by surprise. Immediately, the question of strategy for the Arab armies and overall Arab policy had to be addressed. The British Sirdar of the Egyptian army, wanting to take command of the new Hejaz theatre, urged London to send regular reinforcements to the Hejaz. Without Britain's intervention, he argued, the Turkish army would overrun the untrained Arab fighters. But the High Commissioner in Cairo and the Arab Bureau wanted a different strategy. Political intelligence showed that the Arab uprising was a domestic conflict, motivated by minority political and economic concerns; on top of which, the presence of European Christian infantry in the Muslim holy land of the Hejaz would be anathema to the Arab population. If Britain landed a foreign Christian regular force in the Hejaz, in the Arab Bureau's view, the Sherif would lose his tribal support. In addition, imagery intelligence on road and water conditions showed that a conventional immobile force would be ineffective as a defence against a Turkish advance on Mecca. The British intelligence, army and navy officers working on the ground began to debate the merits of encouraging a war run along guerrilla lines.

The combination of the Arabs' traditional guerrilla skills and the British intelligence officers' access to modern intelligence techniques would prove a potent combination. But the pursuit of an irregular strategy in the Hejaz involved fighting a guerrilla campaign along political as well as military lines. The Arab Bureau saw the military and political dimensions as intertwined, and for the health of one came to argue for support of the other. As the following chapters show, the intelligence officers' attention to the deeper political mechanisms of the revolt on the ground led to several inspired decisions for the campaign, including the rejection of reinforcements, the shift of Feisal's base north to Wejh, the release of Medina as a target and a reorientation of the Arab Revolt to the north, against the railway. These were strategic decisions that kept the Arab Revolt militarily viable; they also created new political conditions for the Arab campaign that were no longer under the control of London's policy. The British intelligence officers in Cairo had already signaled their intent by choosing 'Intrusive' as their telegraphic address. As the campaign in the Hejaz unfolded, the Arab Bureau expanded its traditional intelligence duties to include tactical decision-making, strategic reviews, General Staff responsibilities and even active operations. Their wide-ranging analysis of multiple intelligence sources, their confidence in intelligence as a force-multiplier and readiness to employ irregular methods of warfare would be fundamental to the Arab Revolt's success.

The distinction in practice between intelligence and policy responsibilities, as one intelligence expert recently noted, may often be 'blurred, especially because analytic projections may have policy implications even if they are not explicitly stated. But the distinction is still important'.[14] The Arab Bureau's activities redefined the intelligence-policy dichotomy and skated over that crucial line. London and Anglo-Egyptian authorities allowed operational responsibilities to migrate steadily to this regional office, which both produced policy recommendations for the decision-makers and moved to implement significant changes on the ground. Lawrence emerges during this period as a leading intelligence and strategic analyst who was joined by respected intelligence and army officers in his belief that the defence of Mecca – and the Hejaz generally – hinged ultimately on the attitude of the many Bedouin tribes that stretched across the territory. Lawrence's famous, unauthorized occupation of Aqaba in July 1917 was the culmination of an intelligence commitment that was already unique. While most intelligence experts would hope that their work is utilized regularly as a resource by policymakers, few would propose, for obvious reasons, that the intelligence community cross the bright line and try to influence policymaking directly. The Arab Bureau's success in protecting and advancing the Arab Revolt will be revealed in this respect to be an uneasy exception or, at the very least, a thought-provoking aberration from the received wisdom governing intelligence and those essential boundaries.

On sources

Valuable primary source material was found at the National Archives at Kew; the India Office Library, London; the Imperial War Museum, London; St Antony's College Middle East Centre, Oxford; the Sudan Archive, University of Durham; and the Churchill Archive Centre, Cambridge. The paper record includes intelligence data, reports and summaries; memoranda on specific intelligence topics; private and official correspondence; official records of departmental and cabinet level meetings relating to intelligence and Middle East policy, and intelligence publications. Significant and previously unpublished material was also used, such as the secret reports written by Arthur Brownlow fforde from the Arab Bureau to the Foreign and Political Department, India (India Office Library) and the imagery intelligence produced by General Headquarters (GHQ), Egyptforce's aerial reconnaissance flights in 1916 over the Hejaz and the Gulf of Aqaba (National Archives).

One intelligence source that is used continuously throughout this book requires specific explanation. *The Arab Bulletin* was a secret intelligence publication that appeared several times during the month, depending on the pace of events. Its circulation of twenty-five recipients included the Foreign Office, the Admiralty, the Director of Military Intelligence (London), the Sirdar of the Egyptian army (Khartoum), the Secretary of the Foreign Department (India), the Chief Political Officer at Basra, the Commissioner of Somaliland, the High Commissioner at Cyprus, the High Commissioner of Egypt and an inner circle of military and intelligence officers assigned to the Hejaz. *The Arab Bulletin*'s unofficial audience was certainly far wider. The publication contained pieces of raw intelligence, intelligence reports from intelligence and other service officers around the Near and Middle East and North Africa, scholarly essays on personalities and regional topics, transcriptions of foreign newspapers, and editorial commentary. It has been claimed that after French and Italian representatives in Egypt discovered the existence of *The Arab Bulletin* in December 1916, it ceased to be entirely 'secret' and could no longer function as a forum for discussing sensitive topics such as, allegedly, Anglo-French relations or the future of Syria.[15] It should be noted that such discussions did not appear with any seriousness even before this event. The bulletin's value from the beginning was its swift transmission of all notable intelligence, delivered in an informal workhouse style of reporting, its multi-source analysis and its editorial comment, conveying the Arab Bureau's own impressions and preoccupations. Detailed mission reports, tribal and topographical studies, political and biographical studies, and other essays of a scholarly standard formed the rest of the archive.[16] At times, the scattershot format of much of the material can be daunting, but a close study of the publication is rewarding. *The Arab Bulletin* reflected the ebb and flow of detail that shaped the intelligence community's judgement of events and drove their daily operations.

Special mention must also be given to the biographies of T.E. Lawrence that are an inevitable part of this subject's historiography. Jeremy Wilson's authorized biography of Lawrence is a model of exhaustive research. In the chapters addressing the war Wilson explores many aspects of intelligence activity and offers significant material on French activity in the Red Sea sphere, an important topic which lies outside the scope of this book.[17] John Mack's Pulitzer Prize-winning study, *A Prince of Our Disorder: the Life of T.E. Lawrence* is another first-rate biography, eloquently written, supported by painstaking research and showing a deep understanding of the period. Lawrence James' *Golden Warrior: the Life and Legend of Lawrence of Arabia* adopts a more critical approach to his subject's iconic stature while also providing rich material from military and intelligence archives. A jaundiced scepticism has been a recurrent impulse for historians of this topic since the first charges of fraud were made against Lawrence by Richard Aldington in the 1950s.[18] The post-war blight of celebrity that marks the historiography of Lawrence is another of the bugbears for research in this field. This book has been written without any such agenda. It has aimed rather to restore a sense of the pre-legend Lawrence and his vocation as an intelligence office at a time when the field was beginning to modernize, both technologically and conceptually. As for Lawrence's own historical account, he has described his post-war memoir, *Seven Pillars of Wisdom*, as 'the history not of the Arab movement, but of me in it'.[19] I have used this material cautiously and in conjunction with contemporary intelligence wherever possible. It does include significant references to campaign intelligence. Many sections are clearly adapted or transcribed from his own war-time intelligence reports and can easily be consulted for comparison along with other contemporary intelligence reports. Lawrence's stylized, occasionally contentious flourishes in *Seven Pillars* are well signposted and reflect his attempts at self-judgement more than history; a careful reading can distinguish between the two. Other secondary sources have provided important detail and insights on intelligence and regional history. Works used directly are noted in the Bibliography.

The close focus of this book has inevitably left many important subjects associated with this theatre unaddressed. Egypt's relationship with the Government of India is explored only insofar as it affected the organization of Egypt's intelligence departments and the Hejaz campaign, while other Egyptian–Indian clashes such as the rivalry over control in the Aden sphere and the intricate events in neighbouring Mesopotamia are mentioned only in passing. The wartime aims of the French, which were continually in the background of Hejaz affairs, are addressed only at the most salient points. While this book returns regularly to the interplay between the Hejaz campaign and the agenda of Egyptforce, the latter among other topics has been left to other histories, Yigal Sheffy's *British Military Intelligence in the Palestine Campaign 1914–1918* being one of the finest.[20]

1 Setting the scene

British intelligence and an Arab insurrection, 1913–15

Contrary to the conventional view, the actual course of the British government's alliance with the Hashemite Arab dynasty was not driven by the war's military requirements, Great Power rivalry or even imperial war aims. Although Britain would declare war on Turkey in November 1914, the substance of British policy towards the Turkish government's Arab territories would be contested throughout the conflict by departments and administrations from London to North Africa, from the Persian Gulf to the Indian subcontinent. An official definition of Britain's commitments to the native Arab populations in particular would still be in dispute at the Paris Peace Conference in 1919.

The Arabs of the Arabian peninsula who would become the first army of rebellion in June 1916 were characterized only months earlier by Sir Arthur Nicolson, Permanent Under-Secretary of the Foreign Office, as 'a heap of scattered tribes with no cohesion and no organisation'.[1] Their transformation in London's eyes into a valuable wartime ally of Great Britain was propelled by the British intelligence community based in Cairo. Whether it had been the government's original intention or not, Cairo's intelligence officers were positioning themselves to vie with the political assessments of Whitehall and the conventional military's views, to influence Britain's Arab policy. By the time the Sherif of Mecca launched his revolt in June 1916, the intelligence community was already pushing against the boundaries that separated official responsibilities for intelligence and formulation of policy.

British Egypt: redefining strategic security

Throughout the nineteenth century, the Ottoman Empire, Persia, Turkestan (until its conquest by Russia in late nineteenth century) and Afghanistan acted as a geographical shield for Britain, protecting overland routes to India from the predations of Russian expansionism. After the turn of the century and the rise of German militarism, European governments re-evaluated their security priorities. Great Britain brokered new relationships with Russia and France, previously long-time rivals in the East. The 'Entente Cordiale' between Britain and France in 1904 brought about an end to the 'Great Game' with Russia, an ally of France. After Russia's defeat by Japan in the 1904–5 war, Russian foreign policy began turning from the East and towards the Balkan territories. Sir Edward Grey, British Foreign Secretary, was optimistic about the new Russian orientation.[2] The Treaty of St Petersburg in 1907 introduced Anglo-Russian cooperation on the Northwest frontier and officially ended their respective schemes inside Afghanistan and Tibet. It also divided Persia into British, Russian and neutral spheres of interest. Thus Britain's historical interest in preserving the Ottoman Empire as a territorial buffer against Russia was, in theory, removed. But claims of a new benign international balance were less convincing in the outposts of the British Empire, particularly from the perspective of administrations in North Africa, the Middle East and India for whom the Great Game and threats of expansionist stratagems from Russia, France and soon Germany, far from defunct, continued in force.[3]

The Ottoman government itself was already in crisis long before the war. The despot Sultan-Caliph, Abdul Hamid II (1876–1909), jettisoned the constitution of 1876. He consistently underestimated the nationalist uprisings in his western territories and during the Russo-Turk war of 1877–8, lost the territories of Rumania, Serbia, Montenegro, Bosnia and Herzegovina. The country sank into financial turmoil.[4] In an effort to buttress his public standing, he reached out to the empire's largest disenfranchised minority group, the Arabs. His pro-Islamic policies endeared him to rural Arab communities but outraged secular reformist intellectuals.[5] In 1909 one of the leading opposition groups, the 'Young Turks', ousted Abdul Hamid from the Sultanate and installed his malleable brother, Muhammad V (1909–18). After the Tripolitanian War (1911–13) and the Balkan Wars (1912–13), which ended in further humiliating losses for the empire from the Aegean islands to all Turkish territories west of the Enos–Midia line, the Young Turks seized the capital and declared a new secular government for the country. They promised to rescue the economy, re-establish the suppressed constitution of 1876, modernize the army and navy (with German and British contributions, respectively) and restore the country's national pride with a reformist government, 'the Committee of Union and Progress' (CUP).[6]

Despite their rhetoric, the Young Turks failed to reverse the empire's decline. One of their more injudicious decisions was to renege on the restoration of the constitution, an act that would have protected the rights of all ethnic and religious groups. Instead, they instituted a progamme of *Yeni-Turan* or Pan-Turanism, which designated Turkish ethnicity and language as the dominant culture. Another key decision was to try to bolster national defence by forging alliances with stronger countries. Turkey's northern borders were still vulnerable to Russia and its western border remained unfixed against a restive Serbia, Greece and the shifting Balkan jigsaw. Enver Pasha, one of the founders of the Young Turks and now Minister for War, convinced the rest of the CUP in 1913 that Constantinople should establish a closer relationship with Germany. Germany had already offered generous material assistance and military officers for the training of the Ottoman army. In August 1914, Turkey signed a defensive alliance with Germany against Russia.[7]

The Ottoman Empire's reorientation towards Germany instantly altered the security outlook of its neighbours, particularly that of British Egypt, which had been growing into a powerful hub of colonial and trade policy considerations. After taking control of the Suez Canal from the Egyptian government in 1904, the British Agency in Egypt had concentrated its policy around what it considered its two totems of imperial responsibility, the security of the canal and the holy places in Arabia, to which thousands of British Muslims travelled every year for the *hajj*, or pilgrimage. Its greatest concern with respect to both these investments now became the CUP's deepening partnership with Germany.

Initiated in 1903, the Berlin–Baghdad railway project carried momentous ramifications for international transport and communication. There was substantial international controversy over the significance of Germany's heavy involvement in the construction of the eastern branches. Abdul Hamid had granted Germany the construction rights for the railway from Constantinople to Baghdad and Basra, but under several conditions. Turkey wanted an extension built through Aleppo to Damascus, another tributary from Deraa to Haifa, and the rest of the mainline to continue southward from Damascus to Medina and Mecca. The Arabian portion of the railway was heralded as a symbol of modernization that would bring improved service for pilgrims at the Holy Places. But it quickly became clear that the railway's parallel purpose would be to extend the government's powers of taxation and conscription into the previously remote, autonomous tribal lands of inland Syria, Mesopotamia and the Arabian peninsula, and commandeer the prestigious and lucrative business of the *hajj* along the way.

In Egypt, the British Agency was quick to regard the Turco-German alliance as a strategic threat. As railway construction ensued, the agency envisioned how their neighbours would soon be able to mobilize German and Turkish troops against the Suez Canal and India. The Committee of Imperial Defence (CID) in London was persuaded by Egypt's warnings. In 1913, the CID commissioned the Palestine Exploration Fund (PEF) to make a geographical survey of Palestine, the Lebanon and the Sinai–Negev region that would include intelligence on the railway's construction.[8] The resulting expedition employed three men who would soon be contributing their expertise with regional intelligence to Britain's war effort in the eastern Mediterranean and Egypt. S.F. Newcombe of the Royal Engineers led the expedition as chief topographer. C.L. Woolley and T.E. Lawrence, two precocious archaeologists working for the British Museum at Carchemish in Syria, assisted with the ground survey and provided the mission with its archaeological cover.[9] The PEF's intelligence activity and the attention of CID members, such as future Arab Bureau director, D.G. Hogarth, ensured that some degree of official notice remained fixed on the geostrategic concerns of Egypt during the years before the war.

Field Marshal Lord Kitchener was the British Agent and Consul-General in Egypt, and himself a contributor to the PEF's survey of Western Palestine twenty-five years earlier. Kitchener, molded by over a decade of military and intelligence experience in the Sudan and Egypt, saw the changes occurring in the Ottoman Empire as a clear provocation to British interests. He considered the Arab territories on the other side of the Suez Canal to be a natural extension of Egyptian territory and a vital asset for British security around the eastern Mediterranean, the Canal and the Red Sea. Turkey's collapse was assumed to be imminent, if not through outright war than by internal disintegration. The British Agency's Oriental Secretary, Ronald Storrs, described Britain's envisioned acquisition of Ottoman territories as a 'North African or near-Eastern vice-royalty including Egypt and the Sudan and across the way from Aden to Alexandretta [that] would compare in interest and complexity, if not in actual size, with India itself.'[10] The Arabic-speaking countries would turn their allegiance from Constantinople to Egypt, the Sultan's Caliphate would be dissolved and – significantly – an Arab Caliphate 'restored' in Mecca under the protection of the British administration in Cairo.[11] Kitchener's address to the War Committee in London eighteen months into the war still expressed this assessment of advantage in Britain's becoming the protector of a future Arab 'state':

> [It] is in our interests to see an Arab kingdom established in Arabia under the auspices of England, bounded on the north by the valley of the Tigris and Euphrates, and containing within it the chief Mahommedan Holy Places, Mecca, Medina and Kerbela. In this eventuality the possession of Mesopotamia – as we already hold the Persian Gulf, the Red Sea, and Egypt – would secure all the approaches to the Mahommedan Holy Places. This, in [the British Empire's] position as the greatest of Moslem States, would greatly enhance our prestige amongst the many millions of our Mahommedan subjects.[12]

Notwithstanding the grandeur of this vision, Cairo's administration was beginning to approach the question of empire with some flexibility. In December 1914, the British Agency in Cairo (thereafter, the 'Residency') declared a Protectorate over Egypt, declining to annex the territory outright and thus diverging conspicuously from the example of India's governors.[13] The professional friction and territorial rivalry between Egypt and India, whose areas of control in the Persian Gulf, the Red Sea and Mesopotamia lay adjacent to each other and often overlapped, remained a feature throughout the war.

In August 1914 Kitchener was recalled to London to become Secretary of State for War. He was replaced in Egypt by (Acting Agent) Milne Cheetham, who held the position from 4 August to December 1914, when Sir Henry McMahon was appointed High Commissioner of Egypt. As the tumult of the war spread, the Anglo-Egyptian administration's strategic outlook remained steady. Kitchener in London and the administration in Cairo initially hoped to join the strategic vision of the possible 'near-Eastern vice-royalty' with the larger British war effort against Turkey and Germany. Egypt's intelligence departments played a central role in this project, revealing the actual condition of the Arab territories to the British authorities in Egypt, the Sudan, the Levant and London. What no one could have anticipated, however, was the manner in which Cairo's intelligence community would outun Kitchener and London in their determination to formulate a policy for war against the Turks.

Schemes for subversion: Arab opportunities and British ambivalence

From late 1914 to mid-1916, the British Residency and key members of the intelligence community in Cairo under Brigadier-General Gilbert Clayton pursued a de facto policy of working with Arab activists to explore the possibilities for an armed nationalist movement or army mutiny against the Ottoman government. From early 1914, before the outbreak of war, a number of Arab representatives and Arab defectors from the Ottoman army, largely composed of conscripts, had made contact with the British authorities. They described their communities' widespread resentment of Constantinople's policies, and revealed the existence of dedicated covert revolutionary societies spanning the Arab professional classes of Syria and Mesopotamia, and the Arab divisions of the Ottoman army.

As the British government began to edge towards war with Germany and then Turkey, Cairo intelligence analysed the weaknesses of the Turkish army, militarily and politically.[14] One of the most striking contributors to this evaluation was Aziz Ali al-Masri, an acclaimed former Ottoman commander who led a triumphant force of Senussi fighters against the Italian army in Libya in 1911, one of the few Ottoman victories in that theatre of war. Al-Masri, now in exile, visited the British Residency in Cairo in August 1914. In his debriefing with Captain Russell of Military Intelligence (with the British Force in Egypt), he confided the existence of *al-'Ahd. Al-'Ahd*, or 'the Covenant', was a secret society of Arab officers within the Ottoman army, founded by al-Masri in Constantinople in 1913.[15] He described *al-'Ahd*'s programme for a revolution to form 'a united Arabian state, independent of Turkey and every other power except England, whose tutelage and control of foreign affairs they invite'. He told Russell that *al-'Ahd* would consider an agreement with Britain in exchange for weapons and funding.[16]

Intelligence on a second powerful secret Arab society was also obtained from another human source, a young Turkish officer named Muhammed al-Faruqi who crossed over to the British lines at the Dardanelles. Al-Faruqi claimed to be a member of *al-'Ahd* and also of *al-Fatat*, also known as the 'Young Arab Party'. *Al-Fatat* was an intensely secret, initially civilian nationalist society that was founded in Constantinople in 1909. Its headquarters later moved to Paris, Beirut and finally Damascus. After August 1914, *al-Fatat* was the Arabs' shadowy sentinel keeping watch on the Turkish Fourth Army in Syria, into which many *al-Fatat* members had been conscripted. *Al-Fatat*'s manifesto called for the secession of the Arab territories from Ottoman control and the creation of an independent 'Arab nation.' Its policy was one of religious and ethnic inclusion under the arc of Arab nationhood.[17]

What British intelligence could not have known at this time was that the informants' estimates of the membership in the societies were dramatically inflated, even if unwittingly. Clayton, head of military and civil intelligence in Egypt as well as chief of intelligence for the Sirdar at Khartoum, accepted al-Masri's estimation in mid-1914 that membership for *al-'Ahd* in Mesopotamia reached as high as 15,000. Osmond Walrond (later with the Arab Bureau) was in communication with Syrian-Arab nationalists in Egypt in 1918, and on the basis of their statements he told Clayton that *al-Fatat* membership in August 1914 had totalled 150,000. At the Paris Peace Conference in 1919, the Sherif of Mecca's son Prince Feisal would maintain the fiction, claiming that the societies' membership had numbered in the hundreds of thousands.[18] Recent scholarship has suggested that there were in fact only thirty-seven activists in *al-Fatat* before the war, of which only eight joined the campaign in the Hejaz in 1916. Membership in *al-Fatat* rose to 115 by the end of the war, but of these, just twenty-nine members fought in the Arab Revolt. The numbers for *al-'Ahd* were equally modest: there were fifty-four members before 1916, of which sixteen joined the Revolt at its outbreak. By 1918 there were fifty-seven members in *al-'Ahd*, but only seventeen members fought in the Revolt. The true nature of the Arab secret societies seems never to have been discovered by the British intelligence community, who continued to believe throughout the war that membership for each society numbered well over 100,000. It is also likely that they were influenced in this belief by the Indian government's repeated fears of just such a movement.[19]

Despite this stunning misapprehension of strength by British intelligence, the influence of *al-'Ahd* and *al-Fatat* on the conduct of the pending Arab Revolt was disproportionately strong. The societies' leaders communicated with Sherif Hussein bin Ali before the Revolt and helped set the parameters for his negotiations with the British government (below). Several society members joined the military leadership of the ensuing campaign in the Hejaz. Above all, the society members' express aspiration to launch an internal uprising against the Ottoman authorities persuaded the British authorities in Cairo that this would be a promising campaign strategy: a powerful Arab fifth column preparing to topple the Ottoman government in the Arab territories.

While Great Britain remained at peace with Turkey there could be no serious consideration of al-Masri's offer. In Sepember 1914, one month after Britain's declaration of war on Germany on 4 August, al-Masri returned to Cairo and demanded a private meeting with Clayton. Al-Masri repeated his offer of a partnership with Britain and outlined *al-'Ahd's* scheme for 'an organised revolution backed by a comparatively small but well equipped force', supplied by Britain and constituted of Arab fighters. Al-Masri, as mentioned above, estimated that at least 15,000 *al-'Ahd* members waited in the ranks of the Ottoman army in Mesopotamia, ready to rise and 'serve as a centre round which the forces of the Arab Chieftains would rally'. Al-Masri warned against the inclusion European troops, which he 'deprecated [...] as likely to create an impression that annexation of territory was contemplated'. It was an early warning of the political risks surrounding European troops that would be heatedly debated in British circles over the next three years.[20]

The British administration cast round for a convincing Arab figurehead to lead the revolt, someone with political and religious status comparable to the

Turkish Sultan-Caliph. The most obvious candidate was Sherif Hussein bin Ali, head of the Hashemite dynasty, Emir of Mecca and Guardian of the Holy Places. The Hashemites had become anxious that their traditional autonomy in the Hejaz and lately even their personal security were under threat from Constantinople. The proposed extension of the Medina railway terminus to Mecca and Jiddah on the Red Sea would steal the Bedouin tribes' traditional livelihood from the camel trade and protection of pilgrims on the *hajj*, and transfer the prestige of the *hajj* from the Arab Emirate to the Turks. It would only be a matter of time before a pro-CUP Turkish official was installed in the Sherif of Mecca's place. The Sherif's eldest son, Prince Abdullah, visited Lord Kitchener and Oriental Secretary Ronald Storrs at the Agency in February 1914 to ask whether Britain would support his father if he launched an uprising against the Turks.[21]

Abdullah's invitation took on a new aspect of seriousness after al-Masri's revelations of covert anti-Turk organizations throughout the Arab territories. Clayton and Storrs reviewed the proposals together and drafted a secret memorandum for Kitchener in London. They suggested that if an Arab opposition party (such as *al-'Ahd*) was led by someone of the Sherif's religious status and overthrew the Turkish government, the Arabs might indeed transfer the Caliphate to the Emirate of Mecca. In addition, only someone with the Sherif's influence would be able to quell the Turks' promised pan-Islamic *jihad* against British interests. Kitchener agreed, and on 24 September he instructed Storrs to ask Abdullah whether in the event of a war between Britain and the Ottoman Empire, the Arabs would be 'with us or against us'.[22] It seemed on the surface to be a straightforward and mutually beneficial blending of interests. Lord Cromer, former Consul-General in Egypt, remarked confidently to his former Oriental Secretary Harry Boyle that Arab bitterness towards the CUP was so pervasive that 'a few [British] officers who could speak Arabic, if sent into Arabia, could raise the whole country against the Turks'.[23]

As diplomatic relations proceeded to disintegrate between Turkey and the Allies, Kitchener obtained Foreign Secretary Edward Grey's authorization for Storrs to deliver the following instructions to Abdullah on 31 October: 'If the Arab nation assist England in this war that has been forced upon us by Turkey, England will guarantee that no internal intervention take place in Arabia, and will give Arabs every assistance against foreign aggression.'[24] Kitchener wrote a second letter to the Sherif to make it clear that if the Arabs supported Britain in the war effort, Britain would 'guarantee the independence, rights and privileges of the Sharifate against all external aggression, in particular that of the Ottomans'. Kitchener added, significantly: 'It may be that an Arab of true race will assume the Khalifate at Mecca or Medina, and so good may come by the help of God out of all the evil which is now occurring.'[25] Storrs and Clayton sent Kitchener's proposal to Abdullah, who replied by messenger that his father would welcome their alliance, should the moment come for rebellion against Constantinople.[26] This communication was the first of the rhetorically soaring but highly ambiguous 'promises' exchanged between British representatives and the Arab leadership.

The British government declared war against Turkey on 5 November 1914 and the barrier to action against Constantinople was lifted. Milne Cheetham, Acting Agent in Egypt, wrote to the Foreign Office that 'an excellent effect' would also be made if the British government reassured the world's Muslim populations that, out of respect for the sanctity of the holy places, it had 'no intention to undertake any military or naval operation in Arabia' but wished only to support those efforts 'by Arabs to free themselves from Turkish rule'.[27] Grey agreed that 'the Arab movement should be encouraged in every way possible. Aziz [al-Masri] Bey might be sent to organise with a sum of £2,000, or thereabouts' and promised 'further support' when necessary.[28]

With Grey's approval in hand, the British administration in Cairo could begin a campaign of covert support and funding of Arab opposition movements as their official strategy against the Turks. Cairo's first proposal for the War Council was to dispatch a small Arab mission under al-Masri to Mesopotamia to persuade the *al-'Ahd* members in the Turkish army there to raise a mutiny.[29] Notwithstanding a certain whimsical approach to logistics, the scheme was wrecked by chronic tension and disagreement between Egypt and India. Al-Masri wanted to make the British intelligence headquarters of the Indian Expeditionary Force (IEF) 'D' at Basra his base for penetrating Mesopotamia, but the Government of India, which administered Basra, refused to allow it and denied his entry into the country. Memories of the nationalist violence that sent tremors through British rule in India in 1907, 1909 and 1912 were still fresh, and Indian officials had no intention of risking another eruption of independent political elements in Muslim communities in Mesopotamia.[30] In addition to commandeering the newly discovered oil deposits in the regions north of the Gulf, Indian officials also intended to take over the fertile Mesopotamia regions as a new source of grain production for India. They insisted to Cairo that efforts to launch an Arab revolt and replace the Ottoman caliph with the Sherif would be resented by Muslims across India, and likely worldwide. Sir Percy Cox, the highly respected Chief Political Officer (CPO) at Basra, expressed this view forcefully. He dismissed al-Masri's scheme as 'visionary and impracticable' and noted that to introduce ideas of independence and national sovereignty to 'backward [...] tribes and Sheikhs' at this time 'would not have the slightest effect on them'; in fact, it might even 'do more harm than good and [in any case] would be of no immediate use to us'.[31] On 18 December, the Foreign Office in London deferred to the Indian authorities' judgement and ordered Cheetham to close down the al-Masri scheme. The British officials at Basra apprehended the colleagues whom al-Masri had engaged for the mission and deported them to India for internment.[32]

The administration in Egypt, also engaged on several fronts against a Muslim power, felt similarly vulnerable to the political vagaries of its domestic Muslim population but, unlike India, believed that these 'sensibilities' could be turned. On 3 February 1915 Jemal Pasha, the Ottoman army commander in the Sinai, made his first attempt against Egypt's easternmost defences on the far side of the Suez Canal. His army's failure to establish a foothold on the other side was largely the result of incompetent logistical planning; but equally notable had been the fact that the expected Egyptian Muslim uprising – which Jemal had taken for granted in designing his attack and which many British residents in Egypt had also feared – did not materialize.[33] Ronald Storrs noted that the tension in the country surrounding the Turkish attack on the Canal had confirmed the country's 'constant preoccupation' with invasion scares – although 'less for its military effect than for the repercussion upon a Moslem Egypt'.[34] Referring to Turkey's calls for an international *jihad* against Great Britain, Sir Reginald Wingate, the Sirdar of the Egyptian army at Khartoum, wrote Clayton that 'the matter is of such vital importance that it behoves all the experts, whether they be in India, Aden, Egypt or the Sudan, to consult together and arrive at the best means of dealing with this matter'.[35]

Cairo's second scheme for insurrection hinged on the landing of a British expeditionary force at Alexandretta on the Gulf of Iskenderun. British intelligence estimates placed the Turkish force in Syria at about 50,000 troops; Cairo believed that most of these were 'disaffected' and apt to turn against their commanders along with other minority populations, once an attack was underway.[36] A British force at Alexandretta could threaten a vital junction of the Berlin–Baghdad railway and interrupt Turkish troops moving through Syria, Mesopotamia, Cilicia and Asia Minor. It might even sever the line of communication between Asia Minor and Baghdad, 'where the English are likely to be very hard pressed shortly.'[37] T.E. Lawrence of Military Intelligence (MI) in Cairo, who had engaged in intelligence activity in the Syrian interior before the war and already held personal strong views against the Turkish government, was one of this scheme's strongest advocates. He urged D.G. Hogarth, his former mentor at Oxford who was now working with Naval Intelligence in London, to lobby the War Council, the Foreign Office and Winston Churchill at the Admiralty:

> [Alexandretta] is the key of the whole place as you know. It's going to be the head of the Baghdad line. [...] Point out also that it is a splendid natural naval base (which *we* don't want but which no one else can have without detriment to us).[38]

Despite the full support of Clayton, Sir Henry McMahon (now High Commissioner, replacing Cheetham), General Sir John Maxwell (GOC-in-C in Egypt), and Lord Kitchener for the scheme, the General Staff (GS) in London rejected the proposal.[39] On 13 January 1915, the War Council elected to deploy the available British troops in an attack on the Gallipoli peninsula instead, relegating the Alexandretta landing as an option only 'if the position in the Western theatre [became] in the spring one of stale-mate'.[40] The decision rewarded the priorities of the 'Westerners' on the General Staff who saw France as the indisputable main theatre of war and considered the eastern battlefields as too marginal to justify the diversion of troops. The ignominious conclusion of the Gallipoli campaign would be in some respects a galling vindication of both sides' arguments in the debate.

The regretful denouement of the Alexandretta proposal, quite apart from the tragedy at Gallipoli, was the realization that its central idea of a joint British–Arab attack on the Turkish garrison might actually have succeeded. Humint in late summer 1915 revealed that a high-ranking Arab officer and head of the Aleppo branch of *al-'Ahd*, Major Amin Lutfi al-Hafiz, held the command of the Turkish 136th Regiment at Antioch. His orders had been to fortify the Gulf of Iskenderun outside Alexandretta. Moreover, a second senior member of *al-'Ahd* (and an *al-Fatat* member), Yasin al-Hashimi, was stationed at Aleppo as Chief of Staff for the Turkish 12th Army Corps.[41] Al-Hafiz had won the secret support of the local Ansariya tribes and of the largely Arab divisions at Homs and Aleppo, and had organized extensive acts of sabotage against the Turkish defences at Alexandretta in anticipation of a British landing. But the landing never occurred. Jemal Pasha transferred the Arab Divisions to the Dardanelles and recalled more Turkish troops to Syria in order to ensure the opportunity never repeated itself.[42] Al-Hafiz was arrested and hanged in May 1916, in the second of Jemal's mass executions. Cairo Intelligence, since informed of al-Hafiz's actions by Humint from Ottoman army deserters, reported in their next bulletin that his arrangement of 'a mutiny of all the Mosul and North Syrian troops' and raising of 'the whole country from Payas to Ladikiya [Latakiya]' in expectation of the British naval assault at Alexandretta had been exceptional, and his loss 'is serious for us'.[43]

The Alexandretta scheme was mooted again in early November 1915 during the Dardanelles Committee's deliberations over the Gallipoli beachhead evacuation. It was thought that the landing might help restrain the released Turkish troops from making another attempt against the Canal. But this time, the objections to the scheme came from the French government. The French military attaché in London warned Kitchener that, owing to its ancient interests in Syria, his government would only allow a landing at Alexandretta if it were jointly planned and executed with France. As the French could not contribute to a landing at present, 'for political reasons which it is unnecessary to spell out, any scheme involving action at Alexandretta by England alone is out of the question'.[44] The War Council acquiesced and shelved the scheme. As Basil Liddell Hart later observed:

> [The letter from the French cabinet] must surely be one of the most astounding documents ever presented to an Ally when engaged in a life and death struggle. For it imposed what was really a veto on the best opportunity of cutting the enemy's life-line and of protecting our own.[45]

On 6–8 December 1915, a conference held at general headquarters in Egypt called for a 'complete and immediate evacuation of Gallipoli'. Regarding the security concerns of the Canal, the conference stated that 'although the defence of Egypt was essential in the Allied interests yet it must be undertaken with the least possible force'.[46] A full-scale landing on the Levant coast was no longer an option. Lawrence remarked on the decision to Liddel Hart:

> I am unrepentant about the Alexandretta scheme. [...] A landing at Alexandretta in February 1915 would have handed over Syria and Mespot. to their native (Arab) troops, then all in their home stations, and complete, and automatically established local governments there [...] and that would have been the moment for the Dardanelles naval effort.[47]

As the Turkish government moved its Arab divisions out of Syria, basic material for an Arab Revolt disappeared. Two smaller proposals surfaced in 1915 for an insurrectionist movement supported by a British landing; although neither was approved, both queries strengthened Cairo's impression that large numbers of sympathizers waited behind the Turkish frontlines and required only a show of support by Britain to act. The first scheme originated with an overeager claim by Mohammed al-Faruqi who told his British debriefers in August 1915 that the paramount chief of the Rualla Federation in the Syrian interior, Nuri Shaalan, was prepared to attack the Ottoman army in conjunction with a British landing. The claim turned out to be false, but as al-Faruqi's testimony seemed to be in the same vein as statements already collected from al-Masri and other informants, Cairo Intelligence was prepared to believe that hidden cohorts of Arab revolutionaries stretched from the Hauran to the Hejaz, ready to 'roll up Syria [...] from the tail end' and name the Sherif of Mecca as the new Caliph, as soon as assistance was declared.[48] Lawrence warned that all Arab units in Syria would be transferred to the Dardanelles as soon as Turkish replacements were available, 'unless we some day do something'.[49] In the meantime, with the aim of impressing upon the Syrian and Hejazi Bedouin Arabs that 'a time will come when the Turks will indeed succeed in their endeavour to take Egypt,' the Turks continued to make displays of road and railway construction, despite shortages in materials. By August, the railhead had been extended to Kheimeh and the bankhead eleven miles further to Falluja. According to an informant, a German contractor had anticipated that the railway would reach the Gaza–Beersheba road by end of September 1915.[50]

Cairo's next substantial scheme to catalyse an internal revolt against the Turkish army came in response to an unfolding disaster above the Persian Gulf. In the spring of 1916, 17,000 British Indian troops found themselves besieged by overwhelming Ottoman forces in a bend on the Euphrates River, in central Mesopotamia. The scale of defeat looming at the village of Kut was the greatest humiliation the British would face in any theatre during the entire war. The India Expeditionary Force 'D' (IEF 'D') had been tasked to establish control of Britain's oil installations around the head of the Persian Gulf. Immediately war was declared in November 1915, they mobilized and secured the lower Shatt al-Arab river delta and occupied Basra.[51] Continuing up the Tigris towards Baghdad and buoyed by easy victories, the Anglo-Indian commanders were unaware, or disbelieving, that the troops collapsing before them in the south were radically different from the professional Fourth Army of mainly Anatolian Turks that the German commander, Baron von der Goltz, and the Turkish commander, Nur-Ud-Din, were bringing down from the north. Lawrence later attributed the IEF 'D''s over-confidence to chauvinism and inadequate intelligence on the enemy.[52] There was also the intense desire of the Anglo-Indian authorities to restore some measure of Britain's prestige in the East after the military failures at the Dardanelles and Gallipoli. By November, the reinforced Turkish army had beaten the IEF 'D' back from Ctesiphon to the Kut swamplands. By March 1916, the British commander telegraphed headquarters that they were completely surrounded and facing starvation, without hope of escape or reinforcements. The Government of India ceded control to the War Office.[53]

Cairo Intelligence responded to the crisis at Kut by proposing two schemes, both of which were highly unorthodox and thus galling to many in the British establishment. India blocked the first proposal outright: an Arab mission (comprising al-Masri and al-Faruqi) accompanied by a British intelligence officer to travel to Basra and raise a force of local Arab nationalists to help fight the Turks at Kut. Wyndham Deedes of Military Intelligence in Egypt recorded at the time that 'the atmosphere of Basra is *invincible* to anything of this nature' and that the Indian government's attitude towards the Arab parties was the very reason 'we have been able to do nothing up to date'.[54] The War Office's reluctance to authorize an offer of eventual Arab independence was also an obstacle. Cairo's second solution, which was suggested by Kitchener, was to send a deputation of intelligence officers to bribe the Turkish commander facing the IEF 'D' to lift the seige.[55] Captains T.E. Lawrence and Aubrey Herbert were chosen to accompany Colonel Beach (head of MI, Mesopotamia) up the Euphrates river to the Turkish camp.[56] They offered Khalil Pasha the approved sum of £1,000,000, and then a rise of £2,000,000, but the commander had been ordered by Enver Pasha not to accept any amount; 'the cards were all in his hands', as Lawrence wrote afterwards.[57] In August, 9,000 British and Indian soldiers and a few thousand non-combatants surrendered to the Turkish force. In the months that followed, nearly three-quarters of that number were executed by the Turks, died of exhaustion on the forced march to Baghdad or died in prison camps afterwards.[58]

The shock of the failure at Kut had repercussions on several intelligence questions, including interdepartmental cooperation and the role of intelligence officers in policy formation. Percy Cox, CPO at Basra, suggested to Lawrence in April 1916 that a conference of representatives from Egypt, Aden, Mesopotamia and India might improve interdepartmental consultation on Muslim policies.[59] Lawrence's own report on the mission into southern Mesopotamia, replete with criticism of the Anglo-Indian administration, called for reforms on everything from the organization and technical operation of intelligence in the Gulf, such as the production of Imint, to the policies that intelligence was meant to support. He vented his extensive criticisms in a report (modified by colleagues before submission) that suggested, amongst other complaints, that Indian officials had knowingly sacrificed the IEF 'D' at Kut by ignoring intelligence on potential sympathizers within the Arab tribes of Nejef and Kerbela, who lay behind the Turkish positions.[60]

The Cario intelligence community's efforts to contact the secret Arab nationalist societies in Syria and Mesopotamia and launch a joint Anglo-Arab operation had been repeatedly blocked at the conception stage – by the British Foreign Office on behalf of the French government; by the British General Staff, to protect troop reserves for France; and by the Government of India who refused to sanction the encouragement of Arab independence movements. With British, French and Russian troops beleaguered on Turkish fronts from the Caucasus to the Dardanelles, Gallipoli and Kut, several schemes to foster a rebel army or 'fifth column' behind Turkish lines at Alexandretta and in southern Mesopotamia had been stopped by internal disagreements over Britain's deeper policy aims.

Political negotiations

> One cannot help feeling an uneasy instinct that our whole Balkan, Near Eastern and Arabian policy since the outbreak of the war has been merely opportunist and without any directing spirit. Recommendations from those who are qualified to speak on various subjects seem to have not been called for and, even when volunteered, do not appear to have led to any result [...].[61]

In the spring of 1915, exhausted British troops in France took heavy losses at Ypres. Germany made gains in the Carpathians and Galicia, and escalated their strategy of submarine warfare. British naval forces launched a risky operation at Gallipoli. British authorities in London and Cairo had already debated the military value for the Allied powers of encouraging rebel activity behind the Turkish lines in Mesopotamia and at Alexandretta, and the siege at Kut was still to come. But the negotiations soon to be authorized between the High Commissioner in Egypt and Sherif Hussein bin Ali of Mecca would raise the eastern front strategy to a new level. The specific terms required for agreement with Arab nationalists had always involved political recognition of their cause. McMahon would insist later to a gathering of military authorities that the scheme for an alliance with Arab leaders was 'a purely military business'.[62] But he and his intelligence experts in Cairo understood well that in supporting an Arab rebellion against the Ottoman government, the British administration was engaging with the Arab leaders' aspirations of national self-determination. Some of the officers with experience in the Middle East and Asian countries already looked upon this stage of political reform as inevitable, albeit not ideal for British imperial servants; increasingly progressive rhetoric had been circulating with energy through non-European minority groups since Imperial Japan's 1905 defeat of the Russian army.

On 14 April 1915, the Foreign Office took the first key step and informed High Commissioner McMahon that if he required further means to encourage the Arabs' action, the government was prepared to 'make it an essential condition in the terms of peace that the Arabian peninsula and its Mohammedan Holy Places should remain in the hands of an independent sovereign state'.[63] By

June, McMahon's office had printed this proclamation onto leaflets and distributed them throughout Egypt, the Sudan, Syria and parts of the peninsula.[64] McMahon then sent a personal letter to the Sherif of Mecca to extend the British government's support for an independent Arabian state (of unspecified boundaries) and an Arab Caliphate.[65]

The timing of McMahon's invitation to the Sherif was crucial. Increasingly anxious over his own security, the Sherif hesitated over McMahon's offer. During the spring of 1915, he had maintained a semblance of loyalty to the CUP by sending his third son, Feisal, to Damascus and Constantinople to act as his representative with the government. Feisal met with government ministers and attended official functions, but he was also secretly casting around the Syrian Arab population for allies to aid the Sherif. Both *al-Fatat* and *Al-'Ahd*, whose members were under increasing pressure from Jemal Pasha, welcomed Feisal and explained their societies' war aims.[66] Yasin al-Hashimi assured him that the Arab 12th Corps was ready for action, and other members also pledged their support. Although the societies initially wanted Feisal to declare himself immediately as their military leader, they agreed to accept the Sherif as their titular head and to trust him to conclude fair terms with the British. In an extraordinary joining of purpose, *al-Fatat* and *al-'Ahd* produced a resolution of terms for the Sherif to use as the basis for an Anglo-Arab alliance. It became known as the 'Damascus Protocol', and named four conditions:

> (1) 'The recognition by Great Britain of the independence of the Arab countries [...].'[67] (2) 'The abolition of all exceptional privileges granted to foreigners under the Capitulations.' (3) 'The conclusion of a defensive alliance between Great Britain and the future independent Arab state.' (4) 'The grant of economic preference to Great Britain.'[68]

Feisal accepted the Damascus Protocol and returned to Mecca on 20 June 1915. Inspired by his northern tour, he had planned to raise an army of volunteers that would be described to the Turkish authorities as the Hashemites' contribution for the second Suez Canal campaign. Feisal would then take the army back to Syria where he would combine with al-Hashimi's 12th Corps, and liberate Syria for the Arabs under the banner of the Sherif.[69]

But events to the north disrupted these plans. By June 1915, Jemal Pasha had begun holding public courtmartials of hundreds of Arab nationalists in Syria.[70] Fearing that his scope for action was shrinking, the Sherif replied to the British government on 14 July and gave details for the boundaries of the future Arab state that precisely followed the terms set by *al-Fatat* and *al-'Ahd* in the Damascus Protocol. The Sherif's letter, which was addressed to Storrs, marked the beginning of what later became known as the 'McMahon–Hussein Correspondence'.[71]

McMahon initially questioned the Sherif's authority to speak for all Arab populations on boundary matters north of the Hejaz, but by the time he received the Sherif's reply on 9 September, Cairo had obtained important intelligence that altered their perception of the Sherif's requests.[72] The intelligence came from a young Turkish officer who had crossed over to the British lines at the Dardanelles, Mohammed al-Faruqi. Al-Faruqi claimed to be a member of both *al-'Ahd* and *al-Fatat*, and to be 'accredited' by *al-Fatat* to negotiate with England. He outlined *al-Fatat*'s aims to restore 'an Arab Khalifate in Arabia, Syria and Mesopotamia at all costs' and, with Britain's help, to secure the independence of the Arabian peninsula and Syria. He also said that the society was prepared to accept 'an increasing measure of autonomous government [...] in Palestine and Mesopotamia', as a gesture to Britain, along with independence for the major inland towns of Syria if France demanded control over the Lebanon. Clayton noted the remarkable similarity between the terms issued by the powerfully-described *al-Fatat* and those from Mecca: 'That the attitude of the Sherif is that of the majority of the Arab peoples there can be no doubt.'[73] Cairo's intelligence had now linked the Sherif's demands to the aims of Syria's two main Arab secret societies convinced Cairo. It seemed that here, at last, was an opportunity to detach the Arabs from the Ottoman war effort on a country-wide scale.[74]

McMahon was determined to ensure that London's ongoing confusion over the future of the post-war Ottoman territories did not undermine his negotiations with the Sherif. London's customary deference to India meant that the latter's anxiety about Indian Muslim loyalties to the Turkish Caliph (although never about Arab Muslim loyalties in Mesopotamia) slowed down the deliberations of the War Cabinet. There were also some conservative colonial stalwarts who worried about dismantling the traditional Turkish barrier to Russia's enlargement. But these caveats eventually faded. After Russia bid for post-war control of Constantinople in March 1915 and rumours rose about French plans to colonize not only Syria but Cilicia and Palestine, Lord Crewe appealed to the War Council that 'if we did not block out what we want we might get left in the lurch.'[75]

On 19 March 1915 the War Council ordered an inter-departmental committee to be set up to consider British desiderata in the Ottoman Empire. Sir Maurice de Bunsen of the Foreign Office chaired the proceedings, and its report appeared in April 1915. Contrary to the Arab leaders' aspirations for the territory, the Committee concluded that Asiatic Turkey should be ruled by spheres of European influence (if not outright partition) because it still acted as a necessary buffer to possible French and Russian expansionist aims. The members agreed that an independent Arab state could be established on the Arabian peninsula, but they were not able to agree on its various boundaries. They did, however, emphasize that the Ottoman Empire was the world's last Islamic government and the seat of the Islamic Caliph. Western powers would have to stand forewarned of the repercussions of its dismemberment, should the peace and its aftermath proceed in that direction.

> [By defeating the Ottoman Empire] We should have destroyed the political power of Islam as represented by Turkey, and at the same time, by our annexation of Mesopotamia have made it clear to all Moslems that any hope

> of an Arab Khalifate acquiring material wealth and prosperity sufficient to restore a Moslem State that would count among the Governments of the world was from henceforth impossible.[76]

To protect the existence of a Muslim state organized around an Arab Caliphate and standing alongside other nations in wealth and prosperity was not, as far as can be seen, the express aim of anyone in the British government at this time. Rather, the agreed aim as sanctioned by the Foreign Office was to defuse the threat of *jihad* in Britain's colonial territories and, as far as possible, persuade the Arab population to abandon the Turkish war effort in order to relieve the pressure on British troops. Cairo's view contrasted with that of the War Council and the de Bunsen Committee in that they recognized very quickly that the terms for an alliance demanded by the Sherif and the Arab societies would be sensitive and politically challenging for the British government. Cairo's early deliberations over the future of the Caliphate, for example, foreshadowed several of the policy conflicts that would trail British decision-makers.

The benefits of a 'restored' Arab Caliphate were first advanced to the British government by Kitchener. Part of the diplomatic dance unfolding in Cairo was designed to smooth the course of Anglo-Arab negotiations and establish the Sherif's candidacy for this position. The Sherif had already proven himself to be a shrewd and ambitious regional chief. He had demonstrated independence and courage by publicly separating himself from the CUP and condemning their centralization policies. He had barred the Turkish Vali sent by Constantinople to Mecca and closed the road from Jeddah to Mecca.[77] His tribes controlled the camel supply in the Hejaz, which gave him significant leverage over the Turks' plans to mobilize against the Canal. But most importantly, in terms of public relations, the Sherif was a descendant of the Qoreish tribe, the tribal family of the Prophet Muhammad. He was the country's most prominent Islamic leader, second only to the Turkish Caliph.

Cairo promoted the Sherif to London as the rightful heir to the Caliphate. It would also appear that in their efforts to make the strongest possible case for him, they felt it judicious to misrepresent certain aspects of the Caliphate's function. First, Cairo's communications with London suggested that the true Caliph had to be, like the Sherif, a Sunni and a member of the Qoreish. In fact, those conditions applied only to the classical Islamic definition of the 'universal Caliph'; modern Islam required only that the *sharia* or Islamic law be upheld and that the government be established in accordance with the Kor'an.[78] More seriously, Cairo omitted to point out that the Caliphate possessed both temporal and spiritual power in the eyes of most Muslims, was both 'Imam and Sultan'. The Arabists in Cairo's intelligence offices exchanged many memoranda showing a sophisticated understanding of the position's dual aspects, but they obfuscated the point in official correspondence.[79] They reasoned that if London understood the political nature of the Caliphate, they might decide that negotiations with the Sherif were too risky. France would have greater cause to protest, out of concern for the impact on their position in Syria. The Government of

India would also be able to object, in defence of their aims in Mesopotamia.[80] Thus Cairo portrayed the Caliphate to London as a mainly spiritual figurehead in Islamic government. McMahon reported to Foreign Secretary Grey that general Muslim opinion was in favour of the Sherif's candidacy for the Caliphate for the most uncomplicated reasons. The Sherif was a Qoreish, and as such was already the legitimate Guardian of the Holy Places. In addition, the title of 'Caliph' would only be a religious one, for 'the idea of an Arab unity under one ruler recognised as supreme by other Arab chiefs is as yet inconceivable to the Arab mind'. McMahon added that the election of the Sherif would also suit Britain's interests very favourably.[81]

Indian officials objected that something was not quite straight in Cairo's arguments. In early 1915 when a public announcement of pledges to the Sherif – including the restoration of an Arab Caliphate – was suggested, the Viceroy advised the India Office (IO) not to agree to the pledges because 'it would unnecessarily tie our hands for future':

> The situation is not at present at all clear and it is conceivable that spiritual and temporal claims may become so intermixed, particularly in Arabia, that interference on our part may be imperative on temporal grounds and might be construed as breach of faith.[82]

Clayton dismissed India's concerns in a letter to Wingate, and reiterated the universally held belief that any future Arab state would inevitably be politically feeble: 'India seems obsessed with idea that we mean to form a powerful Arab kingdom. Such was never the intention and would in any case be impracticable.' Although the Sherif might be named the head of an 'Arab confederation', which would 'thus qualify himself to assume the Khalifate, the lack of cohesion which is always quoted is our main safeguard against the establishment of a united Arab Kingdom which might be a threat against British interests.'[83]

Cairo believed that a promise of support for an Arab Caliphate would convince the Arab leaders of their good faith. The other gamble that the Residency in Egypt meant to take, and which India resented, was that by transferring the Caliphate to the Holy City of Mecca, Anglo-Egypt as its nearby protector would win even greater prestige in the eyes of British Muslim subjects.[84] D.G. Hogarth, Acting Director of the Arab Bureau, later clarified the differences in outlook between Egypt and India with regard to this revised definition of the Caliphate. In an in-house intelligence article, he admitted that Cairo had promoted an 'official pretence that the Caliphate is only a spiritual headship, no longer implying temporal dominion over Moslems in general'. None of the official communications from Kitchener and McMahon to the Sherif of Mecca contradicted this definition of the Caliphate but the definition was indeed constructed, 'a sturdy, conscious fiction'. Hogarth recommended that the British government 'persevere' in the pretence that they regarded 'a Caliph as analogous to a Pope,' however; consistency would protect Britain from any complaints of conscious deceit.[85] Of course, Hogarth's cynical outlook did not anticipate the degree to which the Arab leaders' traditional conflation of political, religious and even military authority would create its own pressure on British decision-making, nor the extent to which the eventual campaign in the Hejaz would depend on that conflation.

The Foreign Office and the Sykes–Picot Agreement

While Cairo pursued negotiations with the Sherif of Mecca, London began to consider seriously the eventual status of the Ottoman territories. Despite the central goal of defeating the Turks, and the secondary interest in maintaining a position of influence in the region, a schism opened between the priorities of the Foreign Office, the War Office and the Egyptian Residency. The British Government's private deliberations that culminated in the conclusion of the Sykes–Picot Agreement only widened it further.

In the autumn of 1915, the Foreign Office granted McMahon a significant degree of initiative in his negotiations with the Sherif.[86] Grey made the government's trust explicit: 'the important thing is to give our assurances that will prevent the Arabs from being alienated, and I must leave you discretion in the matter as it is urgent and there is not time to discuss an exact formula.'[87] McMahon's decisiveness in concluding an alliance with the Sherif was later admired by Clayton, who wrote to the Sirdar at Khartoum:

> The High Commissioner came out of it very well, I think, in taking the responsibility upon himself of replying to the Sherif without further reference. The F.O. telegram certainly gave him a free hand but, in their usual way, they left several openings for making a scapegoat in the event of necessity, and there is many a man who would have funked it, and referred his proposed reply for approval.[88]

Nevertheless there was no official mechanism in place that delegated authority for such policy coordination to Cairo. Government ministers were increasingly aware of the Middle East's significance for the Axis agenda; Lord Cromer had come to the conclusion that 'It is no longer a European War. The European side has, for the moment, fallen into the background and the war has become one for supremacy in the East'.[89] The Sirdar, recounting McMahon's 'vast Indian experience', had ventured that his appointment would 'presage an attempt at coordinating British policy in regards to Moslems in India, Arabia and the Near East'.[90] But as India continued to raise complaints about Cairo's activities, it became necessary to make sure that McMahon's negotiations with the Sherif did not intrude upon the interests of Delhi or of Britain's ally, France.

The government in London convened a second inter-departmental committee on 13 November 1915 to discuss the Allies' territorial claims for the post-war Ottoman Empire. Sir Arthur Nicolson, Permanent Under-Secretary at the Foreign Office, chaired the meetings. The committee's priority in Nicolson's mind was to reassure the representatives that negotiations with the Sherif of

Mecca would not compromise the interests of France in Syria or of the Government of India in Mesopotamia. British representatives from the War Office and Foreign Office attended, and two representatives from the India Office. Also present was François Georges-Picot, a former French Consul-General at Beirut and currently Secretary at the French Agency in Cairo. Picot was a well-known expansionist and member of the Syrian party. McMahon described him to the Foreign Office, 'a notorious fanatic on the Syria question and quite incapable of assisting any mutual settlement on the reasonable commonsense grounds which the present situation requires'.[91] No one in attendance questioned the absence of a credible representative from the Arab territories in question. Picot, while outnumbered and outranked at the meetings, was able to make it clear that he was not concerned by Britain's promises to the Sherif, believing, as did most of his British counterparts, that the terms would never become operative. He told Nicolson that it would be pointless to pretend with the Arabs that creating a viable state out of such a multitude of tribes was a realistic aim.[92]

Sir Mark Sykes, Kitchener's agent for Middle East affairs at the War Office, was determined to come to an understanding for the region and offered a series of territorial gifts to France, purportedly based an earlier consulation with Mohammed al-Faruqi on the prospect of working with France. But Sykes' offer was based on a distortion of al-Faruqi's conversation. Moreover, al-Faruqi was not authorized by the Sherif or the Arab societies to negotiate any terms for such an alliance.[93] In a meeting with Sykes, al-Faruqi had discussed the grant of extensive concessions to French interests in Syria and to British aims in the Persian Gulf in exchange for military assistance; he may have been acting from a misguided sense of self-importance or eagerness to force British action. In any case, al-Faruqi asked the Entente to make a 'landing between Mersina and Alexandretta and making good the Cilican Gates or the Amanus Pass; stipulating further that, until this had been done, the Sherif should take no action'. He believed that the Allies' cooperation would enable the members of *al-'Ahd* and *al-Fatat* to cut the railway in Syria and begin their armed revolution.

Sykes reported on al-Faruqi's condition of an Allied landing in his telegram to London on 20 November 1915; but as the Alexandretta scheme had already been rejected on 13 November, this condition was ignored while al-Faruqi's concessions to Sykes were saved. These included a French advisory zone south of a line from Alexandretta through Urfa to the Persian border; a French monopoly on 'all concessionary enterprise in Palestine and Syria'; recognition of French educational establishments; and British control of a similar zone for the remaining regions of Arab self-government, including direct rule over Basra and areas to the south. These gifts were handed to the French without any link to the original stipulation of an Allied landing at Alexandretta.[94]

Finally, the Nicolson Committee report inserted a secret clause into the section dealing with the boundaries of the future Arab state. It made the inclusion of the major inland Syrian towns of Damascus, Hama, Homs and Aleppo conditional on the receipt of material assistance from the Arabs to the war effort; the Arabs would have to liberate the towns themselves in order to retain them.

This clause directly contradicted the McMahon negotiations with the Sherif.[95] The final proposals for French and British zones of direct and indirect control over all of Syria and Mesopotamia (Palestine was designated an international zone), together with the secret clause covering the four inland towns, would eventually form the basis of the ill-famed Sykes–Picot Agreement, ratified on 4 February 1916. The committee also accepted French and Indian arguments that any future 'Arab state' must be contained well within the Arabian peninsula.

As Nicolson later explained to the Viceroy, he did not believe the negotiations with Hussein would 'ever fructify into anything really definite. [...] People talk of the Arabs as if they were some cohesive body, well-armed and equipped, instead of a heap of scattered tribes with no cohesion and no organisation'. He insisted that 'we are trying to treat with a shadow, and it would be a delusion to imagine that we should be able to detach a really powerful Arab force from Turkey'.[96] But other members of the Committee warned that ignoring the agreements already reached between McMahon and the Sherif would not only offend Muslim opinion but probably force the Arabs back into the Turkish camp, an event that would harm French as well as British interests.[97] Colonel A.C. Parker and General C.E. Callwell (now Director of Military Operations and Intelligence) made a special appeal at a committee meeting on 23 November to persuade Picot that they must offer 'the Arabs and Syrians [in the French zone], some measure of independence, conditional on their assisting the Allies, thus putting a check to Turkish and German aims in consolidating Mohammedan religious feeling with them'. Without this gesture, France would only be helping the German and Turkish governments to achieve 'the military co-operation of the whole Mohammedan world in a religious war against the Allies'. Arab resentment would excite uprisings across the Middle and Near East and force the 'removal of a very large part of the British army from France'.[98] But these warnings were dismissed.

The Great Powers' secret designs on the future Arab state would not be finalized in the Sykes–Picot Agreement for fourteen more weeks, but McMahon was already being edged out of London's decision-making. London was also under continuing pressure from Indian officials, who still hoped to undermine both the Arab secret societies' claims and the High Commissioner's authority as a negotiator with the Sherif. Chamberlain, the Secretary of State for India, told Grey that India Office sources suggested that 'the Sherif is a nonentity – powerless to carry out his proposals'.[99] Clayton complained privately about this to General Maxwell, commander of the Force in Egypt. Chamberlain and the Viceroy meant to object to any commitment to the Arab party until 'it is proved that the Sherif and Faroki are willing and able to carry out their promises', insisting that 'unless they act at once [HMG] cannot consider [itself] bound in any way'.[100] Grey was still willing to believe that an Arab movement, if secured, 'would amply compensate us for any future inconvenience as regards Baghdad' (i.e. conflict with the Government of India), but, he insisted to McMahon, 'action must be immediate'.[101]

McMahon cabled London repeatedly to maintain pressure for more assistance for the Arab movement. He stressed to Grey that the 'serious situation' facing British interests in Egypt and Mesopotamia 'renders the alienation of Arab assistance from the Turks a matter of great importance'. He strongly believed that the British government 'must make every effort to enlist the sympathy and assistance, even though passive, of the Arab people.[102] As explicit reassurances from London failed to arrive, McMahon could guess at the implications of London's silence, and he warned Hussein against further inertia:

> It is most essential that you should spare no effort to attach all the Arab peoples to our united cause. [...] It is on the success of these efforts and on the more active measures which the Arabs hereafter take in support of our cause, when the time comes, that the permanence and strength of our agreement must depend.[103]

In the Residency's view, what separated the context of the Nicolson Committee's resolutions from those of the de Bunsen Committee ten months earlier was Cairo's possession of intelligence on the secret Arab nationalist societies working inside Ottoman territory. Buoyed by this information, they had moved forward in their negotiations with the Sherif, confident that his sympathy would activate a wide front of domestic Arab hostility against the Turks. Cairo would not learn of the basic terms of the Sykes–Picot Agreement for four more months, or of the clause concerning inland Syria for at least two years. But in a telegram to the Foreign Office just before the ratification of the Sykes–Picot Agreement, McMahon warned that there would be a penalty for ignoring Cairo's intelligence on the Sherif's supporters and of abandoning the Muslim Arab popular opinion it represented. He believed the French were 'much mistaken in thinking their advent into Arab territory will be welcomed by the Arabs; as the exact opposite will be the case'. The 'considerable danger' for Britain of allowing such French delusions to stand regarding 'her mistake [and] the real state of Arab feeling' was that 'we may hereafter be accused of instigating or encouraging the opposition to the French, which the Arabs now threaten and will assuredly give'.[104] This warning exactly expressed the tenor of the Humint Cairo was receiving from its Arab informants on the scale and seriousness of Arab secret societies in Syria who waited for their moment to act.

The creation of the Arab Bureau

> So far as we were concerned it seemed to be nobody's business to harmonise the various views and policies of the Foreign Office, the India Office, the Admiralty, the War Office, the Government of India and the Residency in Egypt.[105]

Deliberations regarding the future of the disputed Arab movements and Middle East policy might have continued to lurch in different directions if the British government had not itself been exhausted by the various contradictory reports, particularly the clash of counsel from the governments of India and Egypt. In a seminal move, the government was persuaded to try to resolve the confusion by bringing in greater support from regional intelligence, on the assumption that an intelligence staff would be able to deliver some kind of final verdict on the competing claims, free of political bias.

The proposition that a reorganization of Middle East intelligence might help the government formulate a single coherent policy for the Arab territories struck many in the region as self-evident. British officials on the ground had been expressing frustration over the poor coordination between regional offices and lack of information-sharing since at least early 1915. During a visit to Aden, Storrs had discussed with the resident CPO '(what I have tried to advance wherever I have served) the Interchange of Political Officers'.[106] Gertrude Bell would write with the same conviction to Lawrence in March 1916 about the need for intelligence departments to exchange personnel.[107] Sir Percy Cox, despite his and the IEF 'D's emphatic independence from Egypt's policies, was of the same mind as Bell, and told Lawrence at Basra in April 1916 that a Middle East conference with all the administrations represented would vastly improve British policy in the region.[108]

The actual proposal for a new intelligence organization came from the irrepressible Mark Sykes, who had become exercised over the success of enemy propaganda.[109] Sykes appeared before the Nicolson Committee on 21 December 1915 to give a report after his recent tour of Egypt, Mesopotamia and India where he had held regional consultations on the de Bunsen Committee proposals. He announced that he had been shaken by revelations of the virulence and range of enemy propaganda in the Middle East, which the parochial and fragmented commands in Delhi, Basra, Aden and Cairo seemed incapable of countering.[110] His suggestion was to set up a new 'Islamic Bureau' in London, under his own direction, that would 'harmonise British Political Activity in the near East'. It would 'keep the Foreign Office, India Office, Admiralty, War Office, and Government of India simultaneously informed of the general tendency of German and Turkish policy,' and 'co-ordinate propaganda in favour of Great Britain among non-Indian Moslems'.[111] Colonel Parker of the War Office agreed that 'the closest co-ordination and the most direct exchange of information between India and Eygpt, hitherto faulty or non-existent, is most desirable'. He strongly advocated the creation of a specialized Bureau to provide 'a more comprehensive and continuous treatment of the various Islamic problems'.[112]

While there appeared to be widespread agreement on the value of improved regional intelligence and closer coordination on policy in the Middle East, the location of the new intelligence office had still to be decided. Sykes wrote Clayton that India was blocking the idea of the new bureau because they were 'desirous of taking Mesopotamia as an Indian playground, as incorrigible Arabphobes and Turcophiles under seditious Moslem pressure'. But the government in London and the Admiralty, in particular, pressed on. The Admiralty initially contemplated incorporating the Bureau into its own intelligence network, with Sykes on hand in London.[113] Sykes was willing, remarking that despite the

Admiralty's having lost some of its credibility after the Dardanelles, the fact remained that 'it alone achieves anything, has large funds and does things' (including running Britain's main wartime Sigint office). But it was Kitchener's preference that the Bureau be placed under the authority of the Foreign Office, as the institution responsible for directing foreign policy, while simultaneously enjoying full access to the Department of Naval Intelligence, its agent networks, codes and equipment.[114] Captain Reginald 'Blinker' Hall, the Director of Naval Intelligence (DNI), agreed and put the matter to rest by concluding that it would be wasteful to subsume a new intelligence-gathering bureau for the Near East into the Admiralty's London operations. He recommended that the Bureau be located at Cairo for it was the obvious hub of Britain's Arab and Islamic affairs. He told Clayton that 'this seems to be the only successful plan, as you have people on the spot who are able to assess any information at its proper value', and promised that he would be 'delighted to do anything to get the closest co-ordination between all our Intelligences' on the region's Arab affairs.[115]

Clayton was very happy with the decision. He had 'already started the nucleus of a Near Eastern Office' by December 1915 when Sykes first wrote him about his plans for a Bureau. It dealt mostly with 'political suspects of all kinds, and pan-Islamic propaganda', but Clayton hoped they would soon be able to 'take on the study of higher political questions and also the initiation of propaganda on our own account'.[116] He elaborated on this vision for Hall: 'what I want is to start a Bureau here which will be a centre to which all information on the various questions connected with the Near East will gravitate'. Clayton envisioned the Bureau as a means of educating the policymakers in Egypt and in London about the Arab territories' relevance to British policy. He wanted to employ 'a staff of men who are competent to sift and catalogue this information [...] into a form in which it is easily digested by those who may not be experts in the various questions'.[117]

The final constitution drafted by an interdepartmental conference in January 1916 named the new office the 'Arab Bureau'. The Arab Bureau would not be independent under the High Commissioner, as Clayton had hoped,[118] but organized as a section of the Sudan Intelligence Department under the High Commissioner in Egypt (and the Foreign Office). This umbrella of authority would both underscore the emphasis to be given to political matters and provide the new bureau with the valuable association of the High Commissioner's office, whose significance could not yet be guessed at.[119]

The range of the Arab Bureau's mandate was unusually broad, and contentious – not least because it seemed to take for granted the operational constraints implied by an official policy for the Ottoman Arab territories when lack of one was precisely the grievance it had been created to resolve. The Arab Bureau's first responsibility was to 'harmonise British political activity in the Near East' and to 'keep the Foreign Office, the India Office, the Committee of Defence, the War Office, the Admiralty, and Government of India simultaneously informed of the general tendency of Germano-Turkish Policy.'[120] As there was still no single established policy for British interests in the Ottoman territories (and the Sykes–Picot Agreement was still secret), this formulation seemed to give the Arab Bureau an unbounded authority to assert influence over – i.e. 'harmonise' – the various administrations' political priorities in the region. It seemed to suggest that the Arab Bureau itself would be able to direct the content of Britain's Middle East 'political activity', a role normally fulfilled by policymakers. Sir Arthur Hirtzel of the India Office expanded on the worries raised by the Arab Bureau to the CID: 'what is in the back of people's minds is that the Bureau may be the germ of a future Foreign Office, which at present Cairo lacks'.[121] It would have been no comfort to him that T.E. Lawrence of MI, Cairo had already written to his brother in the summer of 1915: 'We are a sort of Levant Foreign Office, and can think of nothing else.'[122]

Worsening the confusion, the Bureau's other responsibility was to act as the central office for disseminating intelligence on enemy propaganda to the government and coordinating 'propaganda in favour of Great Britain and the *Entente* among non-Indian Moslems without clashing with the susceptibilities of Indian Moslems and the *Entente* Powers'.[123] Most of the government ministers, excepting those from the Government of India, had agreed with Sykes' declaration that Muslim Arabs in the Ottoman territories should be targeted more forcefully with pro-British propaganda.[124] But this propaganda function soon became confused with the Arab Bureau's apparent authority to guide 'political activity' after a misstatement by Austen Chamberlain (SSI) to the Viceroy, in which he omitted the context of propaganda and advised that General Officer Commanding (GOC), Basra 'sd. [*sic*] understand that Cairo bureau is central organ through which His Majesty's Government will lay down policy and principles & his dept. must therefore work in strict conformity with indications received from Cairo'.[125] General Percy Lake, GOC, Basra, immediately protested at the implication that he would take instruction from Cairo.[126] The Viceroy also complained to Chamberlain that the Arab Bureau could not be trusted to relay the 'policy and principles of His Majesty's Government in regard to Arab questions' because 'we never know the authority behind their communications'.[127] A senior India Office civil servant only exacerbated those fears by explaining that because 'no "definite decision" has yet been reached as to the lines of our Arabian policy [...] one of the main function of the [Arab] Bureau is to furnish His Majesty's Government with the material for arriving at such a decision'. There was little consolation in his adding, 'It will be for the Irak [*sic*] branch [of the Arab Bureau] to see that the Irak "point-of-view" does not suffer from lack of being represented.'[128] As the Government of India saw it, the Arab Bureau had suddenly risen to a position of privilege with regard to the formulation of Arab policy far beyond that of any other department in the region, with a remit that now crossed over into Indian affairs.

The Arab Bureau had been given a special mandate, however imperfectly understood, to make decisions regarding 'political activity', coordinate propaganda policy for the region as a whole and operate as a new kind of political intelligence section under the Residency. The conference's final notable decision was to reject Sykes for the leadership of the Bureau, and appoint Colonel (later

Sir Brigadier-General) Gilbert Clayton instead.[129] Clayton's style of command would fundamentally shape the running of the Bureau. He was perhaps the only figure before the outbreak of the revolt who fully grasped the new office's unique position within the Egyptian administration and its potential for influence as an intelligence headquarters. For the first few months of its operations, the only official full-time members of the Arab Bureau were D.G. Hogarth (Naval Intelligence), Acting Director; his deputy, Captain Kinahan Cornwallis (formerly of the Sudan Agency);[130] and Arthur Brownlow fforde of the Indian Consular Service, who was attached for 'consultative purposes' on behalf of the Government of India.[131] Clayton immediately augmented this core staff with the most talented Arabists working at the Middle East section of Military Intelligence. Six weeks later, a reorganization of the intelligence departments in Egypt helped facilitate this concentration of expertise. After its evacuation from Gallipoli, the MEF amalgamated with General Sir John Maxwell's Force in Egypt and became 'Egyptforce' (21 March 1916). General Sir Archibald Murray took over as the commander and moved his headquarters from Cairo to Ismailia, closer to the Sinai. The bulk of Murray's intelligence staff accompanied the General Staff to Ismailia but his Middle East experts – including T.E. Lawrence, S.F. Newcombe, W. Deedes, C. Parker, A.H. Herbert, G. Hennessy and G.A. Lloyd – remained behind at the Savoy Hotel in Cairo and continued working for Clayton. Four days later, Clayton's Arab Bureau opened its office on the premises and the two offices combined, openly if still unofficially.

The Arab Bureau's poaching of MI's Middle East experts to engage in political intelligence analysis was made all the easier by the MI officers' enthusiasm for tackling the political subjects. Clayton and Hogarth carefully coordinated the members' responsibilities between the offices so that the Arab Bureau remained at the fore as 'an integral part of the Intelligence section', with the MI officers doing 'work indistinguishable from that of the bureau and in co-operation with it'.[132] As part of their traditional intelligence duties, the staff collected and analysed Humint, Sigint, Imint and open source intelligence on Arabia and other parts of the Middle East (and North African) territories, wrote intelligence assessments for interdepartmental and government distribution and continued to produce the Intelligence Section's daily intelligence bulletins. They revised and expanded the military services' important reference works, including the Admiralty's volume on 'Arabian Personalities' and its Handbooks on the Arabian peninsula's western littoral which were used by naval headquarters on the Canal, the Red Sea Patrol, the administration at Aden and other political officers around the coastline. Other more sensitive, policy-related tasks included communicating with underground Arab movements inside the Ottoman Empire and advising the Egyptian and London authorities on 'communications from, to, and concerning Powers friendly to us in Arabia'.

As the chief directors of the Arab Bureau 'proper', Hogarth and Cornwallis supervised the intelligence focus of the office, contributed reports and editorials for its publications and acted as consultants with the Residency on 'the Arab Question'. The other staff members, while moving informally from one task to another as necessary and all contributing to intelligence on the Hejaz and Syrian theatres, also maintained areas of expertise. For example, Wyndham Deedes with his prewar experience as a captain in the Turkish gendarmerie in North Africa and later the Interior Ministry at Constantinople, specialized in intelligence relating to Ottoman military and political affairs. Philip Graves, previously *The Times* correspondent in Cairo, was the resident expert in intelligence on the Turkish Army. M.S. McDonnell handled the intelligence relating to Arab operations in North Africa. R.W. Graves took primary charge of the new handbook on Egyptian 'personalities'. T.E. Lawrence liaised with the Egyptian Government's Survey of Egypt and the Royal Flying Corps in the production of topographical intelligence in the theatre, organized and edited the material for the daily Military Intelligence Bulletins and interrogated prisoners. In May 1916, he founded *The Arab Bulletin*, a secret publication of Arab Bureau intelligence for a select list of government recipients, the first issue of which appeared on 6 June 1916.[133] Clayton also enlisted Gertrude Bell, from the Indian intelligence office at Basra, to contribute reports on Arab tribal affairs around the Persian Gulf and Mesopotamia.

The High Commissioner's attitude to the Arab Bureau working under his authority was also critical to its success as a new intelligence office. During his twenty-four years' service with the Indian Political Department, McMahon had resolved territorial disputes with Persia, Baluchistan (where he also served as an agent) and Afghanistan. His most famous achievement to date had been the negotiation of the peace treaty between Tibet and China and the redrawing of Tibet's border. These experiences had instilled in him a cautious respect for the complexity of the political forces stirring in the east. He became particularly unique during his tenure in Egypt for the close relationship that he developed with his intelligence staff, especially Clayton.[134] Some histories of the period have characterized McMahon as being overly impressionable.[135] But after some consideration there can be little doubt that McMahon's acceptance of the intelligence judgements delivered to him and his respect for the Arab Bureau's analysis of the Arabs' situation were vital to Britain's engagement with the Arab Revolt. In his private reports to India, fforde repeatedly remarked on the attention that McMahon gave to intelligence in matters of policymaking. He assured India that McMahon and the Arab Bureau did not operate as a closed club, that 'the men who give the orders [also] consult others besides the experts and only act after consultation with London and India'. But fforde's own strategy for communicating India's interests to McMahon would still be to 'try my best to influence the men who advise High Commissioner'.[136]

Over the next year and a half, an air of maverick independence from traditional organizational constraints would continue to characterize the Arab Bureau, which was seen either as a menace to policy procedures or a refreshing corrective, depending on the view. Clayton and his staff would not have been surprised to learn that their wide-ranging intelligence activities and forays into policy judgements only confirmed the India Office's worst fears that the Arab Bureau had seeded the 'germ of a future Foreign Office' in Cairo. McMahon himself remarked to fforde on one occasion that he believed the Arab Bureau did in fact hold 'power over policy'.[137] Another Cairo intelligence officer went further and tried to explain to fforde the logic behind the Arab Bureau's forward-looking role in the region. The rise of Arab nationalism would inevitably and rapidly bring the Arabic-speaking countries together in political sympathy, at which point it would become 'necessary to have the foreign politics of Egypt, South Syria and Mesopotamia under one authority, to keep the balance of these things,' he explained. 'Nobody has yet proposed to put Egypt under India; – and yet the Midde East must be whole. It follows – take Mesopotamia and Arabia from India.'[138] Such progressive attitudes within the Arab Bureau towards the political future of the Middle East invoked something of the spirit of Kitchener's original doctrine. Already the machinery was falling into place to write the policy for the region afresh, based on an aggressive and creative intelligence process and the greater utilization of regional experts versed in the political and military conditions of the Arab territories. The optimistic prediction by an early visitor to the Middle East Section of the MI department in Cairo, which would soon be invited into the Arab Bureau, was perhaps now to be borne out:

> The Intelligence Department [...] have done invaluable work already collecting and tabulating information and initiating ideas which never could have dawned on the heads of the General or his surroundings. [...] A well-run Intelligence Department will really run him as regards policy, and this is what will shortly happen I think.[139]

Such a prophecy, even in jest, could hardly have been made with reference to either the Western or the Eastern Front in Europe.

2 The outbreak of the Arab Revolt, May–November 1916

The Sherif of Mecca launches uprising

The British government's ability to conclude an alliance with the Sherif of Mecca hinged for many politicians on the assumption that its promises to the Arabs, including support for the creation of a postwar independent Arab state, were unlikely to be anything other than rhetorical. The Sherif's promise to withhold support from the Turks, however, might be put into effect immediately and would benefit British forces from the Mediterranean to the Persian Gulf. McMahon assured the Foreign Office in December 1915 that the risks involved in concluding an agreement with the Meccan leader were meagre in light of its advantages. 'The conditions of Arabia never justified an expectation of active or organised assistance such as some people think is the object of our proposed mutual understanding' with the Hashemite dynasty, he said. 'What we want is the material advantage of even passive Arab sympathy and assistance on our side instead of their active cooperation with the enemy.'[1] As late as April 1916, fforde was reassuring his superiors in India that because the creation of a powerful Arab state was a 'practical impossibility, there was no harm in sympathising with the ideal',[2] especially when McMahon's negotiations with the Sherif had enabled Cairo 'to secure the benevolent neutrality of a very powerful Moslem influence, to cause serious embarrassment to the enemy and to defeat the plans for raising a *jehad* which would have made our position in the East far worse than it is today'.[3]

The Sherif could not stop indefinitely at a state of mere 'benevolent neutrality'; he needed to employ every military and diplomatic resource to repel the Turkish government's efforts to remove him from the Emirate. In May 1916, the Sherif sent Feisal to Damascus to meet again with *al-'Ahd* and *al-Fatat*. The societies warned Feisal that Jemal Pasha intended to conscript Hejazi fighters for the next attack on the Suez Canal as a blow to the Sherif's power base. The societies wanted Feisal to name himself the commander of the new force and launch the revolt on the spot. Feisal agreed to the plan. But upon re-entering the Hejaz he found himself out-manoeuvred by Jemal Pasha. Jemal had assigned Feisal a Turkish escort for his journey south, which the prince's obligations as host prevented him from attacking. Once at Medina, Feisal again had to reconsider his options. Fakhri Pasha, the Turkish GOC of the 3,000-strong Medina garrison of the Hejaz Expeditionary Force (HEF), had been ordered to take up a position in the city in preparation for what Jemal had anticipated as a 'disquieting' situation. Bolstering the HEF's numbers were another 3,500 Turkish troops under Major Khairi Bey, who had paused on their way to new postings in the Yemen. The Turkish Forces in the Hejaz now amounted to roughly three battalions, or 6,500–7,000 troops, stationed at garrisons inside the holy cities of Medina and Mecca, at Ta'if (forty-five miles southeast of Mecca), the coastal towns of Jiddah and Yenbo, and in cantonments along the Hejaz Railway in addition to the two battalions for the Yemen.[4] Feisal sent a warning to his father at Mecca that the Turkish army was preparing for hostilities.

The Sherif decided that his moment had come. On 5 June he ordered his sons to launch a collective attack against the HEF troops at Medina.[5] Feisal and Ali called out their armies and declared themselves enemies of the Turkish government. Feisal's force engaged the HEF outside the perimeter of Medina. Ali's men moved out as well and ripped up 150km of railway track to block the progress of Turkish reinforcements from Medain Salih (175 miles to the north).[6] News of the princes' action spread to the populations at Jiddah and Mecca. Turkish documents found later at Jiddah recorded the sudden panic felt by the city's Turkish officers on learning that 3,000–4,000 armed Bedouin had already gathered to charge the garrison in the name of the Sherif.[7]

The speed of events took Britain by surprise, as well. British Egypt's Oriental Secretary, Ronald Storrs, D.G. Hogarth and Kinahan Cornwallis of the Arab Bureau arrived in the Hejaz just days afterwards with the intention of making an assessment of the military situation and giving £10,000 to Abdullah as encouragement for action. The Sherif's youngest son, Zeid, gave them the news of the uprising, announcing that Feisal, Abdullah and Ali had already engaged the Turks and were being supported in the field by the Ateibah, Harb, Billi and Maaza tribes.[8]

At Mecca, as the story has been told, the Sherif leant out of his window after dawn prayers on 10 June and fired his rifle at the nearby Turkish barracks, officially beginning the Arab Revolt. His Arab followers attacked the Turkish units in the city and cut the water supply. To the south, Arabs laid siege to the Turkish fort of Jiyad.[9] The Turks responded; one party fired towards the Great Mosque and struck part of the holy Kaaba [Black Stone], an accident that would be held against the Ottoman government for the remainder of the war.[10] Within days of hearing of the Arabs' revolt at Mecca, the Sirdar of the Egyptian Army and Governor-General at Khartoum, Sir Reginald Wingate, dispatched a battery to the Hejaz to help the Arabs maintain their advantage. On 13/14 June, the Commandant at Mecca, the Ottoman Vali and all his staff surrendered the city to the Sherif's forces.[11]

Meanwhile, at Jiddah, the Turks had reorganized and turned their superior field- and machine-gun fire against the Arab rebels, who began to waver. The Sherif made an urgent request to the British navy to assist by cutting the city's water supply. The HMS *Fox* and HMS *Hardinge*, cruisers on duty with the Red Sea Patrol, responded to the call, while three planes from the seaplane carrier

Ben-my-Chree assisted with targeting and bombing. The combination of force was successful. On 16 June 1916, 850 Turkish troops at Jiddah surrendered to the Sherif.[12] The Arabs' recovery of this chief port for supplying food and materials to the Holy Places was a military and political triumph. The Sherif's fighters spread out and invested the principle blockhouses between Mecca and Jiddah, formed a link and captured more Turkish guns and munitions.[13]

Completing the sweep around Mecca, Abdullah's army surrounded the 1,200–3,000-strong garrison at Ta'if (military and civilian inhabitants), assisted by the Egyptian battery that had finished operations at Mecca. The Sherif ordered Abdullah to reduce the Ta'if garrison by siege rather than direct attack, to avoid the public relations disaster of accidentally harming civilian Muslims.[14] While that siege was underway, the Turkish garrison at the port town of Lith further down the coast surrendered on 23 June, panicked by the threat of similar anti-Turk uprisings and fears of a British naval bombardment.[15]

Reports of the Arabs' surprise victories against the Turkish positions west of Medina put the Turkish and German commands in an awkward position. Their press departments buried the incident and issued official denials. British signals operators intercepted a German message in late June that insisted, 'a rapid end has been made of the local disturbances in the Turkish province of the Hejaz, which has [*sic*] been grossly exaggerated by the English', and another, days later: 'We are in a position to deny absolutely that there has been any rebellion in the Hejaz at all'.[16] Months later, Constantinople still had not admitted that the Sherif had taken Mecca.[17]

One Turkish commander had not been surprised by the Arabs' uprising: the acting Turkish Governor and Commandant at Mecca, Mehmed Zia Bey. Mehmed had been collecting Humint from reliable informants on the city's increasingly angry mood, and had warned his superiors that acts of disobedience and political opposition rallies around the city were multiplying. He had deployed extra troops around government positions and instituted a curfew, but was rebuked for this initiative by his divisional commander who accused him of overreacting to the intelligence with 'extraordinary military measures' and betraying self-doubt to the Arab inhabitants.[18]

Cairo soon learned that the Turkish and German authorities had not only underestimated the degree of local Arab resentment, but misjudged their own ability to protect their war plan against a hostile population. Intelligence obtained by Cairo revealed that a secret Turco-German expedition had recently been launched to convert the Arabian coastline into a German forward signalling base, but it collided with the Sherif's uprising. Major Freiherr Othmar von Stotzingen, a German General-Staff officer formerly with the XIII Army Corps, and his Arabic-speaking colleague, Karl Neufeld, had been travelling south towards the Yemen. They intended to construct a new wireless station with long-range capability either at Hodeida on the coast, or inland at Sanaa. The station would have extended the Axis' network of enemy signalling stations already at Medina, Damascus, Constantinople and Mwanza in German East Africa, and be powerful enough to receive from, if not transmit to, Berlin.[19]

Humint, Sigint and captured enemy documents showed how the 'Von Stotzingen Mission' had been an essential part of the CUP's plan to 're-establish Turkish domination in the Peninsula, and to be an object lesson to the Arabs of the undiminished might of Turkey'.[20] Khairi Bey's force which Feisal found at Medina had been the expedition's military complement, and their few hundred transport animals were carrying the bulk of the wireless apparatus to the Yemen, where they would later stay as an occupying military authority. The Arab Bureau emphasized the significance of this information in their next bulletin, noting that: 'Instead of a handful of German adventurers trying to sneak past our patrols, and set up a wireless station in Southern Arabia,' which presumably would have fit under a more absurdist category, 'we have now an Ottoman Expeditionary Force bound for the Yemen and beyond, on a mixed military and political charter, with a senior German Staff Officer at the head of it,' the most worrying aspect of which was the presence of 'a German wireless detachment to keep in touch with conditions at home and in Africa.[21]

Evidence of the Turkish and German communications moving between Damascus, Constantinople and Berlin showed that the high command had worried about the mission's route and speculated that the Germans' presence in Arabia was precarious.[22] As news of the Arab uprising spread across the Hejaz, the mission's vulnerability increased. On 6–9 June 1916 at Yenbo, an angry Arab population inspired by news of the Sherif's action at Mecca confronted von Stotzingen's party. The Germans were forced to abandon their precious wireless equipment and fled to Um Lejj, where they were again assaulted by Bedouins and also robbed of their baggage.[23] At Medina, Khairi Bey's force was also attacked by local Arabs, and all their wireless cargo lost.[24]

After the Arabs' initial *tour de force* against the Turkish positions around Mecca and the aftershocks that wrecked the von Stotzingen expedition, momentum in the Hejaz started to flag. The Arab forces held on to their gains, contrary to the claims by German propaganda, but the limitations of the Sherif's spontaneous rising of tribal fighters were beginning to surface. It was clear that the tribesmen, who were armed only with rifles, were never going to be able to push through the Turks' machine- and field-gun entrenchments at Medina. According to Feisal, the precipitate start and shortage of arms had also cost them the participation of the powerful Anazeh tribes along the north of the railway.[25] The Sherif's military inferiority in troops and munitions would next be compounded by the challenge of mixing of disparate tribes with Syrian regular officers and local resentment of Hashemites' association with the British.

Complications for British support

The results of a genuine clash of arms between the tribesmen and the Turkish army had clarified several points for Cairo. The Sherif had to strengthen his authority considerably over the Arab tribes and cities beyond Mecca if his Revolt were to succeed. As fforde reported from the Arab Bureau, the entrenched tribal delineation of the Hejaz posed serious difficulties:

> Though the Sherif of Mecca is the most influential and enlightened Arab Chief and writes as the spokesman of the 'Arab Nation', he is not, so far as is known, supported by any organisation powerful enough to enforce acceptance of terms to which he may agree, over all or even the greater part of Arabia. No Arab Chief has, nor is likely to have.[26]

In addition to the traditional tribal distinctions, the Hashemites also seemed to face resistance from the townspeople and merchants on the coast who greeted the prospect of a Bedouin-led government with some scepticism. Yet perhaps even more pressing, the Sherif was having to contend with the expectations of the Syrian officers – deserters from the Ottoman army or British PoWs – who were electing to join his campaign. The Sherif, and the British, hoped that the Syrians would shoulder the task of training a regular Arab army to confront the HEF positions at Medina on their own terms and, eventually, carry the movement north. This northern destination was an integral part of the Sherif's Hejaz strategy and, as Syria was a patently more complex country than Arabia, the Sherif knew he would need the Syrian officers' political and military networks to help his campaign advance.

All of these difficulties were exacerbated for the Sherif by the risk that his association with Great Britain, however cautious and discreet, would undermine his religious and political credibility amongst Muslims and thus his suitability for the Caliphate. In late June 1916, the political liability of bringing a foreign Christian power to the Hejaz was brought home vividly to Cairo when local Arabs at the ports of Jiddah, Rabegh and Yenbo blocked the landing of three British supply ships. Cornwallis of the Arab Bureau, acting as McMahon's representative, Colonel C.E. Wilson, Governor of the Red Sea Province, and Major Pearson from the Egyptian Army (Sudan) had sailed to the Hejaz to deliver money and arms. They brought £20,000 in gold, two Egyptian artillery batteries, munitions, demolition matériel, various supplies and food to the forces fighting for the Sherif.[27] But the Turks had already spread rumours that Britain was deceiving the Sherif and in fact intended to occupy the Holy Land and Syria itself. The townspeople in the ports banded together and, with the few Turkish soldiers still in the town, managed to disrupt the docking of the ships. The hostility shown towards the British visitors came as a particular blow to the officers onboard because they had come in friendship, not to mention their belief that these cities were loyal followers of the Sherif.

The program of landings produced a series of sharp shocks for the British visitors. Cornwallis and Pearson arrived at Jiddah on 28 June and were immediately confronted by the Syrian officers Muhammed al-Faruqi and Jamil Effendi Rafei. Describing themselves as the Sherif's 'Cairo Agency', the Syrians warned that they meant to prevent the ships' disembarkation of British personnel, supplies and even munitions.[28] The British officers eventually managed to telephone the Sherif at Mecca and obtain permission to land the mountain guns and Egyptian escort designated for his own defence. The officers and the remaining artillery sailed on to Rabegh.[29]

Unfortunately the atmosphere of distrust and aggressiveness seemed to grow only more blatant the further the ships sailed from Mecca. When the HMS *Anne* arrived at Rabegh, with Wilson onboard, the reception party on shore threatened to kill any non-Muslim who disembarked and then raised a Turkish flag above the town. The situation was only resolved the next day when a representative from the Sherif arrived on the SS *Surada* and arranged for the supplies to be landed. The Egyptian battery, still considered too provocative, had to return to Jiddah.[30] At Jiddah the stand-off with al-Faruqi and Rafei was repeated but with even more vehemence. The British officers appealed to the town's pro-British military governor who finally secured permission by telephone again from the Sherif to land the remaining batteries, supplies and live transport. The British effort continued up the coastline, to yet worse effect. On 4 July, Cornwallis sailed to Yenbo on the HMS *Hardinge*, hoping to collect intelligence from the shore, but he was barred from leaving the ship and even his Egyptian assistant, Ruhi, was repulsed by threats of violence from the town's chief. Cornwallis's report concluded that, notwithstanding the influence of the few dozen Turks sighted in the town, 'it is probable that Yenbo is in the hands of Arabs who care as little for the Sherif and the English as do those of Rabegh'.[31]

The supply mission had unexpectedly served as a political reconnaissance tour, and Cairo drew two larger lessons from it. First, Great Britain's association compromised the Sherif's legitimacy as an Arab and Islamic leader. Cairo would have to be extremely discreet and sensitive in lending support to the Arab leaders; otherwise the status of the Sherif and his sons, upon which everything depended, would be fatally damaged. The Sherif's control over the larger towns outside Mecca was still 'slender', not least because the townspeople considered the Bedouin to be little better than brigands.[32] The enhancement of his credibility as a leader for Arabs throughout the Hejaz, however, would be as vital for the survival of the Arab Revolt as the provision of guns and food. Cornwallis suggested that the British might raise the Sherif's prestige in the cities by advertizing his guarantee that the *hajj* that year would be flawlessly organized. Cornwallis recommended that a British Agent be quietly appointed to Jiddah to help arrange municipal and medical care for the pilgrims, but with 'some unpretentious title, so as to avoid drawing attention to his real functions'. ('Pilgrimage Officer' was eventually chosen.) He emphasized that a successful *hajj* would confirm the Sherif's political independence and religious leadership for Muslims all over the world, perhaps more than any other single measure.[33]

The other lesson for Cairo concerned the Syrians' impatience to launch their own action, north of the Hejaz border. Their political agenda was a constant notice to Cairo that the 'Arab Movement' was a civil campaign, an insurgency against the Turkish government, simultaneous with but only incidentally connected to the wider world war. Cornwallis had no doubts about the Syrian nationalists' final aims: 'the ultimate intention which [al-Faruqi] frankly avows is to invade Syria as soon as possible. He has instructions to raise the Syrian territorial question and to try to come to some arrangement with the French'. Although al-Faruqi had no authority to negotiate terms with a foreign government, and his plans were clearly premature – as Cornwallis pointed out, the Arab armies were still incapable of taking Medina[34] – the Syrians' determination to press northward using the Hejaz campaign as a springboard served as a reminder for Cairo that local interests were driving each step of the Arab Revolt, regardless of its wider significance to outside powers such as Britain.

The confusion at Jiddah, Rabegh and Yenbo, the tenuousness of the Sherif's authority, the Bedouin tribesmen's lack of regular army training and the diffuse, changeable nature of local interests led Cornwallis to observe that 'the Sherif's dream of an advance on Syria is impossible of realisation for a long time to come'.[35] But the ability of British observers to estimate that Syrian date – or control the next evolution of the Arab campaign – with any real certainty had, equally, been shaken by the Hejazi towns' rejection of Britain's supply ships.

Debating control of the Hejaz campaign

In mid-June, less than a fortnight after the outbreak of the Arab Revolt, India's liaison officer with the Arab Bureau telegraphed his superior at the Foreign and Political Department:

> It is, I believe, a fact that Lord Kitchener dragged an unwilling Cabinet into this Arab business. Possibly Kitchener was preparing for himself a Viceroyalty extending from the Persian Gulf to Dafur. [...] Now Kitchener is dead.[36] You must draw your own inferences. I am not in a position, if I had the grasp, even to suggest a line of action.[37]

Any hope by Egypt's critics, however, that Kitchener's sudden death, which, incredibly, occurred at the same time as the outbreak of Arab Revolt, had left Cairo a rudderless ship would soon be dashed by the performance of the High Commissioner and the Arab Bureau during the summer months of 1916.

Attention was inevitably going to gravitate to McMahon for his role as Britain's primary negotiator with the Sherif. In the absence of any military authority officially assigned to the Hejaz sphere, full responsibility for the conduct of Britain's alliance with the Arabs remained with McMahon. His ability to carry out this function had been enhanced by the arrival of the Arab Bureau, which continued to freely mix its official staff with officers from Military Intelligence, Egyptforce. The military commanders in the region, General Wingate at Khartoum and General Murray, the commander-in-chief of Egyptforce at Ismailia, were less sanguine in witnessing these changes. An active theatre of operations had opened up on the other side of the Red Sea, with Egyptian artillery and British materiél lent to the campaign, but overall control over Britain's engagement still belonged to an official under the Foreign Office.

The Sirdar, former head of Egyptian military intelligence before Clayton and now also Governor-General of the Sudan, was an experienced veteran of British military campaigns in north and east Africa. He had recently defeated the Mahdist rebels threatening Sudan's Anglo-Egyptian government and was credited with restoring order to the beleaguered country. Wingate believed very strongly that he, not McMahon, should be taking over the direction of the Hejaz campaign. After the latest rejection of Alexandretta scheme, Wingate had complained to Clayton about the 'Arabian Policy question & the peculiar situation into which it has drifted owing to the number of "cooks" concerned in its concoction.'[38] He was not overstretched by his responsibilities in the Sudan.[39] The opening of a military theatre in Arabia seemed to be a natural expansion of his own Red Sea sphere. He had responded immediately to the Sherif's request for guns and gunners by sending Egyptian artillery units from Port Sudan to Jiddah.[40] Wingate now began pressing McMahon in his correspondence to institute a sensible system of control over the Hejaz and transfer to him 'general direction of military matters connected with our assistance to Sherif'. He sent a list of demands to the Foreign Office and War Office to facilitate the change of duties.[41]

Wingate's correspondence made it clear that, unlike McMahon, he recognized few, if any, constraints on Britain's possible assistance to the Sherif. Wingate wanted to send trained British reinforcements immediately to bolster the Arab fighters, believing that the inexperienced tribesmen would never be able to stand up to the Turks on their own. He was certain that a British detachment would raise Arab morale and help protect the Meccan base against a Turkish counter-attack. Wingate reminded McMahon that a defeat of Fakhri Pasha's troops at Medina by British and Arab troops would give 'immense prestige' to both governments 'whilst the effect on our enemies by depriving them of the Holy Places would be incalculable'. Wingate also reasoned that if the Sherif refused the offer of regular military assistance, Britain would at least be absolved from the Arabs' failure.[42]

McMahon, who was just beginning to grapple with the political delicacy of protecting the Sherif's domestic standing as well as his military needs, was opposed to sending British reinforcements. Wingate's desire to send a British expeditionary force to the Hejaz seemed to imply a lack of confidence in his reasoning. McMahon argued over several exchanges with Wingate that to dispatch Christian European reinforcements for service in the Muslim Holy Land would not boost Arab morale but cause serious offence to Muslim public opinion, particularly in regions under British rule. Hoping to keep Wingate at a distance, McMahon proposed to turn to GHQ, Ismailia rather than Port Sudan as the official base of supply for the Sherif's armies. He argued that if the Arab Revolt later came to involve 'military activity and demonstrations North of Hedjaz etc.', in Syria, for example, these would be easier to direct if the campaign's military dimension continued to be led by the Residency and, in the north, Egyptforce.[43] But McMahon's tactic failed. Murray did not want responsibility for supplying the Hejaz and McMahon was forced to turn back to Wingate for military provision. This eventually led to a decision by London, in deference to the Sirdar's experience and for simplicity, to accept his offer and transfer 'general military supervision' of the Arabs' campaign to Wingate. Significantly, McMahon asked that Wingate use the Arab Bureau, still under the McMahon's authority, as his 'medium of correspondence and information' with the Residency.[44] fforde summarized the new, uneasy balance of powers to India: 'High Commissioner controls policy and Sardar [*sic*] controls operations, Commander-in-Chief [of Egyptforce] assisting to the limit of his means in supply materials.'[45]

Almost immediately, Wingate announced that working in tandem with the High Commissioner was impossible. He wanted control over policy for the Hejaz transferred to his office, as well. He insisted to McMahon:

> [I]t appears to me that my utility and capacity to assist would be almost nullified unless I am authorized to enter into direct communication with Sherif and given full discretionary powers in putting [?such] matters as I conceive to be already authorized by British policy and therefore unnecessary to refer to you for instructions.[46]

McMahon worried that Wingate might be able to justify any number of decisions from a military perspective that carried significant political implications not approved by the British government.[47] One of Wingate's attempts to bring political control closer to his office was to ask that a portion of the Arab Bureau move to Port Sudan to act liaison office between Khartoum and Jiddah: 'This section, while remaining in close touch with Bureau, should be directly under my orders and would act as my flank executive office.'[48] Wingate was in effect recognizing the Arab Bureau as the de facto headquarters for administering support to the Arab Revolt, as well as being the staff responsible for coordinating traditional intelligence duties. He now wanted the intelligence officers' expertise for continuing liaison responsibilities with the Hejaz and to act as his 'executive arm' in supervising the revolt.[49]

The Sirdar communicated regularly with London and Cairo on the Hejaz situation over the next months, relaying his frustration over the lack of vigour and grand vision in McMahon's leadership. He wanted London to approve a more proactive military strategy: the dispatch of a British or Indian expeditionary force to the Hejaz; a landing of British troops at the port of Aqaba for operations against Ma'an; a French brigade to create a diversion on the Syrian coast with perhaps simultaneous operations by Egyptforce against el Arish.[50] Wingate seized on Cornwallis's recommendation of a British 'Pilgrimage Officer' for the Hejaz and suggested that this officer should also control matters of supply at Jiddah. He should answer to 'whoever is appointed by HMG to deal with political and military questions involved in a revolt in Hedjaz' and 'all communications involved from Sherif should pass through his hands'[51] – the implication being that responsibility for political and military questions, far from being settled in the hands of McMahon, had yet to be assigned. While Wingate pressed his case, London appointed one of his officers, Colonel Wilson, to act as the British Agent or 'Pilgrimage Officer' at Jiddah. McMahon consented, as long as it was 'settled [...] that he is to be High Commissioner's man but repeat all to Sirdar'; an arrangement which, as everyone at the Arab Bureau seemed instantly to understand, Wingate intended to invert. 'There will probably be a squabble as to whether he [Wilson] is to be the Sirdar's man or High Commissioner's,' noted fforde. 'If the latter's, the Sirdar may not be able to spare him.'[52]

The Hejaz campaign also attracted Murray's attention at Ismailia. Murray had three concerns. The amount of military material he was called upon to contribute compared to what he felt he could spare; the potential for a relationship between his Sinai operations and the Hejaz, insofar as the Arabs might tie down or even draw away Turkish forces from the Sinai and the Syrian littoral; and the possibility for a corresponding Bedouin uprising in Syria to act in league with Egyptforce as it advanced into Palestine. Troops and resources were too scarce for two separate campaigns; Murray initially reasoned that if he were put in charge of Hejaz operations, he would be able to keep both within the context of Egyptforce's present and future programme. After the Arab Revolt broke out, Murray cabled General Sir William Robertson, Chief of the Imperial General Staff (CIGS) in London, to point out that the Sherif's activity constituted 'definite military operations against the Turks' and, as such, should 'come under military supervision. [...] I am prepared, if you wish, to assume such military supervision as it is possible to exercise from here'.[53] But Robertson declined to alter the supervision of the Sherif's operations at that stage. There were 'many interests involved in the Arab Movement,' he explained. 'The Foreign Office, the India Office, and the French and Russian Governments [are] all interested and there are many ramifications of the question', so for the time being he preferred to keep the Sherif's operations in the hands of the High Commissioner. The Residency seemed most capable of managing the relationship between the political and operational demands of the campaign.[54] Rebuffed, Murray decided that if the Hejaz theatre were not going to be under his command, then his Intelligence Department officers would no longer be shared with the Arab Bureau to assist with Arab operations that, as far as he could see, had no commander-in-chief. The entry in the Ismailia Intelligence Diary for 24 June 1916 reflected the army's rising exasperation with the unorthodox position and privileges so far granted to Clayton and Arab Bureau:

> Great confusion arises over the Sherif of Mecca's rebellion. It is in no way under Egyptforce. Yet demands are made on us by the High Commissioner and Sirdar independently. It is complicated by the fact that the Arab Bureau is under the High Commissioner: and that Clayton is the Sudan agent of the Sirdar and is, further, liaison between Egyptforce and the Government of Egypt and therefore under us. The Arab Bureau works in the same office as Clayton in his dual regime at Cairo and it is difficult therefore for Egyptforce to know where it stands.[55]

Murray informed McMahon that he would supply materials to the Arabs as far as they could be spared, but his intelligence staff – including Clayton – would no longer be allowed to work on the Hejaz campaign's operations. He ordered Deedes, who was acting for Clayton at GHQ, Egypt while Clayton was in London (mid-June to mid-July), to confine his contact with the Residency purely to intelligence matters and 'not to touch the question of operations'. Murray also asked Wingate to direct all his telegrams on the Hejaz straight to Ismailia, rather than to Clayton in Cairo.[56]

Ismailia's projection of a runaway campaign in the desert led by the High Commissioner was not appreciated at the Residency. McMahon assured Murray that Military Intelligence at Cairo was 'not being used for Operations', and that the Sherif himself held ultimate command over the Hejaz campaign, while 'all that I have been able to do in the matter is to advise him on one or two points such as the necessity for concentrating his efforts in one direction'.[57] But Murray remained sceptical, of the Arab Bureau's role and of the Arab Revolt itself from a military standpoint.[58] fforde, thoroughly delighted with the drama, kept India abreast of these debates. When Clayton returned from London where he had been addressing the War Committee, he would find that Murray 'has ordered him to have nothing to do with the Arab Bureau except give advice when asked,' reported fforde. 'And yet the Arab Bureau is technically a section of the Sudan intelligence according to my orders and I had to report to Clayton'. Lawrence had also been singled out by Murray and told that 'he has nothing to do with the Arab Bureau except give advice when asked!'[59]

Intelligence officers had suddenly become conspicuous players in the conduct of Hejaz affairs; it was a revelation that would not have surprised the Arab Bureau who already believed they constituted the vanguard of support for the campaign. Parker, Sudan Agent and acting head of the Arab Bureau during Clayton's absence, told Wingate that he had managed to get Murray's orders 'somewhat modified so that Lawrence assists in all but where action is necessary, and Hogarth is permitted to consult me [...] so we go on as before'.[60] Lawrence later admired McMahon's struggle to keep the management of the Arab Revolt under the Residency's control, and attributed Murray's obstructionism to professional jealousy. Murray had all but conceded that GHQ, Ismailia lacked the 'ethnological competence' to manage the Arabs' campaign properly; but Murray also knew he 'could make the spectacle of the High Commission running a private war sufficiently ridiculous'.[61]

The purpose of creating the Arab Bureau had been to ensure the proper flow of expert intelligence to the policy-making level. Clayton and Phillip Graves travelled to London specifically to make their 'progressive,' pro-Arab positions known to the War Committee (see Chapter 3). During Clayton's absence from the Arab Bureau, Hogarth briefly stepped in as director. fforde knew that Hogarth had visited McMahon privately and 'opened his eyes a bit', suggesting that Hogarth had not hesitated to weigh in to McMahon on policy-related matters. fforde, despite his Indian association, seemed to approve: 'Hogarth really knows more than anyone else, High Commissioner included, except possibly Lawrence'.[62] The administrators and military chiefs in the region continued to wrangle over the distribution of political authority and command control, but the intelligence community – increasingly confident, engaged and dynamic – kept their attention focused on the practical requirements of the Arab Revolt and the intelligence needed to push it forward.

The Hejaz uprising: a precedent for Syria?

Murray may have objected to the unconventional involvement of the Arab Bureau in operational matters, but he was impressed enough by Cairo's alliance with the Hashemites to try to develop a similar strategy for his own theatre. There had been occasional reports, based on Humint, and hearsay, since 1914 suggesting that Syrian Arabs would welcome 'a swift British occupation'.[63] More consistent was the Humint that described anti-Turk activities in Syria, although the reports also relied heavily on hearsay. Al-Masri in mid-1914 had claimed that Nuri Shaalan, the Rualla chief and head of the Anazeh in the Syrian interior, had joined *al-'Ahd* and desired the overthrow of the Turkish government.[64] In late June 1916, a British agent in Switzerland reported a rumour that metropolitan Arabs and Hauran tribal groups in Syria had indeed rebelled against the CUP and established 'communication' with Mecca.[65] The Sherif told Wilson that he, too, had heard about a Syrian revolt.[66] In early July at Jiddah, al-Farqui told Cornwallis that a 'rising' had taken place in Syria. Cornwallis heard 'several different reports' at the time of such a revolt, which was 'generally considered to be of great importance'. He heard that Nuri and 15,000 Rualla had mobilized with a force of deserter Ottoman Arab officers and entered the Vilayet of Damascus to confront the Turkish authorities.[67] The Sherif had been arguing to McMahon for some months that if British planes bombed the railway between Anatolia and Syria, the population would know that Jemal Pasha was cut off from reinforcements and would feel safe enough to rise up in support. The reports of resistance activity in Syria seemed to confirm these sentiments. In fact, the Sherif was so certain that the Rualla might now be advancing on Damascus that he cancelled his earlier request for the RFC to bomb the Syrian railway junction because there would soon be 'a rapid invasion of Syria by his [own] forces and [...] [he] would shortly need [the railway] himself'.[68]

The idea of a combined operation with the Rualla and Druse tribes as Egyptforce crossed into Palestine and Syria was very complementary to Murray's northern strategy.[69] After the War Committee's approval in early July of a 'forward policy in Sinai and towards Akaba, with naval demonstrations along the Syrian and Asia Minor coasts',[70] Murray ordered fresh Imint to investigate Aqaba's utility as a base for operations around Ma'an and site for an aerodrome. He was already assuming that British aerial attacks would be coordinated with Rualla and Druse ground operations.[71] In late July and early August 1916, Murray ordered reconnaissance flights and photographic surveys over Aqaba and the surrounding mountainous territory.[72] A seaplane attached to HMS *Raven II* conducted the mission. But its pilots estimated that the enemy gun emplacements on the beach would require 'abundant support from ships guns [*sic*]' to clear, although the place was currently held by only a few snipers, and guns would not be effective above the beach. Imint showed a steeply inclined natural bulwark of cliffs wrapped around the north-western road and Wadi Ithm beyond, striated with entrenchments and gun posts.[73] On the strength of the aerial reconnaissance, Egyptforce concluded that any British landing at Aqaba would have to be coordinated with sympathetic Arabs in the high ground to succeed.[74] This Imint would influence later events as well. Nine months later, Lawrence would conceive his alternative strategy for operations around Aqaba with the information produced by these reconnaissance flights, as will be seen.

Remarkable Humint from two deserting Arab officers at the end of September 1916 offered similar visions of a sympathetic Syrian revolt. Both Lieutenant Ahmed Youssef Shaykha, a former station manager, then with the (Arab) 25th Division, and his comrade, Lieutenant Shukri Shurbaji, a member of *al-'Ahd*, told Cairo intelligence that 30,000 armed men waited in the Syrian interior 'ready to rise in event of propitious circumstances'. Shaykha and Shurbaji insisted that these fighters would be able to sabotage the Syrian railway if supported by bombing flights around Ma'an, perhaps from a British aerodrome at Aqaba. Shaykha confirmed the Imint from the HMS *Raven II*; it appeared that a single company of Turkish gendarmes remained at the port, which might easily be overwhelmed by a surprise attack.[75]

A record of the recent deserters' Humint was sent to Mark Sykes at the War Office in London, as the War Committee's expert on Middle East affairs. Sykes' imagination immediately grasped the epic potential of such an enterprise. On 25 September 1916, he informed the War Committee that the Anazeh, Beni Sakhr, Kerak and Druse tribes of Syria were on the brink of joining the revolt, along with 30,000 Turkish Army deserters sheltering at that moment in Jebel-Druse. If provided with arms, munitions and aerial bombing support from a base at Aqaba, these Syrian Arabs would surely cut the railway themselves. In fact, not only did Sykes accept the informants' estimates, he insisted that their numbers were probably 'conservative' and that the War Committee should anticipate 'a rising of at least 65,000 men securely based on natural strongholds and supported by large numbers of Bedawin [*sic*] who are not counted in the above figure'. Excited by the idea that the momentum lost by the Arab armies in the Hejaz might have just resurfaced in Syria, Sykes urged the War Committee to authorize a mission to get in touch with the Syrian elements who, he was now convinced, needed but a spark to launch fire. 'To supply these people with arms, money, and munitions, and get into better communication with them should not require anything in the shape of an independent military operation,' he assured the committee, 'and provided a successful issue attended the presumed military action from Egypt, a very favourable turn might be given to events in the whole of Syria and Palestine, besides putting the Sherif out of all danger'. For both Sykes and Murray, intelligence that supported the likelihood of such a northern Arab uprising – spanning from the Hejaz to Syria, Palestine and perhaps even the Caucasus – was more welcome and thus credible than contrary intelligence, such as reports on *al-'Ahd*'s continuing suspiciousness of western military intentions.[76]

The temptation to favour gratifying intelligence is an endemic challenge for decision-makers. In this instance, Murray chose to rely heavily on informants' opportune statements in formulating his future operations. The rumours continued. Feisal reported to Wilson in early November, probably based on Humint, that Nuri had rebelled and defeated a Turkish contingent.[77] The Arab Bureau referred to intelligence regarding 'minor disturbances' – a train derailed and the railway line cut – undertaken during raids by 'some of Nuri Shaalan's people, but certainly not led by their chief'.[78] Egyptforce struggled to dominate the Turks in front of el Arish but Murray remained optimistic, promising the War Office that soon he would launch aerial attacks 'with very far-reaching results' on the railhead at Ma'an, enemy advance bases in Palestine and the Sinai, and the Hejaz railway.[79] Murray privately asked Wingate 'whether Nuri Shallan [*sic*] can be relied upon', and how he might get in touch with him 'as soon as possible',[80] but to Robertson, Murray maintained a confident tone, again citing Nuri's revolt and his alleged control of tribes along the railway 'between Maan and Damascus' to suggest that Egyptforce would soon be able to enter joint ground-air operations with the Syrian tribes. He pointed out that temporary landing grounds 'in Nuri country' would facilitate attacks against the Hejaz railway 'in conjunction with local levies organized by selected officers conveyed by air to that district'.[81] In the meantime, Murray asked Wilson if he could ask the Sherif to obtain Nuri Shaalan's permission for a landing strip to be built at Jauf to connect the British army with the Syrian tribes east of the railway. As soon as a letter of approval from Nuri was received, Murray would send Captain Royle out by aeroplane to make contact, as his representative.[82]

Events were not helping Murray. In December, he could only refer to a restive, if now still abeyant, Rualla population in his report to Robertson as a palliative for his flagging progress around el Arish. But he assured the CIGS that Egyptforce's future advance and the introduction of aircraft would inspire 'a rising of the Arab population in southern Syria, who are known to be very disaffected towards Turks'.[83] Robertson was willing to allow that Egyptforce's advance 'should encourage the Arabs of Southern Syria to throw in their lot with the Shereef, and it may enable you to get into touch with them by aeroplane'.[84] Murray immediately telegraphed Wingate that the War Office had approved his plans to advance on Rafa 'with a view to operations in south Syria'.[85]

Two intelligence-related matters were being deliberately confused: rumoured claims of an uprising by the Anazeh and Druse tribes in Syria, so far delivered by Humint but as yet unconfirmed by Sigint or even open sources such as the press,[86] and the intentions and sympathies of Nuri Shaalan and the Rualla, and the Druse, which were still being guessed at by intelligence. The documents available from this time suggest that there was negligible if any groundwork laid for this scheme by Murray with Nuri Shaalan himself, and no direct contracts concluded with him by the British or the French. The Humint sources appeared to be from outside the Anazeh confederation, and may have been biased; nevertheless, it is understandable that Murray would have been reassured by the earlier statements from the Arab secret societies and the dramatic precedent of a revolt in the Hejaz by the Sherif, who was their associate. There was also the obvious strategic appeal of a northern uprising. A combined regular and irregular assault on the railway, abetted by Arab insurgents on a mass scale, would wholly rehabilitate the standing of Murray's command of Egyptforce for London.

The War Committee accepted Murray's projections without further intelligence confirmation. The Foreign Office even based a request for future materiel from the French government on this Humint despite there being no real evidence that Nuri had joined, or was prepared to join, an Anglo-Arab alliance. After receiving Murray's November proposal, Grey asked the French ambassador for support of the scheme and the French government authorized the grant of aeroplanes, arms, ammunition and money.[87] Neither the War Office, the Foreign Office nor the War Committee appeared to question the assertion that a revolt had occurred in Syria or was on the brink of occurring, or that an alliance between Egyptforce and rebel forces from the Hauran and Jebel-Druse entailed anything more than logistical attention to put into effect.

Only the Arab Bureau and its like-minded GHQ intelligence officers remained skeptical about the Humint on a Syrian uprising, precisely for lack of reliable corroborative intelligence. Parker reported to Wingate from MI in Cairo that they had 'no confirmation of a serious Syrian revolt, but if it were to materialize I do not see how it could result in anything more than hangings of those in revolt' unless they were part of a larger Allied operation.[88] fforde reported to Delhi in early July 1916 that 'rumours of a Syrian revolt continue to reach us but as yet are not believed'.[89] In the absence of harder intelligence than Humint, such as Sigint from Turkish communications, the Arab Bureau noted in mid-July that reports of action by the Rualla were probably 'greatly exaggerated'.[90] In late July 1916, a 'Damascene notable', perhaps Nesib al-Bekri or Clayton's agent 'Maurice', said that *al-'Ahd* and *al-Fatat*, Nuri Shaalan, his son Nawaf, and the Druse had struck an agreement before the Hejaz revolt to support 'a simultaneous rising' in Syria, but sources in Syria had told the informant that although 'Nuri is ready to support the Sherif', no action had yet been taken.[91] The Arab Bureau published items in their bulletin from Syrian newspapers on clashes between Bedouin from the interior and the Turkish authorities who were ruthlessly trying to enforce mass conscription. Other reports described the trial of Muslim Bedouins from Kerak (east of Dead Sea) who had been charged with assaulting the government's representatives.[92] In such a context, it is more likely that isolated acts of resistance to the CUP's methods such as these were mistaken by informants as signs of a second Arab revolt.

Clayton, through the Arab Bureau, issued a clear one-page statement on 6 November 1916 expressing scepticism that Nuri was on the brink of bringing the Rualla into the Sherif's movement and dismissing the rumours of a rising as 'all groundless'. It was true that Nuri had sent a representative to Feisal's camp, and expressed verbal support for the Sherif; he apparently had 7,000–10,000 mounted riflemen set aside for the Sherif, if he chose. The agent 'Maurice' reported in late October that Nuri had refused to pledge assistance to Jemal Pasha during a private meeting in July, but Clayton interpreted Nuri's behaviour towards both the Sherif and the Turks as typical of his long-held independence from any external ties. He recommended that confirmation be sought, and that even the Sherif's intelligence on the subject be treated with scepticism.[93] In late November 1916, Cairo intelligence learned, probably from Sigint, that a Turkish train had been derailed south of Deraa in early October; it was likely the same intelligence motivating Murray's 10 December communication with the CIGS. But the Arab Bureau noted pointedly that although Rualla tribesmen might have been responsible, in the course of their regular raids around the Hauran, they were 'certainly not led by their chief'. Nor had any parties of the Druse yet joined the Sherif, despite their being armed and probably responsible for recent disruptions to the Homs–Aleppo line. By their reckoning, Jemal's brutal counter-insurgency measures and his reinforcement of Deraa had cowed these groups indefinitely from taking any larger action.[94]

The most informed assessment of Nuri Shaalan's position was provided by Lawrence in response to Murray's inquiries. Lawrence reported that he had talked with Nuri's own agent at Feisal's camp; Nuri himself was hard to locate, moving between the Hauran and Jauf. Lawrence concluded that Nuri would be 'cautious' and remain 'shy of assisting the Sherif till assured of armed support'.[95] Lawrence submitted a detailed account of the meeting to Wilson. The agent, Faiz el Ghusain, was now Feisal's secretary and his emissary to Nuri Shaalan for the first months of the year. Faiz had long experience with the Syrian chiefs and told Lawrence that the Syrian tribes would never fight the Turks in order to hand the country over to a European power. Nor would Nuri enter into an alliance with the Sherif or the British, he said, 'without the backing of a disciplined [Arab] force, or a deep thrust of the British into Syria' and with the ultimate goal being eventual Arab independence. Even in the case of the latter, he added, Nuri would still 'require a deal of persuading'.[96]

Feisal agreed with this portrait, having sent his own emissaries up to the Hauran in 1916 to contact chiefs along the railway and the coast. In Feisal's opinion it was still too early to call for a popular revolt in Syria. The Sherif's armies had not yet gained control of the railway and so were unlikely to be able to sustain a northern advance. He also knew that the Sherif could not guarantee the necessary political settlement to back the Rualla's action. Feisal hoped that in the meantime the Syrian tribes would keep encouraging Arab soldiers in the territory to desert their Turkish units.[97]

Murray's elaborate attempts to contact Nuri continued, without success. Murray asked Wilson, Feisal and the Sherif to write Nuri about the possibility of joint operations and an aerodrome at Jauf.[98] Parker was instructed to arrange a caravan to Jauf carrying petrol and oil as provision for Captain Royle's return flight, once Nuri agreed to the scheme.[99] By 5 December, two consignments of fuel had been sent to Feisal to forward north, when ready.[100] But in early January 1917, Feisal's representative to Nuri Shaalan, Ibn Sheddad, returned from Jauf and reported that the Rualla would not rise up until certain conditions were met. Lawrence reported to Wilson that Nuri and the other Rualla chiefs had decided to withdraw all support from the Turkish government immediately but would only actively support the Sherif after Feisal had occupied the railway junction with Wadi Sirhan, at el Ula.[101]

McMahon and the intelligence community in Cairo had steered Britain's engagement with the Arab Revolt up to this point, with Wingate, Murray and the British navy providing military support. Cairo's attention to the political, cultural and military intelligence for the Hejaz diverged from the approach of GHQ, Ismailia, or even of Sykes, whose assessments of opportunities for combined operations in Syria were distorted by an overemphasis on the military assets of the theatre, and too little attention to its political particularities.[102] The Arab Bureau's greater investment in political intelligence continued to support their alliance with the Sherif's revolt. Distinctly disquieting intelligence on the ambivalence still felt by many Hejazis towards the Revolt and the conditional interest of the Syrian tribes in the north were accepted by Cairo as a central challenge for British policy.

3 Arriving at a doctrine of guerrilla warfare, June–October 1916

The defence of Mecca

The Hashemites' uprising had established a base at Mecca with a fragile corridor to the coastal town of Jiddah, but the military advantage still belonged to the Turks' regular forces and artillery at Medina. Strategic assessments on both sides concentrated on the two holy places, now juxtaposed; one was destined eventually to capitulate to the other. The cities were intensely symbolic; and both depended on external sources of supply, with Medina looking to Damascus and Mecca keeping communication with Jiddah. The city lying midway on the main route between the two cities, the port of Rabegh, became the stress point. Possessing enough wells to water a large army, Rabegh was also the most likely forward base for any future Turkish offensive against Mecca. The eldest Hashemite prince, Ali, was in charge of Rabegh's defence, but it soon became clear that his army was too inexperienced and fractious to meet a Turkish advance. Feisal and Abdullah were trying to hold an extended front to the south-west of Medina, with little artillery and too few rifles. Some British officials began to ask whether a British brigade might some day be necessary to reinforce Rabegh and protect the road to Mecca, in case the Turks made a serious effort to recapture the city.

Over the next five months, a debate over the security of Rabegh would divide British opinion in London and Egypt and set Cairo's political and military assessments against those of Khartoum. In Cairo, the rejection of British supply ships by Arab residents at Jiddah, Rabegh and Yenbo in late June/early July had pushed consideration for the Sherif's survival as a popular Arab leader to the front of the Residency's and Arab Bureau's calculations. They strongly believed that if a regular British detachment were to land at the Hejaz, no matter how dire the Hashemites' military situation, the Arabs would perceive it as a hostile force and the status of the Sherif as a regional leader would be destroyed. McMahon warned that he had also been struck by a statement from the Egyptian Sultan that even Egyptian troops should not be sent into Arabia.[1] The view in Khartoum was different. Wingate, who wanted to assume political control over the Hejaz campaign in order to buttress his military authority, and Colonel P.C. Joyce, the escorting commander of the Egyptian artillery unit currently in the Hejaz, rejected what they saw as Cairo's overly sensitive political reading. In their opinion, only the knowledge of concrete military progress, delivered with the assistance of British troops, would hold the Arab armies together and inspire them to undertake the larger campaign against the Turks' main force at Medina. Wingate referred McMahon to intelligence showing that Turkish reinforcements from Syria were preparing to join the HEF at Medina to help extend their line of communication, an event that would all but guarantee the reoccupation of Mecca. If British troops were on hand, however, to guard the road between Medina and Mecca and protect the Sherif's base, he said, 'there is every prospect that he will succeed'.[2]

Military intelligence reports at this time contributed to the sense of urgency about Rabegh and Mecca. Cornwallis and Pearson had toured the Hejaz in June and made military assessments of the Arab and Turk positions. The Turks had superior firepower. Their siege guns at Medina had a range of 7,000 yards and upwards and their railway forts were defended by machine guns, which allowed little opportunity for a pre-emptive action by the Arabs before enemy reinforcements arrived. The Egyptian maxim battery and mountain battery sent to augment the princes' military capability were, as the Sultan predicted, greatly undermined by the resentment of the Arabs and particularly the Syrian officers for being in their view an extension of the British government. Cornwallis and Pearson concluded that, under these conditions, the Arabs would never be able to deflect a Turkish advance or lay siege to Medina without rifles, trained troops and artillery.[3]

Colonel Parker of Military Intelligence had arrived at the same conclusion after his own Hejaz tour, but explicitly rejected the idea of a British brigade. As fforde noted in his private report, 'Parker is going to try and convince the Sirdar to abandon this idea' of using British troops 'to save the Sherif from defeat'.[4] In Parker's view, Britain would lose too much prestige and trust if such a political miscalculation enabled the Turks to quash the Arabs' revolt after Britain had pledged its assistance: 'accusations would be made that we had callously exploited Islam for our own purposes' and 'our position in the Mohammadan world would deteriorate greatly'. Rather than send Egyptian or European troops, Parker suggested that Britain launch a diversionary campaign north of the Arabian peninsula. Small naval landings and bombardments against the Syrian coast combined with rumours (disseminated by MI) of a larger pending attack would pin down the Turkish reserves in the Syrian theatre.[5] McMahon welcomed the proposal for avoiding the provocation of landing Christian troops and for requiring no further military assistance from Port Sudan (and Wingate).[6]

Gilbert Clayton and Philip Graves of the Arab Bureau believed that the pressures facing the Arab armies and pivotal cities such as Rabegh were sufficiently intricate and urgent to require their personal testimony in London. In early July, in concert with Mark Sykes, Clayton and Graves attended meetings called by the War Committee on future military strategy for the Middle East. They delivered what Graves described as 'a combined attack in favour of a progressive policy' in the Hejaz and the rejection of British reinforcements.[7] Hardinge later noted that he had been 'immensely' impressed with Clayton's testimony, for he had seemed 'thoroughly sensible and comprehending as to what can and cannot be done', in stark contrast to the 'shallowness of the nature of Mark Sykes'. As ever, Sykes was something of a mixed blessing for the Cairo contingent. His prominence in these proceedings is undeniable, even if Hardinge later remarked that he 'inundates the War Committee with a terrible lot of rubbish, and on the only occasion when he came before them talked a great deal of nonsense to the amusement of everybody'.[8]

Sykes was fully prepared to make a passionate appeal alongside Clayton for a 'pro-Arab policy', and he added to that his wish for a curtailment of India's sweeping influence over regional affairs, proposing that all the Indian territories in the Persian Gulf be placed under a new High Commissioner and all policy in the Middle East made 'the policy of London direct'. Sykes berated the Indian Government for its racist ways; in particular he criticized its officers' failure to recognize that the Arabs had a 'physique, fire and a nimbleness of mind and a sense of breed' that negated any claim by Britain to a position of racial superiority. Nevertheless, he advised strongly against making any actual 'pledges or undertakings' to the Arabs, or publicizing Britain's pro-Arab policies. The key to this split devotion may have lain with Sykes' considerable antagonism towards McMahon as High Commissioner.[9] McMahon's responsibility for having negotiated the current Arab alliance, it could be argued, was awkward for Sykes, who had recently authored the secret 1916 agreement with Picot. Thus Sykes opposed any British commitment to future Arab independence, such as had been contained in McMahon's pledges to the Sherif. 'The only tangible result so far', as fforde explained to his chief, 'appears to be the communication [...] not to abuse Arabs'.[10]

Clayton's testimony focused on specific strategic judgements that were now preferred policy for McMahon and the Arab Bureau in Cairo. He told the War Committee that the Arab campaign needed only money, supplies and munitions to maintain their campaign against the Turks, not conventional troops. Clayton's reassurances that British reinforcements were not necessary came as a relief to many members of the Committee.[11] General William Robertson, the CIGS, particularly appreciated Clayton's proposals because they did not disturb his arguments for reserving all troop surpluses in the east for the BEF in France. Robertson wanted a minimum force to be held in Egypt as a 'general reserve' and as protection for the route to India, but the remaining forces, including the five British Divisions still at Salonika, had to be available as contingency troops for France.[12] On 7 July, the War Committee granted the decision to Clayton, McMahon, the Arab Bureau and Robertson, and not to Wingate, by voting against a brigade for Rabegh. They approved Parker's recommendations instead, and asked Egyptforce to progress to Katia and el Arish in the Sinai while the navy and army undertook tactics of deception in the eastern Mediterranean 'to lead the enemy to fear a landing at Alexandretta or Smyrna'.[13] The Committee was in agreement that if any military assistance were to be given to the Sherif in the near future, it would be 'outside the Hedjaz [...] rendered by British troops'.[14]

After this decision, McMahon felt that his judgement of political policy for the Hejaz campaign had been vindicated. As he pointed out to Wingate: 'There is nothing therefore to weaken former objections to transfer of political control, but a good deal to strengthen them and I do not now propose to raise the question with His Majesty's Government.'[15] fforde, who viewed the War Committee's decision as 'a great relief', reminded India that 'the Sirdar has been trying to get full control over policy as well as operations in the Hedjaz, but High Commissioner will not have it [...] High Commissioner has definitely said now that neither Egyptian nor British troops will be used in the Hedjaz, but north of it, if at all'[16] Hogarth was also pleased, believing that British arms and money would be sufficient to enable the Arabs to withstand any Turkish attempt to cross the '250 miles of rugged blistered country between Medina and Mecca'. Once Egyptforce had extended its railway to Gaza and into Palestine, and could target the Syrian railway with bombing raids, the Arab forces would be able to take Medina.[17]

The wisdom of this approach was buttressed further by the knowledge that the most uncontroversial, successful British contribution to the Sherif's cause to date had been delivered by the British navy. British ships operating off the coastline had helped pro-Sherifian fighters dismantle Turkish positions, without disembarking a man. In late June, British ships shelled the port of Yenbo in support of the Emir of the Juheinah, who attacked the local Turkish fort and government buildings with 200 men. On 27 June the last fifty Turks surrendered, and the navy was allowed to land supplies. A month later, seventy miles to the north, another Juheinah unit made its first assault against the Turks' garrison at Um Lejj and declared that more arms and ammunition were all that was required for the whole Arab country to rise in support of the Sherif.[18] Within ten weeks, the surviving Turks at Um Lejj fled to the railway and the garrison folded.[19] The British navy's presence was critical to the capture of this 300 mile stretch of coastline from Jiddah to Um Lejj. The Sherif gained the strategic security of a long secure border opposite Mecca, access to the sea for supply and thus continuing control over the *hajj* for the present. Only the major ports of Wejh, Dhaba and Muweilah on the northern Red Sea coast remained in Turkish hands, supported by the local Billi and Beni Atiyah. The British navy renewed their sea blockade of Wejh and the northern coast, intending to pressure the garrisons to turn inland for supplies.[20]

The value of intelligence, especially political intelligence, had been confirmed by the opening of the Rabegh debate. Members of the Arab Bureau were playing an unusually prominent role in policy deliberations in Egypt and in London, despite their technically meagre budget, handful of official staff and moonlighting MI officers from GHQ. Hogarth insisted to the Viceroy, not disingenuously, that the Arab Bureau had been 'forced' by a 'concatenation of circumstances' to extend its original mandate as an intelligence section, and 'most improperly [...] to fulfil the functions of a small General Staff, as well as of Political Adviser and Intelligence Office' under McMahon. Yet he also chided his friend, 'I know that, in India, you blame us for having disturbed the Moslem pool when its surface all seemed acalm. But what was that peace?' He insisted that he and his colleagues never lost sight of the fact that defeating the Turkish–German enemy remained the consuming priority for Egypt: 'Turkey has to be downed as completely as Germany now, and by using whatever Allies we can get.'[21]

Divided Islam and a military stalemate

There was widespread nervousness in the British colonies over the direction of Muslim public opinion and Muslim loyalty to Turkey, in the wake of the Sherif's uprising. Wingate repeatedly argued that British troops should be sent to protect Mecca from a counter-offensive, because 'the defeat of the Sherif would have a worse effect on India than the use of British troops in the Hedjaz'.[22] British intelligence in Cairo periodically tracked the changes in religious perspectives, Arab nationalist trends, the ubiquitous resentment of Britain's military occupation of Egypt and the wider significance of the Sherif's role.[23] Lawrence contributed an intelligence analysis at this time of the larger crisis facing Islam as seen by local political leaders and Egypt's intelligentsia, using intelligence from informants and personal interviews. It was plainly intended to reiterate to British decision-makers that the Sherif's rebellion against the Turkish government had triggered potentially powerful reverberations inside the Muslim world. He emphasized that the religious stakes for the Sherif in launching the Revolt were extremely high:

> The revolt in Mecca has ruined the edifice of the Muslim solidarity carefully built up in Azhar [University] in the last generation. Pious Moslems are bewildered, and the politicians who led them [will be divided] [...] so long as the issue of the revolt is undecided.[24]

Hogarth described the religious consequences of the Sherif's revolt more bluntly to Lord Chelmsford: 'Well – there he is and, for good or ill, Islam is divided against itself.'[25]

Continuing Turkish military successes in this respect damaged the military and political future of the Sherif – as well as the British. Fakhri Pasha's HEF appeared to be comfortably entrenched at Medina. The Bedouin tribes' sporadic attacks on the railway had done little damage to its service; Humint from an Arab officer from Mecca confirmed that munitions and foodstuffs sent by rail from Syria were still reaching the Medina garrison. The Turks' eastern caravan roads from Medina to Nejd also remained intact, patrolled by the pro-Turk Shammar tribes of central Arabia. In the Hejaz proper, only Sheikh Hussein bin Mubeirig of Rabegh had publicly committed himself to the Turks, but large swathes of the surrounding territory were still unaligned. A prominent Egyptian nationalist, Rashid Rida, announced that he meant to visit the Hejaz soon to encourage greater opposition to the British.[26] Humint in Egypt and Arabia revealed that the Turks were attempting to buy the tribes' loyalty with gold.[27]

The Turkish army in the Sinai was also holding steady. They had pushed Egyptforce out of Katia and a Turkish aerial bombardment of the Suez Canal beginning on 4 August shelled British ships and killed 3,000 British soldiers and labourers. These events only intensified the British administrations' need for the Sherif to secure a victory.[28]

Complicating the Sherif's position further was the fact that the CUP had already named his successor for the Emirate of Mecca: Sherif Ali Haidar Pasha.[29] A British agent at Smryna reported in June that the Pretender had been hesitating to leave Constantinople because he feared for his safety in the Hejaz.[30] In early August 1916, Ali Haidar at last roused himself to assume the office and issued a proclamation. Its publication was banned in Egypt and India,[31] but the Arab Bureau printed a copy in their mid-September intelligence bulletin. Ali Haidar's denunciation of British intentions in the Holy Land reconfirmed the need for the British government to reassure Muslim public opinion of their respect and friendship for the Arab people:

> The enemy [i.e., Great Britain] has invaded Egypt, the Sudan and India, Yemen, Ahkaf, Oman and vicinity, and this time he made an attempt on Basra. […] El Sherif Hussein leagues himself with that enemy, and is now trying to place the House of God, the Kibla of Islam, and the tomb of the prophet, under the protection of a Christian Government, at war with the Turkish Government, and doing what it can to subjugate all Moslem nations […] [He] should have considered the fact that England would not help him unless she was afterwards to govern him, and that the moment she stretches her finger to Hejaz she will not relax her efforts until, by degrees, she annexes it to the other countries which she has already fraudulently occupied.[32]

The Arab Bureau judged that it was only reasonable and realistic, as fforde reported, to assume that 'every Moslem is to some extent pan-Islamic in sentiment'. This political tinderbox was the reason that they opposed the dispatch of British troops to the Hejaz; such an act would only 'be seized upon by the pan-Islamists in Constantinople who would say "I told you so. They have entered the Hedjaz under the guise of deliverers and they will never leave it"'.[33]

In the Hejaz interior, the tribesmen's dwindling successes were depressing morale. Feisal and Ali complained to the British officials that they still lacked the manpower, rifles and artillery to raise any serious threat to the Turkish army groups or their lines of communication.[34] South of Medina, at Ta'if, Abdullah's army was bolstered by the Egyptian mountain battery from the Sudan, but he still believed he could only surround the garrison and wait for it to surrender.[35] Feisal, posted to Medina's southwest, worried that the Arab armies were losing the initiative. Intelligence on possible enemy intentions was not reassuring. Sigint, as Wingate had noted, suggested that the Turks planned to bring down reinforcements of heavy artillery, aircraft and armoured trains to augment the HEF. The Arab Bureau wondered hopefully whether this intelligence might in fact be fictions 'spread *in terrorem*, both by wireless and by post, both of which mediums the Turks know are likely to be tapped'.[36]

In August, concerns over possible Turkish reinforcements were only briefly surpassed by a spate of sightings of 'Germans' arriving in the Hejaz. Humint from a number of Arab informants now claimed that Medina contained as many as sixteen battalions led by fifty to sixty German officers. Feisal declared, most likely on the basis of his own Humint, that amongst the Turkish units facing Ali on the road to Rabegh were '1,000 Austrians and Germans wearing helmets and ignorant of Turkish and Arabic'. The psychological blow to the Arab armies of a German contingent in the Hejaz, even if exaggerated, was obvious and the Arab Bureau tried to verify the claim. Within a fortnight a captured Turkish officer, most likely from the Russian front, had credibly denied the possibility of Germans or Austrians in the Hejaz. The Arab Bureau analysed further intelligence from the Russian GS and reassured Feisal that the 'Germans' he had seen were, in fact, likely to have been Greek soldiers belonging to the 42nd and 55th Regiments of the 14th Division.[37]

The Turks' determination to reach Mecca became undeniable in August, in anticipation of Ali Haidar's arrival. On 3 August, a Turkish expeditionary force pushed beyond the Medina environs in an attempt to reach Mecca but was temporarily blocked by Ali's army. Ali's men ran out of ammunition and pulled back to Ghadir Rabegh [fourteen miles south of Medina] where they were reinforced with tribesmen from the Beni Salim. Feisal moved his force north to the Sultani Road, the route connecting Medina with Rabegh, where he also incorporated fighters from the Beni Salim.[38] At this delicate moment the Turkish commander, despite his advantages in firepower and unit morale, halted his troops to wait for extra reserve battalions to join him from Medina. Ali Haidar was riding with the reserves, and the commander wanted his force to enter Mecca with full military and ceremonial pomp. This gesture towards the symbolic importance of the first Holy City would cost the commander; while he paused in the hinterland, the Hashemite princes recovered some of their momentum and reorganized their forces. On 25 August, Feisal managed to capture two Turkish battalions twenty-five miles south of Medina, a significant gain, although neither he nor his brothers were able to force a conclusion.[39]

The Sherif nevertheless believed a Turkish break-through was imminent and requested further military assistance from the British. He had already accepted that 'he cannot hope to take the place [Medina] with his Bedouin levies alone' but was optimistic that trained Muslim troops, guns and aeroplanes would make up the difference. He announced that he was prepared to permit Christian pilots to fly over the Arabian interior as long as they did not fly over Mecca or Medina.[40] Colonel Wilson, who arrived at Jiddah in early July to take up his post as Pilgrimage Officer, relayed the requests to Cairo. In mid-August, the Sherif's intelligence sources reported that Turkish units had concentrated at el Ula station on the railway in the northern Hejaz. Fearing that these units might soon break through to the Arab-held ports of Yenbo and Jiddah, and strike Mecca, the Sherif asked the British navy to shell the territory inland from Yenbo and send seaplanes along the coastline. The Sherif's worries were worsened by the fact that 100 Arab Ottoman soldiers selected from PoW camps in India for a new artillery unit at Jiddah, on which he had been relying for conventional military help, now refused to fight for him. They had apparently been 'got at' by Turkish prisoners who swore that their families would be punished for their 'treason'.[41] The persistence of the 2,000–3,000 Turks holding out to the south Mecca at Ta'if was also sapping the local tribes' morale. By late August 1916, the Sherif felt compelled to ask for a British aeroplane to skirt the Meccan city limits and fly over the fort as a goad to surrendering.[42]

Crisis at Rabegh: debate over an immobile brigade

Under this atmosphere of increasing military threat, it was Feisal, retreating down the Sultani Road between Medina and Rabegh with his 4,000 men and no artillery, who signalled a weakening towards the idea of British troops landing in the Hejaz. He believed that the Turkish force facing him numbered about 9,000 (Cairo's Humint from PoWs estimated the Medina garrison at 11,000 men). The Arabs' shortage of arms was chronic and debilitating. In July, the Arab armies had fewer than 2,000 working rifles at any of their three camps. The paucity was due partly to faults in arms shipments and partly to the pro-Turk governor at Rabegh, Hussein bin Mubeirig, who pilfered substantial quantities of arms and supplies destined for Feisal. In August, 2,500 English rifles arrived, but these numbers still fell far short of requirements. On 27–28 August 1916, Feisal, now quite pessimistic, met with Wilson on board the HMS *Dufferin* to say that his army had lost all offensive capability and needed greater firepower. If the Turks launched 'a really strong and sustained attack' under the present conditions, the Arab defences would collapse. In addition to the Turks facing himself outside Yenbo, Feisal believed there were 6,000 Turks facing Ali in the centre and 6,000 at Medina as well as along the line of communication.[43] In response to his pleas to Wilson for the 'utmost' assistance in heavy weaponry, Cairo asked GHQ, Ismailia to send another supply of guns and maxims with Egyptian gunners and instructors to the Hejaz, which was done.[44]

Two weeks later, Feisal rattled the working assumptions held by most local British officers and asked for a brigade of British troops to accompany the new guns. He met with Wilson and Parker on board the HMS *Dufferin* on 9 September and explained that his army on the Sultani Road, which had no artillery, faced a Turkish detachment three times larger, and with sixteen mountain guns and two heavy guns. Feisal had set up a headquarters at Kheif, overlooking Bir Abbas, the last mountain gorge before the plains opened to the coast. Ali, whose army was twice the size of Feisal's, still had two maxim guns and two captured Turkish guns, but could not move to assist Feisal because the Turks at Bir el Mashi blocked his advance and threatened Rabegh. There were only small diversions possible further inland, even though another section of Juheinah, led by their head sheikh Saad Ghoneim, now had rifles and were launching more attacks against the railway line.[45]

Feisal's new plan was to draw the main Turkish expeditionary force down towards Rabegh, turn and cut across their line of communication from the north. Ali would strike from the east, and Zeid's force, now at Rabegh itself, would shore up the southern front. Feisal's concern, however, was that Zeid's and Ali's authority was too weak to protect Rabegh in the meantime. Ibn Mubeirig's continuing presence would leave the town vulnerable to reoccupation by the Turks and Mecca undefended. For this reason, he felt that the time had come to land 'a few British troops at Rabegh as a visible sign of British support to reassure and give confidence to the Arabs'.[46]

Wilson and Parker reported to Cairo on Feisal's difficulties and stressed the burden on his fighters' morale. The Arab Bureau had had no positive intelligence in late summer to suggest that the Turks had sufficient transport to advance against Mecca, at least until October's rainy season.[47] The Arabs' raids on the railway and against Turkish convoys were enjoying some success. But Parker cautioned the Arab Bureau that despite the dearth of 'necessary information, topographical and otherwise' which made it 'difficult to appreciate clearly the situation', it was plain that even if Feisal had overestimated the number of Turkish troops, 'the danger of the situation lies in the moral effect of a Turkish victorious advance'. New demoralizing factors were the rumoured preparations by the Turks to bring their *mahmal*[48] to Mecca, and reports of bribes distributed by the Pretender, Sherif Ali Haidar, to the tribes around Medina. Revising his earlier view, Parker now believed that, alongside Wilson's arrival at Jiddah, 'the temporary presence of a small British force entrenched at Rabegh would counter any effect of a Turkish advance, and would entirely clear the situation, at present full of risk'. Once the Ta'if garrison had fallen, the Arab forces south of Medina could relieve the British troops at Rabegh.[49]

On the basis of Wilson's and Parker's conversation with Feisal, McMahon reluctantly allowed himself to be persuaded that an immobile brigade at Rabegh would restore, not weaken, Arab morale. The brigade's visible lack of animal transport might help reassure the Arabs that an invasion of the interior was not only unintended but impracticable. To organize the detail for this new operational policy, McMahon called an interdepartmental conference, held on 12 September at Ismailia, on the Suez Canal, at General Murray's residence. Joining McMahon and Wilson at the meeting were Murray, Clayton, Cornwallis, Ronald Storrs, Admiral Roslyn Wemyss (Naval Commmander-in-Chief, East Indies and Egypt Station), Major-General A.L. Lynden Bell [Chief of GS, Egyptforce] and Lieutenant G.W.V. Holdich [Intelligence, Egyptforce]. McMahon and Wilson presented the new argument for landing an immobile brigade approximately 2,500–3,000 strong at Rabegh, and perhaps even dispatching planes that would 'create tremendous disorganization on a large body of Turks with all the transport they have'. Wilson explained that the aim was to create a 'moral effect [that] would be perfectly extraordinary' and thus provide 'tangible evidence that the English Government is not going to let [the Arabs] be crushed'.[50] McMahon pointed out that 'if the Arabs can keep up their spirits for a little longer they will very likely do all that is necessary themselves. [...] We have endeavoured to do so hitherto by money, big dollops of arms, munitions and guns, by instructors', but now, he emphasized, 'we are absolutely forced to do something drastic and soon to produce the moral effect [that] will avert a big military disaster through a very large area'.[51]

An immobile brigade would partly address the corrosive scepticism towards Britain's intentions in the region, but it would not address the religious issue. Feisal's offer to welcome the force personally might ameliorate the effect somewhat. But Clayton, probably the most versed of all the figures assembled with the latest Humint, Imint and Sigint from the theatre, still demurred. He remained wary of using Christian British troops in the Hejaz and reminded the meeting that Muslim Sudanese soldiers were available at Khartoum; they needed only to be replaced there by British troops. Sending a Muslim deployment would '[do] away with the religious difficulty'. McMahon immediately agreed with Clayon. But Murray and Wilson, both regular army men, held that the 'moral' impact, which seemed to be the key concern, of English troops would be greater because the Arabs 'won't realise that the British government is behind them unless they see British troops – white faced soldiers walking about and smoking'. McMahon repeated his concern that there was a 'great religious difficulty' in landing English troops, but the judgement was conceded in the end to Murray and Wilson who averred that only the sight of English troops would stiffen the Arab resistance.[52]

It is emblematic of the confusion surrounding this subject that, despite this exchange, Murray himself had recently expressed a view closer to McMahon's. In a private letter to Robertson, Murray remarked that, in contrast to Wingate, both he and Clayton opposed any landing British troops at Rabegh because of its negative effect on India 'and the East generally'.[53] But now that a brigade had been requested, his concerns were mainly material. He said that he would only provide the troops if directly ordered by the War Office because of the cost to his own army's capability, especially where it operated in the Sinai with the aim of taking el Arish by January 1917.[54] Perhaps more critically, despite his understanding of the moral effect requested, he believed that an immobile brigade was a practical delusion, no matter what the decision-makers' original intentions:

> From the experience of war [...] it is absolutely clear that you start and you grow. You start with a brigade[,] that brigade wants some artillery, then aeroplanes and camels. Then comes a request that the force may be moved to another point about ten miles which it is absolutely essential to hold. So the campaign grows until we get into a mild form of Mesopotamian campaign.[55]

Murray's final outline for the brigade employed what he called 'a soldier's way' of thinking, which he could assume the CIGS in London would share. He requested not only the brigade of infantry but two batteries of howitzers or a howitzer brigade, a field ambulance, a company of engineers to prepare defences and half a Wing of the Royal Flying Corps, as suggested by Wilson, with details and landing officers.[56]

On 17 September 1916, the War Committee rejected the Ismailia conference's proposal to send a brigade to Rabegh for the present because they were not persuaded that the religious difficulty surrounding the detachment had been resolved, nor were they convinced by the compromise aspect of 'immobility'. Robertson made his objections clear:

> [I]t is futile sending a Brigade to give moral support and equally futile to lay down that the Brigade would not go beyond Rabegh and would be the absolute maximum. Gallipoli and Mesopotamia should have given quite sufficient proof of such futility.

All available troops belonged in France, in his view.[57] India's opposition to the idea had also to be considered, specifically its warnings that India's millions of Muslim subjects would be outraged if Christian troops entered the Holy Land. The War Committee decided that Robertson should consult further with Cairo and Khartoum on the logistics of a brigade, as a possible option in the future.[58]

In the meantime, the Red Sea Patrol continued to deliver its own version of moral support in the open waters off the Hejaz coast. Earlier in the week, on 13 September, a British ship off of Wejh sighted Turkish troops in the town, estimated at less than 100 men by informants. The ship also fired on a nearby Turkish dhow, rumoured to be preparing to reoccupy Um Lejj to the south, and boarded it with a small party of British seamen and Arabs who gave fight and burnt the enemy's stores. The surviving Turks fled to shore and into the interior.[59] Admiral Wemyss was pleased with his ships' effect. When he learned that the government had decided against sending a brigade, he instructed the seaplane carrier HMS *Anne* to stay in the vicinity of Rabegh, 'in the hopes that the sight of the seaplanes in the air may have that moral result on the inhabitants which the Politicals believe; I doubt, but all hope'. He also brought in HMS *Espiegle* because its guns would 'prove a very considerable obstacle to the enemy' should they attempt to reach Rabegh. Finally, Wemyss made sure that he was at Jiddah when the French Military Mission arrived there, to demonstrate to the Sherif and other Arab leaders that Britain was offering even more ready support. The impressive size of his own flagship HMS *Eurylus* resting off the coastline should also, he thought, lend 'some of that moral support for which they are always clamouring'.[60]

Conditions in the interior briefly started to improve, notwithstanding the earlier pleas for a brigade. The Turkish garrison at Ta'if, reduced at last to a state of starvation by Abdullah's seige, surrendered on 22 September. The 5,000 Arab troops under Abdullah, including the Egyptian artillery battery (under Sayed Pasha Ali), were now released to assist Rabegh if necessary.[61] On 23 September, Feisal, Ali, Aziz el Masri and Nuri Bey Said held a war council at Rabegh to organize a new strategy of defence. They agreed that Ali's 5,000 Harb would retire from Bir el Mashi to Rabegh and incorporate Zeid's 1,500 men and a detachment of Ateibah fighters from Abdullah. Abdullah would move his army northward, closer to Medina, while Feisal at el Maksush (mid-point between Rabegh and Yenbo, six miles inland) formed a defensive line with 4,000 men including the Egyptian artillery, and a posting of 3,000 Juheinah at Khaif across the routes heading towards Rabegh or Yenbo. The Arab Bureau commented that after the long-awaited fall of Ta'if and this new configuration for the Arab forces, 'the situation is much easier'.[62]

The Arab Bureau interpreted the recent progress, accomplished by the Arab armies without European troops, as confirmation for the government of the broader ramifications of the Sherif's revolt. The War Committee, however, wanted to make sure that their refusal of a brigade for Rabegh had not left the Sherif in any danger, and asked McMahon and Murray how many troops should be kept as contingency reserves. Clayton wrote a memorandum for McMahon at this time to emphasize the revolt's wider geostrategic context. The Turks' reoccupation of Mecca might not threaten the Sinai campaign or Egypt, in itself; Nuri Said's intelligence had suggested that the 'total Turkish force now in the Hedjaz is only two weak divisions';[63] the real cost would be borne by Britain's Near-East territories, including India. Turkey would acquire control over the Arabian peninsula's Red Sea coast and thus the sea-route to India, while Arabia itself would become a centre for anti-British action in countries across the Middle East and Africa.[64] The Government of India rejected this view. They were more preoccupied with the Sherif's pan-Arab intentions and insisted to fforde that in India's opinion the collapse of the Sherif would be 'viewed [by Indian Muslims] with relief both on religious grounds and as removing a cause of estrangement between the Moslem community and the British Government'. An Arab Bureau member (perhaps fforde) pencilled in the margin of India's letter: 'The collapse of the Sheriff, considering WE egged him on, would be a [?betrayal of trust] – & no Arab wd. thereafter trust us.'[65] Hardinge agreed that the dispatch of any troops, even Sudanese, would be too conspicuous a display of aid.[66] And he accused India of creating an 'awkward' and 'duplicitous' situation for the British government by refusing to give the Sherif greater support.[67]

Meanwhile, intelligence continued to suggest that wider acts of Arab resistance against the Turks had been sparked by the Sherif's rebellion. Dramatic evidence of this phenomenon was delivered by two Ottoman Arab officers who had deserted their units at Kermanshah [Bakhtarān, Iran]. The officers testified in London that the rate of Arab desertions from the ranks was climbing and the Sherif's action had become a focal point for widespread Arab alienation under the CUP. Arab officers in particular resented the Turks' alliance with Germany, whom they blamed for the heinous massacres of Armenians in Iraqi districts.[68] Their detailed statements on internal dissent within the Ottoman units strengthened Clayton's argument that if Britain continued to assist the Sherif, the future Syrian campaign planned by Egyptforce would be 'made infinitely more easy by the Sherif, not only in the absence of Arab assistance to the enemy, the rottenness of the Syrian army, and the block on the Syrian railways,' as already demonstrated, 'but in the general support given to us by all classes of the people and the continual menace of our enemies which will be constituted thereby.[69]

A 'corner turned' for the Arab Revolt, and McMahon

The region's religious sanctity had so far been respected, owing to the cumulative warnings of Cairo and India and to Robertson and the War Office's reluctance to dispatch even an immobile brigade to the Hejaz. On 25 September 1916 the War Committee approved the intermediary measure of a Flight for Rabegh.[70] The planes would provide aerial intelligence and bombing support to the Arab armies. Their presence pushed the debate over military assistance further, with an unfortunate outcome for McMahon. Parker, the Political Officer assigned to prepare for the arrival of the Flight, had so far been a forceful proponent of keeping European troops out of the Hejaz. Over the previous four months he had struggled to create an intelligence network of Arab agents on the ground 'to advise and help' the tribes to undertake raids against the railway, locally and in the north, but had had little success.[71] Wilson and the Arab Bureau had temporarily halted Parker's attempts to encourage more attacks and obtain better information on attitudes north of Yenbo, where the Sherif had yet to win adherents,[72] because of the need to avoid any conspicuous British presence.[73] On 16 September, Parker had taken advantage of the naval demonstrations off the coast of Wejh to try to negotiate permission from the pro-Turk chief of the Billi tribe in the area, Suleiman bin Rifada, for the Arab armies to pass through Billi country for demolitions against the railway. But the sheikh, recently decorated by the Turkish government in Damascus for his loyalty, was 'most uncompromising'. As the Arab Bureau remarked, 'it was obvious that [British] naval demonstrations alone would not persuade him, either of our military strength, or that the Arab cause was going to succeed, and in the circumstances there was nothing that could be done'.[74]

Now, in early October 1916, antipathy to a British presence on the ground destabilized the plans to bring a Flight to Rabegh. Although Parker saw nothing to suggest that the Arabs at Rabegh were 'fanatically adverse to the sight of Englishmen', he did feel 'an uncertain element. [...] Possibly local fanaticism or possibly the jealousy of Arab officers to any interference'. Ali had warned Parker and his assistants to stay close to the harbour and outside 500 yards of the eastern palm groves 'or they might get shot by "irresponsible Arabs"'. Parker wanted to survey the greater area for the aerodrome, but Ali's prohibition and inability to guarantee greater security 'rendered any idea of work futile'.[75] Within days, Parker, increasingly concerned about the political climate and the military requirements of the airplanes, counselled the Arab Bureau against landing the Flight 'unless part of a British force'. The expanded Arab force at Rabegh was still incapable of surviving a determined Turkish advance, but the presence of a British brigade might make a difference. More importantly it would guard the Flight and save it from being 'a half-measure which involves us in land operations without ensuring success'.[76] The Arab Bureau passed Parker's report to the High Commissioner, who cancelled the Flight.[77] The Arab Bureau recommended that instead of the Flight, three Egyptian mountain batteries or QF field batteries should be sent to the Arab armies. They would increase the Arabs' firepower and help keep pressure on the Turkish lines of communication, a strategy 'which [had] always been advocated by this bureau'.[78]

McMahon reviewed the recent events with optimism and relief. Reports began arriving that Feisal had engaged a Turkish advance guard trying to move from Bir Abbas to Jedeida. On 4–7 October Feisal confronted the advance Turkish force at Bir Abbas and, after five days' fighting, managed to occupy the town, taking at least 100 prisoners and pushing the Turks back to Aar. It was also reported that the Arab parties under Sheikh Assaf, who had trained in demolition at Rabegh, had destroyed several miles of the Hejaz track and perhaps blown up a culvert bridge.[79] The pilgrimage, which took place from 26 September to 14 October 1916, had proceeded without mishap, to the credit of the Sherif.[80] Ta'if had fallen. And all this had been achieved without European troops. McMahon believed that 'through the mist of somewhat conflicting reports, we have at last turned the corner, or at any rate a very important corner, of the Arab movement'.[81] Wemyss sent a similar summary to the Admiralty noting that the Arabs' demolition attacks were having 'some success'. Feisal had reportedly defeated the Turks at Bir Abbas. Wemyss believed that the princes' new three-way strategy for attacking Medina 'will be the best guarantee for the safety of Rabegh'.[82]

Despite this sanguine turning, McMahon's grasp on the course of Hejaz policy was already being prised open. Wingate's continued lobbying for a brigade, the heightened military pressure around Rabegh, the military considerations introduced by Parker's recommendation against an unescorted Flight and General Murray's ambivalence towards Hejaz operations led London to decide that a more defined military authority was needed. On 3 October, the Foreign Office informed McMahon that the War Committee had transferred 'military control of arrangements for assisting the Sherif in Hedjaz' to Wingate, 'coupled with large measure of political control'.[83] McMahon protested that such a division of duties had already been 'found quite impracticable' and appealed for a reconsideration.[84] Robertson had hoped that Murray would take military control,[85] but Murray declined, replying, 'Sirdar is undoubtably best man for Military control'. In what amounted to an abandonment of the Residency and the Arab Bureau's judgement so far, Murray concurred with Wingate's opinion that the latter 'could not assume Military control and supervision of arrangements for assisting Sherif unless a large measure of political control were allowed to devolve on him'.[86] One week later, McMahon recommended the assignment to Rabegh of a British Military Mission to provide closer assistance to the Arab leaders and increase intelligence collection, in part to balance the influence of a recent French Military Mission at Rabegh, but likely also to counteract accusations that his office was inadequate to the military needs of the Hejaz campaign.[87]

Wingate had at last won the official authority to direct the Hejaz campaign as he saw fit, namely, along more aggressive military lines. On 12 October he asked Murray to attach an escort of one British company to the Flight and send them to Rabegh, believing the escort would now 'set all doubt at rest' about the ability of European troops to land in the Hejaz without conflict. As he told McMahon, 'Personally, I do not share the view that [a] landing of British troops at Rabegh will be resented by any but a few paid Turkish agents whose opposition will disappear when they see we mean business.'[88] McMahon sent a private plea to Hardinge, warning that Wingate's intentions were bound to shatter the political credibility of the Sherif and the local sympathies underpinning the revolt:

> I regard it as vitally essential in the future interests of the Sherif and his Cause, to avoid using Christian troops in the Hedjaz, and nothing but dour necessity ought to make us do it. The Sirdar however is already agitating for the despatch of aeroplanes with their British escort, and I fear he will soon discover pressing need for a brigade to follow. I will do my best to prevent it [unless genuine necessity arises] [...] the Sirdar has lived so long in the limelight that it may prove physically impossible for him to conduct Hedjaz operations without attracting to them a stronger blaze of limelight than is good for the Arab Cause![89]

Wemyss, always a balanced observer, sounded a calming note at this time that all the necessary assistance for Rabegh was already in place. He had just returned from the port, which he assessed as part of a three-mile-long front held by 5,000–6,000 Arabs. Their left flank was well-defended by the ships' gunfire, although the right flank less so. The Arabs were preparing to construct trenched positions outside the city. Overall, Wemyss was confident that the ships' 'large field of fire in front of the entrenchments, [which was] absolutely flat [...] should make it almost impossible for the enemy to attack except by night'. In any case, the planes' aerial surveillance would 'give ample warning of the enemy's approach'. And yet the Turks' well-reported transport shortages, their proven vulnerability to disorganization by air attack and even the recent arrival of a Cairo *mahmal* at Mecca suggested to Wemyss that the Turks were not, as feared, an indomitable opponent: 'I am of opinion that any immediate advance of the enemy from Medina is unlikely; and that should he still mean to attack Mecca he will postpone his operations until he is better organised.'[90]

The War Committee again weighed the various proposals regarding Rabegh – including the Sirdar's fresh requests for a brigade and Wemyss' report. They had been gratified by the latter's assurance that the port was already secure, especially as the members were still wary of sending Christian troops to the Hejaz. On 17 October 1916, they again declined to approve the dispatch of Christian or even Sudanese Muslim reinforcements to Rabegh. They reiterated their approval for the Flight and any material assistance still available from Egypt, adding only that a Sudanese mountain battery might be held by, in case of emergency.[91] Robertson wrote privately to Murray to express his annoyance with Wingate's proposal for a brigade, admitting that he had had 'great difficulty' blocking the request. 'It would undoubtedly have been strategy gone mad,' he wrote. 'I wish you would endeavour to get [Wingate] to hold a little broader view of the war. [...] The policy is offensive on the Western Front and therefore defensive everywhere else'.[92] Upon finding that the brigade had been refused, Wingate cancelled the Flight and turned it back to Suez, explaining to Robertson that 'their employment [...] was contingent upon the provision of strong British escort and one company British infantry actually accompanied them (Colonel Parker recommended 200 rifles as the minimum)'.[93] Robertson responded that the War Committee wanted Christian personnel kept at a minimum, and any escort for the Flight should be Muslim.[94]

The contest between Wingate, who was avowedly determined to bring European reinforcements to the ground at Rabegh, and McMahon, who opposed the idea but whose political and military authority were being steadily drained from him, was unsettling to the British officers in the theatre. Wemyss commented to the Admiralty that the transfer of authority to the Sirdar had 'created some little confusion'.[95] Lawrence reported from Jiddah that he 'found Wilson in a rather defiant mood: uncertain whom he represented and from whom he was to take orders – uninformed on details, as well as on what he called General Policy'.[96] Even Grant in Delhi was surprised by the War Committee's sudden demotion of McMahon from control over Hejaz policy. Despite his office's differences with Cairo over the Arab Revolt, Grant asked Hardinge whether McMahon was being removed from Egypt because he was destined 'for the shelf or higher things?'[97]

Wingate's ambitiousness for the Hejaz sphere had made an impression in London, despite their frustration with his requests for a brigade. On 25 October 1916, Hardinge informed McMahon that the War Committee was appointing Wingate to take over as High Commissioner at the end of December. The British government wanted 'somebody possessing expert knowledge of the first order' to direct affairs in Cairo, and 'it can hardly be said that you possess an expert knowledge on Egyptian and Arab questions'.[98] The former Viceroy's judgement of McMahon's professional experience, as a former Indian official, may have been reasonable, but the complaint was hardly sufficient, in light of McMahon's focused pursuit of the alliance with the Sherif, his engagement with the Arabs' terms and his successful relationship with the Arab Bureau. The announcement came as 'a severe blow' to McMahon who, not illogically, wondered whether his removal would confuse the Arab leaders who had believed him to be their permanent representative of the British government.[99]

The Arabs' military operations were growing in complexity, and it would appear the War Committee found it too stressful to address its responsibilities while partnering the decisions of a civilian High Commissioner. There had been complaints against McMahon by at least one official in the Anglo-Egyptian administration as well as by Sykes and Wingate.[100] But the change alienated the local British officers who continued to grapple with political concerns that they felt only McMahon had recognized. Lawrence felt strongly enough about the incident to write later that McMahon, 'whose boots the G—-s were not good enough to clean', was unceremoniously shunted out of the Residency through the combined misjudgement of Wingate, 'whose rather facile mind had believed itself the home of political insight in the Arab East', Murray and Lynden-Bell.[101]

He even went so far as to say that McMahon's replacement by Wingate 'confirmed my belief in our essential insincerity.'[102]

Clayton's leadership at the Arab Bureau while he worked under McMahon was characterized by a strong sense of personal initiative regarding the intelligence they were producing, an approach that he passed on to his intelligence officers.[103] He intentionally kept the Arab Bureau's organization informal and flexible to encourage creativity and an individual identification with the region's challenges. He believed that it was his officers' job to educate the policy-makers about the reality on the ground, and they would not be able to do that if reduced to mere intelligence technicians or Sudan office functionaries. He was also aware that the Arab Bureau was working at the convergence of several administrative departments, and would be all the more pressured because of it. 'If you once start asking questions about the Arab Bureau you will get a headache,' fforde joked to his chief in India.

> But seriously the motto of all in the bureau is never refuse a job. One boss says do this and we do it. Another comes along and says 'what in thunder are you at?' We refer him to the first boss and carry on. It is not for us to bother about details of organization. Someone must do the work while that is being settled.[104]

In a personal letter, Lawrence contrasted the tension at Military Intelligence, GHQ (Cairo) where 'voices are [...] drowned by their grinding of axes', with the collegial sense of independence cultivated at the Arab Bureau and its 'atmosphere of being one's own master'.[105]

As General Wingate assumed greater authority over Hejaz affairs, Murray, McMahon and Clayton adjusted their positions in the command hierarchy. Murray shifted to protect his own resources and separate Egyptforce further from the military demands of the Arab Revolt. In late September 1916, Murray removed Clayton from Military Intelligence duties and left him with the Arab Bureau alone.[106] McMahon, the lame-duck incumbent, tried to use the prominent position of the Arab Bureau to guard his office's communication with the Hejaz. Wingate had expanded the Arab Bureau's General Staff function to include executive authority over standard requests for supplies, material and food for the Hejaz, which would now be sent by Wilson directly to the Arab Bureau as a means of streamlining the provision of support. As Wingate told Clayton, 'I do not wish in any way to tie your hands as regards details in this connection'.[107] But McMahon suggested delegating actual discretion over supply to Clayton personally, who would continue to use the Arab Bureau as the executive channel for supply procedures but remain under McMahon's authority. Wingate had a long working relationship with Clayton and did not perceive his loyal successor at Intelligence as occupying the same frame as McMahon. The arrangement was accepted.[108] McMahon also asked to be kept informed – through the Arab Bureau – of all Wingate's correspondence with Arab leaders on political matters; the arrangement would enable

Clayton and the Arab Bureau, with McMahon, to assert some influence over Hejaz policy for a while longer.[109]

The decision to change the leadership at the Residency was accompanied by a review of the Arab Bureau's position, as well. Speaking before the War Committee, Sykes repeated his preference for bringing political and military authority for the Hejaz back to London because the decentralization of decision-making was, he claimed, exacerbating the policy confusion. He complained that 'suggestions are liable to emanate from, or to be criticized by, 18 persons, two civil Departments, the Government of India, and the War Committee, without taking Paris and Rome into account', a situation that was leaving policy questions adrift, such as with the contest over Rabegh. Sykes wanted a special department to be established in London with two Chief Political Officers assigned to each field of operation's GOC to 'co-ordinate the Arab movement, and put it in its proper relation to military operations as a whole'.[110] Hardinge had also mulled over the advantages of installing a new 'Arab Department' at the Foreign Office to handle political policy for all of Egypt, Arabia, Aden, Muscat and Mesopotamia.[111] But the Director of Military Intelligence (DMI) in London did not support the relocation of these responsibilities to London, away from Cairo, Clayton and the Arab Bureau. In early December, the DMI suggested that a Political Intelligence Department incorporating the Arab Bureau and with Clayton at its head might be created, but it should still be located in Cairo, likely under Wingate's new High Commissionership.[112] Now it was the India Office's turn to object: such an enhanced intelligence department (in fact, giving formal structure to what the Arab Bureau was already doing) would be invited to steer policy formulation – and policy must remain wholly under the Foreign Office.[113] Ultimately, none of these proposals to redefine or relocate a new Arab Department outside of Cairo was adopted. By 1 January 1917, the political and military management of the Arab campaign would be tied more firmly to Cairo by Clayton's promotion to Chief of Staff for Hejaz Affairs under Wingate, with continuing charge of the Arab Bureau and two additional Staff Officers to support the office's responsibility for operations.[114] But before then, Clayton and the Arab Bureau had to hold tight to their course through the next months' turbulence regarding the Arab armies.

Lawrence's mission: advancing a strategy of guerrilla warfare

The gains in tactical intelligence for the Arab Revolt from Sigint and Imint were indisputable. In late October 1916, unconfirmed intelligence, probably from Humint, suggested that Turkish troops were evacuating from the Sinai peninsula, raising the possibility that they might be transferred as reinforcements to the Turks' Medina garrison. Wemyss assured the Admiralty that Sigint would give ample warning of such plans for a new Turkish advance, 'as a large number of enemy W/T [wireless] messages transmitted by Stations in Sinai and Arabia are intercepted by us and the Military Stations and decyphered by the Intelligence Department. The news thus obtained is of great value.'[115]

Less successful were the attempts to improve strategic and tactical Humint through targeted or systematic collection on the ground. The Arab Bureau expressed frustration over the continuing lack of 'definite information re enemy dispositions and topographical details' to assist the Arabs in their operations. Humint on enemy movements from informants or PoWs was at times unreliable and needed to be placed in context with other intelligence before assessment. Humint on critical features such as water supplies and road conditions, changing tribal dispositions or the condition of the railway had been misleading on various occasions. As a result, Feisal and the Sherif still had only the 'vaguest information of situation at Medina or North'. There had been discussions in Cairo about building agent networks with regional sheikhs to get 'sufficiently reliable data' – of which Parker's efforts at Wejh to make contact with local tribes were one example – but the failure of these schemes suggested that little could be done until the Sherif's armies took the northern coastal towns and allowed British intelligence officers to enter, with the 'assured co-operation of local Arabs'.[116] Lawrence would later write of this period:

> Things in the Hejaz went from bad to worse. No proper liaison was provided for the Arab forces in the field, no military information was given the Sherifs, no tactical advice or strategy was suggested, no attempt made to find out the local conditions and adapt existing Allied resources in material to suit their needs.[117]

Feisal's victory at Bir Abbas had been short-lived and his position above the Turkish line of advance again became untenable. Fakhri Pasha, seeing that Feisal's army threatened his right flank, sent an airplane to bomb nearby Bir Derwish where some of Feisal's men were camped. By 18 October, the Turks had taken Bir Raha. Feisal evacuated Bir Abbas, sending word that he was 'hard pressed'. He retired to Jedeida and sent the results of prisoner debriefings to the British, describing a strengthened Turkish force.[118] The Arab Bureau's information also showed renewed determination by the Turks. A source, most likely Sigint, revealed that Medina's Turkish governor was reinforcing the track between Bir Nesif and Medina because of the threat posed by the Arabs' raids. He sent out an armoured train, a camel corps detachment and two platoons from the city, as well as a camel corps from Medain Salih. In addition, the Turks at Wejh appeared to be moving south towards Um Lejj and Yenbo, with the intention, should the main force advance against Mecca, of preventing Feisal from retreating northwards near their line of communication. Intelligence suggested that the Turkish force was being joined 'daily' by groups from the Billi and Huweitat tribes.[119]

A surprise solution to many of these problems arrived in mid-October 1916. On the 16th, Ronald Storrs landed at Jiddah to meet with Colonel Wilson and Prince Abdullah to consult on the next stage of the revolt, in light of the rejected brigade and the cancelled Flight. Accompanying him was Captain Lawrence of Military Intelligence, until now part of Murray's staff, who was sent along by Clayton to bring back a military assessment of the ground. Clayton had already sent the War Office his request that Lawrence be transferred permanently to the Arab Bureau.[120] Notwithstanding Clayton's personal estimation, there was little sign that the inclusion of this junior officer would become one of the more dramatic assets for the Arab Revolt. Lawrence maintained a modest profile and only inquired after what he considered crucial information.

After their meeting with Abdullah, the British contingent invited Aziz al-Masri, now in charge of the Sherif's forces, to join the consultation. Abdullah asked that a Muslim brigade and artillery be sent to Rabegh; foreign troops would only be allowed if the Arabs' pending attack on Medina failed and his father was left without protection.[121] Lawrence told Abdullah that he wanted to tour Rabegh personally and review its defences to make his report. He also asked to visit Feisal's encampment on the Sultani Road. Storrs backed the idea and telephoned the Sherif for permission, which was given. Abdullah wrote to Ali at Rabegh that Lawrence must have the necessary transport and assistance to go into the interior.[122] Parker wrote to Clayton a few days later, observing that he himself had long wanted to travel 'up country' and now it was Lawrence who had been given the task. 'Don't think I grudge him, especially as he will do it as well or better than anyone', he remarked. But there seemed little chance that permission for any other trips would be granted in the near future as Ali, pressed into the decision reluctantly, had apparently 'had a reaction on the subject'. Parker noted that 'even Aziz [al-Masri] is not allowed to go north to look around'.[123]

Lawrence's approach to this tour was shaped in part by a recent tutorial in French aims in the Hejaz. Over dinner at Jiddah, Lawrence had talked with Colonel Eduoard Brémond, the head of the French Military Mission. Brémond told Lawrence 'in a moment of confidence'[124] that in order for France to feel secure about their interests in Syria, the Arabs' revolt must not leave the peninsula – which meant that 'above all things the Arabs must not take Medina'. Brémond believed, as did Cairo, that an Allied landing at Rabegh would probably wreck all popular support for the Sherif and leave the Allies (ideally, France) 'the sole bulwark of the Sherif of Mecca'. The French could then counter popular Arab resentment of their Syrian activities by restoring the Sherif to Medina.[125] Lawrence described these schemes in a report forwarded to the War Committee in London.[126] His particular concern was that Wingate would be vulnerable to manipulation by Brémond and send in a European force, sabotage the Arabs' revolt and open the door to French rule in Syria. This concern was expressed by many other figures in Egypt and the Hejaz over the coming months.[127]

Lawrence took instruction on the Arab perspective on nationalist agendas in the Hejaz and Syria by talking with Aziz al-Masri. Al-Masri travelled with Lawrence as far as Rabegh. Lawrence had been asked by Clayton to secure al-Masri's commitment to operations against northern sections of the Hejaz railway, as part of a strategy to open up the northern coast to the Sherif. But it soon became clear that al-Masri was not interested in any operations south of el Ula. Yet he was 'enormously interested in the Hejaz Railway *North of Maan*', Lawrence found. Al-Masri asked Lawrence for intelligence on the Syrian districts of the Hauran, Kerak, Aleppo and Nebk-Salamieh, by which Lawrence concluded that al-Masri meant to 'get up into the Ruallah–Hauran country, not to do very much perhaps, but to sound the people, and cut the line'. Lawrence did not dismiss the idea. He noted that al-Masri did not want to take Hejaz troops along. Lawrence also told Clayton that such a diversion in the Hauran in November might be a useful tactic.[128] The conversation turned out to be a seminal exchange of ideas. Lawrence had been treated to a fairly convincing scenario involving irregular action by Arab fighters around the Syrian railway in Rualla territory, and he was prepared to accept that, with the right leadership, it would have popular support.

Like Parker, Lawrence observed that the absence of a professional intelligence system on the ground was making it difficult to evaluate the Turkish army's movements or intentions, or even tribal motivations with any consistency. An expanded intelligence system would also enable the Arab leaders to better coordinate their respective field operations. Lawrence told Clayton that 'the opportunities are quite good, and at present there is no one to do them. If one stayed there, and worked, one would be able to appreciate the Hejaz situation quite well'.[129] In a report sent to the Arab Bureau on 19 October 1916, Lawrence repeated that 'nobody knew the real situation at Rabegh', but that he and al-Masri meant to assess the situation. Al-Masri wanted better support for a nucleus of 5,000 regularly-trained Muslim fighters to take Medina. He also, with Abdullah, strongly opposed a landing of European troops at Rabegh, believing it was 'neither prudent nor necessary' as the Turks had no doubt abandoned their plans for an attack on Mecca. Lawrence noted to Clayton, 'he does not know much more about it than we do', but he was clearly impressed by al-Masri's confidence regarding the Sherif's troops' fighting capacity and his long-term view of the Revolt encompassing action in Syria. In a telegram to the Arab Bureau, Lawrence forwarded al-Masri's appeals for the British 'to prevent any decisive risk now' that might disturb the Arabs' efforts, such as a dispatch of European troops, and to ensure that the British personnel at Rabegh, where al-Masri planned to train his regular army, dealt directly with Ali and Feisal 'without details being referred to Sheriff of Meca of whom they are all respectfully afraid'.[130] Lawrence later incorporated many of these suggestions into his own reports.

From 20–25 October 1916, Lawrence gathered detailed intelligence from the field on the state of the Arab armies, the Turkish army and the terrain, and drew up his own appreciation of the Hejaz situation for Cairo. On the first day he visited Rabegh with al-Masri and observed his and Ali's efforts to train the 'regular army' of Arab PoW volunteers, Syrians, and Bedouins. On 22 October he rode north to Feisal's camp at Hamra along Wadi Safra, about seventy-five miles southeast of Yenbo. He found in Feisal's style of leadership and demeanour the military and political inspiration that in his view had been conspicuously absent from the Revolt. He stayed with Feisal until 25 October, sitting with him during his conferences with tribal representatives and taking extensive notes. He returned to Yenbo and began writing up his report, catching the HMS *Suva* to Jiddah with Captain Boyle on 1 November. Onboard he met Parker, who, after hearing Lawrence's conclusions, urged him to visit Wingate on the way and deliver his case. At Jiddah Lawrence transferred to the HMS *Eurylus* under Wemyss, who was also travelling to see Wingate. They arrived on 7 November and Lawrence met with the Sirdar over the next four days, before returning to Cairo.[131]

The intelligence reports which Lawrence wrote on the basis of this brief tour of the Hejaz – 'The Sherifs', 'Feisul's Operations', 'Hejaz Administration', and 'Military Notes' – were an extraordinary sequence of analytical essays that managed to overturn many of the common assumptions about the Turco-Arab conflict. One of his most striking points was a recalculation of the Turkish army's ability to reoccupy Mecca. Wingate's arguments for sending a brigade to Rabegh had been based on the assumption that a Turkish force advancing from Medina to Mecca would have to stop at the wells of Rabegh. Lawrence's intelligence identified the existence of two routes out of Medina to Mecca. The larger, more well known route was the Sultani Road. It ran through Rabegh and was used by pilgrims during the *hajj*. There was little water or food along the Sultani Road, however, so a Turkish expeditionary force advancing from Medina would require substantial camel trains for supply. But there was also an interior road, the Wadi Fura, that bypassed Rabegh. It was less frequented, being smaller, but it contained oases of palm trees and water. Although there was little further intelligence about Wadi Fura's current condition, both routes would fill with water sources once the rains began in November. (Aerial reconnaissance in mid-December 1916 spotted abundant water supplies along inland routes, including Wadi Fura.) Lawrence's intelligence on the nature of these roads threw into question the prevailing belief that a conventional force at Rabegh could stop a Turkish advance against Mecca.[132]

One of Lawrence's intelligence responsibilities in Cairo had been the debriefing of prisoners-of-war. In the Hejaz he continued to debrief PoWs for information on the possible intentions and condition of the Turkish army. He learned that the Turks were smoothing roads between Medina and Bir Abbas and improving the water supply, likely in anticipation of an advance. There were also reports that the three Turkish regiments south and southwest of Medina had recently been reinforced to four battalions each, with 800 to 1,000 men.[133] It was not clear whether they had enough live transport to support a full advance by approximately 6,000 troops.[134] Humint from prisoners confirmed earlier reports that the Turks appeared to have enough food for the soldiers at Medina, and enough water, but they were short on forage for their animals. Lawrence reported that 'it is not easy to see why they have not advanced', unless the incidence of cholera at Medina and the overall shortage of food supplies had disrupted their ability to launch a full campaign to Mecca, which would require long lines of communication across the desert. The other possible factor was the prospect of an Allied landing coupled with the unpredictable movements of Feisal's army which, 'as long as [Feisal] preserves its present elasticity and avoids a decisive action', still retained the power to cut off a Turkish column between Medina and Mecca.

If the Turks did decide to advance, despite these obstacles, and chose to take the interior Wadi Fura road over the Sultani Road and Rabegh, the only real barrier to their marching on Mecca was the continued resistance of the Arabs. The tribes' activity had made that intermediate territory a hostile ground for the Turks. Consequently they would require additional transport and reinforcements from Syria to strengthen the HEF so that it could either execute a multi-faceted attack, or set up block-houses along its line of communication from Medina to Mecca to withstand a prolonged resistance. It was Lawrence's personal belief that the Turks were hesitating to move more aggressively against Mecca's advance only because they could not protect their flank while Feisal operated around the Sultani Road.[135] Humint from PoWs stated that the bulk of the Turkish army was two-thirds Turk and almost entirely conventional in organization, apart from 300 Shammar tribesmen lent to the Turks by their stalwart, Ibn Rashid at Hail. This composition underscored the Turks' difficulties in the Hejaz. The Shammar were all mounted and could act as flying columns over long distances, but it was Lawrence's judgement that, 'being tribesmen', the Shammar would not remain long with the Turkish army and their threat was relatively minor. The Turks' flexibility as an expeditionary force was limited.[136]

Lawrence proposed a new strategy of defence for the Arab forces around Rabegh and Mecca that also incorporated intelligence gathered on the Arab forces themselves. It was estimated that 15,000 to 20,000 men were fighting under the Sherif, drawn locally from tribes from Um Lejj to Kunfida. The largest forces were commanded by Feisal and by Ali at Rabegh. Apart from the Sherif's Bishawi 'retainers' and the men training at Rabegh for al-Masri's regular army, which included Syrian and Arab veterans of the Ottoman army, the whole of the fighting force were tribesmen. Desert and hill tribes formed the bulk of the force, with camel corps composing about 10 per cent. The former Bedouin tribes were the groups which Lawrence would examine in detail.

In open country, he acknowledged, a direct assault by a single company of Turkish soldiers would easily defeat a much larger Arab defensive force. But investigations of the Hejaz terrain showed that the ground between Medina and Rabegh was intersected by a steep array of hills. The only passage through it was along a series of chasms and gorges that ran for miles,

> full of turns and twists, without cover, and flanked on each side by pitiless hills of granite, basalt and porphyry; not bare slopes, but serrated and split and piled up in thousands of jagged heaps of fragments as hard as metal.

Lawrence proposed that this terrain, not wider than twenty yards in places, was a formidable barrier in itself against the Turks' regular army which was carrying heavy artillery and leading long lines of transport. Furthermore, the local tribes who occupied the hills outside Rabegh could, in his opinion, provide all the defence necessary for the port. These hill tribes knew 'hundreds of ways from one hill-top to another' and their snipers, whose 'initiative, great knowledge of the country, and mobility, make them formidable in the hills', could be posted in the high ground between Bir Abbas and Bir bin Hassani, to lethal effect. A couple of hundred men would be able to block both the Sultani and the Fura roads against a Turkish advance. The British authorities had only to supply these tribes with 'a kind of sniper's accessory', such as light artillery and light machine-guns; the combination of difficult terrain and determined guerrilla fighters scattered through the hilltops around the pass would form an impenetrable 'cordon' around Rabegh. Lawrence concluded: 'I do not see how, short of treachery on the part of the hill tribes, the Turks here can risk forcing their way through.'[137] Even with limited arms, the hill tribes seemed already to be the main barrier against the Turks; as he wrote a few weeks later, 'Rabegh is not, and never has been defensible with Arab forces, and the Turks have not got there because these hill-tribes under Feisul bar their way.'[138]

The tribesmen's raiding practices worked along pure irregular principles that were effective and need not be altered; 'the tribal armies are aggregations of snipers only,' Lawrence repeated, 'and their sphere is guerrilla warfare.'[139] For this reason Arab raiding parties tended to be comparatively small and they followed the hierarchy set within the tribe, which meant that Bedouin Arabs were particularly unsuited to the practice of working in conventional ranks or accepting commands from outsiders. He recommended that responsibility for the wages, food and military preparedness of the fighters remain with the sheikhs in order to maintain the tribal unit's customary autonomy. Released from ties to any central command, the Arab armies would then be able to function as proper flying columns – and in this way would 'dynamite a railway, plunder a caravan, steal camels, better than anyone, while fed and paid by an Arabic authority'. The traditional reward of the raid – plunder – was sufficient motivation for them to fight the superior Turks, so long as the latter possessed enough camels, horses, provisions and guns to be worth their attention.[140]

Outside the hills, of course, lay the larger target of the railway. Lawrence believed the desert Arabs would continue to harass the Turkish forces along the railway. Feisal, too, meant to follow Cairo's recommendation and focus on cutting the line which, he now realized, was of 'primary importance'. Abdullah was moving to a position on the eastern road out of Medina. Ali (or another leader) was going to reinforce Feisal's previous position on the Sultani Road, while Feisal's army of 2,500–3,000, which was largely Juheinah, at Kheif Hussein attempted to make a full assault against the railway around Bir Nesif. Although the tribesmen insisted on fighting in their own district, Feisal hoped 'to distribute the Arab forces [...] as widely as possible' in order to break up the Turks' present concentration at Bir Derwish and thus relieve Rabegh. Lawrence asked for field wireless sets to be given to each army's headquarters to help coordinate their movements. If these irregular tactics succeeded, the Turks might be forced to pull their outlying units back to Medina and 'allot most of their present force to the duty of guarding their railway communications'. If the Arabs managed to cut the railway, which at present was 'very insufficiently guarded', the garrison at Medina 'may fall more quickly than is expected'.[141] Forcing the enemy to expend precious energy on static defences while maintaining one's own tactical mobility was a classic strategy of guerrilla warfare.[142] As Lawrence wrote:

> The Hejaz war is one of dervishes against regular troops – and we are on the side of the dervishes. Our text-books do not apply to its conditions at all. It is the fight of a rocky, mountainous, ill-watered country (assisted by a wild horde of mountaineers) against a force which has been improved – so far as civilised warfare is concerned – so immensely by the Germans, as almost to have lost its efficiency for rough and tumble work.[143]

Another consideration for British assistance was the Arabs' morale. Wingate and recently the interdepartmental conference at Ismailia had been preoccupied with trying to assess the value of a British brigade for Arab morale. Lawrence broke with their conclusions and recommended supplying heavy artillery to the Arabs instead, because that was what they wanted most.

> From Feisul down to the most naked of his men they all swear 'If we had had two guns we would have taken Medina' – for they will not appreciate that the Turks are not as foolish as themselves in this matter.

'[A]rtillery, artillery, artillery', he emphasized, 'the power and terror of which they have on the brain' had become essential.[144] Lawrence asked the British authorities to send mountain batteries 'to act as amulets to restore public confidence',[145] and instructors to teach the Arabs to man the artillery themselves rather than relying on the Egyptians, who were deeply resented.[146]

The final responsibility for Britain was to provide a financial alternative to the great purse of Constantinople. Because the Arab armies were still floating from base to base, the Turkish army – even if they broke through to Mecca – 'could never feel quite sure that the tribes would not collect again' behind them and across their lines of communication. Thus the Turks were currently trying to secure those flanks by making payments to the local tribes. The Turkish government's long-standing financial arrangements with the tribes – their 'money and suasion', the 'best weapons of all' – would become a significant factor behind the British government's willingness to make such generous payments to the Sherif's administration. By some accounts, the Turks were spending as much as £70,000 a month on the Hejazi Arabs. If transport and supply shortages hindered the Turks' advance on Mecca, Lawrence believed they might try to buy up the tribes along the railway instead. The Billi around Wejh had already been secured with bribes and Turkish propaganda about the Sherif's affiliation with the British. Although they had not sworn a formal alliance with the Turks, they were not yet to be counted as allies of the Sherif.[147] In Lawrence's opinion, the Turkish commander at Wejh might even try to pay his way south between the railway and the coast, collecting not only the Billi but the Juheinah of Wadi Yenbo and the Beni Salem of Wadi Safra to secure the Turkish lines of supply and barricade the Sherif's forces from reaching the railway.

The authorities in Cairo had to recognize that 'money, and money only, is going to give us the breathing space necessary to equip the Arab armies for the taking of Medina,' as Lawrence saw it. The Sherif, who was in touch with many of the same tribes as the Turks, had no choice but to outbid his opponent. His pay schedule was at present more rewarding than the Turks'. He paid a constant rate to the fighters and their families to compensate for the lost income from tribal raids. He also allowed the men to rotate their commitments between the field and visits home. This arrangement meant that more men were being paid than were in active service, but Lawrence applauded the policy because 'the retention in the field of such numbers as the Sherif has actually kept together is unprecedented'. The Sherif's payments to the tribal sheikhs were at times 'little more than disguised bribes to important individuals', but in Lawrence's opinion, 'nothing else would have maintained a nomad force for five months in the field'.[148] The intelligence files from this period show that Lawrence never queried the tribesmen's price for leaving their traditional livelihoods and going to war against the Turkish government. He observed that it was

> customary to sneer at their [the Arabs'] love of pay: but it is noteworthy that in spite of bribes the Hejaz tribes are not helping the Turks, and that the Sherif's supply columns are everywhere going without escort in perfect safety.[149]

He also recommended that the princes be given their funds directly, rather than through the Sherif.[150] It is significant that, as early as October 1916, Lawrence was concentrating on the distribution of the money as a function behind decentralizing control over the tribes' army units, which was essential for the effectiveness of a full guerrilla strategy.[151]

Lawrence's concluding proposal for the Arabs' larger campaign plan can be safely attributed to the inspiration of Aziz al-Masri, with whom Lawrence had travelled from Jiddah to Rabegh. Lawrence stated that the Arab tribesmen could continue to harass the Turks' outposts whilst also composing themselves defensively as a kind of 'screen' or 'shield' around Rabegh, where the training of a regular Arab army would proceed. Ideally, this 'minimum field force with good mobility [would be] capable of meeting a Turkish force distracted by guerrilla tactics, and defeating it piece-meal'. Once the Turkish forces were pinned to the vicinity of Medina and the railway by Arab irregulars, Medina could be taken by a proper Arab force. Five thousand men would be recruited from Ottoman army Arab prisoners sent from India and Egypt and from non-nomadic Arabs such as townspeople, even slaves. Five companies of camel-mounted troops, 200-strong, would support the infantry.[152] After six months of training, these regular soldiers should be able to attack and hold an entrenched position such as Medina. The army would be based at Rabegh and form a 'rallying point' for the Sherifian armies guarding Mecca. Until the regular army was trained, no base could be fortified solely by Arabs fighters 'for the tribesmen will not sit still for a moment'. Lawrence recommended that a monitor – a naval gunship specially designed for coastal bombardment – be employed to defend Rabegh in the interim, as effective a deterrent in its threat of a European landing as any actuality.[153]

The summary argument closing Lawrence's report addressed the political and military risks of landing a European brigade at Rabegh. Logistically, the dispatch of troops would be impossible to organize in time. If the Turkish army did push through the hill tribes' defence, it would reach Rabegh in four days: 'This does not give time for the collection, embarkation, transport, disembarkation, and preparation of a position for a British force to hold the 6,000 yard long front of the palm grove at Rabegh', observed Lawrence. But more importantly, the popular components necessary for an effective guerrilla campaign would be erased by a foreign Christian intrusion. Any attempt to land an allied force, whether Rabegh were threatened or not, would trigger whole-scale political and military desertion of the Sherif's cause. The southern Hejaz Arabs would flee the defensive effort, leading the northern tribes to turn back to the Turks and the British Rabegh force would bear 'the whole weight of the work'. The Sherif had already been accused by Turkish propaganda of allying with an infidel power bent on occupying the Holy Places. Lawrence believed that the anti-Christian rhetoric in fact provided 'an excuse to hide the really political objections to our coming' – which flowed from the near universal conviction amongst the Bedouin that 'an armed landing by us is the prelude of eventual occupation'. Any military assessment of the Hejaz campaign's requirements therefore had to take into account the political nature of the Arab Revolt.

In summary, none of the events which might fatally threaten the Sherif's rebellion would be averted by the presence of a British brigade at Rabegh: it would not compensate for the Sherif's shortage of money, a Turkish occupation of the Arabs' water supplies or palm groves inland, a 'pitched battle' bringing unendurable casualties, or the unforeseen toppling of the Sherif 'as an exclusively Arab sovereign'. The only foreign presence at Rabegh should be advisers and technical units, in addition to the monitor. 'Guns, machine-guns, wireless telegraphy, and aeroplanes' would be welcomed by the Arab fighters as fitting and necessary accessories for their efforts and would provide far more 'moral value' than any foreign combat force. Lawrence emphasized repeatedly that the guerrilla strength of the tribes was the single solid advantage to be played against the conventional weaknesses of the Turkish army: 'It would I think be quite possible for a small Turkish force to re-take Mecca: and if the tribes still kept their present determination, impossible for the Turks to retain it.' Even a successful Turkish offensive against Mecca would have to leave some force outside Rabegh to protect their lines of communication from raids and fend against an allied landing in their rear, and 'at present their whole Hejaz army is not sufficient for this purpose alone'[154]

Lawrence's sympathy with and admiration for the Arabs in undertaking such a revolt was evident. Other British visitors to Arabia were also struck by the heroic status and charisma of the Sherif and Feisal, in particular, even when disappointed by certain individual episodes.[155] Lawrence's respect for the breadth of the Arab Revolt's potential popularity was something he hoped to convey to headquarters. The movement's very singularity across disparate tribal groups might be a source of inspiration to the war planners.

> Looked at from Egypt it loses some of its proportion, in our engrossment in the office telephones, and canal defence, and the communiqués. Yet we have here a well-peopled province, extending from Um Lejj to Kunfida, more than a fortnight long in camel journeys, whose whole nomad and semi-nomad population have been suddenly changed from casual pilferers to deadly enemies of the Turks, fighting them, not perhaps in our manner, but effectively enough in their own way [...][156]

Lawrence did not challenge the general British assumption that the Arab territories would ultimately countenance some European ties, if only to survive. But he did stress that that relationship would depend upon how well Britain played her role as an ally. He no longer doubted the Arabs' ability to create a government superior to the Turkish system in the Hejaz as far as the subjects' interests were concerned, although the Arabs' mainly pastoral and agricultural economy, and their lack of material resources in the Arabian peninsula would preclude their gaining any real wealth or power as a country. Only the annual hosting of the *hajj* promised to project a degree of international power, but still in that regard, in view of its own Muslim populations, Great Britain would have positioned itself well as a friend. He remarked: 'If it were otherwise we would have had to weigh more deeply the advisability of creating in the Near East a new power with such exuberant national sentiment.'[157]

4 Intelligence on trial

The Rabegh crisis, November 1916–January 1917

First alarm at Rabegh: intelligence wanted

The chronic tension surrounding Rabegh, Wingate's campaign to bring in reinforcements and the intelligence community's advocacy of a guerrilla strategy were set to collide. The risks posed by the insertion of foreign troops were still being debated, and the danger for the Arabs of a conventional attack from the Turks' HEF, faced without military help, was another mystery. Wemyss had expressed his confidence to the government in the capacity of Imint and Sigint to give adequate warning of enemy movements against Rabegh, but the Flight was still being organized and Sigint successes depended upon the enemy's communication procedure. Deeper in the field, the Arab armies lacked the targeted intelligence support that would have allowed them to verify single-source warnings of threat quickly, and unnecessary panics inevitably followed.

In late October an Arab informant delivered to Rabegh an exaggerated account of a scouting party of the 80th Turkish Camel Corps on the Sultani Road, which he said was riding towards the port. The HEF's advance units were known to be waiting in the hinterland, impatient to move against Rabegh or Mecca. When Ali and Aziz al-Masri at Rabegh received news of the Turkish mounted patrol moving their way, they concluded that the offensive had begun. They boarded the RIMS *Dufferin* at Rabegh and wired Cairo to send artillery and machine-guns with British crews immediately to save them from being overrun. Abdullah began preparations to transfer to Rabegh with much of his force, to assist.[1]

In receipt of this alarm, Wingate sent London a fresh proposal for sending reinforcements for Rabegh. He ventured that the obvious immediacy of the Turkish threat and the Arabs' direct request for military assistance would have to persuade the War Committee that a regular brigade was inevitable. He told Murray to hold one in readiness at Suez. Murray refused, wanting direct orders from the War Office. He had already sent one 4-gun 15-pdr Q.F. battery, one 4-gun 5" howitzer battery and two additional howitzers to Rabegh.[2] The War Committee had reviewed Wemyss's assurances on the monitor's ability to protect the port only a fortnight earlier. They agreed to trust his judgement and so rejected Wingate's request, explaining that there was still no clear cause to dispatch 'anything in the nature of an expeditionary force, or any such force as may involve us in yet another campaign'.[3] The alarm subsided and by 3 November, the Arab Bureau had assured the DMI in London that a demonstration by the attending ship's guns and the delivery of the field battery, howitzers and aeroplanes on 8 November would soon 'restore confidence' to the Arab armies.[4] Still the incident had revealed the continuing sense of vulnerability amongst the tribesmen and their leaders, and the Arab Bureau admitted to the DMI that low morale and uneasiness hovered over the campaign.[5]

Intelligence officers on the ground turned their attention to the Arab armies' defences and improvements for the system of communication between Cairo and the Hejaz. In addition to Parker, who was still on site at Rabegh, Lawrence returned to Yenbo with instructions from Clayton to make whatever arrangements he could to raise the standard of intelligence-gathering. His first priority, as will be seen, was the establishment of better Imint capability.[6] At the same time, a visiting intelligence officer from the Indian Army, Major N.N.E. Bray, arrived at Jiddah to assist Wilson. Wilson sent him to help al-Masri at Rabegh. Bray's observations led him to the same conclusions as Parker and Lawrence about the region's need for greater intelligence organization and the Arabs' aptitude for guerrilla war.[7]

Concerned that London might be swayed by views such as Wingate's into underestimating the Arabs' ability to hold an effective defence, Bray decided that Cairo must have 'someone from the spot going to England to explain matters' to the government.[8] In late October Bray made a personal trip to London. He met with Sykes, who introduced him to Chamberlain, the Secretary of State for India. Chamberlain listened to Bray's arguments regarding the Hejaz and pressed him to write a report for the War Committee. On 8 November Bray submitted a report asking the government to support the Arabs as a guerrilla army, with all the necessary arms and materiél, but no conventional reinforcements. His testimony reinforced the argument repeatedly advanced by Clayton and McMahon, and matched the conclusions being produced simultaneously in the Hejaz by Lawrence. Bray also argued for the regional staff's request to locate an intelligence organization at Rabegh itself, headed by 'a capable [British] officer [...] who can give us reliable and useful information on improved system of communication'.[9] The CIGS, Robertson, welcomed the proposal. As Bray was still on assignment with al-Masri, he unfortunately could not take up such a post himself. Robertson suggested to Wingate that Lawrence or George Lloyd might be good candidates for heading the new military intelligence system at Rabegh.[10]

Directly after Bray delivered his report, the War Committee approved a second source of counsel on the ground. McMahon had requested the establishment of a British Military Mission in October 1916 to bolster Britain's assistance to the Arab forces and to counter the machinations of the French Military Mission under Brémond at Jiddah.[11] The War Committee approved the proposal on 9 November. The head of the mission, which would set out in four weeks, was Lieutenant-Colonel Stewart F. Newcombe (Royal Engineers) of MI, Egypt.

Newcombe had long experience with intelligence in the Middle East and was Lawrence's CO in 1913 for the Sinai survey. Other members were Major A.J. Ross as Engineer Officer, Majors C.E. Vickery and C.H.F. Cox as Artillery Officers and Captain W.E. Marshall, R.A.M.C., as Medical Officer, all of whom knew Arabic and had worked in Arab countries. One of the Mission's duties would be to assist al-Masri with the training of the Arab regular force.[12] The other was to set up a viable intelligence system in the Hejaz.[13] The British Military Mission would work with the British officers already assisting the Arab forces on the ground: Wilson at Jiddah, Parker at Rabegh (recalled on 1 December 1916 to join Egyptforce[14]), Colonel P.C. Joyce and Captain W.A. Davenport who led the two companies of British troops escorting the Flight,[15] and Major Herbert Garland, an engineer officer based at Rabegh who was teaching the Arabs the art of railway demolition, or explosives.[16]

Wingate welcomed the introduction of a British Military Mission. There is little doubt he perceived it as the first step towards the brigade he still hoped to obtain. One of his first requests to Marshall, the Medical Officer, was to produce a report on the likely sanitation and water requirements of a brigade based at Rabegh.[17] In conjunction with that goal, he believed that his personal assessments of Rabegh's security needs would at last be backed up by creditable military intelligence from the field. As he wrote Clayton: 'the necessity for the presence at Rabegh of a small expert military staff to [...] advise on and appreciate the military situation is very urgent'.[18] Wingate assured the CIGS that full and accurate intelligence would be forthcoming as soon as the Mission arrived in December and the Flight began making tours. The Arab Bureau's latest intelligence on the Turks' transport difficulties and available roads had discredited his own evaluation of the threat at Rabegh. He reminded Robertson that Cairo's reports claiming there was insufficient live transport for the HEF to launch an offensive was based on uncertain or 'inaccurate' Arab Humint. Second, although recent rains had improved the condition of the interior Wadi Fura road – and Abdullah was apparently preparing to transfer thousands of troops down that very route – Wingate was still not convinced that 'large bodies of Turkish troops' would be able to mobilize down it. The Arab guerrilla activity north and south of Medina had created greater pressure and anxiety for the HEF, he agreed. But he and the 'local authorities' (i.e. Parker and Joyce) were still of the opinion that only a British brigade with artillery and naval support would be able to defend Rabegh. Out of respect for religious sensitivities he was prepared to hold the brigade at Egypt until 'the last moment'. Wingate's proposal did not provide any new intelligence on Turkish transport, nor did it solve the logistical problem identified by Lawrence, namely, that there would not be time to embark, transport and disembark a substantial fighting force for Rabegh when the defensive hills at issue lay only a couple days away.[19]

Clayton had no intention of losing his resources or his control over the flow of Hejaz intelligence to another office. Robertson's suggestion to appoint Lawrence or Lloyd as head of the new intelligence system arrived shortly after Clayton had obtained the transfer of Lawrence, officially with MI, Egypt, to the

Arab Bureau as a full-time officer. Clayton also wanted to retain Lloyd's service; although an MI officer, Lloyd devoted most of his time to Arab Bureau work, evaluating political and economic intelligence on the Ottoman territories.[20] Wingate – who, significantly, had not yet read Lawrence's October/November Hejaz reports condemning the idea of a brigade in favour of a full guerrilla campaign – looked forward to placing him and Lloyd more directly under his authority. He told Wilson that Lawrence, 'who knows Feisal well, would be most suitable', although, he added, 'I can imagine Clayton crying out against it, as I am afraid the Arab Bureau is rather hard put to it.'[21] And Clayton did cry out. 'The importance of an Intelligence system as suggested is obvious', he replied. They were so far having to work in the dark, owing to 'the impossibility of getting British officers into the interior and the inaccuracy and unreliability of Arab agents' – but he had to 'strongly deprecate' moving Lloyd but 'especially Lawrence' to the project, because he was engaged in vital work for GHQ and the Arab Bureau.

> [Lawrence's] great knowledge and experience [is] of far greater value at headquarters where he will be almost indispensable. The same applies to Lloyd, whose strong points are politics, economics and commerce, and who [...] does not I believe know Arabic.[22]

Wingate assured Clayton that directly Newcombe arrived with the Military Mission, Lawrence would be released back to Cairo's authority. But in the meantime it was 'vitally important to have an officer of [Lawrence's] exceptional knowledge of Arabs in close touch with Feisal at this critical juncture'.[23] He also anticipated that, with Parker and Joyce assigned to Rabegh, and Wilson working at Jiddah, 'it is quite possible [Lloyd's] services will not be required there permanently'.[24]

Contention over the assignment of intelligence officers would have been a novel topic of discussion in any theatre. Intelligence and intelligence officers had become valuable commodities in the Cairo/Hejaz sphere. Lawrence, despite his youth, already had gained a reputation in Egypt and London as a knowledgeable Arabist with substantial experience in Syria and the Sinai, an authority on the Turkish army's order of battle and now an emerging expert on the topography of Arabia. Most recently he had distinguished himself by winning the Hashemites' confidence and conducting a seminal intelligence tour of the Hejaz interior. His trip's report would have significant repercussions, as will be seen. There were many military and political aspects of expertise in Lawrence's work that Clayton would not have wanted to lose from the Arab Bureau.

The military debate over reinforcements

The debate over intelligence and its relevance to various policy options intensified during the last months of the year. General Murray had been observing Wingate's lobbying efforts with the War Committee. If the Sherif's armies were defeated, their elimination would release Turkish troops for the Russian, Palestinian and Mesopotamian fronts, an outcome which Murray wanted to avoid. And yet, as he pointed out to Robertson, he still 'deeply deprecated' the diversion of a brigade from his force to the Hejaz precisely because the security of the surrounding theatres depended equally upon Egyptforce's maintaining full offensive power, and occupying el Arish and the rest of the Sinai. Once Egyptforce reached Gaza, Murray would be able to open a new front in Palestine and Syria, which would itself draw the Turks away from the Sherif, the Russians and even IEF 'D' in Mesopotamia. Murray asked that London not make Egyptforce so weak as to make it irrelevant to the enemy, for it would only bring worse risk to the other Middle Eastern campaigns.[25]

Murray's great inspiration at this juncture was not to plead his case on behalf of the needs of Egyptforce, but on behalf of the Arab Revolt itself and the Arab forces. The latest intelligence, which Clayton had shared with him from the Arab Bureau, stated strongly that landing a brigade at Rabegh, as suggested by the Sirdar, would be disastrous for the Sherif. When Robertson asked Murray on 16 November which brigade he would send to Rabegh if so ordered by the War Committee,[26] Murray submitted as his reply an incisive report written by Lawrence advising against the dispatch of Allied troops to the Hejaz. Clayton had requested this piece from Lawrence as a précis of his extensive October/November reports. Knowing Murray's concerns, Clayton passed Lawrence's summary report directly to Murray, without reference to Wingate. He introduced Lawrence as 'an officer of great experience and knowledge of Arabs' recently returned from Rabegh and a personal visit with Feisal, whose observations were 'very pertinent to the question of the despatch of a Brigade to Rabegh'.[27] Murray was so impressed by the work that, also without reference to Wingate, he sent Lawrence's report on to the DMI and the War Committee as representative of the political and military views of experienced regional observers, with whom he concurred. Murray stated:

> Lawrence's strongly expressed opinion that no British or foreign force should be sent to Hedjaz is strongly supported by civilian and soldier residents in this country who are intimately acquainted with the delicate nature of the Sherif's position as a religious chief, and the peculiar feelings of the Arabian Moslems towards foreigners. Shortly put, the views held by Moslem experts who have spoken to me on the subject entirely confirm Lawrence's news that the Sherif as a religious chief ceases to exist the moment foreign troops land in Arabia, and that the occupation of Rabegh by a force acting on the defensive is useless.[28]

Quite apart from its professional cunning, Murray's decision to elevate the judgement of a junior intelligence officer over that of General Wingate reflected the remarkable status that expert intelligence had acquired during these policy debates. Lawrence's judgement for London, which was supported by the ongoing reports from Clayton, Bray and the Arab Bureau, was that Britain had only to supply money and 'technical' support such as planes, artillery, instructors, telegraphic equipment and armoured cars for the Arabs to succeed. The tribal fighters should not be forced to adopt conventional configurations against the HEF but allowed to wage a broad guerrilla strategy against the Turks' supply lines and material weaknesses of the railway. Lawrence's report argued that 'to continue the present *guerre de courses* is sooner or later to wear out the Turks completely and force them back on a passive defense of Medina and its railway communications'.[29] Wingate's proposal for a European brigade seemed to be responding to a different, fairly apolitical conflict and appeared myopic by comparison regarding the nature of the Arab armies he was trying so hard to save. Lawrence's report was published along with Bray's report (8 November) in the War Committee's Arabian Report of 23 November, making the divergence of views between the intelligence community and General Wingate clear.[30]

The willingness of Cairo's intelligence community to go outside Wingate's control in commenting on questions of policy was also evident from the reports. Wingate's recommendations on the suitability and expertise of Lawrence and George Lloyd for intelligence posts in the Hejaz, as noted above, had been made before he learned of Lawrence's report to the War Committee. Wingate now found himself being asked by Foreign Secretary Edward Grey if he agreed with Lawrence and whether he thought Lawrence would support a French Algerian force for Rabegh if led by Christian European officers.[31] Wingate could only respond that he was attending to all the necessary intelligence upon which these decisions had to be based. Privately, the episode galled him because his impression after meeting with Lawrence at Khartoum was that they had been in agreement. In Wingate' opinion, the tribes' raiding activity was largely a delaying tactic until a European regular force, an Arab regular army or the British Military Mission could take over. He had not realized that Lawrence was viewing the hill tribes' defensive line as a complete strategy in itself.[32] In defence, Wingate promised Grey that he was submitting his Hejaz case as 'confirmed by information' from Wilson, Parker and a high-ranking Arab figure. He conceded meanwhile that 'the more [the Allies] can publicly proclaim their territorial disinterestedness in Hejaz, the more likely is the Sherif to gain the solid adherence of the tribes and to defeat the ends of the CUP'.[33] But that concession did not reflect a change in Wingate's mind about the necessity of a brigade for the protection of the port and the Flight. His statement for London said that if 'our intelligence and airships clearly indicate that the Turks intend an advance in force', then 'every effort should be made to stop it'. In the event that none of his advice was taken and the Sherif collapsed, Wingate stated that 'he [Wingate] must ask to be absolved from responsibility'.[34]

The War Committee wanted 'direct information' from Wingate in reply to the claims made most recently by Lawrence but also by Bray and Clayton, that the presence of European troops would be worse for the outcome of the Arab Revolt than a poorly defended port. Hardinge wrote privately to McMahon that Robertson was still 'obdurate in his determination that a British brigade should not be sent,' but the Committee would consider approving a French brigade, as offered by the French government, 'if it would be decided that the presence of European troops would not upset the religious fanaticism of the Sherif and his Arabs'.[35] Given that Wingate had already repeatedly expressed his confidence in the psychological and military benefit to the Arabs of a European brigade, the committee's need for explicit reassurance showed that the members were rating Cairo's intelligence conclusions as comparably credible. McMahon assured Hardinge that Lawrence was 'a very shrewd observer' whose tour through Feisal's camp confirmed McMahon's own anxiety 'that whatever the Sherif and his sons may say, our occupation of Rabegh would from one reason or another, have a disintegrating effect on the Arab tribal forces now in the field'.[36]

This extraordinary battle over the intelligence judgements resulted in a reprimand for Murray from the CIGS, who conveyed the War Committee's frustration over the apparent 'lack of co-ordination' as well as their suspicion that information of value was perhaps being kept from the Sirdar – who was 'in charge of the Hedjaz business'.[37] Part of Wingate's isolation was geographical. He was not due to move from Khartoum to Cairo until the end of December 1916. But the more important part of this schism was political and in that sense, cultural. Privately, Wingate appeared to be confused by the divergence of the Cairo intelligence staff from his policy direction; as he complained to Wilson: 'I am rather disappointed at the Arab Bureau being drifted about by any wind that blows.' He felt most aggrieved, however, by 'the apparent want of straightness on the part of certain people who should be above that sort of thing', most likely referring to Murray, who had wired Lawrence's report direct to London without informing him, and to Clayton, who had provided it. It had been awkward for Wingate to admit to Grey that he had not received Lawrence's report himself. But he felt most exasperated by Lawrence's presumption in challenging a policy recommendation decided by himself, Parker and, as he believed, Wilson.

> I have no doubt that Lawrence has done all this in perfectly good faith, but he appears to me to be a visionary and his amateur soldiering has evidently given him an exaggerated idea of the soundness of his views on purely military matters.

Lawrence was not a professional soldier, and Wingate assured Wilson that, 'as you will see from my two replies to the Foreign Office, I am quite prepared to stake my military reputation on the views expressed by yourself and Parker, who are good soldiers and experienced in Arab ways'.[38] Unbeknownst to Wingate, he would not be able to count on Wilson's agreement much longer, either.

The intelligence revelations from Cairo continued to challenge Wingate and his 'good soldiers'' conclusions about the HEF's threat. 'An absolutely reliable source', i.e. Sigint,[39] stated that the HEF at Medina lacked adequate supplies and was under great duress.[40] McMahon referred to this intelligence in a letter to Hardinge to reiterate how foolhardy it would be to send European troops to Rabegh now that the Turks lacked the food and resources for an advance and Arab morale was rising.[41] To put this HEF's condition in greater context,

Lawrence produced an intelligence analysis of the Turks' order-of-battle in the Hejaz, based on GHQ's own intelligence, and calculated the likelihood of their obtaining reinforcements from other Turkish theatres. He estimated that of the Turks' forty-two divisions spread across Egypt, the Caucasus and the Middle East, only the six divisions currently in Syria and unengaged with the enemy were a possible 'strategical reserve' for the Hejaz. But Lawrence did not believe that Jemal would be able to spare them because they supported his own main line of communications, assisted with domestic security and needed to be on hand to defend the Sinai against the British army's advance and the British navy's (rumoured) landing at Alexandretta. Turkish government propaganda was already trying to disguise the army's nearly depleted depôts and their dwindling total rifle-strength of less than 350,000 men. Lawrence concluded that it would 'be hard for Turkey either to form new units or spare old ones, for the comparative luxury of a campaign in the Hejaz' unless Jemal could feel secure about his coastline, convince the German GS of the campaign's necessity and, above all, solve the shortage of live transport.[42]

Cairo's intelligence staff watched those figures on Turkish transport carefully. Like the supply of water, the availability of live transport was a leading indicator for the practicability of a Turkish advance. One of the Allies' most successful agents in Palestine during this time was Aaron Aaronsohn, a renowned agricultural scientist previously employed by the Turkish government to head an anti-locust campaign all over the country. One of Aaronsohn's reports in early December noted that in Syria, 'water-buffaloes now form the largest class of Turkish military as well as civilian transport', suggesting that it was even more unlikely that the HEF would be able to buttress their transport with reserves from the north.[43] In the meantime, Fakhri Pasha was just managing to hold his numbers steady at Medina. By 21 November, a 'certain statement with regard to supplies' from a 'very reliable' source, almost certainly Sigint, placed the total number of Turks in the Hejaz still at 12,000.[44] This intelligence data was used by both the CIGS and Murray to argue against the dispatch of reinforcements. The CIGS, employing the doctrine of superior force, declared that 'nothing less than the despatch of 15,000 [British or Allied troops] would suffice' to protect Rabegh, a figure that would probably require the withdrawal of Egyptforce from el Arish.[45] Murray, taking another tack and denting Wingate's and Brémond's alarmist projections, asserted that the HEF's force of 12,000 men, tied down to increasingly vulnerable lines of communication, was still small enough to be pressured efficiently by arms and money rather than Allied troops.[46]

Intelligence and the strategic detachment from Medina

The Arabs' operations in November ran across the spectrum, from large concentrations of men such as at Prince Ali's base at Rabegh to the smaller tribal raiding parties acting independently around Medina and the railway. Feisal and his force maintained pressure from the Kheif-Milif hills, inland from Yenbo, by attacking a Turkish outpost, raiding a Turkish camel corps and commandeering an HEF supply convoy of more than fifty camels. Zeid acquired 600 tribesmen from Ali and 500 camel-corps and moved to Bir ibn Hassani, between Rabegh and Yenbo. The other important shift, decided by the princes during their 23 September war council, was the migration of Abdullah's army to Wadi Khank, southeast of Medina, with ten guns and three machine-guns, accompanied by anti-Turk/anti-bin Rashid tribal contingents from Nejd. His army attacked a Turkish guard battalion en route before arriving at Henakiyeh, seventy-five miles northeast of Medina.[47]

Sigint and Humint showed changes in the Turks' supply lines and increased raiding activity by the tribes, suggesting that the princes' reconfiguration of force was showing an effect. Intelligence obtained by the Arab Bureau, most likely from Sigint, showed that the HEF had been forced by the Arabs' attacks on the railway to invest in 'the laborious, costly, and also somewhat hazardous task of getting supplies from Hail' in central Arabia, from convoys most likely originating around Nejd.[48] Raiding parties of Harb fighters were harassing Turkish camel corps and caravans east of Medina that numbered in the hundreds, clashing with several hundred of bin Rashid's pro-Turk Arabs around Hail. To the south of Medina, Turkish detachments had been unable to occupy any of the main points along the Sultani Road – Bir el Mashi, Bir ibn Hassani or Jedeida. So far they appeared to be pinned by hostile tribes in bases in the hills northeast of Jedeida, at Bir Abbas and at their advance headquarters at Bir Derwish.[49]

These small gains did not guarantee security for Rabegh, however. Feisal and al-Masri decided they must shift both their bases northward and solidify a broad defensive line. Al-Masri, unhappy working under the close control of the Sherif and Ali at Rabegh, asked to move his regular army training base to Feisal's headquarters at Yenbo. Wingate was baffled by the decision, telling Wilson that it seemed 'strategically absolutely unsound to abandon Rabegh for Yenbo' which was farther away from Medina.[50] But Clayton approved of the move, telling Wingate that 'for strategical *and political* reasons', the Arabs' military base should be moved to Yenbo because it was 'absolutely vital that we should assist the Arabs to prosecute an offensive as soon as possible'. By moving away from Medina, the Arabs' leverage against the Turks' main artery of supply – the railway – would be increased: the Hejaz railway was 'the key of the whole problem and it is the permanent cutting of that railway, or at least the dislocation of its running', that must remain the priority. He also repeated Lawrence's argument that 'as time goes on we are running an increasing danger of finding that the Arabs get sick of the show and begin to melt away. It is only by an offensive that they can be kept together and in the field'.[51]

But the reorganization did not stop there. While al-Masri transferred to Yenbo, Feisal would stretch the top of the Arabs' defensive line still further north, to the port town of Wejh. In mid-November, Feisal, Ali and Abdullah agreed they would have to elongate the Arabs' defensive line 180 miles to Wejh, if they really meant to relieve the pressure against Rabegh and Mecca. The British navy off the coastline could provide fire support. Once al-Masri's base was established at Yenbo, Feisal could use his Wejh base to attack the Turkish rear at el Ula, 100 miles inland on the railway. Not only would such a reorganization of force restore the advantage of surprise and mobility to the Arabs' operations, it would remove permanently any need for European reinforcements. Feisal transferred his Harb and southern Juheinah fighters at Wadi Safra to Zeid, and with his core force began moving up the Wadi Yenbo. He gave notice that he would be organizing agreements with the northern Juheinah for the march on Wejh.[52] Clayton was impressed with these plans and remarked on the same to Wingate. The Arabs' were trying to operate strategically, trying to cripple the Turks' base from behind the head rather than confront the HEF in the field. He also echoed Lawrence's expression in his November report, 'the Turkish force at Medina can stay there as long as it likes, provided it is rendered incapable of a serious offensive'. Clayton assumed that the railway would eventually be cut by a British offensive in Syria, after which point, 'the Medina Division is lost'.[53]

In addition to providing access to el Ula and the railway, Feisal hoped his transfer to Wejh would win over the vital, famously independent Billi tribes to the Sherif's cause. The Hashemites had been courting the Billi leaders since June, trying without success to marginalize the influence of their pro-Turk chief, Suleiman bin Rifada, recently made Governor (Pasha) by the Turks. Although the Turks controlled portions of the Billi, Lawrence reported that most of the tribe were independent and suspicious enough of outside influences to benefit Feisal because they were 'very anti-foreign, and much annoyed with the German–Turk alliance'.[54] Intelligence in October showed that bands of Billi fighters had started harassing Turkish caravans and patrols. Even more encouraging, in late November, one of Suleiman's cousins, Hamed bin Rifada, cooperated in a joint operation with a unit of Feisal's camel corps and attacked a Turkish supply caravan between Wejh and el Ula, intercepting seventy camels and stores headed for the Turks at Wejh. The raid was exceptional in demonstrating that even a portion of the very clan-minded Billi could bury grievances 'for sentimental reasons' and fight alongside their blood-enemies, the Juheinah and Harb.[55] The Arab Bureau reported to the DMI in London that Feisal believed it was only a matter of time before the entire Billi tribe gave their allegiance to the Sherif. He needed only artillery to move his forces with confidence into Billi territory at Wejh. The impression from Sigint continued to support Feisal's argument for this northward strategy: the Medina garrison and outlying detachments still lacked adequate supply for an advance and seemed very unlikely to be able to launch a major offensive in the immediate future.[56]

The senior British regular army officers on the ground disagreed with Feisal, Clayton and the Arab Bureau on the wisdom of transferring to Wejh. The conventional military assessment of the Arab forces was pessimistic; the tribesmen appeared incapable of holding a fixed point and it was doubtful that any regular Arab force would be able to confront the HEF at Medina. Colonel Joyce, posted with the Egyptian artillery units to Rabegh and thereafter with the escort serving the Flight,[57] observed Ali's and al-Masri's efforts with their armies and recorded only poor military leadership, non-existent discipline and blatant dysfunction with regard to operations. His reports expressed his daily frustration over the failure of the Arabs at Rabegh to work in their own best interests against the Turkish threat. He sympathized with al-Masri, as did Parker, over Ali's weak leadership and the Sherif's attempts to control all decisions for the campaign.[58] But Joyce and Parker would have preferred that the princes redouble their efforts to fortify Rabegh – for which 'nothing has even been started,' apart from al-Masri's tattered army – and abandon the move north. The artillery, so emphatically requested by the Arabs, had finally arrived, but the Arabs' performance with it was so ambivalent that its possession now seemed irrelevant. Prince Ali admitted that his constantly postponed operations were due to his own distrust of his armies' commitment. The British officers felt that their presence was not helping and may have even been a liability. All of these factors left the present question of defence for Rabegh, 'from a military point of view [...] an impossible one'.[59]

The regular army concerns were challenged at this juncture by George Lloyd, who worked for both Military Intelligence and the Arab Bureau. Lloyd made a special tour of Jiddah, Rabegh and Yenbo between mid-November and mid-December 1916 to assess the general military situation. He stayed a few days with Lawrence at Yenbo and confided afterwards to Clayton that he had been deeply impressed by the young officer's strategic grasp. He said that Lawrence had given him 'a mass of information', detailing how 'supplies, demolition, communication & intercommunication are the only things we must assist in, plus the political officer at Jiddah to keep relations good with Mecca'.[60]

Lloyd reported on these observations to Murray, echoing many of Lawrence's arguments. He told Murray that the hill-tribes would defend Rabegh better than any conventional foreign force, and that intelligence on new inland water sources and the Turks' continuing supply problems must be accepted for their bearing on Turkish capability. He questioned whether the Turks could do any more than 'make an unsustained coup upon Rabegh' and force the British to evacuate their planes and materiél, 'but that is a trifling loss compared to the expense & risk of white troops even if they helped which they would not. On the other hand', he noted, 'if the morale of the tribesmen fails not [?even] brigades can save the Hejas for the Sherif'. Repeating a favourite sentiment of Lawrence's, Lloyd emphasized the difference between simple military scenarios and the complex political relationships unfolding behind the Hejaz uprising, warning that 'anyone who advises sending white troops to Rabegh or any other spot fails, in my judgement, to appreciate the nature of the movement'.[61] Finally, Lloyd personally visited Wingate at Khartoum to argue these same policy points. The Sherif's survival as the Arabs' religious and political leader had to be Britain's first consideration. Lloyd told Wingate that 'there must be no British troops & British personnel confined to the minimum' because to 'flood' the Hejaz with Christian troops would be 'fatal' to the Sherif's political viability.[62] By giving priority to the political requirements of the uprising before the military ones, Lloyd cast his lot with the intelligence community and a guerrilla strategy against the HEF, and rejected the position taken by Wingate, Joyce and now Parker.

In the final days of November, just before Lloyd's last reports were submitted, a contingent from Zeid's force confronted a scouting party of Turkish camel corps from Bir Abbas in the hills near Bir ibn Hassani, killing fifty Turks while losing only six of their own men. Each report showing growing tenacity on the part of the Arab groups on the ground was interpreted by Cairo as further confirmation that all could be handled without recourse to foreign troops: 'Better and better yet', Lawrence later recalled.[63]

The shield of Rabegh collapses: the Turkish counter-attack, December 1916

All the greater shock, then, in the first days of December 1916 to find that the same meticulously argued theory of the hill-tribe defence around Rabegh had crumbled under Turkish pressure. It seemed for a while that a terrible miscalculation had been made. The Turks at Bir Abbas swiftly advanced westward along a few tracks. A mule-mounted Turkish patrol pushed into Wadi Safra near Hamra on 1–2 December 1916. The Harb's Beni Salem faction were holding a defensive position there but broke and fled. To the south, Zeid and his Egyptian army contingent tried to shore up the Harb but came apart under the Turks' machine-gun fire, and retreated to Yenbo. By 3–4 December, the main Turkish force had reoccupied Hamra and Bir Said. The road to Yenbo lay open and with it, Wadi Safra, Rabegh and Mecca. Feisal, who had been preparing with 3,000 camelry for the great move to Wejh, was forced to abort. On 4 December he turned westward with the bulk of his army from Kheif Hussein to Nakhl Mubarak, hoping to link with Zeid against a Turkish attack on Yenbo.[64] What Lawrence had guaranteed only weeks before as 'the shield of Rabegh', the impenetrable defensive line of hill tribes, had disintegrated.

The Arab Bureau tried to evaluate the extent of the rout. Garland at Yenbo reported that Zeid was panicked and had requested air and naval support, so he had instructed HMS *Dufferin* and a French cruiser in port to remain on hand in case of emergency.[65] Captain Boyle, SNO for the Red Sea Patrol, reported to the Arab Bureau that the situation was still 'obscure' but Zeid's force had clearly been routed. Wilson reported that Feisal was dividing his force between Nakhl Mubarak and Kheif Hussein to avoid being surrounded.[66] The DMI in London tried to clarify subsequent Sigint, asking the Arab Bureau to confirm the substance of an intercepted Turkish communiqué, sent 6 December 1916: 'Our advance towards Yambo [*sic*] is making progress.'[67] But the Arab Bureau was still waiting for news from Lawrence, who had gone to meet Feisal before the Turkish advance.[68]

Lawrence was still the only British officer permitted to travel into the interior. His relationship with Feisal had quickly become one of trust; Feisal treated him 'very well' and permitted him to 'ask hear and see everything, including his agents.' Clayton was also trusting Lawrence. His instructions in sending him back to the Hejaz were characteristically open-ended; he had encouraged Lawrence to use his initiative, 'go ashore and do what seemed best, and it would be hard to be more definite'.[69] On 2–3 December while the Turks were making their advance to Hamra forty miles to the south, Lawence rode east from Yenbo until he found Feisal and his army, making camp in great confusion at the oasis of Nakhl Mubarak.[70] Feisal confirmed the worrying news that much of the Harb had scattered and 'will not rally for a week'.[71] Lawrence stayed in attendance during two days of negotiations, 'alarms and excursions', before returning to Yenbo.

While waiting for transport, Lawrence wrote his most candid remarks on the situation in a private letter sent immediately to Kinahan Cornwallis, now Acting Director of the Arab Bureau, to whom he admitted, 'things are bad [...] the shield of Rabegh on which, in my old report, I relied for all the defensive work is now gone'. The Harb's support had fractured, the Beni Salem had defected – perhaps soon to placate the Turks, and the Hawazim clan 'are almost openly wrong'. It was possible that soon the Subh tribe would also weaken, which would 'lay open the Sultani Road and imperil the holders of the Ghayir and Caha and Fura areas'. Feisal was blocked from moving south to help Ali. He was also almost entirely reliant now on the battered Juheinah who, as mentioned, worked poorly with other tribes.[72] Feisal was still insisting that it was the lack of mountain guns that had lowered Arab morale, 'so that is some chilly comfort for us', wrote Lawrence. But there was now nothing to challenge a Turkish advance upon Mecca except for 'Ali's anaemic force at Rabegh itself, the possibility of a recrudescence of the warlike spirit of the Harb in [the Turks'] rear, or the fear of Feisal behind them all'. Lawrence had little detail on Zeid's 'skirmish' near Kheif but aerial reconnaissance, which he would soon organize, would make the situation plainer. He was going to return to Feisal at Kheif Hussein immediately, adding: 'I hope to clear up that situation' – with information and reassurances regarding Yenbo – 'and expect to be back on Monday night.'[73] Lawrence asked Boyle, with the HMS *Suva*, to support any Arab forces taking up position at Yenbo in the meanwhile.[74] Boyle sent five ships, including a monitor, to Yenbo, with assurances to the Arab Bureau that the port at least would be safe.[75]

The endemic difficulty for the undisciplined tribal fighters remained the maintenance of morale and cohesion in the field when faced with a conventional attack. Observing Feisal's performance inland, Lawrence was impressed to find that superior leadership could compensate to such a degree for the armies' lack of training. Despite the collapse of the Harb and of Zeid's force, Ali's difficulties and the Sherif's hunkered base at Mecca, Feisal had remained focused and purposeful in the field. He alone seemed capable of holding a wavering camp together despite the proximity of the Turks and the forced postponement of Wejh, which had wrecked his previous six months' efforts 'tying tribe to tribe and fixing each in its proper area.' Privately, Lawrence told Cornwallis that he was recognizing in Feisal 'the *beau ideal* of the tribal leader,' in contrast to the command style of the other princes. The Harb's flight had reduced his options for the moment, but his ability to motivate a complex force of fighters and conclude negotiations with the neighbouring tribal chiefs was still impressive.

Lawrence felt that the last three days had given him 'a very great insight to what [Feisal] could do in a pinch.'[76] When Lawrence wired Wilson and the Arab Bureau the next day, he stressed his strong impression of Feisal as a leader who was 'holding his force [of] about 5,000 [men] together with his personal prestige, and though himself much depressed, keeps splendid'.[77]

The crisis had also emphasized the Arabs' painful lack of working tactical intelligence. Lawrence made note of the paltry results produced by the debriefing of informants at Feisal's camp, and concluded that poor intelligence probably outranked even the famously wished-for artillery, feuds and the tribes' lack of regular training as the Arabs' greatest disadvantage against the Turks. As he reported to Wilson, 'the situation is certainly not good – and in the maze of conflicting reports and obvious exaggerations afloat here one can hardly see more'.[78] 'Unreliable reports' had placed the main detachment at Bir Said, a Harb village forty miles south of Yenbo, with food for one month, but Feisal's agents could not tell him whether the Turks intended to move on Yenbo, turn north against Nakhl Mubarak or reverse southward to reoccupy Rabegh and Mecca. On 6 December, Feisal complained that he could still not tell whether the main Turkish force was at Bir Said and possibly heading towards Yenbo, or had moved to Wadi Safra and now aimed at Rabegh.[79] The uncertainty was affecting his followers. Lawrence said they now had 'urgent' need of aerial intelligence of the fifty miles between Bir Said and Wadi Safra, to determine which course the Turkish contingents were taking so that Feisal could plan. He prepared a rudimentary landing ground at Nakhl Mubarak before he left, and assured Wilson that he would be happy to accompany the flights himself to prevent the pilots from 'simply flying in the dark'.[80] Wilson had already instructed Lawrence to stay with Feisal.[81]

As Lawrence had reported, the Arab armies' efforts to reorganize were plagued by unsubstantiated rumours. Despite the cumulative impression from earlier intelligence that the Turks were incapable of advancing against Rabegh, new if unconfirmed intelligence sources suddenly suggested that an advance might be imminent. George Lloyd, still in the Hejaz, telegraphed Clayton on 6 December to say that 'very scanty intelligence', probably Humint, suggested that the Turks were going to send advance parties to Bir Said to cut off Feisal and Zeid, while their main force pushed through Ghayir to Rabegh. Worse, Feisal's sources claimed that Turkish reinforcements of artillery and infantry had arrived at Medina from Syria and the Sinai. Feisal telegraphed Murray that 'the relief to you should be great, but the strain upon us too great to endure'. Feisal did not ask for reinforcements, but urged Murray to move on Beersheba 'or feign landing in Syria as seems best, for I think the Turks hope to crush us soon, and then return against you'.[82] In Cairo, the Arab Bureau was already reviewing Humint from two deserters from the 42nd Regiment which confirmed the Medina garrison figures.[83] But claims of reinforcements from Sinai caught them by surprise.[84] While these were being investigated, Wilson recommended holding a brigade of troops with artillery at Suez in case of emergency, and Wingate agreed, pointing out again that, despite the vulnerability of the HEF's line of communications, they may still be able to undertake 'a resolute offensive which, having regard to the nature of the Arab forces in the field, would almost certainly result, within the space of a few weeks, in the entry of the Turkish force into Mecca'.[85]

The Turkish army pushed through Feisal's position within twenty-four hours of his dispatch to Murray. Three Turkish battalions armed with three guns and four machine guns advanced against Feisal's force at Nakhl Mubarak on 8 December and tried to cut his line of communication with Yenbo. Feisal fought back with his artillery but when the Juheinah on his left flank suddenly crumpled he was forced to retreat on Yenbo. The Juheinah's later explanation – that they had only paused for 'a cup of coffee' before resuming battle, then without artillery or Feisal, until pushed back themselves to Yenbo the next day – only made for a more miserable postscript.[86] Feisal sent the Juheinah fighters back to Kheif in Wadi Yenbo to harass the Turkish line of communication with raids and sniping parties and disrupt their ability to ride en masse against Yenbo.[87] Boyle noted, nevertheless, that Feisal's unnecessary withdrawal had only underscored the 'constant and apparently irreparable factor in the Hejaz military situation', namely, 'the incapacity of Arab levies to meet regular Turkish troops in the field',[88] Ali and Aziz al-Masri, still at Rabegh, moved north on 12 December with the main force of 7,000 (including 1,800 trained troops) to Bir ibn Hassani, in order to draw any engagement away from the port. Ali sent another 350 camel corps to help Feisal, and posted guards at Rabegh and on the Fura road.[89]

It was Feisal again, bearing the brunt of the Turkish pressure, who began to consider bringing in Allied reinforcements. With the enemy occupying Wadi Safra, and the Harb and apparently much of the Juheinah dispersed, Feisal believed the situation had 'entirely changed' and that 'everybody sees how serious the Arab position is'. He sent the Sherif a description of the Turkish force facing him at Nakhl Mubarak, promising to work the enemy flank as long as Rabegh held out. The Sherif wired Wilson at Jiddah about the crisis, who wired Wingate on 10 December 1916. Wingate wired the Foreign Office the same day. Feisal sent a second message directly to Wilson, through Lawrence, which was even more candid about the threat and explicitly requested a landing of British troops at Rabegh, whom he promised to welcome personally.[90]

Reports of the withdrawal of Zeid and Feisal to the coast caused a stir in London. On 8 December, Wingate wired Wilson's relay of Lawrence's telegrams sent on 6–7 December from Yenbo, communicating the flight of the Harb and the request by Feisal for a diversion at Sinai to lessen the Turks' pressure.[91] On 9 December, the War Committee decided to ask the French whether they would still contribute troops, if an Allied landing at Rabegh were required. Robertson asked Murray to hold a detachment from Egyptforce at Ismailia, in case this approval came.[92] The Foreign Office alerted Wingate, who replied that the guns from the Egyptian artillery batteries had been landed for the Arabs at Rabegh, leaving the remaining artillery personnel and aeroplane escort to help Joyce prepare defences.[93] Wemyss had already ordered the monitor *M.31* from Suez to stay at Yenbo until further notice, confident that the navy could protect the port from inland attack.[94]

Wingate viewed the collapse of the Harb and the apparent irresolution of Feisal's and Zeid's followers as proof of his long argument that without Allied conventional assistance, the Arabs would break before any determined Turkish assault. Joyce agreed, adding that their 'slackness and unwillingness to accept expert advice' made it highly unlikely they would ever raise and field an adequate regular force of their own, despite al-Masri's dreams. Wingate advised the Foreign Office that a brigade with artillery should be sent directly to Rabegh, or else preparations made for the worst-case scenario of a successful Turkish advance and the evacuation of all planes, materials and personnel, which would have a 'very bad' effect on Arab morale.[95] Wingate also wired Wilson instructions to challenge the Sherif with these risks, so that he might finally make a formal request for Allied reinforcements.[96]

Unfortunately for Wingate, the crisis coincided with reports by the Sherif's informants that Turcophilic elements in Medina were spreading black propaganda that the Hashemites had given the Hejaz to Britain. Throughout the interior the Turks were still paying 'large sums of money' to the Harb, Juheinah and Billi to try to keep or win back their loyalty. Burdened by these reports, the Sherif met with Wilson, Lloyd, Brémond and the Italian Military Mission's representative at Jiddah on 10–11 December. He stressed that because the Arab population looked to him to personify the integrity of the revolt, he could still only accept help in the form of Muslim troops. He rejected the offer of 3,000 British troops but agreed to Brémond's offer of a French Senegalese contingent, still three weeks away. The next day he cancelled that request, as well.[97] The Sherif told Wilson that a strategy of deception was really all that was required: if Britain sent 1,500–2,000 Muslim troops to Rabegh and Yenbo, he would spread word that they were only the advance units of a much larger force. The Turks would panic, and his reputation would be saved. Wilson recommended the idea to Wingate, suggesting that Murray's detachment be held at Port Sudan as an emergency reserve only.[98] Wingate passed the request for a Muslim brigade along to London but omitted Wilson's and the Sherif's remarks about the attendant possibility for deception, noting only that 1,500 British Muslim troops were unlikely to be able to repel a serious Turkish attack, according to the 'experts on the spot'.[99]

At the same time, trials with Imint and aerial support were beginning over the active field, as Lawrence had urged, with important returns for Feisal. The first reconnaissance flight from Rabegh on 4 December spotted over 100 tents in the valley bordering Hamra to the north, but the pilot had not been able to verify them as Turks or pro-Turk Arabs.[100] On 8 December, a reconnaissance flight sighted a possible Turkish headquarters at Kheif and an enlarged camp at Hamra, and although the pilot was not able to locate Bir Said – confirming Lawrence's concern that the pilots required close instruction – he could confirm that no significant Turkish force had approached the coast.[101] Imint by seaplane on 10 December spotted a large body of Turks at Nakhl Mubarak,[102] but on the same day a seaplane from Yenbo 'successfully fired into and bombed a force of about 400 Turks' in camps twenty miles to the northwest of that place, boosting the morale of the Arab armies at Yenbo and Rabegh.[103] Such obvious benefit from the Flight and the seaplanes made Lawrence impatient to incorporate Imint more smoothly into Feisal's operations. He told Wilson that he would ask Captain Ross, the RFC Commander of the Flight at Rabegh, to reroute the flights using his (Lawrence's) instruction on the terrain, or base a plane permanently at Yenbo, because the pilots arriving from Rabegh had been flying for four hours and were 'too dazed to see anything' on the ground. Worse, it seemed the pilots had been given no intelligence on the key terrain, 'only the old map, and no notes on what the places looked like, on what to look for. So they saw nothing, though they passed over Nakhl Mubarak during the battle'.[104] Even so, Feisal was soon able to admit to Boyle at Yenbo that it was now clear that 'the strength of the Turkish force opposing them had been exaggerated, and that their own retirement was not a necessity'.[105]

Intelligence and the gainsaying of Wingate

It must have been frustrating for Khartoum to learn that most of the British officers in the Hejaz seemed to be finding their understanding of the Hejaz campaign reinforced, not overturned by events on the ground. Even the Arab leaders' own vacillations over reinforcements had not changed their views on the deeper political principles drawn from the previous six months' intelligence data. Few British officers were prepared to believe even Feisal's promise that 'there would be no local opposition' to a British landing.[106] Lawrence, always careful not to disparage the judgement of the Arab leader he lauded in his reports, noted to Cornwallis merely that he could see Feisal's 'arguments [for a brigade] have force', suggesting still that it was he who had to be persuaded, not Feisal.[107] Lloyd was more frank. He informed GHQ, Egypt that Feisal's offer was merely a lapse from better instincts, for surely Feisal maintained 'fundamentally' the same aversion to Christian troops as the Sherif and had simply panicked after the recent threats.[108] Wemyss reported the same to the Admiralty, and advised that the British government should respect the Sherif's political caution above all else.[109] Wilson repeated to Wingate that the British government should not let the Arabs' current disarray distract them from the necessity of obtaining the Sherif's explicit permission before landing British troops.[110]

With no direct request arriving from the Sherif nor yet any consensus materializing behind Wingate from the British officers on the ground, the sense of urgency in London and Paris regarding Rabegh drifted away. The French government, increasingly exhausted by the continuing demands of the Western Front, retreated from their earlier enthusiasm for sending in infantry. They now preferred to hold their Muslim artillery units at Suez until 'a base of resistance' could be organized at Rabegh (i.e. by British infantry) that would allow the French to 'intervene without being exposed to useless sacrifice'.[111] The British government reiterated that they would only send troops to help the Sherif 'in last extremity'; as that condition was not yet met, they authorized Wingate to hold a British brigade with artillery at Suez only as a precaution.[112] Murray was glad of the decision. He promised Robertson that Egyptforce would cross Sinai and cut the railway in Syria very soon, whereupon if the Turks hoped to maintain their position in the Arabian peninsula or attempt any large-scale operations, the redoubled pressure from Egyptforce at Gaza would require them to withdraw troops from Europe or their near-Eastern theatres, which they would be loath to do.[113]

Wingate held course on his own. He passed on Feisal's now outdated request for British reinforcements to the Foreign Office on 13 December as further evidence of the risk to Rabegh and Yenbo. He sent another warning to the Sherif that by holding these troops at Port Sudan only as an emergency reserve, it would be the Sherif's sole 'responsibility for the collapse of the Arab movement, should this come about'.[114] He eagerly awaited Lloyd's return from the Hejaz on 14 December, hoping for more sympathetic first-hand information, but when Lloyd pressed only for his agreement to keep the Hejaz clear of European troops, Wingate ignored his observations and reported to London that, based on Feisal's distressed request, a British brigade was essential to provide a great 'moral effect' and 'a rallying point' for the Arab forces, while striking a blow to the Turks' intentions. 'The immediate question for HMG to decide is whether we shall make a last attempt to save the Shereef and his Arabs *in spite of themselves*', he insisted, and recommended dispatching a British brigade, two battalions of infantry, and the French Senegalese contingent currently at Djibouti to Rabegh, while pressuring the Sherif to accept them in the meantime.[115] In the same vein, Wingate instructed Wilson to 'induce the Sherif to send me a satisfactory reply', i.e. a written request for British troops, or the Sherif would carry responsibility for the ensuing catastrophe.[116] Wingate asked the Foreign Office for permission to demand a final decision within a fortnight.[117] The Foreign Office agreed, but repeated they would need the Sherif's explicit request before approving the dispatch of British and French units. Apparently oblivious to the nature of the Sirdar's impasse with the Sherif, the Foreign Office asked the Sirdar whether the Sherif might be willing to use his great influence to inspire Arab populations in southern Palestine and Syria to rise against the CUP.[118]

The Foreign Office might have been unfazed at the tenor of these communications but Wingate's tactics disturbed both Wilson and Lloyd. When the Sherif, predictably, again refused Wingate's offer of troops, Wilson averred to his chief that without the former's consent, no detachment should be sent.[119] Wilson had recently demonstrated his own sensitivity to the Sherif's political position by declining to accompany the latter's procession out of Jiddah, 'as it may have been seized upon as an argument by anti-Sherif individuals that he was "completely in our hands", etc.' Wilson believed that the strain already in evidence at Jiddah and at Rabegh, and which Parker had described, stemmed from 'the ever present fear of the Arabs that we are getting too much control in the Hedjaz' and that the British activity 'was only a prelude to occupation'.[120] Lloyd argued the same. He warned Lynden-Bell at GHQ against (Wingate's) threatening the Sherif with further ultimata, 'for in these circumstances *further pressure would be equivalent to force* and I think it probable that acquiescence so obtained could only end disastrously for ourselves and the Arab cause'.[121]

While these voices weighed in, a stream of Imint arrived from the battlefield showing that the source of Feisal's distress had passed.[122] Only Imint – in this instance, a consummate force-multiplier – could have demonstrated so quickly that the threat against Rabegh and Yenbo had fallen back, that the Turks were withdrawing wholescale from the coast and contracting their force around Medina. The Arabs' operations in league with the British navy's presence had been effective. The release of pressure around the Arab forces at Yenbo was swift and dramatic. The final reckoning had apparently occurred during the night of 11 December, shortly after Feisal's plea for help. A determined Turkish assault force approached the outer limits of Yenbo – only to find themselves confronted by the awesome sight of the night-lit British ships in harbour and naval searchlights flooding the intervening ground. The Turkish unit turned and drew away.[123] On 12 December, Imint showed a Turkish evacuation from Wadi Fura, north of Rabegh.[124] On 16 December aerial reconnaissance observed a diminished camp at Bir Said (forty miles southeast of Yenbo), and an estimated 1,200 men, probably the lead Turkish unit, moving eastwards to Hamra. Reports, most likely from Feisal's agents, claimed that the Turks were also moving eastwards out of Nakhl Mubarrak towards Kheif Hussein. To spur this eastward tide, Feisal ordered the Juheinah out of Yenbo to harass the enemy's flank. Intelligence, possibly Sigint, on 18 December confirmed that the Turks had retired from Wadi Yenbo and redistributed themselves in the interior at Wasta, Hamra and Bir Said. On 19 December, Imint showed Ghayir also to be empty, and it was then concluded that no Turkish troops remained between Ghayir and Rabegh.[125] Major Ross, commander of the Flight, later reported that Imint 'proved of real value while the Turkish advance on Rabegh was impending'.[126] On 26 December, the Arab Bureau reported that the Juheinah had blocked an attempt by a Turkish mounted patrol to extend their front from the Turks' main encampment at Hamra to Kheif Husein.[127] Independent parties of Bedouin were now 'playing the mosquito round the communications of the Turks', as George Lloyd had put it.[128] The Arab Bureau informed the DMI that at last 'the Arabs have recovered their morale',[129] and in their final bulletin for 1916, they declared with confidence that the Turkish advance force had now 'evacuated and renounced (if it ever seriously intended) the profitless venture of an attack on Yambo itself'.[130]

Lawrence, Wemyss, Wilson and Lloyd had all been willing to promote an irregular Arab campaign against the HEF because they took as written the ability of modern intelligence to enhance the Arabs' capability in the field, both as a warning system and through direct surveillance of the enemy. As new intelligence continued to arrive, such as Imint on the supply of water and available roads, Wemyss was repeatedly struck, as he told London, by 'how imperfect is our knowledge, and how difficult it is to appreciate the local circumstances'.

> A reconnaisance by our seaplanes has revealed the fact that water exists some 20 miles to the Eastward of Rabegh. The early information from the Arabs that the Rabegh Wells were a necessity to an advancing Turkish force is therefore incorrect [. . .] What we do know for certain is that the Turkish

> Transport is defective, that the country is difficult, and that if the Arabs are capable of carrying out guerrilla warfare, the fall of Mecca to the Turks should be as nearly impossible as anything can be.[131]

Wilson stressed to Wingate as well that the discovery from Imint of alternative water supplies for the Turks only confirmed the need for caution in pushing London for a brigade. He, too, was optimistic about the Arabs' talents as guerrilla fighters.[132] With recent intelligence in hand, McMahon remarked on the same to Hardinge at the Foreign Office, noting that 'with their weak railway communication in rear and their long transport line', the Turks would have serious difficulty reaching the coast.[133] As for Lloyd, he saw the panic over Rabegh and the recurring debates over possible British action as the penalty for London's still not having a consistent, long-term Arab policy in place nor an adequate intelligence system on the ground to protect it. A clear central policy for the Middle East supported by improved intelligence in the theatre itself would remedy all the 'exaggerated reports both of failures and success' and resolve the debilitating schisms over Britain's future aims.[134]

Of all these officers, it was Wilson, 'the Sirdar's man', who showed the greatest alteration in outlook after his familiarization with local intelligence at Jiddah. In late December 1916, Wingate issued his last ultimatum to the Sherif. The Sherif responded by returning all responsibility for judging the wisdom, or error, of an immobile brigade to Wingate himself.[135] Three days later, on 28 December, Wilson called a conference at Rabegh with Brémond and other Allied officers to consider the port's immediate security and troop requirements. Brémond stated that there were 10,000 Turkish troops standing ready for an attack, a suitably daunting figure. And in view of that threat, the Arabs only chance of defence was an (immobile) Allied force on the ground at Rabegh, behind the enemy's rear, should the Turks attempt to advance against Mecca. But Wilson objected that, to his knowledge, based on recent intelligence, the Turks would have difficulty mustering even 6,000 men for an attack. He also noted that the greatest obstacle to the Turks' even attempting to mobilize was not a force at Rabegh but the availability of live transport. The overwhelming impression from intelligence was that the camel supply available to the Turkish garrison had been dramatically depleted by Arab raids on Turkish convoys and camel buyers.[136] Wilson told the gathering that he was convinced that any Turkish hope of extending their supply lines farther from Medina would be absolutely futile:

> 'Can the Turkish forces in the Hejas [*sic*] provide the men and camels for such an undertaking, as well as garrison Medina, safeguard the railway, guard against the constant threat of Feisal's force on their flank, and block approaches to Medina via the [Fura], Ghayer, Eastern and other roads?' he asked. 'Personally, I doubt it.'[137]

Wilson publicly separated himself still further from Wingate's and Brémond's preferences by declaring that he would not countenance 'running the risk of *forcing* the Sherif to give a written request for British troops to be sent' when all political intelligence on the Arabs' likely response in addition to the latest intelligence on Turkish capability counselled against it. He insisted that only non-Christian troops be sought for dispatch, 'as soon as possible', along with any available mountain battery.[138]

Within the week, Wilson's stand on this policy was nearly sabotaged by Brémond and Wingate. Wilson left Jiddah briefly on sick leave and during his absence, Brémond tried to engineer a rush dispatch of an Allied brigade behind his back. Brémond not only pressured Major Pearson, Wilson's less experienced replacement, to encourage the Chief Cadi of Mecca to issue a *fatwa* proclaiming only the Holy Cities as sacred ground, thereby allowing non-Muslim troops access to the rest of the territory, he also suggested that a brigade should be landed without the Sherif's permission because Arab public opinion would surely welcome the Allied troops, even without the *fatwa*.[139] Lloyd discovered Brémond's ploy and confronted him, finally obtaining his agreement that 'negotiations of this character on any subject behind the Shereefs back highly undesirable, and especially so in regard to such a delicate matter as this'.[140] Pearson relayed these events to Wingate. But Wingate managed to draw encouragement from them and resumed his correspondence campaign for a brigade with the Sherif.[141] Over the next week, numerous telegrams travelled between Cairo, Jiddah and Mecca. The last from Mecca, signed not by the Sherif but by his secretary Fuad el Khatib, expressed sympathy with Wingate's concerns but again made no explicit request and left all responsibility to Wingate for sanctioning a brigade.[142] Pearson, naive as to the nuances of this kind of negotiation, interpreted the telegram as a positive request for a British brigade, and wired the positive result to Wingate.[143] Wingate wired Murray to dispatch the brigade from Suez to Rabegh. Murray expressed distaste for Wingate's stratagem, replying:

> I need hardly say what a blow your letter and the Sherif's telegram is for me. It is not for me to criticise your actions or views in this matter, but I do consider that the Sherif has been more or less obliged to accept this assistance.[144]

No less appalled was Clayton. But his earlier relative independence in assessing policy courses had been recently complicated by his being made Chief of the General Staff for the Hejaz by Wingate after the latter's arrival as High Commissioner, a position that tied Clayton all the more firmly under his old chief. He vented his apprehension in a private letter to Lloyd, describing the chasm in perspective which lay between Wingate and himself:

> I have never viewed with anything but grave foreboding the deliberate entry of Christian troops into the Hejaz; it is a step which may invoke results which we today cannot gauge, and in the face of the Sherif's considered warning it alarms me still more. [...] Moreover, I am by no means convinced of the military soundness of the plan.

But, under the present circumstances and despite his still being head of the Arab Bureau and General Murray's chief adviser on local and political affairs, Clayton was now 'bound to carry out the policy of my Chief, when he has definitely decided on one. [...] One is damnably tied by official tradition & etiquette'.[145]

One more turn of the wheel followed. Just as it appeared Brémond's duplicity was complete, Wilson, now at Yenbo, reviewed a copy of Pearson's latest correspondence and immediately shot a wire back to Pearson asking him to retransmit his telegram to Wingate with the warning that the message from Mecca could not be considered a legitimate request as it was not from the Sherif and had not been put in writing.[146] On the evening of 4 January 1917 Pearson telephoned Mecca, and on the morning of 5 January sent another message by wireless. Wilson returned to his post at Jiddah on 6 January, in time to interpret this exchange. He confirmed that the Sherif was evading responsibility for the order and telegraphed Wingate, the Arab Bureau and Murray his strong opinion that to consider a dispatch of troops under such vague conditions would be a grave mistake. '[T]he Sherif must himself make the request in writing for British troops without any pressure from us,' he insisted. 'Moreover, it should be stated in his request that he accepts complete responsibility for consequences.'[147] Wilson also challenged Brémond's efforts to accelerate propaganda activities for the hypothetical brigade, reminding him that they had not received the Sherif's full support and without his approval, a landing of Christian infantry would not only risk 'general Moslem trouble' but imperil the Sherif's candidacy for the Calipate – which, apart from the 'getting the Arabs on our side during war', was 'the greatest asset we will obtain from his revolt'.[148] Brémond later described Wilson's determination to not bring European forces to the Hejaz as a return to the position advanced by Lawrence, specifically, who had recently visited Wilson at Yenbo.[149]

This extremely strained episode came to a close in early January 1917 after further intelligence was received on the continuing withdrawal from the coast of the Turkish forces and the end of any visible threat to Rabegh. With Egyptforce progressing across the Sinai and bombing flights in force, the War Committee felt it could at last lay aside the question of Allied reinforcements to the Hejaz. On 30 and 31 December 1916, Imint spotted little activity around Bir ibn Hassani though some movement at Bir Said. Meanwhile Ali believed that 5,000 Turks north of Wadi Fura were still advancing towards his positions outside Rabegh, leaving three battalions at Hamra in Wadi Yenbo facing Feisal.[150] Closer to Medina, Imint in January 1917 clarified that Turkish forces were indeed contracting at Ghayir, Bir el Mashi and Bir Derwish.[151] On 6 January, Robertson asked Murray for reassurance that he would be advancing soon with mounted troops and air operations against the Hejaz railway.[152] Murray responded that aerial bombing would begin presently and that the moral effect would be great, even if permanent damage could not be assured until Egyptforce got closer to the line.[153] Three days later, Murray assured Robertson that the planes were already bombing all enemy camps within a 100-mile radius, but any further penetration of the peninsula would require advance landing grounds with mobile guard postings and supply schedules, all of which were still impossible given the religious prohibitions.[154] In the meantime, Turkish planes posed little opposition to the RFC. Humint had stated that two, perhaps three of the five Turkish planes at Medina had been grounded and one pilot was killed.[155] Turkish flights were not only rare, but intelligence suggested that the planes remained far behind the Turkish frontlines because of petrol shortages.[156]

With multiple intelligence statements, operational updates and policy warnings from Egypt and the Hejaz in hand, the War Cabinet[157] decided on 8 January that no troops would be authorized unless the Sherif sent a written request for them which took responsibility for the presence of Christians in the Hejaz and provided a 'suitable proclamation [...] for issue to the Mahommedan world' to be reviewed before circulation by the British government.[158] In the meantime, the War Cabinet asked whether there might be more bombing raids made from Rabegh against Turkish camps and 'particularly transport'.[159] Wilson certainly felt the weight of his role in opposing the landing of the brigade, with regard to London's decision. In September 1917, he wrote his recollections to Clayton:

> The WO may have been under the delusion that I have been properly running the show directly under you, in which case I presume it will be set right [...] they rate your services in connection with the actual military operations [...] which are considered on a par with Cornwallis. Whereas I think I can say with truth I directed the show, shouldered the responsibility many times (the case of the British troops coming and the move to Wajh [February 1917] to name but two) and I would probably have been rightly 'Hung' if the revolt had failed.[160]

The last months' frantic debates over the question of Rabegh had shown bursts of independent thought, courageous analysis and principled stubbornness from intelligence, army and naval officers grappling with Wingate and Brémond's efforts to get a regular detachment on the ground. In effect, their consensus on the political intelligence constituted a kind of policy revolt regarding strategy. The past six months had also proven the ability of modern intelligence techniques to provide tactical advantages for an irregular Arab army in the field. Arab and British authorities could now turn their sights to the railway and northern part of the peninsula, away from the shining symbol of Medina and towards more ambitious targets to the north.

5 Reorientation

The Arab Revolt shifts north, January–April 1917

Wejh: filling the strategy vacuum

Conventional principles of war were giving way to unconventional tactics and even strategy in the Arab Revolt. Before 1917, ill-fated campaigns in the east such as Gallipoli, Kut and Salonika had ended with the defeat of an ill-prepared British expeditionary force by an unexpectedly fierce defending force. There was certainly a case to be made that these peripheral eastern operations were, as Keegan notes, too often 'a drain on resources instead of a threat to the enemy'.[1] By the opening of 1917, Cairo intelligence and the Hejaz's supporting regional commanders believed they had avoided this error by withstanding the pressure to send Allied reinforcements. In opposition to Wingate, they had argued that only by withholding troops and maintaining the Sherif's political legitimacy before other concerns would they genuinely serve the Arab Revolt. Intelligence now showed that Rabegh was no longer in danger. Cairo anticipated the next stage of the campaign and soon found itself forced to consider – mainly by nature of the Arab armies themselves – relinquishing plans for a direct regular attack on Medina in favour of a guerrilla strategy against the Turks' lines of communication. If successful, the Arabs might be able to isolate Medina and force the HEF to surrender.

Intelligence at the end of the year showed that the tribesmen's harassment of the Turkish positions at Medina was affecting the HEF's means of supply. Reports claimed that the Turks were suffering from scurvy and dysentery, and diminished troop strength as a result. The Harb and the Juheinah were continuing to raid points around the railway, all of which made the Turks' patrols of the track 'more and more arduous'.[2] Humint in December 1916 from the Sherif's informants showed that the Turks were turning east for food and other materials. Turkish supply caravans now travelled to Nejef and Kuweit, using Ibn Rashid's capital at Hail as a depot. The Arab Bureau noted that if Abdullah with his 2,500 men, currently at Henakiyeh and Wadi Khank, east of Medina, could squeeze the traffic along those routes, 'he will do as much for the campaign as any of his brothers' in accelerating the fall of the HEF. Damascus was 'hard enough put to it to feed themselves without having to feed Medina'.[3] Shortly afterwards a detachment of Abdullah's men intercepted a caravan of camels and supplies from Qasim as it neared the outskirts of Medina.[4] Lloyd commented to Wingate that despite the 'pretty useless' performance of Feisal and Abdullah recently, 'even this [activity] is better than sitting immobile at Yambo in so far as it must create some uneasiness in the minds of the Turks as to their intentions'.[5]

Positive though these developments were, they were not producing swift results against Fakhri Pasha. Wemyss voiced a popular thought when he wished that Ali 'could be persuaded to be more resolute' as a leader and cut away the Turks' positions south of Medina.[6] But Ali was having difficulty asserting control over his cordon of mixed fighters, and was unequal to the complaints being produced by his disgruntled Syrian officers whose real interests lay north at Damascus. The Arab Bureau regretted in January that the 'friction and intrigue among the Syrian and other Arab officers at Rabegh' were still weakening Ali's capability, though it was 'in consonance with the recent traditions of this somewhat ill-starred place'.[7] Feisal's operations around Yenbo showed greater command, but his tribes were reluctant to follow in any direct attack against Turkish regulars. In late December, Feisal's and Ali's armies encircled the large Turkish concentration at Kheif and Hamra, but panic broke out. Feisal's Juheinah splintered and a rumour spread from the south that the Subh fighting under Ali had defected. The princes aborted the operation and withdrew.[8] Feisal was stuck again 'in very bad temper' at Nakhl Mubarak at the head of only part of his force. His main army was still with Sherif Sharraf and Zeid at Yenbo. Ali withdrew to Rabegh. Abdullah, at Henakiyeh, sixty miles south of Bir ibn Hassani, and could offer no help.[9]

The Arab armies needed a new strategy against Medina, one that did not involve pitched battles between Arab tribesmen and Turks. At Yenbo on 28 December, Feisal met with Wilson, Bray and Lawrence onboard the HMS *Hardinge*. They decided that the Arabs' best option was to manoeuvre on a large scale. Feisal would resume his earlier base transfer from Yenbo to Wejh. The Royal Navy would ferry supporting Arab units to Wejh. Abdullah would act as the vital flank for Feisal and cross west from Henakiyah to Wadi Ais, 'a natural fortress [...] astride the Medina Lines of Communication' on the coastal side of railway. He would continue to pressure the supply caravans and railway contingents around Abu Na'am station. The RFC Flight at Rabegh would provide support for Feisal's rear. Even though the Turks were known to erect decoy camps and disguise movements on the ground,[10] regular aerial reconnaissance would help ensure that the Turks did not launch a surprise attack against Yenbo or Rabegh during the move. To convince Feisal that by transferring he was not leaving a fatal vacuum behind him, Wilson took the exceptional step of personally guaranteeing the safety of Rabegh. He promised that the Navy would fend off any Turkish advance against Ali or the Sherif at Mecca, while Feisal completed his march. Lawrence praised Wilson for this initiative in *The Arab Bulletin*, noting that although 'there was no means of giving force to this assurance', his promise as the British government's representative was a 'reasonable and necessary risk to take, since without it Feisal would not have moved north'.[11]

A number of advantages would be secured by this move. As Wilson explained to Wingate, Feisal wanted to restore the Wejh plan because the threat to the Turks of a new, greater tribal offensive around the railway would remove 'all fear of any Turkish advance on Mecca'.[12] Wemyss had already promised Feisal that the seaplane carrier *Raven II*'s sea and air support would assist his operations, if needed.[13] He reported optimistically on the new plan to the Admiralty, noting that 'if properly guided and led [the Arabs] should be able to seriously hamper any movement on the part of the enemy by guerrilla warfare', particularly with their new ability to apply pressure against the Turks' rear at el Ula.[14] Hogarth wrote a special memorandum for the Arab Bureau in early January 1917 expressing confidence in the Arabs' ability to employ irregular operations in defence of Mecca. Recent intelligence confirmed the existence of additional smaller interior roads between Medina and Mecca, but even if the Turks advanced successfully down one of them in the spring and reached Mecca, the tribesmen's raiding activity would soon sever the HEF's supply lines and they would be 'starved out again in a comparatively short time'. The Sherif could always retire to Jiddah under the protection of the British navy and continue his subsidies to the tribes, who would certainly return to help recapture the Meccan base.[15]

Even more dramatically, the reorganization of force would enable an expansion of guerrilla activity against the northern sections of the railway and open up a new passage northward into Syria. Wilson reported on the implications to Wingate. Once Feisal was established at Wejh, his army would be able to organize attacks against the Turkish garrison at the opposite station at el Ula. From el Ula, Feisal would have access to Wadi Sirhan and the Syrian interior on the other side, and from there be able to begin serious negotiations with the Huweitat, Rualla and other northern tribes.[16] Bray agreed. He believed that Feisal's shift away from Medina would convey an 'earnestness' about the Arab Revolt's scope to the northern Juheinah, Billi and, most importantly, the Rualla tribes around Jauf upon whom the Arabs would have to depend for reinforcements, supplies and safe passage.[17] The Arab Bureau reviewed the possible new tribal relationships for the DMI in London. The Arab armies had so far been drawn mainly from the Harb, Ateibah and Juheinah tribes in the districts of Mecca, Medina, Rabegh and Yenbo. Feisal's ability to advance north from Wejh would depend, in addition to the Billi, on the co-operation and sympathy of the Beni Atiyeh, the Huweitat and the southern Anazeh tribes bridging into Syria, of which the Rualla were indispensable.[18] The Sherif had already been given provisional promises of allegiance by the Aida, the Beni Sakhr, the eastern Huweitat and the Rualla; thus '[t]he movement of Feisal northwards is, it appears not unconnected with the negotiations which have been going on between his father and the northern tribes'.[19]

Humint arrived in early January suggesting that the Arabs were holding a slight psychological advantage. On 4 January, Feisal sent a small raiding party, including Lawrence in his first active operation, to investigate the Turkish presence at Hamra, east-southeast of Medina. It was a somewhat tense rite of passage, as the Turks had recently offered a reward for 'the capture of the British officer (Captain Lawrence) who is with Feisal'.[20] The raiding party failed in its assault against Hamra but did capture two Turkish engineers whose statements were more than adequate compensation.[21] They were Ali Besim Bey, an inspector of the wireless telegraph system with the Corps of Engineers, and Hassan Siam, a sergeant major also with the Corp of Engineers, 2nd Battalion, 129th Regiment.[22] Lawrence interrogated the men on Medina's communication capability and found that their information confirmed earlier intelligence on the HEF, its increasing isolation and the psychological strain of being surrounded by greater numbers of hostile tribes. Ali Besim Bey explained that he had been sent to build a large wireless facility at Medina to provide the HEF with an alternative to the landline and to allow the HEF to transmit to Damascus. At present, the garrison could only receive wireless messages. And there was such a small number of competent Turkish signallers in the Hejaz that, even though they did occasionally intercept the British ships' transmissions, they had been ordered to ignore them and concentrate only on Turkish signals.[23] The lack of signalling capability meant that most of the Turks' intelligence on the identity, movements and capability of the British personnel at Rabegh was drawn from Arab informants, confirming the Arab Bureau's earlier impression that the Turks' intelligence in Arabia was still 'almost entirely derived from native sources'.[24]

The informants enlarged on the psychological duress felt at Medina. The Arabs' uprising against the Turkish detachments and supply lines had infected the imagination of the Turkish GS and made them so 'exceedingly distrustful' of the Arabs in their ranks that they now meant to replace all those soldiers 'with men of Turkish race'.[25] Most of the 10,000 Arabs conscripted for service in the Hejaz had been moved to bases on the railway, said one informant, because their loyalties were viewed as so 'doubtful'.[26] The Arab Bureau was pleased to note that despite the Arabs' being 'fairly quiet' around the Turkish camp at Hamra at the moment, the Turks still viewed the surrounding tribesmen as a 'continual source of uneasiness'.[27]

As for Medina itself, the garrison was intact, if not immediately capable of launching an offensive. Both informants believed Fakhri Pasha remained determined to recapture Mecca and had only been temporarily unbalanced by the extent of the Arabs' resistance. The Turkish GS would soon request reinforcements for Medina. In the meantime, the Arab Bureau concluded that enough food still arrived by the daily train from Syria and by eastern caravan routes to prevent the starvation and rampant sickness that they had hoped would topple Fakhri Pasha. According to the engineers, the actual garrison now consisted of just one company with two field-guns and no heavy guns. But the railway had been transformed by the reorganization's infusion of troops into an elaborately guarded system of small blockhouses, each with patrols that communicated with the main stations.[28]

The Turkish forces were now hunkering along a defensive line from Kheif and Hamra to Bir Said.[29] The Arab Bureau did not believe any of these units were likely to move against Yenbo or Rabegh in the near future, nor were they at all 'ready to take immediate advantage of the disorganization of the Arabs'.[30] It seemed the Arabs' activity had indeed halted the Turks in their operations: '[The Turks'] difficulties seem to increase in geometrical rather than arithmetical progression the further they move from Medina.' Further south at Wadi Safra, there seemed to be only Turkish reconnaissance troops.[31] The continuing withdrawal by the HEF from the Rabegh and Yenbo roads appeared to the Arab Bureau to be 'the end of the second stage of the Hejaz Revolt',[32] despite claims from the Turkish government that the HEF were 'confident they can reach Rabegh whenever they like', and proclamations by Jemal Pasha in Damascus which had 'publicly insisted' on the recapture of Mecca.[33] Sigint and other intelligence on the Turkish forces' weakened state continued to reinforce the Arab Bureau's conclusion that 'any [Turkish] advance from Kheif Hamra district would appear improbable'.[34]

All intelligence supported the wisdom of Feisal's moving to Wejh before the HEF acquired any greater leverage or obtained reinforcements. Lawrence emphasized Feisal's courage under these conditions.

> [Feisal would be embarking on] 'a flank march of about 200 miles parallel to the Turkish communications, [with] an inferior fighting force, leaving its base (Yambo) entirely undefended, and evacuating its only possible defensive position (Wadi Yambo) in the face of an enemy force of nearly divisional strength in Wadi Safra, not thirty miles away across easy country'.[35]

The British navy was ready to give support along the coast. Abdullah's new position at Wadi Ais was intended to prevent the Turks from advancing against Yenbo, Mecca or Ali at Rabegh because Fakhri Pasha would first need reinforcements to remove him. The Turks' advance bases at Ghayir or Hamra were unlikely to be stripped any further,[36] which left only Syria as a source. But spare troops were at a premium in Syria, particularly after the pressure created by Egyptforce's capture of el Arish on 21 December 1916 and Rafa on 9 January 1917.[37]

The advance to Wejh was launched.[38] Feisal rode out of Yenbo on 10 January 1917 at the head of a combined force of Juheinah and Harb tribesmen numbering 4,276 infantry, and 3,862 mounted troops, fourteen pieces of artillery and 100 mule-mounted cavalry led by Maulud el Mukhlus.[39] Feisal's 'further objective' of eventually advancing to el Ula depended upon his success at Wejh and the sympathy of the local Billi tribes along the way.[40] Lawrence recalled that Feisal was 'very nervous during this period', worrying that something might disrupt the effort, a feud amongst the tribes, ambivalence towards fighting fellow Muslims or sudden abandonment of the operation.[41] Abdullah moved west to Abu Na'am with 6,000 men, picking up a demolition party from Feisal.[42] To the south, British planes spotted Ali's movements outside Rabegh.[43] Ali was not able to assist the planes' local bombing raids owing to continuing difficulties in camp, but he was eventually able to distribute his men along the approaches to Rabegh and add fresh reinforcements from Mecca.[44]

At the outskirts of Wejh, Feisal incorporated a further 1,200 mounted men and 808 infantry of the Northern Juheinah, under Saad Ghuhein.[45] Lawrence saw in the army's progress a sign of greater success to come, writing to Newcombe: 'you cannot imagine greater fun for us, greater vexation and fury for the Turks. We win hands down if we keep the Arabs simple [...] to add to them heavy luxuries will only wreck their show, and guerrilla does it'.[46] Several ships of the Red Sea Patrol ran parallel to Feisal's march, including the HMS *Hardinge* carrying two contingents of Arab fighters from Yenbo and Um Lejj (400 Juheinah under Saleh ibn Shefia and 150 Bishawa under Sheikh Amr) to Hassani Island and then Wejh, where they were to rejoin Feisal's army. As Wemyss reported the scheme: 'The original plan [was] that the enemy should be attacked by these two forces and the ships' guns simultaneously.'[47]

The attack on Wejh, while eventually successful in several respects and a turning point for Arab operations, ran into difficulties en route that nearly terminated the mission. As far as they were based on human error, they served as valuable instruction for the future. The most vital lesson in Lawrence's opinion was the importance of reconnoitering the ground beforehand and conducting a proper intelligence survey. The Arab leaders had almost entirely neglected the preliminary review of water supply, forage and road conditions for the 8,000 men marching to Wejh, and the oversight almost proved fatal. Lawrence reported that Feisal's first stage from Yenbo to Um Lejj took twice as long as planned when the force's nine sections of men led by their respective sheikhs and sherifs had difficulties obtaining water.[48] The second stage also suffered because Feisal relied on the local Musa Juheinah for details on water sources. On the basis of their testimony, he split his force between an interior road and coastal road, with plans to reunite at Abu Zereibat, forty miles southeast of Wejh. When that testimony proved 'most unreliable', the men were left to march the final fifty miles with only a half-gallon of water per man and no food, while the animals went without food or water for the last two and a half days.[49] In Lawrence's opinion, the root of all trouble had been the lack of accurate intelligence: 'a great deal of delay, confusion, and actual danger for lack of water and food [...] would have been obviated had time allowed of previous reconnaissance of the route'.[50] It was a lesson he incorporated fully from that point onward. The meticulous and thorough collection of intelligence would become a hallmark of Lawrence's preparation for future operations in the field.

The rest of the Arabs' advance achieved much of the hoped-for political effect. It attracted positive attention from northern Bedouin tribes and unnerved the Turks, who crumpled with surprising rapidity. Feisal had issued invitations to the Billi, Huweitat and Beni Atiyeh to join his attack on Wejh.[51] By the time Feisal reached Abu Zereibat, on the southern limits of Billi country, he was joined by the Wuld Mohammed Harb, Sherif Nasir of Medina and three Billi notables who were close relatives of the Billi chief, Suleiman Rufida. The opportunistic Suleiman, long in the pay of the Turks while simultaneously declaring loyalty to the Sherif, had gone into hiding in the hills outside Wejh to await the battle's outcome.[52] When news of his defection reached the Turkish garrison in the town, they also fled into the interior. The Turkish commander of the Ageyl camelmen, Ahmed Tewfik Bey, held his nerve for one day longer. But when the British navy became visible off the reef, he posted 100 Turkish infantry in the town and another 100 infantry on the nearby high ground overlooking the plain, and escaped.[53]

The major failing of the march was that it was not Feisal's ambitious but beleaguered force that took the town of Wejh, but the second-string Arab contingent under the command of Saleh ibn Shefia, brought by ship to supplement the attack. The contingent arrived on 22 January, as planned, days before Feisal. Unable to stay longer in the ships, the attack had commenced.[54] Bray recalled that the 550 Arabs troops were not even expert fighters but 'consisted of inferior material, which was not fit to accompany Feisal's army, and had no real leaders'. Yet despite most of the group's poor showing, one unit of 100 fighters and another party of snipers struck Bray as being particularly effective and cemented his confidence in the tribesmen's potential as a striking guerrilla force.

As an improvised action, Wejh offered several demonstrations of the strengths and weaknesses of the mixed Arab forces in confronting a fixed target. On the morning of 23 January, a British warship opened fire on the Turkish trenches to the east while an Arab landing party disembarked with a naval escort and quickly split into three groups. Bray's description of the Arab parties would foreshadow the frustration of many British observers to come. They comprised:

1 About 100 who really meant fighting, and advanced directly against the Turkish position on the eastern scarp;
2 about 300 who moved along the beach and incontinently went off to loot and fight in the town;
3 about 100 who sat on the beach and did nothing during the whole operations.

But Bray, who watched the action closely from the ship, also took careful note of twenty singular Juheinah under Sheikh Salih, who advanced 'at a very sharp pace towards the Turks' in position against the inland scarp, a couple of thousand yards away, to carry out the following extraordinary assault:

> At 1,000 yards they came under fire, but took no notice, and showed no excitement. Indeed, they appeared, but for the pace they were walking, to be out for an ordinary constitutional. When within 500 yards they halted a moment or two to see exactly where the fire came from, and without taking advantage of any cover or extending to any unusual extent wandered on till they eventually halted in some dead ground within fifty yards of the Turks. Here they remained, firing snap-shots and crouching down again, suffering no casualties whatever, but inflicting a fair number on their opponents. There was no noise or confusion, and the affair might have been a manoeuvre with blank.[55]

The Juheinah's bravery under fire made a strong impression on Bray, particularly after the next morning's inspection revealed three Turkish corpses and eight 'large pools of blood' from an initial force of thirty-five, while Sheikh Salih's twenty men had escaped without a single casualty. Bray also praised another eighty Arab fighters who had engaged the Turkish trenches to the south and fought steadily, until instructed to move aside for the British naval guns: 'They retired quietly and extended, walking slowly away and taking no notice of the stray Turkish bullets amongst them.' The remaining tribesmen contributed little to the assault, choosing instead to plunder the town; seaplane reconnaissance flights taken on 23 January tracked the Arabs' haphazard corralling of the Turks through and beyond the town in the direction of el-Ula.[56] It was left to the ships' guns, British artillery and a naval landing party to take out the last fort and tower where a cohort of Turkish snipers were sheltering.[57]

Despite the tribal armies' uneven showing at Wejh, the capture of this new forward base rejuvenated the Arabs' campaign, exposed the northern coastline and panicked the local Turkish groups who felt their room for manoeuvre was fast disappearing. Some sections of the legendary Huweitat, whose southern territory stretched across this part of the peninsula, decided that this was the time to enter the field against the Turks. On 5 February 1917 at Dhaba, ninety miles north of Wejh, the Turkish commander and 250 men fled to the railway but were intercepted by the Huweitat Ahmed Rafiyah and his clan. They killed fifty Turkish soldiers before a Turkish cavalry unit from Tebuk station rode to the rescue. The Arab Bureau noted that this event was the first mention of active assistance by Ahmed Rafiyeh; Auda abu Tayyi, 'the principal Huweitat chief', and Mohammed Dheilan, his cousin, had pledged their loyalty to Feisal's movement several weeks before. Another Huweitat raid cut down or captured fifty more Turkish cavalrymen at Khoreitah, on the road from Dhaba to Tebuk. These reports of Huweitat participation signalled a dramatic loss of authority and influence for the Turks, who had now lost the last of the five main roads of supply from the railway to the coast to Arab hands. Wemyss remarked on the progress to London: 'the capture of [Wejh] has had an excellent effect on all the surrounding Tribes, who are now openly joining the Shereef, and who had been only waiting to do so for some practical sign of his power'.[58] The British navy found the Turkish garrison at Muweilah had also evacuated to Tebuk, just days later.[59] According to Lawence, the garrison was being driven into the interior by yet another Huweitat sheikh, Ahmed Teqeiqah of the Midianite clan, who controlled the territory east of Dhaba. Apparently he had attacked both Dhaba and Muweilah in advance of the British ships and was pursuing the Turks to the railway.[60] Wemyss reported triumphantly after the news of Muweilah that 'the whole of the Littoral from Lith to the Mouth of the Gulf of Akaba is now in the hands of the Grand Shereef'.[61]

Intelligence soon confirmed that it had been dread of geographical isolation amongst newly hostile Arab tribes that had triggered the Turks' domino-like abandonment of Wejh, Dhaba and Muweilah. Sigint, Humint and seized Turkish documents from Wejh showed that the Turks had been anxious watching the

Billi, Harb and Huweitat tribes melt away to Feisal. The British navy had already sealed off the coast. Now the garrisons, unable to protect their limited land supply routes and facing an increasingly inhospitable interior, had decided the coast positions were no longer tenable.[62] Not only were bases like Wejh suffering from forage, clothing and food shortages, about which the Wejh commandant protested 'frequently, and with growing insistence' to the Military Governor of Medina. Captured documents showed they also lacked cash enough to make the necessary payments, or 'great solicitude', to local Billi and Juheinah chiefs to stop them from reverting to 'uppish' behaviour and joining the Sherif.[63] Open source intelligence confirmed that Constantinople was equally concerned about the loyalty of the southern Syrian Bedouin potentates. Government officials, hampered by the gold shortage, had been handing out decorations as another means of purchasing friendship.[64] Jemal Pasha had personally decorated several leaders of the Huweitat and Anazeh in order to retain their support in regions east of the railway. But he could not reach Auda abu Tayyi, or the head of the main Jazi section, Arar ibn Jazi, for they were already pledged to the Sherif. The Arab Bureau was sanguine, despite the reports, that 'most, if not all, these decorations have been wasted on the desert air', for the Fuqara and Aida sections of the Anazeh had picked up their decorations and ridden to Feisal.[65]

At Medina, Fakhri Pasha had long passed the stage of dispensing decorations. By the middle of January, intelligence repeatedly suggested that the Arabs' harassment of the HEF's supply lines outside Medina had transformed the Turks' environment into 'hostile territory, whose inhabitants are a perpetual source of danger to their supplies and communications'.[66] The Sherif's intelligence office in Mecca reported that Fakhri had withdrawn outposts, imprisoned town notables and allegedly brought twenty-two German officers to Medina. While the Sherif's details could not immediately be confirmed, the Arab Bureau did believe that Fakhri's behaviour was tending only to 'stiffen the tribes against him, neutralize his propaganda, and alienate the city'. As they noted in their intelligence bulletin, 'there is much that is symptomatic in the situation at present. [...] Something is evidently rotten in the Turkish position at Medina'.[67]

The Arab Bulletin thus lauded the capture of Wejh as 'a fresh nail [...] hammered into the Turkish coffin'.[68] The action had extended the Arab front northward more than 200 miles, and the unprecedented congregation of Bedouin tribes volunteering for service under the banner of the Sherif had overthrown the Turks' assumptions about their loyalty. The Arab Bureau reported on 'The Political Situation' in their bulletin, noting that, contrary to traditional habits, several of the Sherif's 'contingents have consistently served far from their homes', and these 'same tribes and clans have already kept the field through a summer and autumn and most of a winter'. Further, many had 'been serving with, and among their blood-enemies'. The Turks had not been able to coerce or buy 'any but very partial and short-lived tribal defections'. Indeed, the Arab Bureau emphasized:

> [W]e have never yet heard of any Hejaz tribe or clan within the area of active operations, coming out as a whole, or even in any proportion, on

> behalf of the Turks. [...] Wherever there have been active operations the Bedouins have come out when and where required and have kept out, and no tribe or clan in those areas has operated against the Emir.[69]

The Arab Bureau concluded that 'what was said, therefore, by T.E. L[awrence]. (in our [*The Arab Bulletin*] No. 32, p. 483) about the political attitude of the tribes is borne out sufficiently by the facts'.[70] The Bedouins defined nationality as 'the independence of tribes and parishes, and their idea of national union is episodic combined resistance to an intruder'; they had only been willing to alter their 'immemorial habits' because of their political identification with the removal of a non-Arab government.[71] In this context, the British government's gold payments to the Sherif to support the tribes' livelihood while they fought were only marginally significant. 'We are not here concerned with the means, pecuniary or other, by which its [i.e. the Arab movement's] allegiance has been gained and maintained, any more than with its military value', noted the Arab Bureau:

> We have merely to record the fact that at present the King of the Hejaz has the political support of these tribes, and that their support is, perhaps, as nearly unanimous as that accorded to any other Sovereign by an equally large proportion of his subjects. They have kept a fighting strength of about 3,000 volunteers in the field.[72]

Regular support for an irregular campaign

The British Military Mission arrived in the Hejaz in late January 1917, after the capture of Wejh. While Feisal's army incorporated new adherents from more northern territories, the British Military Mission reviewed its instructions to organize and broaden the British staff's liaison role between the British government and the Arab leadership.[73] They were entering a sphere already occupied by the Arab Bureau and officers on the ground such as Wilson, Wemyss, Bray and Lawrence. This team had been pursuing an irregular campaign that employed guerrilla tactics as well as, for several, genuine attention to the Arab Revolt's political components. The British Military Mission might have tried to revise the Arab Bureau's *modus vivendi* and supplant its philosophy with a more conventional practice. They might have dismissed the alleged political intricacies and reasserted a regular army policy against Medina, as Wingate no doubt hoped months earlier when he agreed to their assignment. But their own intelligence gathering on the ground led them to a different conclusion.

The confusion that greeted the Mission's arrival only highlighted the ramshackle lapses of responsibility regarding general policy that still existed between the Hejaz and London. The British officers on the spot assumed that the Mission's instructions were to support, not reform or replace, relationships and practices already in place with the Arab leaders. Both Wilson and Lawrence wrote to Lieutenant-Colonel Newcombe, the Mission's CO, with advice on how not to disturb the fragile sense of trust they had built between Britain's representatives and the Arab tribesmen. Wilson, always attentive to the Arabs' suspicion of Britain's ulterior intentions, advised Newcombe and the other members to act with respect and discretion towards the Arab armies because 'too much interference or "riding rough-shod" over Arab leaders or their men could have no good result'.[74] Lawrence expressed the same concerns. He encouraged Newcombe, his former chief, to efface himself and make friends with the Arab chiefs before presuming to instruct them or his efforts with them would fail: 'After all, it's an Arab war, and we are only contributing materials – and the Arabs have the right to go their own way and run things as they please. We are only guests.'[75]

The British Military Mission's official instructions did not refer to such niceties; they were supposed to establish a military executive arm on the ground for Wingate. They were told to establish agreement with Wilson on 'all plans and future policy', bring order to the Hejaz proceedings, assist in training the Arab regular army, and 'advise and report' on the campaign to Wingate.[76] Their arrival was also supposed to change some of the current officers' responsibilities. Newcombe was instructed to relieve Wilson of some of his workload, which by all counts was overwhelming; Newcombe was to take charge of affairs at Yenbo and northwards, and act as Wilson's representative in all matters involving Feisal and Abdullah. He was also supposed to replace Lawrence as liaison officer with Feisal. Lawrence's presence in the Hejaz, now undefined, had been extended indefinitely after a strong request arrived from Feisal that he stay, 'as he has given such very great assistance'.[77]

Neither of those transfers of duty proceeded as planned. Within two weeks Vickery reported to Wingate (through the Arab Bureau) that Wilson had been reluctant to relinquish any control or authority and this had '"ipso facto" disbanded the mission' as conceived. As an alternative, Vickery suggested actually strengthening Wilson's position: just one officer, i.e. Wilson, should be given 'complete control of the British Staff with representatives at the various ports and with the various armies as he may determine' so that he might institute 'co-ordination of operations, of opinion and of general policy', thus obviating the 'present absurdity' of British officers with 'divergent views and opinions each advising his Sheref [*sic*] to adopt a different plan or line of operations'.[78] The last remark almost certainly referred to officers such as Joyce and Lawrence, who held expressly 'divergent' views on the campaign and had been to some extent improvising their advisory roles with Feisal and Ali. Vickery's recommendations expressed trust in Wilson's judgement and designated him, not the Military Mission, responsible for deciding what were, in essence, policy-related questions of support. Vickery believed the Mission should be transferred up to Feisal's headquarters at Yenbo, where it could advise on operations.

If Wingate had hoped that the assignment of these regular officers to the field would make the conduct of the Hejaz campaign any more biddable or conventional, he was mistaken. After two weeks' observation, both Newcombe and Vickery were convinced that the Arab armies were right to be committing to a full and permanent rather than partial or temporary campaign of irregular warfare against the railway, and to be doing so from a position north of Rabegh.

Both men wanted the Arab armies to cut the railway using raiding and demolition tactics, isolate the HEF at Medina and force Fakhri to surrender. Vickery, who had been present as an observer at the assault on Wejh, emphasized that the latter operation had had uneven results because conventional tactics had been pressed upon untrained nomadic fighters: 'the value of the Sheref's Armies as a military force is nil if they are exploited on wrong principles and if they are asked to undertake tasks which would tax trained troops'. Feisal's advance to Wejh afforded just such an example of wrong principles. But Vickery was optimistic that 'as irregular armies confining themselves to guerrilla operations, they are a force of some potential value'.[79] Newcombe was also confident in the Arabs' ability to conduct an effective irregular campaign, and asked only for more technical assistance, such as enhanced supply services between the ports and wireless sets for the Arab bases currently still relying on naval signalling facilities.[80]

Where Newcombe and Vickery diverged was in their wider strategic observations of the campaign. Vickery, with his long colonial military experience, was more alert to the political and military burdens constraining the Arab armies because he understood the basis of guerrilla warfare. In fact, he noted in his report that 'it is difficult to separate the military and political situation and easier to discuss them under one heading'. In addition to the now familiar request to send modern artillery to the Arab armies, if only 'to put heart in his [Feisal's] army and as a moral asset', Vickery's great concern was that valuable political capital would be wasted if the Arab armies were thrust into contests where they were sure to fail, such as undertakings to seize and permanently occupy railway stations. All intelligence suggested that the Turks had retired most of their troops to the railway, which meant that the stations 'have in all probability been put in a state of defence and are in fact small forts'. Under such circumstances, 'anyone who advises the Sherif that such stations can be stormed by a small body of irregular troops with rifles and hand grenades, undertakes serious responsibility,' he said. Vickery also urged every care be taken to help Feisal negotiate successfully with the surrounding tribes and ensure that he held the advantage before taking action. Rash or haphazard raids undertaken by ambivalent tribesmen, especially those that brought large numbers of casualties, would damage the Arabs' morale and the fragile consensus upon which Feisal relied to sustain his movement:

> The political situation is a very serious matter for [Feisal], he has to think of the future, he has to win the tribes over to his side, not for a day, but for good. Precipitation in such matters would be disastrous. To advance until he is certain of the attitude of the tribes whom he will leave in his rear is foolhardy.[81]

Feisal wanted to establish a forward base at Jeida, halfway between Wejh and el Ula. From this base, Feisal could send raiding parties to the railway, twenty to 100 men in size, and conduct reconnaissance of the line. Vickery approved of the plan. Feisal's force included well-trained camel corps, infantry and horse units. Vickery believed that, buoyed by Ali's pressure from the southwest and Abdullah's activity either at Wadi Ais or back at Henakiyeh, Feisal's army would be able to cut the line and hold it long enough to isolate Medina. They needed only to ensure that 'all the armies work on some concerted plan, controlled and advised from central channel. Spasmodic operations undertaken by one army not in conjunction with the others cannot give the best results'.[82]

Newcombe was preoccupied with a different vision of Arab operations altogether. Having surveyed the field and the course of the railway, he concluded that he might be able to cut the railway himself. Vickery had already queried the wisdom of the Mission members' taking 'an active part leading and assuming Military control of small raiding parties' in his report,[83] but Newcombe felt no such hesitation. He knew that Lawrence had taken part in action inland, and Garland was just setting out to mine the railway from Wejh with a raiding party.[84] Newcombe was already thinking about the next stage of demolition. Once Dhaba and Muweilah had fallen and supplies arrived from Egypt, Newcombe wanted to lead a demolition expedition against the railway at Tebuk station or north of it and cut the line. He only required the promise of a naval assault on Aqaba: 'the sooner Akaba is attacked after Dhaba, the easier will operations be for me on the railway towards Tebuk'. A joint Anglo-Arab landing at Aqaba would both act as a diversion and provide a new base for aerodromes from which to make bombing runs against the railway, as had been envisioned several times previously. Once he had ensured the railway was cut for a fortnight, Newcombe would send word through Wejh to start dismantling the supply base at Rabegh. The planes, the Egyptian contingent and Aziz al-Masri's force would transfer to Aqaba 'directly that place is taken' – although 'the situation may not be quite so hopeful as that of course'.

Newcombe's only other requirement was that Feisal give him permission to ride inland. Feisal wanted 15,000 more rifles with which to arm the Billi and the Beni Atiyeh, after which he should 'have all the country up to Tebuk in 1½ months time'. Newcombe felt impatient with Feisal's preparations but conceded that Feisal 'has really been waiting till he got the tribes safely on his side before letting me move on the railway, and thinks that once we give them the lead the Arabs will destroy it wholescale'.[85] It can be assumed from these accounts that Newcombe, because he intended to conduct the demolition raids himself, did not regard Feisal's political dependence on the goodwill of these disparate tribes with the same degree of seriousness as did Vickery. It was a gap in perception that would close by April 1917, after Newcombe's experience in the interior.

The treatment of Aqaba as an operational target also separated the two officers' accounts. Newcombe's evaluation made no reference to any possible political repercussions in occupying Aqaba, the first major port lying above the Hejaz border, a gateway into Syria and the Sinai peninsula. Vickery, by contrast, touched on the approaching political mire in his criticism of the Syrians' presence in the Arab armies. He stated that he very much regretted that the Syrians had 'crept into the Army' because they were hindering the Bedouin forces, who worked awkwardly around them. Worse, he warned Cairo, the Syrian officers' ultimate goals were inevitably going to collide with those of the 'higher' – i.e. British or Allied – authorities after the fall of the HEF, for 'it is assumed that the Syrians have not joined the Arabs to stop at Medina, and that they had some deeper object than the desire to serve the Grand Sherif when they joined their fortunes with the Arabs'.[86] Warnings from the field about the political complications of operations in Syria would only grow stronger over the coming months.

Imint and Turkish redeployment to the railway

Intelligence during the Wejh advance showed that Arab operations continued to disrupt Turkish positions. One of the most stunning raids was carried out by Abdullah's army. On their way to Wadi Ais, they engaged and captured an armed Turkish convoy riding eastward out of Medina on 13 January 1917. The 'notorious Turkish bravo' and protégé of Enver, the commander, Eshref Bey, was amongst the prisoners.[87] He had been carrying letters for Ibn Rashid, Ibn Sa'ud and leaders in the Yemen, as well as *l.*20,000 in gold, munitions and gifts.[88] The capture epitomized the crescendo of Arab raids across Turkish territory, and its benefit to the Arab cause rolled still further. Three months earlier, a Smyrna intelligence agent stated that Eshref Bey had been ordered by Constantinople to form a contingent of irregular fighters for service in Arabia, presumably to fight the Arab guerrillas on their own terms.[89] Whether he still held this mandate, as the Arab Bureau believed, or was trying to buy safe passage to the isolated Turkish garrison in the Yemen, as Lawrence later wrote,[90] his capture proved 'an outstanding item of intelligence' for the Arab Bureau and only intensified the Turks' 'uneasiness about communications and shortage of supplies'. Abdullah posted a triumphant advertisement of the attack on the railway to humiliate Fakhri Pasha, and sent Eshref Bey's ornate Meccan gold dagger 'as a trophy' to Feisal, who presented it to Colonel Wilson.[91]

In mid-January, an 'authentic source', most likely Sigint, but perhaps a well-placed informant, confirmed that Fakhri's defensive line was still contracting.[92] Whereas the earlier impression by Imint and Humint had been of a moderate retirement of Turkish forces, Imint and Sigint now showed 'a very considerable measure of [Turkish] withdrawal on all the Rabugh roads, as well as from the Yambo direction'. Imint during the last two weeks of January 1917 tracked and confirmed the evacuation of advanced posts at Hamra, Khafia, Bir Zeid, Hafah, Bir Raha and Ghayir, while two raids by British planes bombed Ghayir and dropped pamphlets urging the Ottoman soldiers to surrender.[93] The cumulation of intelligence showed that 'much material of all kinds has been or is about to be retired to Medina'. The Arab Bureau now had 'little doubt' that the Turks had given up operations against both Yenbo and Rabegh. They also interpreted Abdullah's capture of Eshref Bey to have been one of the 'causes' precipitating the Turks' sudden withdrawal. In this context, the Imint and Sigint returns for January were 'outstanding items of intelligence [...] which [...] represent cause and effect' on the battlefield.[94]

Fakhri Pasha responded to the Arabs' Wejh advance by increasing the number of infantry garrisons on the railway, using troops 'from Medina as far as we can see and not from Syria', reported Lawrence.[95] The Arab Bureau confirmed in mid-February 1917 that the Turks were indeed 'weakening' Medina in order to reinforce the railway to the north; 'isolated posts are being withdrawn and concentrations made at [el Ula], Medain Salih and Tebuk'.[96] Further intelligence, most likely Sigint, confirmed that 'a considerable part' of the HEF had withdrawn to the railway in late February. The largest force on the railway now stood at Medain Salih, followed by garrisons at el Ula and Tebuk.[97] The latter, recently bolstered by a 900-horse cavalry unit and groups from the coast, now stood at a half-battalion.[98]

The Arabs' expanded operations also upset Ibn Rashid at Hail, who had been overseeing Medina's supply caravans from the Nejd and the Persian Gulf. He confessed to Ibn Saud that because 'he could not cope with the British and the tribes supplied by them with war material', the Turks had sent him a guard detachment of 150 Turkish gunners and, it was rumoured, one or two German soldiers.[99] Despite this, Saud es-Subhan, a dedicated rival of Ibn Rashid, managed to attack a Hail caravan carrying *l*.6,000 to markets in Kerbela to buy supplies for Medina.[100] The action not only removed precious cash from the Turks' supply but provided valuable propaganda for the Sherif's pan-Arab platform.[101] Around the same time, news arrived that an auxiliary force of North Asir tribesmen wanted to join the Sherif's army.[102]

The Arab Bureau celebrated how cannily they had read the intricacies of the Hejaz situation. A member of the bureau, most likely its director, Cornwallis, wrote a triumphant summary of recent events. He declared that not only had the intelligence community been vindicated in their judgement of political affairs in the Hejaz, they had resisted the Turks' crude attempts to provoke the British government into landing a brigade and violating the religious sanctity of the Hejaz, an action which would have wrecked the Sherif's movement. 'Considering his small strength, one wonders why the Turkish Commanding Officer ever undertook these fruitless and abortive offensives,' the author observed:

> It is just possible they were intended only as demonstrations, to create panic, and induce us to land troops in the Holy Land, to the advantage of the Turkish Sinai operations, and of pan-Islamic propaganda directed from Medina. If so, we have avoided a very pretty trap.[103]

The Flight folded easily into Ali's operations at Rabegh, giving aerial bombing support to his fighters and supplying valuable Imint of the wider battlefield. The Turks had evacuated from Bir Abbas but remained in full occupation of Ghayir and an outpost at Mijz. Ali's force, tracked by Imint, engaged the force at Mijz[104] and, in a remarkable turn, dispatched a detachment to blow up the Turkish barracks at Kubah in Medina on 21 January. Three days later, a larger force under Ali attacked and completed the seizure of the Mijz outpost. The Turks ordered a bombing raid but failed to dislodge them.[105] Humint from the

Sherif's agents now suggested that, apart from two outposts south of Medina, the Turks' only defensive line was along the Ghayir and Fura roads. A Turkish plane strafed Ali's camp on 1 February. A British plane from Rabegh promptly retaliated for two days with strikes against Turkish positions and a munitions dump around Sath el-Ghayir, causing considerable damage. Aerial observation on 4 February around the Wadi Fura road discovered that the Turks had since evacuated their outposts south of Medina. Two days later, British planes travelling from Rabegh to Ali's camp encountered and chased away a Turkish plane flying out of Medina.[106] Aerial reconnaissance on 22 February confirmed the Turks' evacuation of Sath el-Ghayir and Khunigat-ar-Rim.[107]

Ali now viewed the planes as essential support to help compensate for his army's recurring problems with cohesion. On 25 February he announced that the religious prohibition against non-Muslims did not apply to pilots: 'There is no objection to a plane flying over the environs of the city [of Medina] and taking photographs, provided it does not fly over the city itself, photograph it or drop bombs into it.'[108] By 28 February Ali's army had cleared a landing ground at Mijz. On 5 March, Major Ross of the RFC flew two planes over Medina, reconnoitering Turkish positions at Bir el-Mashi, Bir Derwish, Bir Ali and the intervening roads. At the Medina terminus, the pilots sighted three planes in the air but saw no train engines and little rolling stock. Imint and Humint also kept watch on the status of the outpost at Jebel Ohod, outside the southern gate of Medina, for signs that it might evacuate.[109]

The combination of aerial bombardment and Arab raids, particularly by independent sections of the Beni Salim and Rahalah, forced the Turks to retire yet further and accelerated their fortification along the railway. By the end of February, the Arab Bureau reported that the Turkish army had evacuated all but one advance post on the southwest perimeter outside Medina. Zeid's force harassed the Turkish reserve units moving out of these camps.[110] The Turks moved their headquarters back from Bir Derwish to a site nearer Medina, chased all the way by the Rahalah Harb who managed to capture two officers, many rifles and camels. At Medina itself, Fakhri Pasha remained entrenched but the Governor of Medina evacuated to Syria. The pretender, Sherif Haidar, was also said to be preparing his departure.[111] Reports on the city's conditions stated that basic rations of food such as bread were cut to almost half in February and March, and most city inhabitants and government officials were trying to relocate to Syria, Yenbo or Mecca.[112] The Arab Bureau noted one report estimating that, with most of the HEF now distributed north along the railway, perhaps only six battalions remained in the Medina district.[113] This figure would pose little threat to the Hashemite positions in future. In effect, the Turks were assuming 'a passive defence of trenches [...] a static position which endured till the Armistice ended the war and involved Turkey in the dismal surrender of the Holy City and its helpless garrison'.[114]

By late February 1917, representatives from all the northern tribes apart from Suleiman Rifada and the Billi clans had visited Wejh to pledge their support to Feisal.[115] Feisal welcomed thousands of volunteers from the dynasties of the

Rualla Anazeh, the Sherarat, the Beni Sakhr and the Huweitat. He now needed rifles to make good their commitment. The War Office managed to supplement the 54,000 rifles already sent with an additional 30,000 by taking a few thousand from British forces in Egypt, Sudan and Salonica who were awaiting new arms from England.[116] Abdullah also received letters at Wadi Ais from Nuri Shaalan of the Rualla, promising to join the Sherif's movement and requesting funds.[117]

Tribal politics and a northern migration

With the debates over European reinforcements and Feisal's move to Wejh successfully resolved, awkward rumblings began over the ultimate direction of Britain's policy. Guerrilla tactics north of Medina had restored the Arab armies' enthusiasm and attracted additional Bedouin tribes, but the British government had yet to confront the question of their long-term goals. As the Hejaz campaign neared the north of the peninsula, Feisal's promises to local chiefs that they were fighting for local autonomy after the overthrow of the Turkish government would begin to push against Allied post-war aims for Syria and the Levant coast, as Vickery anticipated.

Wishful assumptions had been made in some British circles about the inevitable partnership of Nuri Shaalan's Rualla Federation. Feisal's negotiations with him were ongoing but, as only an attentive few in Cairo seemed to register, still inconclusive. Lawrence tried to clarify the situation at the beginning of the year. No operational agreement with the Rualla had been reached. The supply and fuel caravans which Murray had envisioned for his Jauf scheme had not yet been organized and the petrol consignment given to Feisal languished at Kheif Hussein – albeit fortunately, according to Lawrence, for Ibn Shaddad had said that if sent north, 'it would be looted inevitably'.[118] Despite the encouraging 'rumours of friction' between the Syrian Bedouin tribes and the CUP that continued to reach Feisal's camp, Lawrence had been urged by Faiz el Ghusain, Feisal's secretary, not to extrapolate further about the Bedouin's willingness to mobilize against the Turks as 'we do not know the local conditions'. Faiz doubted, as noted above, that any Syrian potentate would 'enter into any premature scheme of co-operation with the Sherif or his allies' without strong military backing or British action in Syria to ensure that the Turkish army was besieged on all sides.[119] Ibn Sheddad, Feisal's former envoy to Jauf, told Lawrence that Nuri, his son Nawwaf, and Fawaz ibn Faiz of the Beni Sakhr had decided in a council to terminate relations with the Turks immediately, but not to actively support the Sherif until Feisal had taken el Ula, the junction from which they could market their crops to the Hejaz and establish communication with Jauf. But to hold el Ula, Feisal would also have to take the village of Teima to the east and confront the Shammar Ghazzua tribe of central Arabia. Teima was currently held by a Shammar ally of Ibn Rashid, Abu Rumman, although only 'with seven men: – and offers to surrender to eight', reported Lawrence. It was possible that the Rualla were hesitating because Nawwaf had long wanted to defeat the Shammar and Ibn Rashid himself, to validate his future position at the head of a

Shammar-Rualla confederation.[120] The Rualla were a famously powerful and self-sufficient tribal group; in that light, Lawrence described the overall 'tone' of Nuri and Nawaf's pledges to Feisal as 'excellent' and their request for preliminary guarantees of the Sherif's stability and strength as quite reasonable.[121] He shared his report with Wilson and the Arab Bureau, where members such as Bray and Lloyd submitted comments.[122] Clayton wired the DMI in London, stressing that once Feisal took el Ula they would be able to supply and arm the Rualla. A similar promise of alliance had also been received from the Mujali of Kerak, from Auda abu Tayyi of the Huweitat, and from Ibn Awajawoun of the Wuld Suleiman of the southern Anazeh.[123]

Lloyd revealed even more about the political complications underlying these negotiations. He reported that he had seen a letter that the Sherif had drafted to Wingate, before [apparently] changing his mind and cancelling it. Lloyd wrote to Wingate that despite the Sherif's optimism about securing the alliance of the Rualla, the Sherif was feeling a 'vague uneasiness in his mind as to the possible outcome' of Nuri's allegiance. He expected Nuri to ask for certain guarantees regarding Syria's future which he, as the leader of 'the Arab Revolt', should be able to give but knew he could not without the British government's consent. In the Sherif's letter to Wingate, he stressed his embarrassment over the discrepancy between his real and perceived authority, saying that in his negotiations with Nuri he 'felt somewhat handicapped by his agreements with us to which equally he had to be loyal'. As far as is known, the Sykes–Picot Agreement had not been discussed with Mecca, so the Sherif may have been referring to London's insistence that his title be 'King of the Hejaz', and not 'King of the Arab Nation', as he had asked, or was merely alluding to suspicions.[124] As Lloyd explained, Nuri 'was not of course aware of the agreements between HMG and himself, and estimated the Shereef's power at a wider geographical valuation than that which HMG had been able to do'.[125] It was equally possible that the Sherif hoped that by negotiating with Nuri without interference from Great Britain, he might secure an alliance with the northern tribes that would thus pivot on him and increase his leverage with the Allies.[126]

Despite the tension caused by their presence in the Hejaz, a number of British observers had continued to assume that Anglo-Arab military co-operation in Syria, because it lay outside the Holy Land, would be relatively straightforward, abetted by but not dependent upon the Sherif whose ambitions the British government still hoped to confine to the Hejaz. Lloyd, for example, hoped that the Sherif would intuitively understand that 'the limitations imposed by us upon his authority in regard to the Syrian area may be taken to include the use of Shalaans [*sic*] forces in that area, but of course one has nothing to do with other'.[127] Lloyd, however, unlike many of his Cairo colleagues, was at this point prepared to leave the Syria question to France because his greater priority was Britain's take-over of the former Ottoman Bank in the Hejaz. In his mind, almost any compromise was worth ensuring that 'the greatest engine of political influence namely financial power should be British'.[128]

Yet, within weeks, as will be seen, even Lloyd would revise his views on

Britain's imperial interests in Syria.[129] The defensive solidarity of Arab and other minority races in Syria against the CUP's ethnic policies had created a political climate as delicate for the Allies as religious sacrosanctity had been in the Hejaz theatre. Despite the relative independence of the Rualla, Anazeh and Druse from the CUP's conscription and taxation laws, there had been years of penalties against non-Turks in Syria, constraints placed on Arab officers, a systematic isolation of Arab divisions and executions of Arab leaders that had driven thousands of Arab soldiers to desert into the interior of the Hauran. Few Allied observers seemed eager to speculate at the time on the implications for their war aims should it be impossible to detach the Hashemites' revolt from the Syrian secret societies' pan-Arab rhetoric; although it was precisely that rhetoric which, ironically, had infused the Sherif's defiance of the Sultan-Caliph's call for *jihad*.[130]

The geography of operations would force more of these questions into the policy sphere, particularly as Egyptforce approached Palestine. In the third week of February 1917, as Murray's troops approached Tell-el-Sharia, the War Cabinet gave in to French pressure and agreed to assign a British Chief Political Officer, Mark Sykes, to accompany their French Commissioner, F. Georges-Picot, so they might provide 'political' advice to Egyptforce after it crossed the frontier into Palestine and Syria.[131] The tenuousness of the Anglo-French understanding over Syria was underlined again in March, but this time by Clayton who had to reject the British Military Mission's suggestions for a landing at Aqaba.[132] In a significant memo addressed to Lawrence and sent to the Arab Bureau, Clayton cited the lack of seaplanes and transport ships, and the port's insecurity from inland attack. More tellingly, he referred to the question of 'whether, in the present circumstances, the presence of an Arab force at Akaba would be desirable, as it would unsettle tribes which are better left quiet until the time is more ripe'.[133] It is possible that this timing referred to Egyptforce. It is also possible that, with decisions pending over the future position of France in Syria, Clayton did not want to encourage an Arab rising in support of British army operations which the French would then feel obliged to suppress.[134] But what is also clear from later correspondence is that Clayton might have already been anticipating Great Britain's need to possess Aqaba itself, as an essential base for the post-war defence of Egypt.[135] The inconsistent decision-making of the British government towards this phase of the Arab campaign would cause increasing confusion and frustration between London and the men on the ground, and only heighten the latter's sense of urgency with regard to the Arabs' progress.

Sigint and a vanished option

In early March 1917, a remarkable piece of Sigint presented an unparalleled opportunity to the Arab armies. The proposals that followed reflected the degree of confidence invested by decision-makers in this theatre's military intelligence sources, especially in Sigint. GHQ, Egyptforce intercepted a Turkish wireless communication relaying orders from Jemal Pasha to Fakhri Pasha to evacuate Medina and retire the whole of the HEF north to Palestine. The implications of this release of troops for Murray were crucial. Since mid-February, the RFC had been subjecting the Turkish forces at Beersheba to bombing raids. Now Egyptforce was anticipating its advance against the Ottoman Fourth Army's stronghold in Syria.[136] Murray shot off a telegram to the CIGS regarding Jemal's decision: 'It is now quite obvious that the Turkish campaign in Arabia has failed, and that the Hejaz Expeditionary Force is about to be withdrawn to Palestine.' He also cautioned Robertson to keep the intelligence source absolutely secret: 'no premature announcement of any kind should be made on the subject, either in Parliament in the Press or elsewhere'. Murray considered this intelligence source so valuable that he even asked Wingate to not inform the Foreign Office; he proposed that Robertson, if necessary, make only the most 'strictly secret communication to the Foreign Office regarding the situation'. Murray added, 'For obvious reasons I have not told the French.'[137]

The Sigint was brought to Lawrence at Wejh on 9 March by MacRury, a Cairo intelligence officer, aboard an Egyptian patrol ship. Newcombe and Garland were working inland against the railway, so Lawrence reviewed the information with Feisal alone. The 'long telegraphic instructions from Jemal Pasha to Fakhri [...] emanating from Enver and the German staff in Constantinople', ordered the HEF to withdraw through Hedia (the largest water supply between Medina and el Ula) to el Ula, Tebuk and finally to Maan where they would form a new defensive line. The instructions confirmed previous intelligence on the HEF's shortage of live transport by showing that Fakhri would be using all available train capacity to carry freight, while his troops were left to walk in columns alongside the cars, a decision considered by Lawrence to be an extraordinary display of vulnerability.[138] Nevertheless, Lawrence was ordered by Clayton not to let Feisal know that the entire HEF was being withdrawn because the Arab fighters might simply cheer their progress – and Murray wanted the Turkish garrison stopped. Lawrence violated his orders slightly; he knew that by preventing the HEF from evacuating the peninsula the Arab armies would only protract the Hejaz campaign and delay any critical move into Syria, which he was already coming to believe was essential for the Arab movement's success. To fulfil his trust with Feisal, he gave the latter a candid explanation of the situation. He then argued that 'Allied interests in this case demanded the sacrifice, or at least the postponement of immediate advantage to the Arabs.'[139] Feisal wrote instructions to his brothers and various Arab leaders to begin a multipronged attack against Turkish troops wherever they were found along the railway. Lawrence personally carried these instructions to Abdullah, who was critically placed for these operations at Wadi Ais but had lately been showing little interest.[140]

In the meantime, Feisal worked with Newcombe to devise a strategy to 'develop maximum force' along the railway during the Turks' attempted evacuation. They decided that Ali would strike between Muheit and Bowat stations from his base near Bir Derwish. Abdullah would raid the track from Bowat to

Hedia, using his base at Murabba in Wadi Ais. Saad Ghranein [probably Ghuhein], 115 miles up the Wejh–Medina road in Wadi Hamdh, at Faqair, would wait for machine gun support and then attack stations north of Hedia. Feisal and dynamite experts would make their base at Jeida, eighty-five miles west on Wejh–el Ula road, and raid the track between Toweira and el Ula. A machine-gun detachment would try to dynamite the track around el Ula while other demolition parties attacked north of Medain Salih and the Dar el Hamra-Muaddham section and moved towards Tebuk.[141]

Feisal had received a declaration of continuing hostility to the Sherif from Ibn Rashid in mid-March. Humint from Turkish prisoners stated that Ibn Rashid was expecting to receive 200 camels, arms and money, which he would combine with 300 camels at Dar el Hamra; all of which suggested an imminent offensive. Feisal sent word to Nuri Shaalan and asked him to attack Ibn Rashid from the north to draw him away from Medina. He also warned Abdullah that Ibn Rashid might be hoping to recapture Nakhail and Henakiyeh, and to make those bases secure. Wingate wrote to the GOC of Force 'D' at Basra to ask if he might induce Ibn Saud or any of the other Gulf Sheikhs to threaten and absorb Ibn Rashid's men away from the Hejaz.[142] Another 500 camelmen from the Rualla and Beni Sakhr chiefs arrived at Wejh to pledge their service to Feisal, and provided further weight to these proposals.[143] The RFC Flight transferring from Rabegh to Wejh would help maintain pressure on the Turks' withdrawal.[144]

Intelligence returns were analysed at Cairo to compose a picture of the distribution of force facing the Arabs. The Arab Bureau was certain that since January 1917 no reinforcements had reached Medina, nor had any of the Turkish forces south of Maan since that time been withdrawn north to Turkish garrisons in Syria.[145] The only exception to this stasis was the reported arrival of two battalions of the 163rd Regiment at Medain Salih and el Ula in late February. These units would have constituted a considerable opposition, but as the 163rd was part of the 53rd Division now headquartered at Ludd in southern Palestine, the Arab Bureau believed these two battalions might have been pulled north again. As for the force facing Feisal at Tebuk, it was known that the Turks had stationed a new force there to help guard the railway. But the Arab Bureau calculated that without the infusion of reinforcements from the north, this force could only have been organized from former railway companies and the old HEF of which a major part at least seemed to be in the process of evacuating Medina. There were native reports identifying a Circassian cavalry arrived at Tebuk, and on the southern portion of the railway a new camel corps had been organized from Huteim or other tribesmen, but the Arab Bureau believed that these would be withdrawn as soon as the HEF were safely evacuated.[146] Medina itself seemed destined to become a ghost town. Reports from native agents suggested the city was near collapse. The number of sick was increasing, food was scarce, most shops were closed and the great mosque had been 'stripped bare'. Trains evacuating the civil population of Medina were now stopping after twenty-one miles and disembarking passengers, who continued by foot.[147] By early March

1917, as a symbol of the CUP's complete loss of confidence, Sherif Ali Haidar finally left Medina for Damascus.[148]

The appearance of incipient withdrawal, as tracked by Humint, Sigint and Imint, continued for a few weeks. Outside the city, the Turks had evacuated Bir Aar[149] but still occupied Bir el-Mashi and Bir Derwish, which they could not evacuate due to lack of transport. Throughout March, Zeid and Ali had surrounded these districts and harassed the Turkish lines of communication with raiding parties. Zeid's men attacked a series of outposts as far as the gates of Medina before retiring, cutting telegraph lines, capturing horses and camels, and taking prisoners.[150] Ali's men fought the Turks at Bir Derwish for two days before driving them out and capturing one of their captains and nine men, 200 rifles and ammunition. The Turkish advance force had now withdrawn to Manjur, just sixteen miles from Medina to which Ali believed they would finally retire. Jebel Ohod appeared abandoned as well, and the Turks were having difficulties at Bir el-Mashi.[151] 'No doubt', the Arab Bureau noted, 'at the same time, other troops are being withdrawn northwards from that city.'[152]

Unfortunately, these positions constituted the extent of the Turkish withdrawal. Cairo's treatment of the special Sigint and its interpretation of all the subsequent movements were flouted by the determination of Fakhri Pasha to ignore orders he considered unnecessary or irrelevant. Intelligence agents had 'reported more than once' that the Turks planned to move the bulk of their HEF north to el-Ula and beyond, but it now looked as though Fakhri's garrison would remain exactly where it was, only with reduced numbers. The Arab Bureau announced in their weekly bulletin that the Turks' 'original plan of complete evacuation' of Medina had apparently been 'modified either by realization of the difficulty of withdrawal in face of the Arabs along the railway, or by remonstrances from Fakhri Pasha, who appears still to be in Medina'.[153] One month after this assessment, the DMI in London received information from the agent 'Maurice' showing that Fakhri had warned the Turkish government that if he were not supplied with more ammunition, he would be forced to surrender Medina.[154] The Arab Bureau printed this new information with scepticism, as 'given here for what its worth'.[155] What was clear was that Fakhri Pasha had resolved not to be pressured – by the Arab tribesmen or the needs of the Turkish Fourth Army – to abandon his hold on Medina.

This episode was outstanding for two reasons. It demonstrated the British authorities' tremendous confidence and fluency in handling Sigint for the region. Moreover, the unpredictable reaction of Fakhri to his orders meant that the Arab armies' combined attack on the railway, which was essentially a regular operation taken under what could have been ideal circumstances, was never executed. Without such a (successful) test of their potential for conventional action, there was nothing to prevent the resumption of the earlier proposals for an irregular strategy along the railway towards the north. British intelligence officers in Arabia had arrived repeatedly at the conclusion that military and political considerations were indelibly intertwined; now, in Feisal's successful advance to Wejh, they knew that he had not only solidified the Arab front against the HEF but drawn vital sustenance from the tribes of the northern peninsula and demonstrated credibility to the tribes of northern Syria. The Anglo-Arab partnership was now set to confront 'the Syrian question'. It was a central and unresolved policy question that, while inevitable and clearly overdue to many figures in Cairo and the Hejaz, was hardly a matter that the War Committee and the Foreign Office in London would have delegated to a regional administration at the perimeter of the empire. The intelligence community in Cairo did not wait for the invitation.

6 An unauthorized policy triumph

Intelligence and Aqaba, February–July 1917

Destination: Medina, Jauf or Aqaba?

The Arabs' capture of Wejh had altered the essential balance of strength between the Arab and the Turkish armies in Arabia. The Turks' ability to project force from the railway and Medina had been shut down. Feisal's and Abdullah's armies had shifted to positions around the northern portion of the line that would allow for a concerted attack on a withdrawing enemy, only to be halted by Fakhri's decision to defy even his superiors' expectations and remain rooted at Medina. With that strategy now defunct, earlier proposals re-emerged to confront the lingering issue of Medina.

Feisal found himself surrounded by a preponderance of counsellors. Joyce had already recommended an Arab operation to cut the railway permanently and isolate the HEF, again with the aim of forcing Fakhri to surrender. The natural targets for attack remained el Ula and Medain Salih stations, the last enemy strongholds north of Medina. In February, Wingate had agreed with Joyce's evaluation and asked the War Office for 40,000 new rifles, ammunition and two 4-gun mountain batteries to support the strategy, claiming that Feisal and Abdullah would be able to seize the line and force a state of starvation on the 10,000–15,000 Turks left at Medina within six months.[1] Less sure of this proposal were Newcombe, Vickery, Wilson and Lawrence. The preceding eight months of experience had led them to question the ability, even the willingness of Arab fighters to hold a defensive position for more than a few days, especially on the railway where a Turkish counter-offensive could come from two, possibly three directions. These officers wanted London to pay greater attention to Feisal's need to keep his followers enthusiastic in the field by supporting his raiding operations around Wejh and his political negotiations with tribes north of the Arabian peninsula.

The relevance of Aqaba was also a source of disagreement. Vickery and Newcombe's proposals involved a multi-stage attack on the railway using Arab fighters supported by British technical and logistical support, such as had been the case at Wejh; but it did not end with the collapse of Medina. They wanted an Anglo-Arab force to seize Aqaba as well because it was the best and most obvious base for supporting future joint operations in Syria. Anglo-Arab parties would conduct simultaneous demolition operations in the north Hejaz, such as Newcombe envisioned for his scheme north of Tebuk. But it was a widely-held view that 'the whole movement to Akaba depends on ships: movement by land [alone] will be too slow and laborious'. The French Military Mission in the Hejaz heard that an Aqaba landing was being discussed and moved quickly to protect French interests. Brémond cornered Feisal at Wejh and promised to transfer French battalions currently at Djibouti to Aqaba, provided that the British contributed a battalion with aeroplanes to ensure the operation's success. Feisal confided to Newcombe that while he welcomed British assistance, he 'did not want any help from the French or to have anything to do with him [Brémond]'.[2] Brémond pressed his offer on GHQ, Egypt, as well, but Murray was as reluctant as the next Englishman to allow the French a lead role in his military advance. He also knew from Brémond's own testimony that in injecting a European conventional dimension to the Arabs' effort he hoped to sabotage the political basis of the Arabs' movement before it reached Syria. Surpassing any of these considerations was the possible toll of an Aqaba scheme on Murray's attenuated Egyptforce. To land at Aqaba while the Turks still held the high ground above the beach would require a more robust military detachment than Murray could spare. Imint on the hostile terrain above the shoreline at Aqaba in the summer of 1916, as discussed earlier, confirmed Murray's pessimism about the entire undertaking.[3]

Lawrence had helped to prepare the Imint on Aqaba for GHQ, Egypt. He could see that a landed force on the beach burdened by artillery would be helpless against enemy fire from the cliffs as long as Turkish reinforcements remained safely entrenched in Wadi Ithm, the winding route connecting Aqaba to Ma'an. After Wejh, the political necessity of creating a viable northern Arab force was growing daily. In Lawrence's mind, the two considerations pointed to a single solution. By early 1917, Lawrence recalled, he had decided that 'Akaba, whose importance was all and more than [Brémond] said, would be best taken by Arab irregulars descending from the interior without naval help'.[4] The scheme would spare Egyptforce and bypass the French altogether. It would also give support to Feisal's domestic requirements by precluding the participation of European manpower. This revised Aqaba concept began to shape Lawrence's private counsels with Feisal over the coming months.

The British advisers meeting with Feisal reported on the latter's great determination after Wejh to send his men northward as soon as possible. They did not know that Lawrence was contributing to Feisal's sense of urgency. Lawrence encouraged Feisal to gain access to the Wadi Sirhan roadway connecting the northeastern Hejaz with the Syrian interior, and make full use of Nuri Shaalan's support. Once Feisal's Arab force had recruited enough fighters from the Syrian tribes, they could make 'an extreme example of a turning movement' westward and cross the railway, enter Wadi Ithm and clean out the Turkish garrisons down to the port of Aqaba.[5] To ensure that Brémond would not be able to sway Feisal's confidence, and that Feisal understood fully the significance of Aqaba and the Syrian inland towns within the Allies' secret post-war agreements,

Lawrence seems to have confided the terms of the Sykes–Picot Agreement to Feisal at this time. He urged Feisal to concentrate on establishing an independent military command in the Syrian interior from which the Bedouin armies could assert their advantage in conjunction with European troops entering from the coast. France would have to take the Lebanon after the war, and Britain would probably control the Palestinian coastal territory west of the Jordan River. But if an Arab force seized Tripoli and still dominated the interior, Lawrence said, Feisal could help ensure that the future Arab state in Syria would be economically solid and have access to a Mediterranean port.[6] Feisal and Lawrence agreed that his first step had to be to take Aqaba as his base for supply outside of the Hejaz. Feisal believed that there was only one warrior capable of carrying out such a daring operation: Auda abu Tayyi, the chief of the Eastern Huweitat, who was soon to arrive at Wejh. This legendary fighting chief would guarantee that Feisal's deputies won over the tribes lying between Ma'an and Aqaba, before taking the port.[7]

The other British officers in the Hejaz were unaware of Feisal's discussions with Lawrence. They continued to respond to the March Sigint containing withdrawal orders for the HEF by urging the Arabs to organize a trap for the HEF as it attempted to evacuate. Joyce, now Senior British Officer in charge of the RFC flight and armoured cars that moved from Rabegh to Wejh on 20 March, pressed this railway strategy on Feisal for two weeks. But Feisal seemed uninterested in the railway, Joyce noted, and far more preoccupied with pushing the campaign into Syria.[8] On 31 March, Arab and British authorities decided to transfer the main part of Feisal's army with two machine guns and four maxims under Sherif Sharraf inland, to Abu-Raka, to increase their attacks on the railway.[9] But Joyce reported that he still felt uneasy, due to the continuing rumours in camp about operations planned for Syria. A gap seemed to be widening between the British government's immediate war aims and the nationalist Arabs' programmes for independence after the war. He warned Wilson that all of Feisal's work was 'now concentrated on the north with the idea of getting the tribes in this region to cooperate and make general attack on the line between Derra [north of Amman] and Tabuk'; he added that Feisal's ambitions 'probably go even further and aim at getting the whole line south of Damascus'. If the boundaries of the Hejaz operations were not clarified, he said, there would only be resentment and conflict between the British and the Arabs later. Joyce knew that Feisal was unnerved by whispers that the French planned to land an army in Syria, and had warned the Syrian tribes to prepare for his call to action.[10] But too much of this activity appeared premature and uncontrolled to Joyce. 'From somewhere [Feisal] has developed very wide ideas', he reported, 'and I would like to feel certain they are in accordance with the general plan'.[11]

Feisal navigated his cautious way around these disparate counsels. In early April, the great Auda abu Tayyi arrived at Wejh and his magnificent Toweiha force mingled with the several hundred sheikhs and thousands of camel riders in camp from the Rualla Anazeh, the Sherarat, the Beni Sakhr and Huweitat subtribes. Feisal called a strategy meeting with Auda and representatives from the northern tribes, and Newcombe and Joyce.[12] Newcombe and Joyce had been discussing possible routes with Feisal for an Arab extension northward, after the HEF was defeated at Medina. The first option was for an Arab army to advance up the railway and seize Ma'an, before advancing north and 'using Akaba as a base for clearing up Turkish posts on the way'. But this plan was conditional on a successful Anglo-Arab landing at Aqaba beforehand. The rest of the proposal resembled Lawrence's suggestions for Feisal, in that it anchored an Arab presence in the Ma'an–Aqaba area.

But Newcombe and Joyce dismissed the Ma'an plan in favour of a second option. They may have been influenced by Clayton's recent memorandum prohibiting an Aqaba landing, or they may have genuinely believed that the second proposal was 'more economical, more rapid, and if successful [...] attaining the same results' as the first. It involved a smaller Arab force, that would ride north to the Druse mountains in the Syrian interior and secure the help of the Druse and other Anazeh tribes.[13] From there, the Arabs would launch an attack on the railway between Ma'an and Damascus. This scheme bore greater resemblance to the proposal put forward earlier by Murray for joint operations with the Arab tribes at Jauf, and did not involve Aqaba. The operation could only proceed, however, after Feisal had managed to 'clear up [the] situation at Medina, el Ula and Medain Salih', and end the HEF's occupation of the peninsula.[14]

Feisal agreed to the British officers' condition regarding Medina. It is possible he wanted to prepare for as many schemes northward as available; it is also possible that he felt unable to resist the British officers' requests. Before the grand tribal council at Wejh, Feisal sent an urgent letter to Lawrence, who was currently participating in demolition raids at Wadi Ais, and asked him to return to Wejh as soon as possible: 'You are much needed here more than the destruction of the line because I am in very great complication which I had never expected.'[15] In the meantime at the council, Feisal won the tribes' agreement for a combined move north into the Syrian interior in two months' time, but along the lines suggested by Newcombe and Joyce, with the preliminary condition being that the railway was permanently cut. Feisal assured Newcombe and Joyce that once his men reached Syria, the Druse would supply food and the Anazeh would provide 3,000 transport camels for the mobilized Arab force. Feisal requested another 20,000 rifles with ammunition from Britain, and more funding from his father.[16]

Running parallel to these discussions on strategy was the flow of intelligence on the Arab raids. Each success and failure fed into calculations concerning Medina as a target for Arab operations. The intelligence reports on these raids show vividly how the British officers' negative assessments of the Arabs' capacity to fight or achieve a decisive position on the battlefield influenced their views on future strategy. Ali's force was still problematic. Deprived of the Flight's Imint and the British staff's technical support after their transfers to Wejh, Ali again seem unable to confront the Medina garrison. He missed at least one excellent opportunity due to failed nerve. Intelligence in late March suggested again that Fakhri Pasha was 'in difficulties'. Raids along Feisal's section of the line were diverting the Turks' attention. Ali's men had a brief advantage and pressed forward against the outlying bases to the south of city, particularly Bir el-Mashi. Ali sent a bold message to Fakhri Pasha, daring him to surrender. Fakhri asked for three days' armistice instead, and Ali rejected it. But there the engagement ended. Without the Imint assistance upon which Ali expressly stated he had come to rely for anticipating Turkish movements, he hesitated to charge the Turkish positions. Turkish reinforcements from Medina broke through to Bir el-Mashi soon afterwards.[17]

Feisal's army's demolition activity against the north Hejaz sections of the railway grew more ambitious in early April and wrecked a considerable amount of track, but none of the raids permanently damaged the line.[18] There were a number of inhibiting factors. The Turks' repair gangs were dogged in their patrols and had ample reserves of track at Medina, deposited for the planned extension to Mecca.[19] The Arabs' raids were also inhibited by the presence of the British advisers, as Newcombe and Garland reluctantly admitted. Despite the British officers' professional and technical contribution, their participation was a liability for the Arabs' sense of cohesion and purpose. Newcombe's and Garland's reports on a major demolition raid on 14 April against Muadhdham and Dar el-Hamra that involved 1,000 of Feisal's men repeatedly turned to details of exasperation and complaint over the tribesmen's poor discipline, disdain for taking orders and recalcitrance at almost every step of the mission.[20] Only the Arab trained infantry, led by the Baghdadi Yuzbashi Malaud, maintained discipline and coherence under enemy machine-gun fire. The Bedouin fighters made only the most 'desultory' effort in the attack. Worryingly, it also appeared that the Turks may have been 'expecting the attack', for their mountain guns were already in position and they had instantly taken cover in well-dug trenches. Within twenty-four hours of the Arabs' assault, Turkish repair gangs had repaired the demolished sections of the railway.[21]

Newcombe's experiences with the Arab parties on these raids dampened his earlier optimism about joint operations in the interior. The Arab Bureau remarked that Newcombe's reports from later operations in the area of Khishm Sanaa, Muadhdham and Abu Taka continued to be 'a record of disappointments, of missed opportunities and of good plans spoilt by the indiscipline, instability of purpose, cowardice and general untrustworthiness, not only of the Bedouin forces accompanying him, but also of the Sheikhs at their head.' In Newcombe's opinion, 'the obstacles put by the Turks in the way of his efforts at [railway] destruction are far less serious than those proceeding from his own people'.[22] He proposed creating a proper camel corps or a new scheme for training regular Arab fighters, rather than continuing with mixed demolition work: 'It is obvious from this and former reports that either all of us are wasting our time here, instead of getting on with the war, or an entirely new line must be taken'.[23] His views were echoed by the other officers in the field, such as Garland and the engineer Lieutenant H.S. Hornby, who also candidly expressed their sense of discouragement, despite the considerable amount of track demolished.[24] Garland now urged Abdullah to use the regular Syrian soldiers rather than tribesmen for operations. He concluded his report to Cairo on the latest disappointing foray with a typical view: 'Such are Bedouins. The trials of an energetic white officer obliged to depend on them are indeed considerable.'[25]

These officers' disappointments while serving with the Arab tribesmen in the field had a bearing on deliberations over future strategy because they emphasized the extreme difficulties of combining British advisers and Arab irregulars for demolition operations. It had been generally accepted that Bedouin fighters could not carry out regular operations such as taking and holding fixed positions, but the latest composite operations against the railway had been heralded as a compromise, an improved arrangement that might have led eventually to the cutting of the railway and the capture of Medina. The British officers' frustrations threw these plans into disorder. It seemed increasingly unlikely that the Medina garrison could be taken with any Bedouin troops at all.

Lawrence's epiphany on Medina

A fresh view from the British camp was delivered by Lawrence. While the plan for a combined pincer operation against the withdrawing HEF was still active, Lawrence was sent to Abdullah's camp at Abu Markha in Wadi Ais to motivate him to mobilize against the railway and cooperate with Feisal. En route, Lawrence was struck down by fever and an attack of dysentery. Shortly afterwards, one of the Arab tribesmen in his party murdered a man from another tribe. Although still extremely ill, Lawrence judged that the offence against the Ageyl victim had to be resolved immediately and, in his capacity as expedition leader as well as the single neutral figure amongst the tribes, he executed the Moroccan who had confessed. He later explained that it had been vital to adhere to customary tribal law regarding acts of murder, or his inaction would have invited the inevitable chain of inter-tribal reprisals 'by which our unity would have been endangered'. Nonetheless, his sense of personal responsibility for the 'horror' of the execution haunted him.[26] He collapsed upon arrival at Abdullah's base and spent ten days in seclusion to recover. During that time he started questioning whether the fundamental strategy of taking Medina and even taking the Hejaz railway itself might be misconceived. The Bedouin were ill-suited to the operation; this point was widely accepted. Feisal was operating with a volunteer force and could not afford to throw away lives on costly conventional battles with Turkish troops. But Lawrence also now considered the fact that the Turkish bases, as they stood, had ceased to pose any threat to the Arab movement. In fact, the Turks' retirement to the line had transformed the railway bases into de facto holding pens, keeping the enemy far from any active front.

Lawrence's reconsideration of the Arab armies' strategy aimed not only to match future operations to the tribesmen's preferred style of warfare but to challenge again the prevailing assumptions about the Arab–Turk contest of strength. There were nearly 5,000 Turkish troops still stationed south of Hadiyeh [Hedia]. If the Arabs left Medina intact, he reasoned, and continued to conduct raids against the line to prevent the Turks' evacuation, the latter's conventional capability would be useless and their most precious materiel, the engines and rolling stock, would be sacrificed. The Arabs would be free to extend their front along as broad a line to the north as they dared. As Lawrence later explained:

> [The Turk] was welcome to the Hejaz Railway, and the Trans-Jordan railway, and the Palestine and Syrian railways for the duration of the war, so long as he gave us the other nine hundred and ninety-nine thousandths of the Arab world.[27]

Clayton had touched on a similar concept the previous November, when he had questioned whether in the interests of economy Medina might act as a kind of repository for the enemy until 'our activities further North' were able to cut the railway.[28] Lawrence's unique amendment to this idea was to see that the railway's entrapment of the enemy released the Arab forces for a far more ambitious guerrilla strategy than enabling Egyptforce to cut the line.[29]

The Bedouin fighters' irregular skill-set and refusal to conform to conventional military hierarchies would, in Lawrence's opinion, be the Arab Revolt's greatest guarantee of endurance once the movement reached Syrian interior. If the British were 'patient and superhuman-skilled', the Arabs' advantages in manpower and popular motivation would enable them to follow a strategy of extreme manoeuvre and 'reach victory without battle'.[30] To encourage his British colleagues not to lose heart in this larger enterprise, he urged them to show greater tolerance towards the Bedouin, to not judge their differences as evidence of inferiority, and to give greater consideration to the tribes' strengths as guerrilla fighters. The Arabs' 'processes are clear, their minds moving as one's moves, with nothing incomprehensible or radically different, and they will follow us, if we can endure with them, and play their game', he wrote in *The Arab Bulletin*. 'The pity is, we break down with exasperation, and throw them over.' Lawrence had been watching Feisal's leadership achievements with the unprecedented amassing of tribes at his camp. He reminded his British colleagues, 'I think Europeans could not or would not spend the time and thought and tact their Sheikhs and Emir expend each day, on such meagre objects.'[31]

The Arab Bureau applauded Lawrence's call for greater stamina, patience and optimism on the part of British officers in the Hejaz, and noted his success in getting Abdullah 'to do a great deal' more at his camp, after the 'dreary catalogue of difficulties [...] with inadequate human material [i.e. Bedouin]' reported in the same issue by Newcombe.[32] There was no such welcome for Lawrence's case on the strategic irrelevance of Medina. Back at Wejh, he found Newcombe, Joyce and Wilson holding meetings with Feisal on the details for a possible attack against the railway to force the capitulation of the Medina garrison, still believed to be essential before the Arab armies could risk mobilizing into Syria. Lawrence declared himself against the plan because irregular fighters would not hold the railway even if they did cut it, whereas they would be effective in any operation involving continual manoeuvre and sabotage. Wilson, Newcombe and Joyce disagreed and dismissed his alternative suggestion for beginning operations behind Aqaba: 'All I gained was a hearing, and a qualified admission that my counter-offensive might be a useful diversion.' Feisal, on the other hand, was impressed by Lawrence's view and gave him permission to consult with Auda abu Tayyi. Auda agreed and said privately that the small Huweitat clans around Aqaba could be persuaded to join a raid against the Turkish positions at Wadi Ithm and the port – as long as their expedition proved itself first against an impressive local target, such as Ma'an.[33]

Fresh intelligence regarding Aqaba arrived to reinforce Lawrence's calculations. Shortly after meeting with his colleagues, Lawrence debriefed a group of Turkish prisoners who had been brought to Wejh by Captain Boyle. They provided precise information on the condition of Aqaba and its defences. Their capture was a windfall. Wemyss had sent the HMS *Lama* and the HMS *Espiegle*, warships with the Red Sea Patrol, to the Gulf of Aqaba to investigate a previous item of intelligence, perhaps Humint, that had placed a 'European' (in fact, a German) officer at Aqaba with a store of mines for the waters off the gulf. The ships, aided by the HMS *Northbrooke*, collected at dawn on 20 April and fired at the shore, scattering the Turks' defensive positions. A landing party of sailors overran the first trenches and took eleven prisoners, leaving the rest of the garrison, estimated at sixty to eighty Turks and Syrians, to flee into the hills.[34] The intelligence that Lawrence gleaned from the prisoners revealed a brittle Turkish presence at Aqaba and gave him further confidence that the port could be taken from the interior. Visiting Turkish units, such as the 2/161st Regiment from Ma'an that had camped at the port six weeks earlier, were rotating out after one week. The permanent garrison comprised mainly gendarmes from Syria and Medina, but most had now decamped to the three posts in Wadi Ithm under Dhurush Bey, Officer Commanding (OC), joining Turkish and Arab soldiers, an Arab camel corps and Huweitat fighters totalling about 130 men. At Aqaba itself, just ten Turks remained, and a company left by the 2/161st as reinforcements for Dhurush. The prisoners said that no other Turkish troops remained in western Arabia or south of Aqaba. Although some initially inflated their estimates to interrogators, claiming that 14,000 Turks remained at Aqaba, they told Lawrence that they had only done so out of anger at being captured by the British. After landing at Wejh, their attitude had changed and they wanted to give accurate information. Several Syrians asked to join the Sherif's cause.[35]

The rest of the Aqaba expedition was set discreetly in train. Feisal appointed Sherif Nasir as the expedition's commander, and he invited Lawrence to accompany the party. Both Nasir and Lawrence kept the expedition's destination a secret from other Arab leaders and British officers. Lawrence recalled later that he had reasoned that he was only depriving Newcombe, Joyce and 'the railway scheme' of 'negligible' assistance:

> The desert route to Akaba was so long and so difficult that we could take neither guns nor machine-guns, nor stores nor regular soldiers. Accordingly the element I would withdraw from the railway scheme was only my single self; and [...] this amount was negligible, since I felt so strongly against it

> that my help there would have been half-hearted. So I decided to go my own way, with or without orders. I wrote a letter full of apologies to Clayton, telling him that my intentions were of the best: and went.[36]

Nasir departed into the interior on 9 May 1917 with Auda, Lawrence and some forty tribesmen. It was assumed by onlookers that their destination was Jefer, and that they were an appendage (discussed below) to the grander combined Syrian campaign under discussion: specifically, a small advance party to set up food and arms supply depôts to the east of Ma'an, Deraa and Damascus once the interior campaign was underway.[37]

Another 'revolt': the Sykes–Picot stratagem stumbles

Lawrence's concerns over the duplicity of British policy decisions in the Arab territories were not as unique in the region as popular histories have tended to imply. The conflict between the British Hejaz staff's priorities and those pursued by the government in London was sharply outlined by a perverse act of diplomatic double-dealing in April/May 1917. Sir Mark Sykes and François Georges-Picot came to Egypt to act as CPOs for Murray's next advance, 'to advise [Egyptforce] on political situation beyond Eastern frontier of Egypt and to co-operate with a French Commissioner'.[38] Lloyd, who was visiting London, reported back to Egypt that Sykes and Picot's 'task will be to relieve [Murray] of any political embarrassments or questions affecting the future of Palestine or Syria'.[39] But Lloyd, who could discover few details on the diplomats' actual program, became particularly sceptical after finding that Sykes and Picot were also planning to make personal contact with Arab leaders in the Syrian hinterland. The Syrian chiefs had already informed the Hashemites that they would not break publicly with the Turks until the Sherif held el Ula, made a strong entry into Syria and provided them with weapons. Lloyd also knew that the only meaningful communications from Nuri Shaalan had been issued to the Sherif and his sons Feisal and Abdullah, not to European officers, a point he raised with Lynden-Bell: 'There is some idea that there will be a great deal of interviewing of neighbouring Sheikhs, and through them getting into communication with the Hauran, Jebel-Druse, Ruala, and other neighbouring tribes by means of this mission.' If successful, well enough, Lloyd observed:

> but I am not sure that they fully appreciate the difficulties of getting into touch, the reluctance of the Arab chiefs to negotiate with us ahead of our advance &c; but it may be that long experience of work on the spot in these kind of matters makes me too pessimistic.[40]

Some Arab Bureau members were already wary in their estimation of the mission. fforde reported to India that Sykes' area of expertise was believed to be Anglo-French relations more than Arab issues, and Picot 'apparently dreams even of Egypt returning to French domination'.[41] Wilson asked Clayton whether

Sykes and Picot would be addressing the future of Syrian and Arab territories with the Sherif. Wilson did not want 'the settlement of Syria etc.', to be resolved behind the Arabs' back. He believed the Sherif was 'well deserving of the trust of the British Government and I feel sure we shall greatly regret it in the future if we are not quite open and frank with him now over the whole matter' of post-war territorial agreements. For moral but also strategic reasons it was also important that the Sherif's own wishes would be honored in any such agreement:

> [T]he Sherif has considerable spiritual power but it is also essential that his temporal power should also be great and such territories should be included in the 'Independent area' as will not only satisfy the legitimate ambitions of the Arab peoples (the flame of which we have fanned by encouraging the Sherif to revolt and assisting the movement) but will also form a sufficiently large and independent Moslem territory which will to some extent replace the pre-war position of Turkey in the eyes of the Moslem world. [...] We now have a chance which is not likely to occur again of winning the gratitude of millions of Moslems of the Empire.[42]

The Sykes–Picot mission would be a disappointment to all concerned. From 11 April, Sykes and Picot toured Egypt and the Hejaz with the aim of winning support for their post-war guardianship of those lands along the lines set out in the still unacknowledged Sykes–Picot Agreement. Syrian nationalist groups whom Sykes met later in Cairo would denounce any vision of a French destiny for Syria. The original dramatic plan to visit Rualla and Druse representatives in the Hauran was soon abandoned as unfeasible, as Lloyd had anticipated; in any case, Egyptforce's latest attack on Gaza on 1 April failed to win the territory.[43] And then there was the unexpected dissension from the Sherif and the British officers in the Hejaz.

Sykes' official report to the Foreign Office presented one perspective. He met with Feisal on 2 May at Wejh and, 'after much argument', Feisal had finally accepted the 'principle' of the 'Arab Confederation', as it was now called, and 'seemed satisfied'. Sykes met with the Sherif the following day at Jiddah, where the Sherif stressed to him two points: 'unless Arab independence is assured [...] posterity would charge him with assisting in the overthrow of the last Islamic power without setting up another in its place', and second, 'if France annexed Syria he would be open to the charge of breaking faith with the Moslems of Syria by having led them into a rebellion against the Turks in order to hand them over to a Christian Power'. Sykes agreed that these concerns were 'important' but they were remedied by his proposal for an Arab Confederation or State with certain special relationships with Britain and France. The Sherif, he said, 'after a very lengthy argument', finally agreed.[44] Sykes later admitted that his goal in meeting various Arab representatives in the region was 'to manoeuvre [them] without showing them a map or letting them know that there was an actual geographical or detailed agreement, into asking for what we are ready to give them'.[45]

The view was less congratulatory on the ground in the Hejaz. The cunning exhibited by Sykes in his discussions with the Sherif baffled the British officers. Wilson had assumed that Sykes came to represent the interests of both the British government and the Sherif in their negotiations with France. He had taken for granted that the commission 'came expressly to fix things up with the Sherif' regarding Syria, a matter which he did not think would be too complicated.[46] Thus he assumed, along with other British officers in the region, that the mission would obtain the Sherif's consent to the final agreement, which, while not absolutely necessary, would follow proper protocol. The Sherif was the Arabs' legitimate political spokesman and rebel leader, and the obvious candidate for the caliphate/leadership of the future Arab 'state'. It was with this understanding that Wilson initially supported Sykes' meetings with Feisal. On 30 April, aboard the HMS *Northbrook* from Wejh to Jiddah, Wilson had counselled Feisal to do as Sykes advised but also to 'state quite plainly what he considered necessary in Syria for the Arab State and argue the matter out', advice which suggested that Wilson assumed Sykes would be trustworthy.[47]

Having witnessed Sykes' complete avoidance of these issues at Jiddah with Feisal and the Sherif, Wilson seemed even more determined to support the Arabs' upcoming military operations in the north. Wilson had recently approved the scheme devised by Newcombe, Joyce and Feisal for moving into the Syrian interior. He described it to Clayton as ambitious but manageable, and, if successful, the new Arab configuration would be invaluable to the British operations in Palestine.[48] On 12 May, Sykes, Wingate, Wilson, Lloyd and Clayton held a meeting in Cairo to approve the new plan. Wilson distinguished himself further by proposing a significant change: Feisal's army should be released to move immediately into Syria without the precondition of cutting the Hejaz railway or taking Medina. They were the only force with access to the interior who were also mobile enough to threaten the Turks' lines of communication into Palestine. All they needed was a safe supply route to a base in the Hauran, probably through Mesopotamia, and Murray's approval.[49] Whether or not Wilson had been persuaded by Lawrence's arguments at Wejh for an immediate northern strategy, he had come to the same conclusion about the waning value of Medina and the greater premium to be placed on an active irregular force in Syria, regardless of the implications for France. His suggestion was not adopted. But Sykes had been confronted with the difference in outlook presented by the stalwart Colonel Wilson towards Britain's Arab partners.

If Wilson or anyone else had hoped to suggest to Sykes that the latter's agenda with Picot was ill-conceived, their instruction was ignored. Sykes and Picot visited Jiddah again on 19 May 1917, with a new agenda. Sykes met with Fuad el Khatib, now the Sherif's Foreign Secretary, onboard the HMS *Northbrook* and asked him to persuade the Sherif to request two particular but unspecified points at the next day's meeting. At the next day's meeting with Sykes, Picot, Wilson, Fuad and Feisal, the Sherif produced a note for Fuad to read which contained these two points. Both points, Wilson immediately recognized, were intended to confine the Arab state to the peninsula. The Sherif asked that

Sykes and Picot grant that (1) 'relations between the Arab Government and France should be the same in Syria as those between the King and British in Baghdad' (Wilson later wondered whether 'Syria' meant Greater Syria, including Damascus, or only the Levant coast), and (2) 'the Missions being sent by Syrians to N & S America, Europe, etc., should not be sent under his protection'.[50] Sykes and Picot were delighted with the 'agreement'. But Wilson, present only as an observer, felt extremely distressed at the new equation of 'the French in Syria as the British were in Baghdad', and worried that:

> the Sherif, one of the most courteous of men, absolutely loyal to us and with complete faith in Great Britain, was verbally agreeing to a thing which he would never agree to if he knew our interpretation of what the Iraq situation is to be.

Wilson expressed his concerns candidly to Clayton in a private and secret letter:

> From George Lloyd I gather that Baghdad will almost certainly be British, if this is so then I consider that we have not played a straightforward game with a courteous old man who is as Sykes agrees, one of Great Britain's most sincere and loyal admirers, for it means that the Sherif [consented] verbally to Syria being practically French which I feel sure he never meant to do.[51]

Wilson's worries deepened after hearing from Newcombe that Fuad and Feisal had said it was Picot who concocted the equation of 'the French in Syria as the British in Baghdad' during the previous day's private meeting. The Sherif at first refused, saying 'I withdraw because I am not anxious to make a Kingdom but I wanted to save the critical situation of the Mohammedan world and join a cause which I believe is honourable'. But Sykes persuaded Fuad to obtain the Sherif's agreement. Fuad explained that he had only agreed to do so because it seemed Sykes must have 'some very good plan of proposal which will enable the formation of a whole Arab Empire to be realised' if everyone followed his advice.[52] Moreover, the Sherif declared himself to be reassured by a letter received from McMahon the previous year which conveyed a guarantee by the British government that 'Iraq was promised to the Arabs except Basra about which there was some money arrangement'. Neither Feisal nor Fuad had seen the letter, but it was now worrying to Fuad that 'the King has a fixed idea of the meaning of this letter which may possibly differ from that held by the British Government and hence also from the interpretation given by the French Government'.[53]

The Hejaz staff reacted angrily to the possibility that their good faith was possibly being manipulated or exploited by Sykes and Picot. Wilson complained to Clayton that he had 'all along been a strong advocate of being as open as possible with the Sherif' but that that attitude was clearly not shared by Sykes and as such Sykes had betrayed the personal trust and commitment of British representatives:

> [B]y urging the Sherif to agree to the formula re France and Syria Sykes has undoubtably taken a very heavy responsibility on his shoulders and if I had known (at the meeting) that the Sherif had only agreed to the formula on Sykes urgent persuasion I should certainly have tried hard to get some principal facts re our position in Iraq stated at the meeting.[54]

Two months earlier, Wilson had heard from Lawrence that Abdullah believed the Arabs' future was 'assured with Syria and Iraq irrevocably pledged to the Arabs by Great Britain's signed agreements'.[55] The spectacle of the Sherif's now being toyed with by Sykes and Picot while the Sherif vouched for Great Britain's trustworthiness to the Arab public and even, on occasion, to his own sons so disturbed Wilson that he concluded his report with a threat to resign if the deception was not remedied:

> Is the Sherif living in a fools paradise? If so he will have a very rude awakening and once his trust in Great Britain has gone we will not get it back again [...] if there is any chance of the Sherif being under any delusion about what he has verbally agreed to, the matter requires serious and immediate attention. [...] If we are not going to see the Sherif through and we let him down badly after all his trust in us the very 'enviable' post of Pilgrimage Officer at Jeddah will be vacant because I certainly could not remain.[56]

Wilson's and Newcombe's discomfort at the widening schisms in official policy were reinforced by Fuad's reiteration that 'all people in Mecca look on Faisal as their hero because he is destined for Syria and all enthusiasm for Medina has died as being a "fait accompli"'. Fuad visited Cairo in person to ask that Sykes and Picot be sent back to speak truthfully to the Sherif. If they did not, the Sherif might have to renounce the Allies and leave the Hejaz with his family, a threat that worried Wilson greatly, as he reported to Cairo.[57]

Newcombe's report on Sykes' behaviour was equally dark. He accused Sykes of purposeful manipulation and bad faith. He described Sykes' intimidation of Fuad and condemned his dissembling with the Sherif who had obviously consented to the two points only because he had 'absolute trust in the British Government'. Newcombe stressed that by agreeing to the terms, the Sherif '*is sacrificing his independence by leaving all things to the British Government*'. The Sherif had never been given a copy of the Sykes–Picot Agreement, 'the full text of which he was apparently told yesterday and asked to give a final decision upon a moment's notice: *while the French and English Governments have had months to consider their point of view*'. Newcombe's remarks suggest that he, too, assumed the future of Syria would be decided by some manner of agreement and consent among British, French and Arab leaders, not by the Great Powers alone.[58]

The British officers' emotional protests at Sykes' and Picot's deception of the Sherif foreshadowed the more public objections made by Lawrence after the war, in print and at the Paris Peace Conference. Indeed, while Lawrence was quietly embarking on his more famous challenge to official policy by targeting Aqaba alone, a second front of resistance had been opened up by his colleagues in the Hejaz. Complaints and warnings of resignation punctuated the correspondence of the officers on the ground. Newcombe warned his superiors that Sykes must return and negotiate honestly on the future of Syria:

> otherwise we are hoodwinking the Sherif and his people and playing a very false game in which officers attached to the Sherif's army are inevitably committed and which I know causes anxiety in several officers' minds: in case we let them [the Arabs] down.

The officers were greatly burdened by their awareness that if the northern Arab leaders could not believe in the promise of future Arab independence, they would not support Feisal's entrance into Syria. Newcombe remarked angrily that the government should let itself be guided at such times by the region's experts, rather than uninformed diplomats such as Sykes and Picot.[59] Wingate and Murray read the various reports and advised the War Cabinet that they were of one mind on the matter: Sykes and Picot should return.[60] But these appeals were ignored, and the Sherif's remarks to Lawrence later in the year suggested that he continued to be 'hoodwinked' in his misunderstanding of Picot's equation of Syria with Iraq.[61]

Intelligence assessments: Medina fades to Syria

Intelligence collected from human sources, Sigint and Imint during late April, May and June gave little encouragement that the HEF would be leaving Medina or the railway. A valuable informant, Ramadan Effendi, a Bedouin son of a sheikh who became an Ottoman commander of Fakhri Pasha's camel corps outside Medina, deserted and provided detailed intelligence on the Turks' distribution in the Hejaz and Syria. His descriptions of Medina confirmed Humint from other deserters and refugees who attributed the city's endurance to the tenacity of Fakhri Pasha.[62] The Turks were refortifying the Hejaz railway. The railway south of el Ula appeared to hold three battalions of the 55th Regiment, with the main concentration between Hedia and Medina. Medina itself had been largely emptied, with the 42nd Regiment's remaining three battalions dispersed between Bir el-Mashi and Bir Ali and the outer environs. The reinforced garrison at Medain Salih had been joined by a mule-mounted company from Tebuk, although it was rumoured that an Arab staff officer sympathetic to the Sherif's cause might be in their party.[63] Reports, possibly inflated, were picked up that as many as two or three trains still passed through Medain Salih station each day, defended by armoured trucks and carrying out supply and evacuation duties. The railway's only supplies of water north of Medain Salih were said to be at el-Muadhdham, Qalat el-Akhdar and Tebuk.[64] The Turks were later found to be blowing up most of the other wells near the track to deter Arab raiders.[65]

Hogarth despaired of the Arabs' lack of progress around Medina. He wrote an article for *The Arab Bulletin* to mark the Revolt's first anniversary which attributed the tribesmen's 'comparative ease' in pushing the Turks out of Mecca and the coast primarily to their opponent's isolation in the peninsula, an exposed 300-mile line of communication with Damascus and a substandard supply of munitions and equipment. The Arabs' failure in June and July 1916 to take Medina or the crucial Sultani Road he ascribed to the Bedouins' being 'simply *guerrileros*, and not of good quality at that'. The now hastily trained Arab force assembled from tribesmen, Ottoman Arab PoWs and army deserters, Syrian refugees and a handful of townspeople was as unlikely as the preceding Bedouins to capture Medina, its main outposts at Bir el-Mashi or Manjur, or the railway. The British policymakers could only hope that the HEF never recovered its supply of men, live transport or munitions.[66]

Hogarth was not alone in his frustration over Medina.[67] Ali's command around Medina seemed to be sliding backwards. Joyce complained that 'unless a competent commander takes over charge of the operations, it appears to me very doubtful if any important military success will be obtained'. The tribesmen were reluctant to attack fellow Muslims, and the Syrian officers' obstreperousness was mounting. Joyce questioned whether Britain's unending supply of arms and money was dissuading the Arab fighters from pushing towards a conclusion. Relations between British staff and the sheikhs and tribesmen were growing somewhat easier, he admitted, but the Egyptian troops were still unwelcome: 'old prejudices are slow in changing', he warned.[68] In the meantime, Fakhri rearranged his defences as best he could. Intelligence in late May, most likely from Sigint, suggested that he was reinforcing his artillery sections and moving companies from Bir el-Mashi to the railway. The Arab Bureau hoped that the Arabs' harassment would disrupt traffic from both directions.[69]

But the political effect swelling behind the Arabs' stance against the Turks, regardless of its ambiguities and cycles, was undeniable. The Arabs' small-scale raids along the length of railway between Medina and Tebuk and the assistance from bombing sorties by the Flight at Wejh continued to be effective. In mid-May, Abdullah's men raided the station at Toweira while another party attacked at Dizad station. Subsequent intelligence showed that the Turks had been forced to reinforce the Muadhdham district with troops from Palestine in response, and were starting to run short of rails and other materials. On 16 May, a British plane dropped bombs on the main building at el Ula station and on a freight train; the pilot noted that the garrison had dwindled over the last month.[70] In late May, Arabs near el Matalli station attacked sixty Turks, killing the commander and inflicting many casualties, capturing rifles and prisoners.[71] By June, intelligence from refugees suggested that the HEF was preparing to deport the rest of the civilian population from Medina, allowing only the poorest classes to remain who couldn't pay for passage north. Because of the hazards for the trains, many deportees had to walk to the city limits and hope to be picked up by Bedouin. The deportees arrived at Zeid's and Ali's camps and provided regular information on the besieged city.[72]

At last, in early June, the Bedouin Arabs' guerrilla tactics punched a hole in the Turks' eastern supply lines through central Arabia. A pro-Turk Arab chief from the central region, Ibn Leilah, and a contingent of Turkish troops tried to shepherd a large caravan of supplies from Hail to Medina under the protection of Ibn Rashid and his Shammar. But outside Medina, Ibn Leilah and Ibn Rashid were surprised by Prince Zeid and a force of Harb tribesmen. During the battle, those two great chiefs of central Arabia fled into hiding, and handed Zeid a great moral victory. Zeid returned with hundreds of prisoners, artillery and 3,000 loaded baggage camels.[73] The propaganda value of his success was even more fortunate. Reports soon arrived that several Shammar chiefs such as the Abdah had left Ibn Rashid's sphere in order to join the Sherif's forces.[74] Feisal also received letters from two paramount chiefs of the Amarat tribe (Anazeh), including Fahad bin Hadhdhal, paramount chief of the south-western Anazeh, and from Ajeimi Saadun of Iraq pledging support as soon as he arrived in their territory.[75] The British authorities in Cairo politely declined an invitation by the Sherif to include a British reply to these offers, out of consideration that 'independent Arabs' might react with suspicion.[76]

Intelligence that projected promising conditions for a Syrian insurgency, especially around the Aqaba district, undercut the value of Medina still further. The deserter informant Ramadan Effendi confirmed Cairo's earlier intelligence reports that 10,000 Arab deserters from the Ottoman army were hiding at Jebel Druse and many more at Nablus. He believed that only two Turkish infantry companies remained at Ma'an, their mounted troops having been transferred to Gaza to face the British. The Ma'an hospitals were full with sick and wounded. The line between Ma'an and Deraa was now defended by a single railway battalion, and the Beni Sakhr around those two stations were 'very strong and anti-Turk'.[77] Humint from an Ottoman prisoner whom the Arab Bureau described as 'a good source' described the severe shortages afflicting the Syrian railways, engines and rolling stock.[78] Other intelligence sources confirmed Ramadan Effendi's claims. The tribes around Aqaba and Ma'an who had already claimed to favour the Sherif were already undertaking small-scale operations against Turkish posts. In late May, intelligence, probably Sigint, revealed that a contingent of Beni Atiyah occupied Ramleh station, fifty miles east of Aqaba, while another section raided a Turkish labour corps in Wadi Ethil, south of Tebuk. Also around Aqaba, the Amran section of the Huweitat under Ibn Jazi was said to be negotiating with the Beni Atiyah for joint attacks on the remaining posts between Ma'an and Aqaba.[79] Other lesser Syrian chiefs, including some among the Druse, were also promising to support the Sherif and assist the British advance. Intelligence from the agent 'Maurice' stated that the German and Turkish authorities felt such great anxiety over this rise in rebel activity that the Germans were sending agents to the Anazeh and Rualla in order to shut down any progress towards the Sherif. Only Nuri Shaalan's son, Nawaf, not for the first time, was rumoured to be wavering towards the Turks, and the DMI urged Murray to do everything he could to make sure that Nuri Shaalan did not join the enemy.[80]

Feisal tried to keep open as many options as possible for a transfer to Syria. He continued to prepare the northern scheme into Druse country with Wilson and Newcombe, yielding to their insistence that the railway be cut first and Medina isolated. Under this scheme, a coordinated advance by Feisal's army and the Farhan and Anazeh tribes, Abdullah's force with the Egyptian escort, and Newcombe with trained Arab fighters from Wejh would launch simultaneous attacks against the stations of el Ula, Bedia and Medain Salih around 31 May 1917. Feisal and Newcombe also agreed to two additional actions that would be significant. First, a little-remarked upon assignment for Lawrence and Auda around the Ma'an area: it was agreed that, concurrent with the railway assault, supplies of food and munitions for 1,000 men and transport animals would move up to a new supply base at Jefer, twenty-five miles east of Ma'an, under the charge of Auda abu Tayi and Lawrence. The depôt would enable Feisal's entire party to move to Kasr el Azrak and begin demolition attacks against the northern Syrian railway, alongside the Druse. Lawrence was also to consult with the local Beni Sakhr and set up a main line of communication for Feisal from Azrak to the west, to the British bases at el Arish. From these points, it would appear that Feisal was engaging in a strategic gamble, pursuing two schemes at once. He had dispatched Nasir's secret expedition to Aqaba and then prepared a second scheme to enter Syria, which not only provided an alibi for the first but had British support, and which would be in place if Nasir's expedition failed.

Feisal's other request concerned targets. He was now convinced after talking with Lawrence of the necessity of holding Aqaba. He told Newcombe that he wanted to launch a seaborne attack at Aqaba using Arab troops only, without French involvement. The landing would occur after the railway had been cut, but Arab fighters had to compose the force for 'both political and tactical' reasons, to convince the Beni Sakhr, Huweitat and Druse chiefs of the campaign's seriousness. Feisal said he had already sent orders to the Huweitat under Auda abu Tayyi and to the Amran tribe to clear the Turks from Wadi Ithm; a statement that again described Auda's actual movements without revealing the true context of his activity with Nasir and Lawrence. Newcombe apparently never guessed at any alternative operation in the Ma'an area. Feisal would collect 1,500 Meccan fighters at Wejh harbour by 24 June for transport to Aqaba. Once Aqaba was taken, the 'Turks would not move towards [Aqaba] from Ma'an though a hostile country, any more than they did from El Ula after Wedj was taken, though water was ample'. Once the 5,000 rifles and 1,000 boxes of ammunition stored at Dhaba and the 10,000 rifles and 1,000 boxes of ammunition due from Egypt arrived at Aqaba, Nuri Shaalan's Bedouin would 'start raids in Syria in order to get the necessary excitement and expectation amongst the people'. Feisal's army at Jebel Druse would raid between Damascus and Deraa, while another force at Tadmor (140 miles northeast of Damascus) would raid the Homs–Hama district.

The Turks would soon be pinned to the railway in defensive positions. Druse tribesmen and deserters would be enlisted to form a conventional force, while local people conducted smaller raids on Turkish posts. Newcombe approved the plan to Cairo, including the seaborne assault on Aqaba, and said he felt confident now that the port 'will be easy to take' even with untrained Arab fighters. His report, submitted in the aftermath of Sykes' and Picot's tour, reiterated that in order to bring the campaign successfully into Syria (an aim he appeared to take for granted), Feisal 'must have a political propoganda [*sic*] which will induce the people to risk their lives. It must be a clear statement, showing that they will be fighting for an Arab Govt'. Feisal added another request for more rifles and pushed his anticipated arrival date at Jefer to the end of July, possibly to give Nasir's actual expedition more time.[81]

London's chronically confused policy towards the Arab uprising meant that more than one operational policy was now being pursued at the same time. The programme discussed by Wilson and Newcombe and the Cairo staff anticipated some of what Sherif Nasir's expedition set out to do, but with the important difference that Nasir's party meant to operate only in alliance with other Arabs, while Feisal's army would be moving in conjunction with and with support from the British navy and Egyptforce. Nevertheless, both strategies aimed to bring the next base for the Arab campaign into Syria. Due to the unusually responsible intelligence and liaison roles assumed by Lawrence, Wilson and Newcombe with the Arab leaders, these officers were working alongside the mainsprings of the Revolt and as such, felt motivated to launch active initiatives and bear the repercussions for high policy in a manner unthinkable in any other theatre of war at the time. Lawrence, Nasir and Audah were riding in secret on a mission to attack Aqaba at the same time as Feisal's plans to begin a northern campaign with a force expected to reach 15,000-strong continued to be blocked out by Wilson, Newcombe and the Residency. Concurrently, Sykes and Picot were touring the Red Sea region in the van of a concealed European agenda for Syria.[82] Adding to the surreality, the Sherif assisted British intelligence with propaganda through leaflet drops and the dispatch of emissaries, informing the Arab communities north of the Hejaz that his negotiations with McMahon had guaranteed Arab independence after the war.[83] And Clayton, in his capacity as CGS for the Hejaz, reminded Wingate that British forces should maintain pre-eminent in any operation at the port for it was most likely that 'after the war Akaba may be of considerable importance to the future defence scheme of Egypt'. If an Arab force occupied Aqaba, he anticipated, it 'might well result in the Arabs claiming that place hereafter'.[84]

Humint obtained by Feisal and British military intelligence in early June suggested that the situation around Aqaba was in flux. For a while, local Huweitat sections harassed Turkish outposts around Aqaba and Wadi Ithm. Thirty Ageyl tribesmen deserted the Turks and rode to Feisal at Wejh, reporting that the Turks now stood at only one and a half battalions in Wadi Ithm, although other Turkish patrols continued in the interior.[85] Sinai intelligence confirmed this activity when ten Turkish soldiers fleeing Aqaba stated that 100 Arabs had deserted to fight with the Sherif.[86] Within the week, however, the Huweitat's gains had been reversed: an Arab eye-witness described as 'reliable' reported that fifty Ottoman infantry with 300 Arab irregulars had occupied Aqaba. His sighting of 'a number of "foreigners" [...] wearing peaked caps' in tents on the beach was understood by the Arab Bureau to be of a German naval detachment sent in support; British intelligence had already learned, most likely through Sigint, that such a force under German officers had been dispatched from Galilee in April.[87]

The best laid plans: political and military intelligence on Aqaba

The nearing Aqaba campaign would be a triumph of intelligence in its strategy, identification of feasible targets and tactics of deception; in the resiliency of its leadership despite unexpected set-backs and competing goals; and in the self-sufficiency of its execution. Sherif Nasir's expedition of forty men rode into central Syria and turned towards Ma'an and Aqaba, securing its passage through the continual collection of intelligence and local negotiation. The efficiency and comparative coherence of this operation as well as its recruitment successes with Nuri Shaalan were a testament to the political judgement of Nasir, Auda and Lawrence. The forging of these Syrian contacts without British or French participation seems to have been a possibility that had not occurred to Egyptforce or the War Committee, who continued to look forward to making those arrangements themselves. In his meetings with Syrian leaders, Lawrence would maintain the British government's trustworthiness with regard to the Arabs' future independence; despite its obvious conflicts with the Sykes–Picot Agreement, Lawrence believed the capture of Aqaba might in turn negate all that went before. 'The Arabs needed Akaba; firstly, to extend their front, which was their tactical principle; and, secondly, to link up with the British' who would provide 'food, money, guns, advisers'. Then from Aqaba the Arabs could establish their value by acting 'as the right wing of the Allies in the conquest of Palestine and Syria' and take the territory they needed, to 'assert the Arabic-speaking peoples' desire or desert of freedom and self-government'.[88]

On 9 May 1917 the expedition left Wejh and crossed the railway at Dizad to ride north-eastward up Wadi Fejr and then Wadi Sirhan, the northern passage into Nuri's Rualla territory where Auda's Abu Tayyi's Huweitat were waiting. Auda rode to Jauf to see Nuri, bringing £6,000 in gold for the chief's continued indulgence of their presence, while Nasir, Lawrence and the Damascene, Nesib el Bekri, acting as Political Officer, began recruiting fighters in Wadi Sirhan. By 18 June, the camp numbered over 700 Huweitat, Rualla, Shererat and Kawakiba (Anazeh) tribesmen. The fittest 500 embarked for Aqaba.[89]

The political complexity, practical and rhetorical, of moving the Sherif's revolt into Syria soon became apparent. Syrian officers with the Sherif had been pressing him to fulfil his obligations to Syrian nationalists, although the advantages for both Syrians and Hejazis of combining forces against the Turks, and perhaps even the Europeans, had been well argued. For Syrians such as Nesib el Bekri, obligations to the Hashemites ended when the Revolt entered Wadi Sirhan. To him, the Aqaba scheme was unnecessary. He wanted to take his share of arms and money and muster the Druse and Rualla, not the Huweitat, and launch attacks against the main railway junctions at Deraa and Damascus. Lawrence counselled Nasir and Auda strongly against this course. Aqaba was indispensable if they were going to anchor an extended Arab front with a new supply and communication base; without it, the Arabs would be stranded in the interior. Holding Aqaba would also prevent the Turks from using it to attack Suez and el Arish, collapsing the British right flank and threatening all future Anglo-Arab operations in Syria with it. Moreover, Nesib's action would rob the Aqaba party of the element of surprise and risk the Turks' retaliation, and Lawrence did not want 'even a half-baked rising [around Deraa], to spoil our future material'. Auda and Nasir agreed. Nesib declared himself independent, and Lawrence released him – though not before recovering most of Nesib's portion of gold by promising to send along any funds left over after the occupation of Aqaba.[90]

Nesib's arguments had unsettled the expedition's leadership, all the same, and a divisive debate over targets in Syria followed. Lawrence volunteered to resolve the issue decisively with further intelligence. Privately, Nesib's 'optimism' had also forced him to consider the 'liberation of Syria' as a nearer possibility than assumed and he wanted to adjust the campaign. He rode out of Nebk on 4 June with two companions. His aims were twofold: to reconnoitre the area up to Damascus and construct an intelligence profile of the districts; and to undercut Nesib's influence by meeting with the northern leaders, including members of *al-Fatat*, and giving them information about Nasir's and Feisal's campaigns before Nesib began his propaganda. On 8 June, Lawrence arrived at Tadmor and visited Sheikh Dhami of the Kawakiba Anazeh. Dhami refused to be reconciled to the Huweitat but expressed interest in the demolition operations and rode out with Lawrence, bringing twenty-five men. They rode west to Ras Baalbek and on 10 June, dynamited a small bridge. Lawrence then rode south to el Gabbun, three miles outside Damascus, and on 13 June he met in secret with Ali Rida al-Rikabi, whom he described in his debriefing report as 'the well-known Turkish Engineer General, President of the Syrian branch of the Arab Secret Society', i.e. *al-Fatat*. After the outbreak of war, the Turks removed al-Rikabi from the Ottoman army. He became mayor of Damascus until February 1917, when the Turks decided he still harboured nationalist loyalties and removed him from that post as well. He told Lawrence that he now had only 500 Turkish gendarmes and three unarmed labour battalions, and so 'was not in a position to demonstrate his real feelings unaided'.[91] Lawrence set out again and made contact with the Leja head sheikh, who agreed to a 'provisional plan'. He then rode to Salkhad and met with the leader of the Druse, Hussein Bey el Atrash. The Druse had conditions for joining the uprising, but Lawrence believed these points offered 'a basis for negotation'. Finally, Lawrence rode west to Azrak where he met in person with Nuri Shaalan and Nawaf. Nuri emphasized that he would not act unless the Druse did, also. Until then he would remain silently pro-Sherif and, according to Lawrence, 'playing double till we require him'. Lawrence returned to Nebk on 18 June.[92]

Reflecting the truism that deception works most effectively when it is employed 'to fit in with and magnify its target's own preconceptions',[93] Lawrence decided to exploit the inevitable rumours following Nesib's defection north and Nasir and Auda's progress from Wadi Sirhan. The Aqaba party's movement towards the railway could not be kept entirely secret, as he wrote later, for 'we lived by preaching to the local people', but Lawrence made sure he 'dropped hints' during his journey north to suggest that the main Arab force was heading to Jebel Druse, east of Deraa, not Ma'an. Nesib, who would be moving 'noisily' in the north, would confirm the impression. Nuri Shaalan sent the Turks word of the same.[94] The Turks, already nervous for Ma'an and Aqaba, had tried to preempt the Arabs' making a base near the railway junction. Nasir's party arrived at Bair on 30 June, seventy-five miles northeast of Ma'an, and found that three of the four wells had been blown up. A scout sent on to Jefer reported that all seven wells there had been dynamited, too. The expedition had enough water at Bair for the time being to continue visitations with the local Huweitat. Lawrence took the opportunity to continue 'a prolonged campaign of deception, to convince [the Turks] that our objective lay nearer to Damascus'. To buttress the impression that they were still camped near Azrak and oriented towards Deraa, Lawrence and Zaal, Auda's nephew, carried out raids to the north of Ma'an.[95] Around this time, as Lawrence understood it, Newcombe helpfully staged a classic ruse of disinformation. He deliberately dropped documents for the Turks outside Wejh that contained details of an Arab plan to march up the Wadi Sirhan to Jefer and then Tadmor, from which base a large Arab force would strike at points around Damascus and Aleppo. The papers mentioned an advance guard for Jefer, purportedly Lawrence's and Auda's assignment to arrange the supply depôt. 'The Turks took the documents very seriously', Lawrence wrote, 'and chained an unfortunate garrison in Tadmor till the end of the war, much to our advantage'.[96] Shortly afterward, the Jazi Huweitat sent word to Nasir that the sabotage at Jefer might not have been complete. The Arab party moved to Jefer and, unbeknownst to the Turks, dug out one of the wells. A messenger from Nuri Shaalan arrived soon afterwards to confirm that the Turks did believe the main Arab force had been trapped at Wadi Sirhan. A relative was escorting their search parties in a long bogus chase.[97]

The Turks were not the only authorities misled by disinformation about the true aims of Nasir's and Auda's mission. The British authorities at Cairo and Wejh received only glimpses of their movements from fragments of hearsay and then Sigint, in effect relying on the reports of others for news. A sherif at Dhaba wrote Feisal on 24 June 1917 about a northern visitor's claim that Nasir, Auda and Lawrence were travelling towards Jebel Druse and had blown up 'a very high bridge near Maan'. Feisal reported this news to the Arab Bureau, but added that it was 'only an Arab rumour and possibly not true'.[98] It may not have been strictly true; the raids on Minifer and Atwi were not quite near Ma'an, and did not occur until 24 and 27 June respectively; but the rumour did mention the main figures and the Druses' support. As part of their deception, Lawrence's and Zaal's raiding party had spread disinformation that a main force was camped at Azrak, south of Jebel-Druse. Lawrence's ride through this region on his secret tour north would have provoked similar rumours.[99] As a consequence the Turks, and thus British intelligence in Egypt who were intercepting their communications, knew that some vague activity was occurring both to the northeast of Ma'an and amongst the Huweitat to the west, but no one guessed that any of these flashes represented anything outside of ordinary inter-tribal disturbances.

On 30 June, a flying column of Huweitat detached from Nasir's force at Jefer to join the Dhumaniyeh Huweitat in an attack against a Turkish gendarme post at Fuweilah, seventeen miles southwest of Ma'an en route to Aba el Lissan. The Turks repulsed the raid and massacred a nearby Huweitat village as punishment. The Dhumaniyeh retaliated by charging a nearby Turkish post and killing almost everyone (later PoW statements suggested that at least one Turkish survivor made it to Ma'an with this information). Informed of these events at Jefer by a Huweitat messenger the next day, Lawrence concluded from the Turks' revenge against the villagers that the Turks must have believed the Arabs' initial attack was 'only an ordinary tribal affray', substantiating Nuri Shaalan's claim that the Turks had been fooled in Wadi Sirhan.[100] Hoping to sustain the deception and also draw attention away from the Huweitat action at Fuweilah, Nasir sent out another diversionary detachment northwest of Ma'an to strike at three points – Tafileh, Shobek with its large camel herds, and Wadi Musa – while his main force demolished points in the railway around Ghadir el Haj station, twelve miles south of Ma'an. He and Lawrence reasoned that Ghadir el Haj's telegraph message to Ma'an for help would take priority over any message arriving from Fuweilah, and it would be forgotten. The Arab force would then be free to ride on to Wadi Ithm.[101]

The plan encountered some surprises. The main force headed west after Ghadir el Haj, but were met by Huweitat messengers from Fuweilah who warned them that the Turks had occupied Abu el Lissan, twenty miles west of Ghadir el Haj.[102] Auda and Nasir joined forces with the Dhumaniyeh on 2 July and led a massive charge against the Turks at Abu el Lissan, who immediately surrendered. The Arab fighters ignored their pleas and tried to massacre the battalion. Three hundred Turks were killed before urgent intercessions by Lawrence and Nasir spared the remaining 160, including the battalion commander, whom they took prisoner.[103] Lawrence's interrogation of the commander and the other prisoners revealed that this detachment – the 4th Battalion, 174th Regiment, just arrived from the Black Sea – was the only reinforcement unit that Ma'an could spare, as its own defence now relied on a mere two companies. The prospect of such a weakened target, combined with the Arab party's looming shortage of food, threatened to distract some of the Huweitat. But Nasir, Auda and Lawrence were agreed that it would be impossible for their force to hold Ma'an without regular troops, more munitions and more money. Aqaba had to remain the critical target. Nasir and Auda wrote to the Huweitat sheikhs along the Gulf of Aqaba to announce their advance, and ordered them to seize the nearest Turkish garrison. They then marched towards Guweira, closing in on Wadi Ithm, while sending a detachment to raid Mreigha back towards Ma'an as another feint, taking the entire garrison.[104]

Cairo continued to pick up intelligence on the shifting Arab–Turkish front above Aqaba through several sources. The patrolling HMS *Slieve Foy* stopped at the small port of Magnah on the Gulf of Aqaba and was greeted in a friendly fashion by the local Arabs, who reported that the Arabs of the interior and to the north were now also friendly towards the British. The captain wired the information back to Egypt and sailed on to observe the port of Aqaba, where he was surprised to find the beach entirely deserted. The Turkish garrison had in fact taken refuge in the cliffs above the beach. The captain, who knew nothing of this, bombarded the empty post for good measure and unwittingly drove the Turks inland where they took sanctuary at the post of el Khadra. Around this time, another 'report' was received that the Sherif of Muweilah was 'assembling Arabs for the purpose of attacking Aqaba'; the captain was asked to verify the claim, if possible.[105]

The last stage of the Turks' occupation around Aqaba was approaching. In the high ground behind the cliffs, with the help of a Turkish PoW, Nasir and Auda wrote the Turkish commanders hunkered at the remaining posts of Guweira, el Kethira and el Khadra, and demanded their surrender. The garrison at Guweira, seeing they were surrounded by Ibn Jad's Huweitat, gave up their post. El Kethira was disabled in part by Lawrence's foreknowledge of the following night's eclipse; the Huweitat timed their attack with the darkness and captured that garrison, as well.[106] El Khadra, the last post before Aqaba, held the 300-strong garrison driven back by the fortuitous British naval fire days earlier. Smaller local tribes and Huweitat sections heeded the written requests by Nasir and Auda, and pinned el Khadra down until the Aqaba party arrived. Nasir and Lawrence rode immediately between the hundreds of Arab fighters and the Turks this time, to prevent any unnecessary bloodshed. The Turks surrendered at once, declaring themselves 'anxious to go on fighting foreigners and Christians till they dropped, but with no intention of adding a Moslem enemy to the powers already against them'.

On 6 July 1917, Nasir, Auda, Lawrence and 2,000 Arabs rode down to touch the sea at Aqaba. Their 600 prisoners included forty Ottoman officers and a German engineer. The German and Turk prisoners were transferred to Egypt, while most of the Arabs and Syrians stayed to join the Arab army. In total, 700 Turks were killed in the Aqaba campaign, and four Arabs.[107] An irregular Arab contingent had seized one of the key ports of the region from both Turkish and European hands, and altered the balance of power in the war.

Aftermath: intelligence revelations

It was only by raiding the enemy's wireless communications that British intelligence learned there had been any significant operations occurring between Ma'an and Aqaba. The Hejaz railway was still intact, Medina was still under Turkish control and there had been no Allied assistance, but an all-Arab tribal force had taken and occupied Aqaba and all the inland roads to Ma'an, in the name of the Sherif. Cairo assembled various items of intelligence. During the first week of July a statement was received, almost certainly from Sigint, claiming that the Huweitat around the station of Ma'an had 'broken into active revolt and have already caused considerable embarrassment to the enemy'. Cairo also learned that tribesmen had cut Turkish communications from Ma'an to Akaba with the attacks against Fuweilah and Mreigha. Various reports arrived describing disparate Arab attacks, including the demolition of rail and telegraph lines. Other intelligence, most likely Sigint, stated that the Arabs had reopened the wells at Bair and now 'appeared' to have based their headquarters there.[108]

The Arab Bureau's hesitant response to these intelligence receipts emphasized how independently Lawrence and Feisal as well had operated during those weeks. The Arab Bureau did not know the full extent of the Huweitat's activities or whether other tribes were involved; they could only note that 'the results already achieved have proved a very timely diversion and must have distracted the attention of the Turks from the Arab preparations further south', i.e. Feisal's activities around el Ula.[109] At the end of June, Feisal relayed news, probably brought by messenger, that Auda was receiving adherents at Azrak with Nasir, Nesib el Bekri and Lawrence: these details matched the disinformation spread by Nuri to cover the Aqaba expedition. Feisal had also received news, confirming earlier Sigint, that the Turks had tried to stop Auda's army from reaching the railway by destroying the wells at Jefer.[110] These expanded references to the effect of Auda's and Lawrence's movements must have confused Cairo: Newcombe's plan had suggested that Auda and Lawrence would be guarding Feisal's stores at Jefer in four weeks' time; and there had certainly been no discussion of Auda's party going to Azrak or negotiating with Nuri before Feisal's arrival. The Arab Bureau tentatively tried to connect Auda's mission with news from other quarters on activity around Ma'an, but professed complete ignorance as to the whereabouts of Lawrence, whose participation at Azrak they decided was unlikely but who seemed to be operating in some capacity with Nasir, Nesib and the Huweitat, 'whose activity without this direction it is difficult to account for'.[111]

A full account was at last provided by Lawrence himself, who passed through Suez on 9 July 1917. He wrote his first report on the Arab exploits around Ma'an and Aqaba at the Canal before continuing on to Cairo the next day. He posted a more detailed account to the Arab Bureau in the first weeks of August 1917.[112] The acclaim given to Lawrence in aftermath of the Aqaba campaign was extraordinary for an intelligence officer, especially in light of his having clearly blurred the lines separating responsibility for intelligence, operational policy and the conduct of operations itself. Wingate sent an encomium on Lawrence's achievement to General Robertson:

> The fact, of which he was well aware, that the Turks had put a reward of 5,000 *l.* on his head considerably enhances the gallantry of his exploit. He was moving among a highly venal population, of whom some at least were definitely hostile. In spite of this, he seized every opportunity of damaging the railway, interviewing tribesmen and obtaining information regarding the country and its inhabitants and finally directed successful operation in

> Ma'an region, the result of which was that 700 Turks were destroyed and 600 captured. I strongly recommend him for an immediate award of the Victoria Cross, and submit this recommendation is amply justified by his skill, pluck and endurance.[113]

Lawrence was now clearly identified as the key to Britain's success with the Arab forces, despite his junior rank to the officer soon appointed commander of the British forces fighting with the Arabs in Syria, Lieutenant Colonel Joyce. Allenby considered Lawrence to be an expert judge of intelligence material as well as a leading guerrilla commander, whose opinion on the formulation of strategy in Syria should be taken as essential by the British government in London.[114] The capture of Aqaba brought Lawrence a promotion to the rank of major for the coming operations alongside Egyptforce, and a Companion of the Order of the Bath, ostensibly for the operations leading to the occupation of Aqaba but actually for the secret reconnaissance mission to the north, which could not be publicized.[115]

This is not to say that the independent, even surreptitious political aspect of Lawrence's action was addressed or reconciled publicly with British policy, inchoate as it still was. Allenby, who was particularly happy with Lawrence's military results, insisted to London that Lawrence's operations in the Ma'an-Aqaba region were not politically problematic because they were 'outside the French sphere' and the French political officers were being kept informed. If Lawrence ever did act in the French zone (i.e. north of Jerusalem – the Sykes–Picot Agreement designated the south-Syrian region a British sphere of influence), Allenby promised, the French Mission would 'be informed as fully *as military exigencies permit*'.[116] The French military attaché tried to obtain a personal guarantee about Lawrence's future activities but Allenby refused to be swayed from this military argument, as he later wrote to the CIGS: 'Lawrence must not be hampered while engaged on delicate and dangerous tasks *which are purely tactical*, which may be of great importance to the success of my operations, and which he alone can carry through.'[117]

Throughout the first year of the Revolt, Lawrence, Wilson, Lloyd, Newcombe and even Joyce had warned the British authorities in Cairo and London that the Arabs were fighting the Turkish army because the Sherif had promised they were fighting for their independence and Great Britain backed their aims. The occupation of Aqaba affirmed the promise for the Arab Revolt's extension into Syria because its execution – apart from Lawrence – had been entirely Arab and its target a genuine territorial asset. As Antonius observed, the Arabs' leading propaganda message in Syria after the occupation of Aqaba was that through the joining of purpose between McMahon and the Sherif and the launch of the Revolt, the Arabs' aim of independence was adopted into the policy goals of the Allies.[118]

This equation of interests served both the Arab leadership, eager to demonstrate their claims of popular support to the Allied powers, and the British authorities, who wanted access to the Syrian/Palestinian battlefield. The potential for 'an adverse political situation [...] to cramp a purely military operation'[119] was, however, anticipated by Allenby when he warned the War Cabinet three months after Aqaba that Britain could not expect the Arabs to fight alongside Britain if behind closed doors the Allied governments were investigating terms for a possible negotiated peace with the CUP which would leave the Turkish government in power after the war. 'Any idea in their [i.e. the Arabs'] minds that we intend separate peace with Turks, with possibility of their being left under Turkish rule, would bring them against us and endanger my communications.'[120] In this way, Nasir's and Auda's occupation of Aqaba with an all-Arab force had fulfilled Lawrence's and the Arab Bureau's most ambitious ideal for this guerrilla strategy: even Allenby was fixing the Arabs' political aspirations for independence into his army's own context for operations.

After the capture of Aqaba, the Arab Revolt in the Hejaz developed into a new manner of campaign extending throughout Syria. Demolition raids against the railway continued in the Hejaz, but Feisal's main base for the Arab army transferred to Aqaba and became the right wing of Allenby's campaign in Palestine and Syria with Lawrence and other intelligence officers such as Clayton and Cornwallis assuming a more prominent role. Eventually bringing Syrian leaders such as Nuri Shaalan himself into their operations, the Arab armies conducted extensive guerrilla attacks against Turkish communication lines, bridge and railway infrastructure and other bases east of the Jordan river, harassing Turkish positions from Ma'an up to Deraa and finally Damascus – which was occupied by Arab and British forces on 1–2 October 1918.[121]

The Aqaba expedition stood as a culmination of the Hejaz campaign and all the debates that had marked the Arab Revolt since its first negotiations in 1915. With the force-multiplying effect of intelligence and intelligence principles, the irregular capability of the Arab fighters could now 'be likened to water', avoiding the proverbial heights while exploiting lowlands to their advantage.[122] The success of these intelligence activities also raised the profile of the intelligence officer to a new and unexpected position of command over the field. The collectors and interpreters of intelligence during the Arab Revolt not only broke with tradition in their initial organization but transcended each new mandate and chain of command. By participating in the conduct of operations and becoming part of their own intelligence subject, they sought to influence Cairo and London by shaping a policy for the Arab campaign that responded principally to intelligence. The fact that their argument managed to persuade so many influential British figures involved in the Hejaz, in telling contrast to the experience of theatres such as the Western Front was, in the longer historical view, perhaps the ultimate triumph for intelligence.

Conclusion

The Arab Revolt was one of the British success stories of the Great War. The abiding image of the revolt as a minor and exotic, even quixotic episode on the periphery of Europe's main theatre has discouraged any serious attention to the unorthodox design of this campaign until now. Because the Middle East sphere was linked so vividly to British adventurism and Great Power political opportunism, its greater significance as a British intelligence and military triumph has been neglected.

Because the asymmetric aspect of the Arab–Turk confrontation was evident from the beginning, many histories have simply let float the impression that a genuine guerrilla strategy in Arabia, so shrewd in retrospect, was inevitable. As this book has shown, the decision to pursue a full irregular campaign in the Hejaz was fitful and vigorously contested. The struggle for British decision-makers – and, even occasionally, for the Arab leaders – was that unlike the players in any other guerrilla model, the Anglo-Arab alliance had other alternatives. The British government had the capacity to employ conventional assets against the Turkish army, land a regular army detachment on the Hejaz coastline and even move inland, however laboriously, against the Turks' main garrison at Medina. Powerful figures in the British establishment urged such a choice. But a different decision was made and the basis for that decision was intelligence. This history has reconstructed the impressive cycle of intelligence and debate that produced a consensus behind conducting an irregular Arab war against the Turks. It argues that it was intelligence rather than existing policy or military convention that persuaded the British intelligence officers in Cairo to attend to the political dimension of the Arabs' uprising, block proposals for regular British reinforcements and focus on the original conflict's military asymmetry.

'Most wars are wars of contact', Lawrence noted, but 'our victory depended on our just use of speed, concealment, accuracy of fire'.[1] The Arab Revolt in its full incarnation was a model of guerrilla 'detachment' in which outgunned, untrained Bedouin fighters attacked Turkish assets and avoided direct combat, rejecting the sacrifice of casualties or indeed any defensive burden for most of the war. 'The corollary of such a rule was perfect "intelligence", so that we could plan in complete certainty.'[2] Intelligence furnished British and Arab leaders with a powerful tool in tactical and strategic planning: foreknowledge of risk and assurance of opportunity. Accurate, targeted intelligence acted as a tactical force-multiplier for the Arab fighters, bolstering their raiding capability, lending protection and opening up opportunities in the field. Humint, Sigint and especially Imint allowed the British to track distant Turkish – and Arab – activity and assess changes on the ground, at times almost instantly. Dominance over the flow of information on Turkish and Bedouin movements, changes in water supplies and road conditions protected the Arab fighters from ill-fated gambles and gave their movement an aura of advantage. Intelligence was as valuable for the conduct of this irregular campaign as the provision of weaponry or funding.

It was the strategic role of intelligence, however, that was even more striking. British intelligence on Arab political activity, Bedouin tribal interests and Arab–Turk relationships persuaded Cairo that the Arab uprising could not be treated as an extension of the British front but had to proceed as a domestic Arab insurrection, without the intrusion of foreign Christian troops. In the majority opinion of British intelligence and like-minded service officers on the ground, the only viable strategy model under these circumstances was a full-scale irregular campaign driven by the domestic political aim of ending Turkish rule. British assistance included an invaluable naval presence along the coast, aerial support, demolition training, armaments and funds, but no landed regular British infantry. The distinction was critical. Guided by intelligence and relying on inter-tribal negotiations rather than foreign troops to open up territory, the Arab forces were able to keep the field, extend their front northwards and anchor a new base of operations at Aqaba. By maintaining their irregular profile, they accrued greater numbers of tribes and territorial control. Their success vindicated Cairo in its resistance to European reinforcements. The multi-dimensional role that intelligence played in supporting the Arab campaign reflected what intelligence expert Herman has described as a '*transformation* effect', where intelligence 'not only optimizes but [...] determines the nature of operations and campaigns as well as outcomes'. As these chapters have shown, the influence of intelligence on the tactical and strategic design of the Arab Revolt distinguished this campaign as the first modern 'intelligence war'.[3]

Theatre challenges

The grinding deadlock of the Western Front would extinguish millions of soldiers' lives, and along with them the nation's presumption of an easy victory against the Central Powers. The War Cabinet believed that a blow to Turkey would remove a well-placed strategic ally of Germany and make the latter vulnerable to defeat from the east. But the Ottoman Empire was a challenging theatre for Britain, for geographical as well as political reasons. Britain's early attempts to breach the Turkish front became bywords for incompetent planning and lack of foresight in a hostile theatre – the disastrous offensives at the Dardanelles, Gallipoli and Kut. The reasons behind the debacles were several but underlying all was Britain's ignorance of the enemy and the ground. Under these circumstances, complacency and overweening insularity regarding intelligence at the command level amounted to a death sentence for many of the soldiers in these battles.

The political status of the Ottoman Empire as the world's last great Islamic power was the other great complication for Britain in light of its own millions of Indian Muslims, most of whom looked to the Turkish Sultan-Caliph as their religious leader. London and its near-eastern colonial administrations feared that the Sultan's call for a *jihad* against the British and Allied powers would create chaos in the empire during wartime. It was thus electrifying for Cairo to learn from defecting Ottoman Arab officers that two powerful secret Arab nationalist societies, *al-Ahd* and *al-Fatat*, had established themselves inside the civilian population and the Ottoman army and were already preparing to overthrow the CUP. The Muslim Arab aspect of such a revolt would certainly impair the Turks' ability to proclaim a true *jihad*. Yet armed insurrection by a genuine political insurgency in the view of many British colonial officials remained a vexatious solution. The War Office and the Indian administration invested heavily in networks of native informants, agents and anti-Turk operatives in western Turkey, the Sinai, and around the Arabian Sea without engaging with the political groups' aspirations. The Sykes–Picot Agreement (1916) and the Balfour Declaration (1917) are only the most well known examples of such expediently misjudged minority interests. By contrast, Cairo's High Commissioner and the intelligence community not only believed that the Arabs were Britain's natural ally but that the intricate political forces inside the Ottoman Empire were the key to its defeat.

From late 1914, Cairo intelligence explored a number schemes for assisting Arab sabotage or resistance against Turkish military positions – at Alexandretta, outside Basra and at Kut. The schemes were daring and inventive, if of dubious quality; each was undermined in its execution or quashed outright by India, or the Foreign Office (on behalf of the French), for encouraging political militancy in Arab territories earmarked for Great Power colonization. By mid-1915, with the death toll mounting in France, the War Cabinet in London decided to give Cairo's proposals greater latitude, though with little expectation of success. London authorized the High Commissioner to pursue negotiations with Sherif Hussein bin Ali of Mecca for an Arab revolt against the Turkish government in return for a vaguely defined promise of Arab independence and the restoration of an Arab Caliphate. When the Sherif launched a successful surprise attack against the Turkish garrisons at Mecca and Jiddah in June 1916, the British government's lack of a coherent political or military policy for the conflict presented the intelligence officers on the ground with a rare opportunity. Because the Bedouin tribes were fighting without sophisticated weaponry, trained troops or even an effective command structure, it was widely assumed that unless assistance was given, the Sherif's flash rebellion would be overrun by a Turkish counter-offensive. Sustaining the Sherif's uprising against the Turks became Cairo's highest priority, second only to the defence of Egypt. In concept and in execution, Cairo's intelligence support for the Arab armies soon showed a more creative treatment of the field than witnessed in almost any other theatre. The intelligence officers' holistic approach to intelligence analysis and strategy produced a policy view on the Hejaz that was independent from the rest of the government.

Regional expertise: the Arab Bureau

Decision-makers in other First World War campaigns would be criticized later for relying on unexamined preconceptions and obsolete military conventions in their planning rather than on proper intelligence from the theatre. In the Arabian theatre, perceptions and convention in 1914 were already in dispute. Influential figures complained about the lack of an agreed policy for all the regional administrations to cover future British aims, territorial authority and the challenge of anti-British *jihadist* propaganda. The War Office's Middle East expert proposed the creation of an 'Islamic Bureau' in London to coordinate British political activity for the Ottoman territories, including counter-enemy propaganda, and intelligence collection on the German–Turk war effort. Britain's intelligence chief in Egypt refined the idea by asking that the bureau not only focus on Arab and Islamic matters but be located in Cairo, in order to instruct London policy-makers from the region itself. Naval Intelligence agreed with Cairo that local expertise was essential. A senior War Office figure with political experience in the Middle East spoke in the same vein when he recommended a special bureau to provide London with 'a more comprehensive and continuous treatment of the various Islamic problems'.[4] Most intelligence sections until this time were organized to provide operational support to military branches, so to design a new intelligence office with a policy-level focus on political and religious affairs, located in the region itself, was highly innovative.[5]

In early 1916 the unique hybrid intelligence office of the Arab Bureau was sanctioned for Cairo. Gilbert Clayton, Britain's subtle and prolific intelligence chief in Cairo and head of the Arab Bureau, chose an eclectic team of intelligence officers from civilian and military backgrounds, men with regional and professional expertise ranging from archaeology, military intelligence, British politics, journalism, the Turkish gendarmerie, the Sudan Service and the Royal Engineers. These officers saw political and military intelligence, cultural and historical knowledge as intertwining strands of instruction. Set up under the Foreign Office rather than the War Office or the Admiralty, the Arab Bureau was asked to centralize regional intelligence on Arab affairs for the benefit of London and to 'harmonize' Britain's political engagement in the Arab sphere. The outbreak of the Sherif's revolt led to a spontaneous expansion of the Arab Bureau's responsibilities. D.G. Hogarth, the Arab Bureau's first director, apologized to the Government of India for the Arab Bureau's having assumed unofficially the functions of political advisor to the High Commissioner and General Staff to the Arab armies, but insisted it had been 'forced' to expand its original intelligence duties by an extraordinary 'concatenation of circumstances' – though 'most improperly', of course.[6] Whether proper or not, the Arab Bureau was a war-engendered office already granted unusual liberties by its constitution and unrestrained by competition in the Hejaz from any local military authority.

The effect of the intelligence community's enlarged powers of decision-making on the course of the Arab Revolt would be crucial.

Until this point, Britain's strategic enquiry had focused largely on the British/Turk conflict and the potential of Arab resistance to undermine the Turkish government's war effort. After the outbreak of the revolt, the Arab Bureau refocused their attention on the Arabs' motivation and method in the field. British staff were shocked during the first days of June 1916 when Arab villages along the coast blocked the British supply ships carrying artillery, food and arms, and threatened to kill any foreigner that disembarked. Notwithstanding inflammatory Turkish and Syrian elements in the towns, the spectacles drew support from the people's widespread distrust of British intentions and fears of a European occupation. Cairo's intelligence community saw that Anglo-Arab relations themselves were a factor, and incorporated the information into their planning. The Sirdar, Sir Reginald Wingate, who eventually became head of Hejaz military and political affairs, repeatedly promised the War Committee that if British regular troops landed in the Hejaz, their superior military capability would be welcomed by the Arab fighters with gratitude. The Arab Bureau and the High Commissioner, by contrast, warned London that a landing of European Christian infantry would be seen as an invading force of infidel imperialists. Political and field intelligence reports from intelligence officers such as Lawrence, Lloyd, Newcombe and Bray, as well as from liaising officers on the ground such as Wilson (Jiddah Agent), Admiral Wemyss (Red Sea Patrol), Vickery and Newcombe (British Military Mission) came to the same conclusion. They argued that if a British brigade were landed, the Arabs would desert the British–Hashemite effort and join with their fellow Muslims, the Turks. Topographical intelligence also challenged Wingate's predictions by revealing changes in road and water conditions that altered the enemy's likely path of advance. Several officers in Cairo and the Hejaz believed that a proper analysis of the Arab conflict was sufficiently urgent, and the costs of misjudging the field so high, that they travelled to London to address the War Committee in person. In November 1916 both Clayton (head of the Arab Bureau) and Murray (GOC-in-C of Egyptforce) expressed the same sense of seriousness when they forwarded Lawrence's intelligence conclusions directly to the War Committee and the DMI in London, bypassing Wingate, who was the sphere's named chief officer. In allying themselves with Lawrence's recommendations for supporting an irregular campaign fought by Arab tribal fighters and Ottoman army defectors rather than a modified, combined conventional engagement led by Allied regular troops, Clayton and the other service officers were advocating an intelligence-led policy for the campaign.

It was the first of several fateful decisions for Hejaz policy that were based on intelligence rather than ideology or convention. Over the course of six months, the War Committee was persuaded repeatedly, and finally, by the intelligence community and sympathetic officers on the ground that no British reinforcements should be sent to Arabia. It would be difficult to overstate the significance of this policy debate. If the intelligence community, High Commissioner

McMahon and Admiral Wemyss had sided with the Sirdar's analysis and requested British troops, it is very likely that the War Committee would have complied and overridden the CIGS's desire to save all force reserves for France. It is also almost certain that the Arab movement would have collapsed after the landing of a British brigade. Subsequently, Egyptforce's operations in Palestine and Syria would have lost an indigenous ally and the Ottoman army would have been strengthened as a result. Over the next several months the British intelligence community, repeatedly spearheaded by Lawrence, managed to push through three more pivotal decisions. Each of these decisions contributed to the Arabs' winning campaign. All were based on intelligence assessments and required the continuing use of modern intelligence techniques and principles for support, especially Imint and Sigint (although Humint was particularly valuable during the Aqaba expedition). The transfer of Feisal's base from Yenbo to Wejh (January 1917) supported by the British navy along the coast empowered the Arab armies to apply pressure to the HEF without requiring a British landing at Rabegh. The shift from a conventional offensive to an irregular campaign targeting the railway garrisons above Medina, supported by Imint and Sigint, forced the Turkish army to withdraw most of its coastal and inland troops to bases on the railway line. And the relinquishment of Medina as a target, coupled with the capture of Aqaba with an all-Arab expeditionary force (July 1917), a strategy shift based on intelligence as analysed by Lawrence, put an independent Arab army north of the Hejaz border, a new military and political force to be reckoned with.

Lessons: the Lawrence conundrum

The Arab Bureau's officers were not, as is occasionally suggested, a collection of political neophytes, nor were they rogues or opportunists taking advantage of a distant command structure in order to pursue a private agenda. The decentralization of intelligence to the Arab Bureau had the opposite effect on performance: it increased, not decreased, the officers' sense of official responsibility and led to informed debate on all manner of intelligence. The analytical work produced by these officers was more sober and meticulous than is often portrayed. In ways, their rigorous and independent approach resembled the research methods and 'character of a university gone to war'.[7] They were convinced that without their expert advice, the Arab uprising would dissipate through the government's inattention or mismanagement. The records also show that many of the British officers on the ground who managed the flow of information between the field and London identified strongly with the integrity (or lack thereof) demonstrated by their government. Clayton, Graves and Bray travelled to London to argue for an irregular Arab campaign without British troops. Lawrence and Lloyd of the Arab Bureau made personal visits to Khartoum, as did Wemyss, to persuade the Sirdar to change his policy appeals for British reinforcements. The repugnance felt by Newcombe (Cairo Intelligence and British Military Mission) and Wilson over Anglo-French duplicity towards the Arab leaders during an official visit in spring 1917 moved them to threaten their own resignations. The fragility and complexity of the tribes' attitudes as British allies were a source of constant concern for these officers. Their determination to convey the events in Arabia as they were in fact occurring, not as London, Khartoum or India might have preferred, foreshadowed one of the most remarkable demonstrations of intelligence command: Lawrence's unauthorized facilitation of a secret Arab expedition to capture Aqaba.

Lawrence would survive the war with extraordinary renown for a young man who had been only twenty-six years old and a junior subaltern when the war began. He became an internationally recognized figure after Lowell Thomas's wartime propaganda films. His attendance at the Paris Peace Conference in 1919 as Feisal's deputy, public condemnation of the post-war bombing of Iraq and appointment by Churchill to the Cairo Conference in 1921 confirmed his standing as a champion of the Arab cause. His account of the Arab Revolt, *Seven Pillars of Wisdom*, has been continually in print and is one of the most well known historical memoirs of the twentieth century. Equally enduring associations with Lawrence have been the psychological difficulties and controversy that haunted him after the war until his death in 1935. Well-meaning hagiographies have vied with a counter-trend of inculpation, and scholars have had to peer through a long lens of both idealized fabrications and character assassinations, psychological and sexual speculation, political polemics and a postmodern scepticism of anything resembling 'the Great Man' theory of history.

The result has been a regrettable distortion of not only Lawrence's history but by association the history of the Arab Revolt and Britain's intelligence achievements in the campaign. The intelligence officers' influence over the direction of the Revolt and in particular their drifting without ado into active operations were unique to this war. Their decentralization of tactical intelligence and semi-autonomous operational control to the field foreshadow the microcosmic organizations of the Special Operations Executive (SOE) in France during the Second World War, the Navy SEALS and the Special Forces operating in Afghanistan and Iraq nearly 100 years later. In all these cases, mobile, self-sufficient irregular field units acted with high degrees of intelligence and operational authority because their success, not to mention their survival, depended upon their ability to respond efficiently to unpredictable incoming information. Lawrence never questioned the logic behind this evolution of tasks. We have seen that Lawrence was one of the first and most enthusiastic proponents of Imint/aerial support for the Arab armies; he cleared landing grounds on his own initiative, coordinated flight plans to meet the Arabs' operational needs and contributed extensive topographical information for the improvement of their maps. He interrogated Arab and Turkish informants and PoWs and made sure that the Arab Bureau kept him informed in the field of all latest intelligence, especially Sigint. Once he entered operations, he developed the practice of reconnoitering the ground personally before planning or taking action, and seems to have rarely, if ever, embarked on missions that were not based on the fullest possible collection of intelligence and preparation of personal relationships.

It is clear from the records that, for the first twelve months of the Revolt at least, Lawrence defined himself primarily as an intelligence officer who came only by force of circumstance to act as leading saboteur, guerrilla leader and strategist. He opens *Seven Pillars* with a reminder that he held a subordinate position in Arabia, had 'no office among the Arabs, was never in charge of the British mission with them. Wilson, Joyce, Newcombe, Dawnay, and Davenport were all over my head'.[8] Nevertheless, his actions reflected what he and the other officers on the ground felt had become a morally charged relationship between information and leadership responsibility. 'The chief agent had to be the general's head [...] and his knowledge had to be faultless, leaving no room for chance. We took more pains in this service than any other staff I saw.'[9] This quotation brings us to the back to the question of boundaries and the more difficult challenge inherent in Lawrence's example.

It is a cardinal principle of intelligence that it must be kept separate from policymaking to protect its objectivity. The price of that separation, of course, is that policymakers are under no obligation to attend to intelligence. Lawrence's conflation of the roles of 'chief agent' and 'general', particularly in the seizing of Aqaba, eliminated the danger that vital intelligence – on Arab political requirements, on irregular military opportunities – might be ignored. Similarly, it was on the strength of 'faultless knowledge' from political, military and topographical intelligence that Lawrence and his colleagues decided to oppose a British brigade, argue for an irregular strategy against the railway and a reorientation of Arab forces to the north, and support the establishment of an Arab military capability in Syria. In purely military terms, these decisions produced a clear advantage against the Turks; as proposals that responded to political intelligence on the uprising, they were responsible for guaranteeing the progress of the Arab Revolt beyond the Hejaz. By enabling a mobile insurgent Arab army to move out of the Hejaz and into Syria, these decisions affected British policy and contradicted the official, if secret, policy aims expressed only weeks earlier in the Hejaz by Sykes and Picot. General Allenby tried to deflect the political implications of Lawrence's occupation of Aqaba in July 1917 by insisting that it was solely a military action and the French had no need to protest. Owing to Aqaba's advantages with regard to the approaching Palestine campaign, further questions about Lawrence's action were waived aside. And yet this encroachment by an intelligence officer into the field of operations, with the express aim of influencing policy, had in one stroke solved the Hejaz campaign's Medina crisis, provided a new flank for Allenby's army and empowered a new Arab nationalist force in the north.

The challenge for intelligence studies is that the augmented intelligence role in the Hejaz, while successful and passionately pursued by intelligence officers with the support of other service officers on the ground, is almost impossible to distil into a universal rule. Lawrence's reports to Cairo and his activity in the field would be described pejoratively by intelligence professionals today as 'policy prescriptive'.[10] Ideally, such prescription should not be a temptation. If policymakers were guided by the best information available, eschewing biased or mythological views of the world, their judgements would reflect much of the objectivity attributed to intelligence analysts.[11] The Arab Revolt was a particular case in that so many of London's serious policy questions for the Ottoman territories were left unresolved or addressed only imperfectly during the war. The boundary dividing intelligence management, field analysis and policy judgement in the highly irregular environment of the Arabs' uprising became blurred under the duress of the campaign, or was deliberately breached. The political analysis performed by Cairo's intelligence community attempted to fill the policy vacuum and provide strategic consistency within the context of the Anglo-Arab alliance.

Without venturing any ruling as to when such an unconventional intelligence and military arrangement might be desirable – i.e. when that 'bright line' might safely be crossed – this case study has emphasized the innovations and entrepreneurial problem-solving that contributed to victory in this theatre. Understanding the intelligence community's robust engagement with the Arabs' campaign and the success of its tactical and strategic response should help provide a sharper historical context for judging other, past and future, intelligence-dependent campaigns.

Glossary of names

London

Herbert Henry Asquith	Prime Minister, 1908–16.
David Lloyd George	Chancellor of the Exchequer, 1908–15; Minister for Munitions, 1915–16; Secretary of State for War, 1916; Prime Minister, 1916–22.
Charles Edward Callwell	Intelligence branch, War Office, 1887–92; attached to Sir Redvers Buller during Boer War, 1899; retires, 1909; Director of Military Operations and Intelligence, War Office, 1914–16; Major-General and KCB, 1917.
George Russell Clerk	Head of War Department, 1914.
Sir Eyre Crowe	Assistant Under-Secretary, FO 1912.
Sir Edward Grey, Viscount Grey of Falloden	Secretary of State for Foreign Affairs, 1905–16.
Sir Arthur Nicolson	Permanent Under-Secretary for Foreign Affairs, 1910–16.
Sir Maurice Hankey	Secretary to the Committee of Imperial Defence, 1912–18; Secretary of the War Cabinet, 1916–18.
Charles Hardinge, Lord Hardinge of Penshurst	Permanent Under-Secretary, 1906–10; Governor-General and Viceroy of India, 1910–16; Permanent Under-Secretary, 1916–20; censured by Commission of Inquiry into Mesopotamian expedition, 1917.
Sir George M.W. Macdonogh	General Staff, GHQ, BEF, 1914–16; Major-General, 1916; Director of Military Intelligence, 1916–18.
Sir William Robert Robertson	Quarter-Master-General, 1914–15; Chief-of-Staff, BEF, 1915; Lieutenant-General,

	1915; Chief of the Imperial General Staff, 1915–18; General, 1916.
Sir Tatton Benvenuto Mark Sykes	Conservative MP for Central Hull, 1911–19; Assistant Secretary, War Cabinet, 1916–18; Sykes–Picot Agreement, 1916; attached to Foreign Office and chief advisor on Near East policy, 1916.

India Office and Government of India

Sir Austin J. Chamberlain	Secretary of State for India, 1915; Resigned after mismanagement of Mesopotamian Campaign, 1917.
Robert O.A. Crewe	Secretary of State for India, 1910–15; President of Board of Education, 1916.
Sir Arthur Hirtzel	Secretary, Political Department, IO, 1909–17.
1st Viscount Chelmsford	Governor of New South Wales, 1909–13; Viceroy of India, 1916–21; Signed Chelmsford Report, moving India towards responsible government, 1918; First Lord Admiralty, 1924.
A.H. Grant	Deputy-Secretary, Indian Foreign Department, 1912; Foreign Secretary, Political and Foreign Department, 1914–19.
Sir Percy Zachariah Cox	Political Resident and Consul at Bushire, Persian Gulf, 1904–14; Resident, 1909–14; Chief Political Officer, IEF 'D' and MEF, 1914–18.

Egypt

Edmund Henry H. Allenby 1st Viscount Allenby of Megiddo	Inspector-General of Cavalry, 1910–14; commanded cavalry at Ypres and Mons, 1915; Third Army at Arras, 1915–17; GOC-in-C, Egyptforce, June 1917.
Sir Milne Cheetham	Acting High Commissioner, Egypt, December 1914–January 1915.
Gilbert F. Clayton	Egyptian Army, 1898; Private Secretary to Sir Reginald Wingate, 1908–10; Sudan Agent and Director of Intelligence, Egyptian Army, 1913–17; Head Military Intelligence at British Headquarters,

	Egypt, 1914–17; Colonel, 1914; Director of Intelligence, Egypt, 1914–16; Chief, Arab Bureau, 1916; Brigadier-General, April 1916; CGS, Hejaz; Special Service Officer GSO (1), attached to Intelligence Corps, to SSO under High Commissioner, Egypt, January 1917; Chief Political Officer, October 1917; Advisor to Ministry of Interior, 1919–22.
Major Kinahan Cornwallis	Sudan Civil Service, 1908; Egyptian Civil Service, 1912; Intelligence, GHQ, Cairo, 1914; Arab Bureau, 1915; Director, Arab Bureau, 1916–20; Personal advisor to King Feisal of Iraq, 1921–33.
Wyndham H. Deedes	Seconded to Turkish Gendarmerie, 1910–14; Intelligence, London, Gallipoli and Cairo, 1914–18; Major and DSO, 1916; Brigadier-General, 1918. Political Intelligence department, Military Intelligence, Egyptforce/Arab Bureau.
Sir Ronald W. Graham	Adviser to the Egyptian Ministry of the Interior, 1910; Assistant Under-Secretary, 1916–19.
David George Hogarth	Keeper of Ashmolean Museum, 1908–27; Commander, Royal Naval Reserve Volunteer Reserve, 1915–19; Acting Director, Arab Bureau, Cairo, 1916.
Lord Horatio Herbert Kitchener	Governor-General, Sudan, 1898; Chief of Staff under Lord Roberts in S. Africa, 1899; C-in-C, Boer War, 1900–2; C-in-C, India, 1902–9; Field-Marshal, 1909; British Agent and Consul-General, 1911; Secretary of State for War, 1914–16.
Thomas Edward Lawrence	Commissioned in Geographical Section, General Staff, War Office, Military Intelligence in Egypt, Middle East section, November 1914; liaison officer with Survey in Egypt; Arab Bureau (full-time) October 1916.
George Ambrose Lloyd	Conservative MP for West Staffordshire, 1910–18; Military Intelligence, Egypt and Arab Bureau, 1916–17; DSO, 1917; Governor of Bombay, 1918–23; MP for Eastbourne, 1924–25.

Lieutenant-Colonel A.L. Lynden-Bell	Chief of Staff, Medforce, 1915; Chief of Staff, Egyptforce, 1916.
Sir John Grenfell Maxwell	GOC-in-C, Egypt, 1908–12; GOC, Force in Egypt, September 1914 through December 1915.
Sir Arthur Henry McMahon	Secretary, Foreign Department, to the Governor-General in Council, 1911–14; High Commissioner, Egypt, 1914–16.
Sir Archibald James Murray	Chief of General Staff, BEF, August 1914 through January 1915; Deputy Chief of Imperial General Staff, February–September 1915; GOC-in-C, Medforce, September–December, 1915; GOC-in-C, Egyptforce, January 1916 through June 1917.
Colonel A.C. Parker	Military Intelligence Branch (Ib), Medforce and Egyptforce; Liaison officer between Arab Bureau and Sirdar at Khartoum, 1916–17.
Sir Ronald Storrs	Oriental Secretary to the British Agent and Consul-General, Egypt, 1908–17.

Sudan

Sir (Francis) Reginald Wingate	Sirdar of Egyptian Army, 1884; Director, Military Intelligence, 1889; Governor-General, Sudan, 1899–1916; High Commissioner, Egypt, 1917–19.

Arabia

Major Cox	British Military Mission.
Major Davenport	Egyptian army, escort (Artillery).
Colonel Pierce Charles Joyce	Egyptian Army, escort (Artillery).
Major Herbert Garland	Demolition, Explosives training at Rabegh and Yenbo.
Lieutenant-Colonel Stewart F. Newcombe	Military Intelligence Branch, Egypt; Head of British Military Mission, 1917.
Major Vickery (Artillery)	British Military Mission to Hejaz.
Colonel Cyril E. Wilson	Egyptian Army, 1902; Sudan Government, 1902; Governor, Khartoum, 1909; Governor, Red Sea Province, 1913–22; H.M. Representative at Jiddah, July 1916.

Royal Navy

Admiral Sir Rosslyn E. Weymss	Rear Admiral 1911; Commander, 12th Cruiser Squadron, in charge of western patrol in English Channel, August 1914 through February 1915; Governor of Lemnos, 1915; Mudros, Dardanelles Campaign, DKB and Vice-Admiral, 1916; C-in-C, East Indies and Egypt Station, 1916–17; deputy Sea Lord, 1917; supports Allenby's advance into Palestine, 1917; first Sea Lord, December 1917.
Captain William H.D. Boyle	Commander of Red Sea Patrol.

The Hejaz

Sherif Hussein ibn Ali	Emir of Mecca, Guardian of Mecca and Medina.
His sons:	Prince Feisal
Prince Abdullah	
Prince Ali	
Prince Zeid	
Sherif Nasir of Medina	
Sherif Ali Haidar	Turkish-appointed Pretender to the Emirate of Mecca.

Hail

Ibn Rashid	Pro-Turk chief of the Shammar.

Ma'an – Aqaba

Auda abu Tayyi	Chief of the Eastern Huweitat.
Ibn Jazi	Chief of Central Huweitat.

Jauf

Nuri Shaalan	Paramount chief of the Ruallah, Anazeh.
Nawaf Shaalan	Son of Nuri Shaalan.

(Turkish) Medina

Fakhri Pasha	General-Officer-Commander, Hejaz Expeditionary Force.

Notes

Introduction

1 M. Handel, *War, Strategy and Intelligence*, London: Frank Cass, 1989, p. 197.
2 M. Sykes, 'Appreciation of attached Arabian Report No. XIV', 20 October 1916, FO371/2781/210071.
3 See C. Andrew, *Her Majesty's Secret Service: the Making of the British Intelligence Community*, New York: Viking Press, 1987, pp. 1–33 *passim*.
4 See J. Ferris (ed.), *The British Army and Signals Intelligence during the First World War*. London: Army Records Society, 1992. The Admiralty's Room 40 produced such Sigint successes as the decryption of the Zimmerman telegram and the tracking of submarine fleets hunting British convoys.
5 Andrew, *Her Majesty's Secret Service*, pp. 86–173 *passim*.
6 C. Andrew and D. Dilks (eds), *The Missing Dimension: Government and Intelligence Communities in the Twentieth Century*, Illinois: University of Illinois Press, 1995.
7 C.E. Callwell, *Small Wars: A Tactical Textbook for Imperial Soldiers*, London: Presidio Press, 1990, p. 53.
8 See Callwell, *Small Wars*, pp. 25–33, 43–56 *passim*. These distinctions in warfare were clearly familiar to commanders outside the French theatre, who did not require the example of Haig or post-war hindsight. General Sir Archibald Murray (GOC-in-C, Egyptforce) asked the War Office in the autumn of 1916 to send 'a special type' of officer for a command position on the West Frontier of Egypt, emphasizing: 'What I am in search of is a young up-to-date soldier, not obsessed with the conditions of trench warfare.' A.J. Murray to W.R. Robertson (CIGS), 21 October 1916, M.S.889 WO33/905 No. 5971.
9 R. MacLeod (ed.), 'Introduction', in *Government and Expertise: Specialists, Administrators and Professionals, 1860–1919*, 1, quoted in M. Herman, *Intelligence Power in Peace and War*, Cambridge: Cambridge University Press, 1996, p. 259.
10 The phrase 'imperial archive' described the Victorian concept of extending and maintaining empire through the accumulation of knowledge. T. Richards, *The Imperial Archive. Knowledge and the Fantasy of Empire*, London: Verso, 1993, pp. 1, 5.
11 Michael Herman observes that the First World War showed the degree to which 'total war needed total intelligence'. His examples of non-departmental inter-service intelligence bodies that collected topical Sigint, Imint and Humint on the enemy's domestic politics, economy, morale and refugee movements, or dealt with 'covert action and political warfare', such as the Special Operations Executive (SOE), all occur during the 1930s and the Second World War. The Arab Bureau's treatment of the Ottoman Arab territories could be included on the list. Herman, *Intelligence Power*, pp. 25, 260.
12 The territory above the Arabian desert corresponding roughly to modern-day Syria, Jordan, Palestine, Israel and western Iraq, to the Euphrates. The Lebanon, or Vilayet of Beirut, was considered both part of yet distinct from Syria.

13 Dr Rohrbach, *Deutsche Politik*, 11 February 1916, quoted in memorandum by the India Office, dated 25 May 1916, L/P&S/11/103 P962.
14 '[N]ational security abounds with problems that are clearer than the solutions to them.' P.R. Pillar, 'Intelligence, Policy, and the War In Iraq'. Reprinted by permission of FOREIGN AFFAIRS, Vol. 85 (March/April 2006), p. 17. Copyright (2006) by the Council on Foreign Relations, Inc.
15 Westrate dismisses *The Arab Bulletin* as 'disappointing fare' for anyone seeking information on the Arab Bureau's perspective on complex policy questions, such as those regarding French war aims or Zionism. B. Westrate, *The Arab Bureau: British Policy in the Middle East, 1916–1920*, University Park, Pennsylvania: Pennsylvania University Press, 1992, pp. 104–5.
16 When T.E. Lawrence prepared to stay in the Hejaz for an extended period from late 1916, he asked to have copies of *The Arab Bulletin* forwarded to him. Lawrence, Yenbo to K. Cornwallis, Cairo, 27 December 1916, FO882/6 HRG/16/90A-B.
17 J. Wilson, *Lawrence of Arabia: the authorized biography of T.E. Lawrence*, New York: Atheneum, 1990.
18 R. Aldington, *Lawrence of Arabia: A Biographical Enquiry*, London: Collins, 1955.
19 Lawrence wrote that *Seven Pillars* was 'intended to rationalize the campaign, that everyone may see how natural the success was and how inevitable, how little dependent on direction or brain, how much less on the outside assistance of the few British'. Lawrence, *Seven Pillars of Wisdom: A Triumph*, New York: Penguin, 1981, p. 21.
20 Yigal Sheffy, *British Military Intelligence in the Palestine Campaign 1914–1918*, London: Frank Cass, 1998.

1 Setting the scene: British intelligence and an Arab insurrection, 1913–15

1 A. Nicolson to Lord Hardinge, 16 February 1916, Private letter, FO800/381, fo. 135.
2 For more on Britain's perception of Russia's position before the war, see Zara Steiner, *Britain and the Origins of the First World War*, London: Macmillan, 1977, pp. 79–93. For Russia's long-term strategic aim to occupy Syria, Mesopotamia and North Africa in addition to Persia and Afghanistan, see Sir J. Glubb, *A Short History of the Arab Peoples*, New York: Dorset Press, 1969, pp. 251–2.
3 David Fromkin remarks on the 'intellectual time lag' in foreign policy between Whitehall and the colonial administrations during the first decade of the twentieth century. D. Fromkin, *A Peace to End All Peace*, New York: Henry Holt & Co., 1989, pp. 31–2. See also E. Monroe, *Britain's Moment in the Middle East, 1914–1956*, London: Chatto and Windus, 1964, p. 24.
4 The financial and consular privileges granted to Europeans, the 'Capitulations', were another irritant. Western capital had been lent to Turkey in exchange for trade advantages after its defeats in the Crimean War (1853–6) and the Peace of Paris (1856). Twenty years later, Constantinople was bankrupt. An international administration took over the Ottoman public debt in 1881. Despite the cost to Turkey's national revenue, European powers continued to resist the concessions' abolition.
5 Glubb, *Short History*, pp. 248, 252; for further discussion see pp. 252–3, 256–8.
6 The Young Turk party was founded in 1889–91 in Constantinople by a coalition of army officers from the 'Freedom and Progress' Committee and from Mustafa Kemal's party. P. Hitti, *The Near East in History: A 5000 year story*, New Jersey: D. Van Nostrand Co., Inc., 1961, pp. 347, 362–4.
7 The CUP considered Italy, Austria-Hungary, Greece, Bulgaria and Russia to be potential aggressors. A number of ministers approached the Great Powers to ask for protection. Djavid (Minister of Finance) favoured Great Britain. Djemal (Minister of Marine) hoped to negotiate with France. Talaat (Minister of the Interior) even appealed to Russia. Only Enver's appeal to Germany was accepted, with enthusiasm

by Kaiser Wilhelm II. The CUP signed a defensive alliance with Germany on 1 August 1914. Fromkin, *A Peace*, pp. 49–50, 58–9.

8 Major C.E. Callwell recommended a scientific cover for the Palestine Exploration Fund (PEF): 'If the Turkish Government understood that the survey was for exploration purposes it is probable that their consent would be more easily obtained.' (Callwell) Director of Military Operations (DMO) to the Under-Secretary of State for Foreign Affairs, 20 September 1913, FO371/1812 (orig:43118), fos 279–80. See also Lawrence, *Military Report on the Sinai Peninsula* (Fordingbridge, 1990; first published 1915 for restricted circulation by the War Office, General Staff, Geographical Section).

9 The expedition's official report, *The Wilderness of Zin*, confirmed its legitimacy. See: Palestine Exploration Fund Annual No. 3, 1914–15, Palestine Exploration Fund (London, 1914). Woolley and Lawrence, *Wilderness of Zin*. See also Monroe, *Britain's Moment*, p. 26.

10 R. Storrs to O.A.G. FitzGerald (Kitchener's personal military secretary), 3 August 1915, quoted in J. Nevakivi, 'Lord Kitchener and the Partition of the Ottoman Empire, 1915–16', K. Bourne and D.C. Watt (eds), *Studies in International History* (1967), p. 320.

11 The vice-royalty's proposed northern limit would be the top of the Levant, its western boundary the eastern Mediterranean, western Egypt and the Sudan, its southern boundary would extend down to Aden, and its eastern boundary would follow the Persian Gulf and the Tigris and Euphrates rivers. The idea of supplanting the Ottoman Sultan/Caliph and moving the seat to Mecca was probably first expressed by the Khedive of Egypt, for his own benefit. See Fromkin, *A Peace*, p. 85; U. Trumpener, *Germany and the Ottoman Empire, 1914–1918*, Princeton: Princeton University Press, 1968, p. 31.

12 Kitchener wanted to ensure that no other Great Power dominated the line of communication between India and the Mediterranean Sea.

> It should obviously be no part of our programme to create a frontier coterminous with that of Russia [...] [but] even a frontier coterminous with Russia, with all its grave drawbacks, would be preferable to a Franco-Russian domination of the line from the Gulf of Iskanderun [*sic*] to the Persian Gulf.
>
> Kitchener memo on 'Alexandretta and Mesopotamia', 16 March 1916, CAB27/1, fo. 104.

Included as Appendix X (fos 100–15) to 'Report of the Committee on Asiatic Turkey', 30 June 1915, Maurice de Bunsen (chair), addressing the question of British desiderata and possible partition of Turkey after the war.

13 The British Agency's rhetoric of (even eventual) self-government for Egypt had no parallel on the sub-continent. R. Storrs, *Orientations*, London: Nicolson and Watson, 1945, pp. 136–43.

14 As early as 1913, Arab representatives of other smaller underground movements in Egypt, the Lebanon and Syria had paid visits to the British Agency and to General Maxwell, GOC-in-C of the British Force in Egypt, to ask for assistance in a rising against the Turks. The British government, not yet at war with Turkey, rejected the invitations out of hand. For details on the programmes espoused by the Decentralization Party, *al-Fatat* and other early Arab nationalist communities, see: 'Arab Committees before the War', *The Arab Bulletin*, No. 90, 24 May 1918, pp. 165–7. See also E. Tauber, *The Emergence of the Arab Movements*, London: Frank Cass, 1993, pp. 33–42, 90–7, 155–9, and Tauber, *The Arab Movements in World War I*, London: Frank Cass, 1993, pp. 10–13, 58–9, 121–34.

15 R.E. Russell, 'Abd El Masri: transmits summary of conversation between him and Capt. Russell [on 16 August 1914]; his aim in Arabia & Syria, etc.' 17 August 1914, FO371/2140/46261, fo. 1. Tauber, *Emergence*, pp. 90–7, 250. Tauber, *Arab Move-*

ments, pp. 7–8. Al-Masri also approached Turkish figures periodically throughout the war.

16 Al-Masri also reassured Cairo that they did not have to fear a revolt by Muslims in Persia or India because his 'Central Committee''s programme (Baghdad) did not contain Pan-Islamic or Arabian Khalifate aims. Russell, 'Abd El Aziz El Masri [...] Capt. Russell [on 16 August 1914]', 17 August 1914, FO371/2140/46261, fos 1–2.

17 G.F. Clayton, memorandum, 11 October 1915, W. Ormsby-Gore, 'Summary of historical documents from outbreak of war between Great Britain and Turkey until the Rising', 29 November 1916, FO882/5 HRG/16/65, fos 207–8.

18 Report, Clayton, 30 October 1914, FO371/2140, fos 180–1. Clayton, memorandum, 11 October 1915, fos 208–13, and J.G. Maxwell (GOC-in-C, Egypt) to Kitchener (WO), 16 October 1915, tel. 2030, fos 205–6 in Ormsby-Gore, 'Summary of historical documents', 29 November 1916, FO882/5 HRG/16/65. See also Maxwell to WO, 16 October 1915, Sudan Archive, W/135/4/17–34. T.B.M. Sykes to FO, 21 November 1915, tel. 709 and to DMO, tel. 20, Sudan Archive, W/135/6/77. Memorandum, 'The Arab Movement', Walrond, July 1918, FO882/14 PA/18/11. Tauber, *Arab Movements*, pp. 113, 184–5.

19 Tauber, *Arab Movements*, pp. 111–13.

20 Sir Louis Mallet (British ambassador to Turkey) told Grey that an Arab movement would be a 'most effective' weapon against Turkey, but he recommended supporting Ibn Saud rather than the Hashemites, if only to allay Indian and Arab Muslim concerns over the safety of the Holy Places. L. Mallet to E. Grey, 4 September 1914, tel. 692 [46520], K. Bourne and C.D. Watt (eds), *British Documents on Foreign Affairs: Reports and Papers from the Foreign Office Confidential Print, Series H, The First World War, 1914–1918*, University Publications of America: 1989, Vol. I, 68. Clayton made special note of al-Masri's concern that the Turks recently been 'assiduous' in courting the Bedouin Arab chiefs with material rewards. This intelligence underscored the strategic value of the tribes' allegiance. Clayton, report, 30 October 1914, relayed by M. Cheetham (acting British Agent), Cairo, to Grey, FO, London, 30 November 1914, FO371/2140/46261 (orig. 7708), fos 180–1.

21 Bourne and Watt (eds), *British Documents*, Vol. II, p. 357.

22 Kitchener to Storrs, for Sherif Abdulla, repeated in FO, London to M. Cheetham, tel.219, 24 September 1914, FO371/2768, fo. 76.

23 Correspondence from October 1914, quoted in Monroe, *Britain's Moment*, p. 26.

24 Kitchener, in FO to Abdullah, 31 October 1914. tel. 303, Bourne and Watt (eds), *British Documents*, Vol. II, p. 358.

25 Kitchener to Sherif Hussein of Mecca, 31 October 1914, FO371/2768. Kitchener to Cheetham, repeated in FO, London to Cheetham, tel. 303, 31 October 1914, FO371/2139.

26 Abdullah's reply relayed in Cheetham to FO, London, 10 December 1914. tel. 310. See also Abdullah's more expansive statement of Mecca's position in letter, brought by messenger to Cairo on 30 October 1914. Cheetham to FO, London, *c*.30 October 1914. tel. 233. Bourne and Watt (eds), *British Documents*, Vol. II, pp. 357–8.

27 Cheetham to Grey, 13 November 1914, tel. 264, FO371/2140, fo. 158.

28 Grey to Cheetham, 14 November 1914, tel. 327, FO371/2140, fo. 159.

29 Cheetham reported to Grey that agents from a 'pan-Arab movement in Cairo' were being dispatched to Palestine, Syria, Mesopotamia and throughout the Arabia peninsula, but there seemed to be concrete details only on the Basra expedition. Cheetham to Grey, 28 October 1914, tel. 228, [64467] Bourne and Watt (eds), *British Documents*, Vol. I, p. 136. The War Council was formed in November 1914 to advise on the general conduct of the war, but met infrequently. In May 1915, 'the Dardanelles Committee', which was composed of permanent members of the CID, replaced the council and took responsibility for a wide range of naval and military operations, in addition to general war policy. In November 1915, the Dardanelles Committee was

renamed 'the War Committee'. In December 1916, after David Lloyd George's election as Prime Minister, the War Committee was replaced by a 'War Cabinet' comprising the five members of the Secretariat of the CID.

30 The Director of Criminal Intelligence in India wrote a report in 1913 on the dangers of Muslim political activism which was still quoted years later by the Foreign and Political Department of the Government of India in defence of their opposition to negotiations with Arab nationalists or Pan-Islamists: 'The discontented Muhammadan naturally becomes a pan-Islamist since his rebound from loyalty to the [British] Government throws him into sympathy with the established though distant fact of the Ottoman Empire in which he already has a religious stake. His sympathy supplies him with endless matter for abusing and embarrassing Government, and for swaying the masses to hatred'. V.P. Vivian, Director, Criminal Intelligence, 'Pan-Islamism in the Moslem League', 30 September 1913; contained in communication from A.H. Grant to A.B. fforde, *c.* April 1916, 662W (item 6), R/20/A/1569 IOLR.

31 Cox to Secretary to the Government of India, Foreign [and Political] Department, tel. P, No. 82-B, 3 December 1914 (rec'd 4 December), FO371/2479/1385, fos 308–9. See also Lord Hardinge: 'We have always regarded [...] the creation of a strong Arab state lying astride our interests in the East and in the Gulf as a not unlikely source of ultimate trouble [...] [To relinquish British claims to Mesopotamia] will not only be abandoning enormous potential sources of revenue, but will also be resented by the Indian people, and the European commercial community, who look to Mesopotamia as a field for commercial expansion and emigration in return for the blood of their countrymen there shed.' Hardinge to Lord Crewe, Secretary of State, India, 4 November 1915, FO371/2486, fo. 254. See also GOC, Mesopotamia, Sir Percy Lake, the following spring: the 'political views and schemes [of the Arab nationalists] are much too advanced to be safe pabula for the communities of occupied territories', in addition to which they were 'undesirable and inconvenient.' Lake to Secretary of State, India, tel. 1040B, 30 March 1916, FO371/2768, fos 36–7.

32 T.E. Lawrence, *Seven Pillars*, pp. 76, 59, 478, 171–2. Callwell, DMO, informed the Sirdar at Khartoum that 'the whole trend of opinion is now all against these side-shows and [Britain must] concentrate on the main theatres'. Sir F.R. Wingate to G.F. Clayton, 3 January 1915, Sudan Archive, Box 469/8/2.

33 Storrs, *Orientations*, pp. 132–5, 149. Fromkin, *A Peace*, p. 121. Wilson, *Lawrence of Arabia*, 174.

34 Storrs, *Orientations*, pp. 131, 149.

35 Wingate to Clayton, 13 February 1915, Sudan Archive, Box 469/8/36.

36 Cairo estimated 200,000 enemy troops in the Dardanelles, 200,000 in the Caucasus and 50,000 in Mesopotamia. Lawrence to Hogarth, 18 March 1915, D. Garnett (ed.), *The Selected Letters of T.E. Lawrence*, London: Jonathan Cape, 1938, pp. 85–6.

37 Lawrence to Hogarth, 18 March 1915, Garnett (ed.), *Letters*, p. 86. The IEF 'D' had secured the Basra vilayet and was moving up the Tigris river towards Baghdad.

38 See Lawrence to Hogarth, 18 March 1915, Garnett (ed.), *Letters*, pp. 85–6.

39 Kitchener told the War Council that a landing of 30,000–50,000 men at Alexandretta would be 'a minor but useful operation. [...] It would strike an effective blow at the Turkish communications with Syria'. War Council meeting, 'The General Policy of the War', 18 January 1915, CAB/42/1/12, fos 3–4.

40 War Council Meeting, No. 18, 13 January 1915, CAB22/77. E. Kedourie, *England and the Middle East*, Sussex: Harvester Press, 1978, p. 43. The Mediterranean Expeditionary Force (MEF) attacked the Gallipoli head on 25 April 1915, and evacuated in January 1916. The War Council directed the War Office to prepare memorandum on the 'strategic advantages of Alexandretta' again in March 1915, in light of a

Russian *aide-mémoire* on post-war desiderata. War Council Meeting, No. 17, 10 March 1915, CAB42/1.

41 The 12th Corps comprised the Iraqi [Arab] 35th, 37th, and [partly Arab] 36th Divisions, and was nicknamed 'the Army of Salvation' (Jaysh al-Khalas) because of its high proportion of Arab and in particular *al-'Ahd* members, one of the few such army groups still located in Syria. See Tauber, *Arab Movements*, pp. 59–60.

42 As part of his crack-down on potential Arab subversives, Jemal 'promoted' 300 Arab officers in Syria and transferred them to Anatolia, Thrace and the Straits. He dismissed a further 1,100 Arab officers as undesirable or unfit.

43 *The Arab Bulletin*, No. 2, 12 June 1916, 15. Tauber, *Arab Movements*, 19–21.

44 French Government to Kitchener, tel. 9918, cipher, 14 November 1915, WO33/747/2800B, fo. 815.

45 B.H. Liddell Hart, *'T.E. Lawrence' in Arabia and After*, London: Jonathan Cape, 1934, p. 56; see also pp. 54–5. In October 1917 the French would re-evaluate their position and propose their own joint landing at Alexandretta, but this time the British government declined.

46 FO371/2482, Box 2 (miscellaneous), file 2, fo. 33A.

47 Lawrence to Liddell Hart, 31 March 1929, commenting on the latter's *Decisive Wars of History*, quoted in Garnett (ed.), *Letters*, p. 87.

48 Around this same time, Cairo learned that 300 Armenian rebels in the area of Jebel Musa had risen against the Turks but fell after six weeks for lack of guns and ammunition. Lawrence remarked to his intelligence colleague George Lloyd, currently stationed with the Gallipoli forces, on yet another missed opportunity:

> So N. Syria is full of unarmed battalions of Armenians & Christians, fit men, with no relations or home ties. In addition there are many outlaws, Mohammedan & Christian, in the hills: – all of it good material for a rising backed by us: a few hundred men, a company or two of machine guns, 10,000 rifles, & acceptance of Armenian officers of volunteers arriving daily from America, & we'll have all the Armenians & Cilicia in a horrible tangle [...] Sherif in rear & Armenians in front.
>
> Lawrence to Lloyd, 19 September 1915, GLLD 9/1 in M. Brown (ed.), *The Letters of T.E. Lawrence*, New York: Oxford University Press, 1988, pp. 77–8.

49 Ibid.

50 Intelligence Summary, Egyptforce, 'Railways in Syria and Palestine', 'Syria', 19 August 1915, WO157/694, fos 1, 4.

51 Wilson, *Lawrence*, p. 160.

52 For Lawrence's report, 'Intelligence IEF "D"', May 1916, see Clayton to Wingate, 12 June 1916, Sudan Archive, W/137/7/5–23.

53 For the government's evaluation of the causes and aftermath of the failure at Kut, see *Report of the Commission appointed by Act of Parliament to enquire into the Operations of War in Mesopotamia* (London, HMSO, 1916, Cmd.8610), p. 113.

54 Diary entry by Deedes, 31 March 1916, in J. Presland (pseud, Gladys Skelton), *Deedes Bey*, p. 256.

55 Wyndham H. Deedes [later Sir] had been Kitchener's first choice to head this mission, but he declined when the Government of India and the War Office made it clear that they did not intend to co-operate. Deedes to his mother, 18 March 1916, in Presland, *Deedes Bey*, p. 251. Deedes had been a Captain with the Turkish Gendarmerie in North Africa and the Ministry of the Interior at Constantinople, before moving to the Turkish section of Military Intelligence, London in 1914. He led I(b) Secret Service Section of Military Intelligence for the MEF during the Gallipoli

campaign and helped organize its evacuation. Kitchener transferred Deedes to the Intelligence Department, Cairo in December 1915.

56 Lawrence, who had worked closely with the Survey of Egypt and the RFC photography section, was also ordered to instruct Basra Intelligence on new aerial photography techniques for map-making. Aubrey Herbert of MI, Egypt, was a fluent Arabic and Turkish speaker and a regional expert with naval intelligence for the Mediterranean, Mesopotamia and the Persian Gulf.

57 Lawrence to his mother, 18 May 1916, Garnett (ed.), *Letters*, pp. 92–3. Lawrence met with a number of pan-Arab party members in Basra but found them too inexperienced and unreliable. Wilson, *Lawrence*, pp. 266–8.

58 For further discussion see Aubrey Herbert's Papers, KCL; Paul K. Davis, *Ends and Means: The British Mesopotamian Campaign and Commission.*

59 Lawrence to Clayton ('Intrusive', Cairo), 8 April 1916, FO882/15 PNA/16/2, fo. 73.

60 Lawrence observed that the tribes of the Shatt al-Hai had not risen to support the British precisely because they dreaded conquest:

> I rather sympathise with them, though of course their pretensions to remain an independent little state of freebooting freelancers in the middle of Mesopotamia is absurd. [...] If we had played our cards better at first, I do not think there would have been even the fighting there has been – but we have entered their country (for it is their country, and not the Turks') like sphinxes, never saying why we came or what we meant to do.
>
> Lawrence, 'Intelligence, IEF "D" ', in Clayton to Wingate, 12 June 1916, Sudan Archive, W/137/7/14–15.

61 Clayton to Wingate, 9 October 1915, 'Strictly private', Sudan Archive, W/135/4/10.

62 Sir H. McMahon, 'Report on the proceedings of an interdepartmental conference at Ismailia, 12 September 1916', FO882/4 HRG/16/46, fo. 342.

63 FO to McMahon, 14 April 1915, tel. 173, recorded in Ormsby-Gore, 'Situation in the Hejaz', 10 December 1916, FO882/6 HRG/16/77.

64 Bourne and Watt (eds), *British Documents*, Vol. II, pp. 363–4.

65 McMahon to Sherif Hussein, 30 August 1915, Bourne and Watt (eds), *British Documents*, Vol. II, p. 364.

66 Telegram from [CPO Sir P. Cox at] Basra, 2 June 1916, relaying statement from Faiz Bin Ghusain. Faiz, an *al-Fatat* member who had escaped Jemal's order of exile to Diarbekr and joined the Sherif's movement. *The Arab Bulletin*, No. 1, 6 June 1916, p. 7.

67 The boundaries were given as follows: 'North: The line Mersin–Adana to parallel 37°N. and thence along the line Birejik–Urfa-Mardin–Jazirat (Ibn 'Umar)–Amadia to the Persian frontier; East: The Persian frontier down to the Persian Gulf; South: The Indian Ocean (with the exclusion of Aden, whose status was to be maintained); West: The Red Sea and the Mediterranean Sea back to Mersin.'

68 G. Antonius, *Arab Awakening*, Beirut: Khayats, 1938, pp. 157–8.

69 Lawrence, *Seven Pillars*, pp. 50–2.

70 The mood of the Turkish government was defensive after the army's failure to take the Suez Canal. Jemal Pasha, GOC of the Fourth Army based in Syria, ordered his security police to collect evidence on hundreds of prominent Arab nationalists. A number of French diplomats failed to destroy their records of contact with the nationalists, thereby handing evidence of the Arabs' treasonable activities to the Turkish security police. *The Arab Bulletin*, No. 2, 12 June 1916, pp. 13–18. For more on the betrayal of the Arab representatives by consul-general François Georges-Picot, later a co-architect of the Sykes–Picot Agreement, see Tauber, *Arab Movements*, 35–56. Jemal responded to the evidence with a new policy of terror against Arab nationalists in June 1915. Arrests, imprisonment,

torture, courtmartial proceedings and deportations continued for the rest of the year. Two public mass executions were held, on 21 August 1915 and 6 May 1916 (Amin Lutfi al-Hafiz was amongst the victims). After the revolt broke in the Hejaz in June 1916, the courts in Constantinople stayed Jemal's ruling for the execution of political prisoners. The Sherif added his warning to Constantinople that he would match any further executions of Arabs with executions of captured Turkish officers and of the captive Vali of the Hejaz. 'Extracts and precis of articles in *El Akha el Othmani*, Beyrout, 6 May 1916'. *The Arab Bulletin*, No. 2, 12 June 1916, pp. 13–15. Tauber, *The Arab Movements*, pp. 35–56.

71 'The Arab Question', D.G. Hogarth, FO882/2 AP/16/2, fo. 199. 'Arab Revolt in the Hejaz', *The Arab Bulletin*, No. 5, 18 June 1916, p. 43.

72 'The Arab Question', Hogarth, FO882/2 AP/16/2, fo. 199.

73 The inland towns of Syria referred to Damascus, Aleppo, Homs and Hama. Al-Faruqi's concession was nevertheless ambiguous for he promised that any French rule over the region would be 'strenuously resisted' by the Muslim population. Clayton, memorandum, 11 October 1915. Ormsby-Gore, 'Summary of historical documents', 29 November 1916, FO882/5 HRG/16/65, fos 207, pp. 209–12.

74 Lawrence to Lloyd, 19 September 1915, Brown (ed.), *Letters*, pp. 77–8.

75 War Council Meeting, No. 17, 10 March 1915, CAB42/1.

76 'Report of the Committee on Asiatic Turkey', 8 April 1915, CAB42/2.

77 Storrs, *Orientations*, p. 123; Lawrence, *Seven Pillars*, pp. 49–50.

78 A memorandum by an Arab nationalist, sent internally by Clayton to Storrs in September 1915, represented the modern view that the Turkish government's chosen Caliph (Muhammed V) was a poor guardian of Islam who had lost the 'Muslim countries' of Rumania, Serbia, Bosnia and Herzegovina, Montenegro, Cyprus, Tunis and Algiers, and should be replaced. 'The Future of the Islamic Khalifate', memo by Mohammed Rashad, 17 August 1912, fo. 5; and 'the Champion of the Koreish', 17 August 1912, fo. 7. FO882/18 TU/12/1, fos 1–7; contained in Clayton to Storrs, 4 September 1915, FO882/15 PNA/15/5, fo.20. The Sherif would also argue that the Turkish Sultan lost his legitimacy as Caliph when he denigrated the Islamic *sharia*, i.e. when he lost Muslim territory to enemies, permitted the westernization of the country's administration and armed forces, and elevated Turks to key government positions to the exclusion of Arabs and other minorities.

79 Storrs, 'The Khalifate', 6 May 1915, FO882/13 MIS/15/3, fo. 344. For more on this debate, see: Ormsby-Gore, 'Note on the Khalifate', FO882/3 HM/16/2, fos 131, 136; C.A. Nallino, *Appunti sulla natura del 'califfato' in genere e sul presunto 'Califfato Ottomano'*, pp. 5–7, 10, fo. 221.

80 A non-temporal Caliph also fulfilled the terms established by the British government in their stipulation of support for a 'Moslem entity,' as stated by Grey and the Foreign Office in March 1915 in negotiations with Russia and France: once the Allies took Constantinople, Britain's 'first desideratum would be the establishment of a Moslem entity. It would have to include Arabia, and the question would arise as to what was to go with it'. War Council Meeting, No. 18, 'The Partition of Turkey in Asia'. 19 March 1915, CAB42/1.

81 McMahon to Grey, 14 May 1915, No. 188, FO371/2486, fo. 60357.

82 Viceroy, 17 January 1915, FO371/2482, fo. 8281c, item 2. The Viceroy most likely had in mind the possibility of Allied 'interference' in defence of the Holy Places or Aden, or in the IEF 'D''s operations in Mesopotamia. But in retrospect his remarks most anticipated what was least expected at the time, a serious conflict of claims with the Sherif over Syria.

83 Clayton to Wingate, 28 January 1916, FO882/12 IND/16/1, fo. 70.

84 India Office estimates for this period reported that 66.6 million Muslims lived in India, amounting to one-fifth of the total population. 'Memorandum on Indian Muslims', India Office, London, 11 October 1915, Sudan Archive, W/135/4/14.

85

> Though Moslems as a whole do not regard a Caliph as analogous to a Pope, it is perfectly reasonable for us to say that we, for our part, do so regard him; *i.e.*, in his relations to our Moslem subjects and those of our Allies, and indeed, everywhere outside his own realm, he has, *qua* Caliph, a spiritual position only.
>
> Hogarth, 'The Next Caliphate', *The Arab Bulletin*, No. 49, 30 April 1917, pp. 191–2.

86 McMahon suggested a draft agreement with the Sherif based on al-Faruqi's statements. McMahon to Grey, *c.*19 October 1915. For McMahon's official invitation to the Sherif for an alliance, its terms and the definition of a future Arab state 'in which Great Britain is free to act without detriment to the interests of her ally, France' (referring to British and French spheres of control), see McMahon to Sherif Hussein bin Ali, 24 October 1915, Bourne and Watt (eds), *British Documents*, Vol. II, pp. 367–8.
87 Grey to McMahon, tel. 796, 20 October 1915, FO371/2486, fo. 208.
88 Clayton to Wingate, 27 October 1915, Sudan Archive, W/135/4/77.
89 Cromer to Wingate, [undated but *c.*October 1915], Sudan Archive, W/135/4/38.
90 Wingate to Clayton, 9 January 1915, Sudan Archive, Box 469/8/14.
91 McMahon to Foreign Office, London, tel. 761, 10 December 1915, FO371/2486, fo. 480.
92 Andrew and Kanya-Forstner, *France Overseas*, London: Thames and Hudson, 1981, p. 90.
93 Al-Faruqi was appointed the Sherif's official spokesman in January 1916.
94 Sykes to DMO, London, 20 November 1915, tels 19, 20, 21. Repeated verbatim by High Commissioner to the Foreign Office, 20 November 1915, tel. 707. Ormsby-Gore, 'Summary of historical documents', 29 November 1916, FO882/5 HRG/16/65, fos 225–32. Sykes' correspondence is also contained, under heading 'Franco-Arab difficulties about Syria and Palestine', in FO882/13 MIS/15/17.
95 McMahon diverged from the de Bunsen proposals in his negotiations with the Sherif by assigning the Syrian coast to France for direct rule rather than as a sphere of influence and reserving the inland Syrian towns of Damascus, Homs, Hama and Aleppo for inclusion in the independent Arab State. McMahon to Sherif Hussein bin Ali, 24 October 1915. Bourne and Watt (eds), *British Documents on Foreign Affairs*, Vol. II, pp. 367–8. For Lawrence's influence on this separation of the inland towns from the coast, delivered first to Clayton, see Lawrence, 'Syria: the Raw Material. Fragmentary notes written early in 1915, but not circulated'. *Arab Bulletin*, No. 44, 12 March 1917, pp. 107–14. See also Wilson, *Lawrence*, pp. 183–6.
96 Nicolson to Hardinge, 16 February 1916, Private letter, FO800/381, fo. 135.
97 A.C. Parker to Clayton, 25 November 1915, Letter, Sudan Archive, W135/6/34, 1. Aubrey Herbert also made personal recommendations in London to Nicolson, George Clerk and Grey for immediate support of the Arabs; see Herbert to Clayton, 7 November 1915, FO882/2 AP/15/7, fo. 133.
98 'Note on the Arab Movement', Parker and Callwell, 29 November 1915, FO882/2 AP/15/11. Callwell had earlier regretted to Parker that 'We have got to keep in with our infernal Allies'. Parker to Clayton, 19 November 1915, Letter, Sudan Archive, W/135/6/13. George Clerk of the FO had urged Parker to enlist Callwell to make such a case to the French 'on military grounds', namely, that failing to negotiate fairly with the Arabs would eventually require France and Britain to withdraw troops from France. Parker to Clayton, 25 November 1915, Letter, Sudan Archive, W/135/6/34, 1. For the Sherif's warning (expressed in a letter to Sayed Ali Morghani, a pro-British Sudanese religious leader and rival of the Mahdists) that without the desired boundaries, the Arabs would soon be persuaded by German and Turk propaganda to raise a *jihad* against the British, see McMahon to Grey, 5

November 1915, tel. 674, in Ormsby-Gore, 'Summary of historical documents', 29 November 1916, FO882/5/ HRG/16/65, fo. 198.

99 Sir A. Chamberlain to Grey, relayed in Grey to McMahon, 11 November 1915, tel. 874, in Ormsby-Gore, 'Summary of historical documents', 29 November 1916, FO882/5 HRG/16/65, fo. 199.

100 Clayton to Maxwell, Egypt (Mudros), 'Sherif of Mecca and preparations for the Rising', 12 November 1915, FO882/12 KH/15/12, fo. 151.

101 Grey to McMahon, 11 November 1915, tel. 874, in Ormsby-Gore, 'Summary of historical documents', 29 November 1916, FO882/5 HRG/16/65, fo. 200.

102 McMahon to FO, London, tel. 736, 30 November 1915, FO371/2486, fos 447–8.

103 McMahon to Sherif Hussein, 14 December 1915, Cmd.5957. English translation in *Correspondence between Sir Henry McMahon … and the Sherif of Mecca*, HMSO, p. 12.

104 McMahon to the FO, London, 24 January 1916, FO371/2767, No. 20954.

105 Storrs, *Orientations*, p. 154.

106 Ibid., pp. 195–6.

107 G.M. Bell to Lawrence, 18 March 1916, FO882/13 MES/16/2, fo. 264.

108 Lawrence to Clayton ('Intrusive', Cairo), 8 April 1916, FO882/15 PNA/16/2, fo. 72.

109 Sykes' engagement with the Arab cause was fervent if not always coherent. While negotiating the Ottoman Empire's partition with Picot, he could still complain, somewhat bizarrely, that the German–Turk efforts to separate the Arabs from the Entente were designed not merely to weaken the latter but to 'eliminate the last centre of uncontrollable intellectualism from Ottoman Enterprise'. Sykes to DMO, London, [undated, but probably *c*.21 November 1915), tel. 21, Sudan Archive, W/135/6/19.

110 Anglo-Egypt was keenly aware that Germany 'sedulously maintained' its propaganda efforts in Egypt. See Storrs, *Orientations*, p. 133.

111 Memorandum by Sykes, 23 December 1915, FO882/2 ARB/15/3.

112 Statement by Parker, in Wingate to Clayton, 4 December 1915, tel. 863, FO882/2 AP/15/12.

113 Sykes to Clayton, 28 December 1915, FO882/2 ARB/15/4, fos 1–14.

114 Ibid. Minute by Arthur Hirtzel (Sec. Political and Secret Dept, IO) on SSI to Viceroy, 18 January 1916, L/P&S/10/576 P182 #218. For more on the British navy's enthusiasm for modern technologies, in contrast to the army, see Keegan, *First World War*, pp. 279–82.

115 W.R. Hall, DNI to Clayton, 20 December 1915, FO882/2 ARB/15/2.

116 Clayton to Sykes, London, 13 December 1915, FO882/2 ARB/15/1.

117 'The Bureau will be quite a new child and must be allowed to grow up and expand in the directions indicated by experience'. Clayton to Hall, 13 January 1916, FO882/2 ARB/16/5, fos 24–6.

118 Minute by Clayton (to the Residency), 4 January 1916, FO882/2 ARB/16/3, fos 20–1.

119 The conference was conducted by nine members representing the War Office (including the DMI and the DMO), FO, IO, Admiralty (DNI) and CID. Committee of Imperial Defence Paper, 'Establishment of an Arab Bureau in Cairo', Report of an Inter-departmental Conference, 7 January 1916, FO882/2 ARB/16/4, fos 22–4.

120 CID Paper, 'Establishment of an Arab Bureau in Cairo', 7 January 1916, FO882/2 ARB/16/4; also in Creedy Papers, WO159, Box 2, Misc., file 2, #33A.

121 Hirtzel, minute, 31 August 1916, attached to 'Note by Sir Percy Cox [CPO, Basra] on the newly formed Eastern Bureau [Arab Bureau] and the functions of the Basra Branch', No. 6162, P3404/16, #108 R/20/A/1569 IOLR.

122 Lawrence to Will Lawrence (brother), 17 July 1915, Garnett (ed.), *Letters*, p. 90.

123 CID Paper, 'Establishment of an Arab Bureau in Cairo', 7 January 1916, FO882/2 ARB/16/4, fos 22–4.

124 SSI to Viceroy, 10 December 1915, L/P&S/10/576 P4522/1915 #236; CID Paper, 'Establishment of an Arab Bureau in Cairo', 7 January 1916, FO 882/2 ARB/16/4, fos 22–4. It was eventually resolved that India retained the right to decline propaganda policy suggestions from Cairo. For more on this debate, see: memo by Sykes, 'Constitution and Functions of the Arabian Bureau', 23 December 1915, FO882/2 ARB/15/3; SSI to Viceroy, 10 December 1915, L/P&S/10/576 P4522/1915 #236; Viceroy to SSI, 24 December 1915 (rec. 27 December), L/P&S/10/576 P4744 #229; SSI to Viceroy, 18 January 1916, L/P&S/10/576 P182 #218; A.H. Grant to A.B. fforde, 22 May 1916, D.-o., No. 593, W. R/20/A/1569 IOLR.

125 Chamberlain to Lord Chelmsford, Viceroy, Foreign Department, 26 April 1916, L/P&S/10/576 P1495? [*sic*] #167.

126 General P. Lake to Chamberlain, 11 June 1916, L/P&S/10/1576 P2255 #154, IOLR. Copies to MI, FO, DMI, Sykes.

127 Lord Chelmsford, Viceroy, to SSI, 20 June 1916, R/20/A/1569 P2379 A16 #146.

128 Memo by John E. Shuckburgh, 13 June 1916, P2255 #151 IOLR. Hirzel minuted after the above:

> We seem to be getting into a tangle [...] The intention was to make it clear that neither the Bureau nor General Lake is to have an independent Arab policy – which both of them wd. like to have. The policy is that of HMG, & the Bureau is the organ through which, for purposes of propaganda only, that policy will be revealed to Genl. Lake. It is difficult to make this clearer than previous telms [*sic*] have made it.
>
> Hirtzel, minute, #144, attached to Viceroy to SSI, 20 June 1916, R/20/A/1569.

For the Arab Bureau's 'consternation' at India's suspicions, see fforde to Grant, 27 June 1916, item #27, and 6 July 1916, Item #31, No. 140, W.C. R/20/A/1569 IOLR.

129 See: 'Establishment of an Arab Bureau in Cairo', 7 January 1916, ARB/16/4, fos 22–4; Chamberlain to Lord Hardinge, Viceroy and Governor-General of India, 18 January 1916, L/P&S/10/576 P182, tel. 218. Clayton commented diplomatically on the fact that Sykes would not be directly involved in running the Arab Bureau. 'I do not think it will be necessary to tie [Sykes] down as a permanent member of the Bureau; he would be more useful as a freelance, available to go wherever it was necessary to obtain information.' Clayton to Hall, 13 January 1916, FO882/2 ARB/16/5.

130 Captain (later Major) Cornwallis, who had read Arabic at Oxford, entered the Civil Service in the Sudan in 1906 and later worked the Egyptian Ministry of Finance. In early 1916 he transferred to the Arab Bureau. After Hogarth was recalled to the Admiralty in August 1916, Cornwallis replaced him as Director of the Arab Bureau. 'Arab Bureau Report for August 1916', K. Cornwallis, 4 September 1916, FO371/2681/188311. He held the post until 1919 when he was invited by Prince Feisal to be his Adviser in the new state of Iraq. Herbert Garland took over as Director of the Arab Bureau in 1919.

131 For background on A.B. fforde's appointment to the Arab Bureau, see correspondence between SSI and Viceroy, December 1915 (L/P&S/10/578 P4522/1915, fo. 236 and P4744, fo. 229), January 1916 (L/P&S/10/576 P182 #182) and February 1916 (L/P&S/10/576 P570 #207).

132 Hogarth, 'First Report, Arab Bureau', 1 May 1916, Enclosure No. 2, Serial No. 8, R/20/A/1569 IOLR. fforde described the Arab Bureau's informal attitude to staff recruitment to Delhi:

> 'There are several officers who are technically in the Arab Bureau when they are doing Arab work and out of it when they are not'; 'Everyone does whatever turns up [...] There are many ephemeral Bureaux in Cairo at present, containing all sorts of men drawn from all sorts of pursuits and all sorts of places'.
>
> fforde to Grant, 16 June 1916, No. 140, WC item #23 R/20/A/1569 IOLR.

133 Hogarth, 'First Report, Arab Bureau', 1 May 1914, Enclosure No. 2, Serial No. 8, R/20/A/1569 IOLR

134 fforde observed that McMahon seemed to be in the habit of consulting Clayton exclusively about the Arab Bureau's activities, at least during the first months of the Arab Revolt: 'He only worked through Clayton and did not even send for Hogarth'. fforde to Grant, 14 July 1916, No. 187 W/C R/20/A/1569 IOLR.

135 Typical of this perspective is Fromkin's description of McMahon as 'notoriously dull-witted and ineffectual'. Fromkin, *A Peace*, p. 95.

136 fforde to Grant, 30 June 1916, 140 WC item #29 R/20/A/1569 IOLR. See also fforde to Grant, 16 June 1916, 140 WC item #23 R/20/A/1569 IOLR.

137 Ibid., 6 July 1916, 140 WC item #31 R/20/A/1569 IOLR.

138 Ibid., 8 June 1916, item #18. D.O. No. 100 W.C. R/20/A/1569 IOLR, relaying a conversation with a colleague at the Arab Bureau whose name was deleted in this copy. For more comments on the Arab Bureau's possible post-war role, see: T.W. Holderness, India Office, minute, 4 September 1916, No. 6162, P3404/16, #108 R/20/A/1569 IOLR; Cox to Secretary, Foreign and Political Department, Government of India, 2 November 1916, P5127/16 #100 R/20/A/1569 IOLR.

139 Diary entry by S.P. Cockerell (friend of George Lloyd), 27 December 1914. GLLD 9/1.

2 The outbreak of the Arab Revolt, May–November 1916

1 McMahon to FO, London, 10 December 1915, tel. 761, FO371/2468, fo. 480.

2 fforde to Grant, 16 April 1916, D.O. 684, No. 662W R/20/A/1569.

3 'The fundamental aim of Cairo policy is to frustrate the attempts of Germany and the CUP to unite Islam against Great Britain,' insisted fforde. 'The Arab Question. – Cairo Policy', fforde to Grant, 25 April 1916, No. 662 W, item 4, fos 5–6. R/20/A/1569. IOLR. Grant declared that it was 'incredible that the Sheriff and his Arabs will be able to raise any kind of revolt in the Hedjaz against the Turks who have guns'. He also seemed to suggest that India took comfort from the secret clause limiting Britain's obligations to the Arab leaders. 'Whether we are to remain the absolute rulers of the occupied territory must depend of course on the extent to which the Sheriff [*sic*] of Mecca and his party carry out their engagements to McMahon.' Grant to fforde, 22 May 1916, D.-o., No. 593 W, fos 10, 12. R/20/A/1569 IOLR.

4 Cairo Intelligence calculated that the HEF [formerly the 22nd Army Division] were distributed between Medina with 3,000 troops, Ta'if with 1,200 troops, Mecca with 1,000 troops, and Jiddah with 1,000 troops, plus the train troops, the local (Arab) gendarmes, and the force maintaining Yemen's garrison. The Turkish 21st Division, numbering ten battalions or 4,000–5,000 troops, garrisoned the Asir province south of the Hejaz. The 3rd Division in southern Syria was a possible reinforcement for the HEF. *The Arab Bulletin*, No. 6, 23 June 1916, pp. 47–8.

5 The Sherif's original date for an Arab uprising had been August 1916. McMahon, 'Record of a Conference called by Sir H. McMahon to discuss the military situation', [at Ismailia.] 12 September 1916, FO882/4 HRG/16/46, fo. 343. *The Arab Bulletin*, No. 16, 18 August 1916, p. 169; No. 22, 19 September 1916, p. 274; No. 52, 31 May 1917, p. 249.

6 'Arab revolt in the Hejaz', *The Arab Bulletin*, No. 5, 18 June 1916, p. 43. By 22 June 1916, Turkish repair crews were spotted on the railway. *The Arab Bulletin*, No. 6, 23 June 1916, pp. 47–8.

7 'Arab revolt in the Hejaz', *The Arab Bulletin*, No. 5, 18 June 1916, p. 44; 'Extracts from Official Turkish correspondence, dated about June 15, 1916, captured at Jeddah', No. 25, 7 October 1916, p. 345.

8 *The Arab Bulletin*, No. 5, 18 June 1916, pp. 43–4; No. 6, 23 June 1916, p. 47. See also McMahon to Viceroy, 28 May 1916, No. 700 W/C #62 R/20/A/1569 IOLR.

9 'Arab revolt in the Hejaz', *The Arab Bulletin*, No. 5, 18 June 1916, p. 44. 'Translation of an Account … by Bimbashi Mehmed Zia Bey, Acting Governor and Commandant at Mecca', *The Arab Bulletin*, No. 21, 15 September 1916, pp. 258–60. Tauber, *Arab Movements*, p. 81.
10 In his official proclamation of revolt on 26 June 1916, the Sherif condemned the Turks' attack: they had damaged the Kaaba, set fire to the Kiswe [Curtain] and endangered the Sepulchre of Abraham. *The Arab Bulletin*, No. 9, 9 July 1916, pp. 7, 10.
11 The Jiyad and Nekato forts outside Mecca surrendered on 4 and 10 July 1916, respectively. Nearly 1,000 Turks in the Hejaz surrendered to or were captured by the Arabs in the first four weeks, bringing the number of Turkish PoWs to 2,500, plus 150 administrators in July 1916. Said Ali Bey (CO Egyptforce at Mecca) to C.E. Wilson, 4 July 1916. Transcript of telephone message. Sudan Archive. W/138/3/18–19. Said Ali Bey to Wilson (undated, but *c*.4 July 1916) telegram (unnumbered) Sudan Archive W/138/3/20. *The Arab Bulletin*, No. 5, 18 June 1916, p. 44; No. 11, 17 July 1916, p. 5; No. 13, 1 August 1916, p. 130.
12 A Persian consul told an agent working for the Arab Bureau in Jiddah that although the Turks were prepared to bear food and water shortages for months, British naval and air power had left them panicked and in fear of being 'butchered' by the Arabs. Report dated 21 June 1916. *The Arab Bulletin*, No. 7, 30 June 1916, p. 8. See also: *The Arab Bulletin*, No. 5, 18 June 1916, pp. 43–4; No. 6, 23 June 1916, p. 47; No. 15, 10 August 1916, p. 166; 'Extracts from Official Turkish correspondence', No. 25, 7 October 1916, p. 345; Liddell Hart, *Lawrence of Arabia*, pp. 60–1.
13 *The Arab Bulletin*, No. 5, 18 June 1916, p. 44. From an agent's report, dated 16 June, *The Arab Bureau*, No. 7, 30 June 1916, p. 8.
14 Wilson to Wingate, 20 June 1916, tel. 522, Sudan Archive, W/137/7/120. *The Arab Bulletin*, No. 6, 23 June 1916, p. 47; No. 11, 17 July 1916, p. 5; No. 13, 1 August 1916, p. 130
15 *The Arab Bulletin*, No. 9, 9 July 1916, p. 6.
16 The Arab Bureau's decision to publish an explicit transcript of this message suggests that it was probably sent *en clair*. *The Arab Bulletin*, No. 9, 9 July 1916, p. 1.
17 *The Arab Bulletin*, No. 25, 7 October 1916, p. 341.
18 'Translation of an Account … Bimbashi Mehmed Zia Bey … Mecca', *The Arab Bulletin*, No. 21, 15 September 1916, pp. 250–2.
19 'Stotzingen–Neufeld Mission to Arabia', Translation of 'Report or Letter by Baron von Stotzingen at El-Ala on or about May 5, 1916', *The Arab Bulletin*, No. 13, 1 August 1916, pp. 134–5, 137–8. Von Stotzingen's interpreter's notebook contained Berlin's signals transmission hours, von Stotzingen's call sign and his radio wave-length. Lt F. Grobba's notebook, *The Arab Bulletin*, No. 22, 19 September 1916, p. 266.
20 'Further information of the Stotzingen Mission', *The Arab Bulletin*, No. 22, 19 September 1916, pp. 272–3. See also: 'Stotzingen–Neufeld Mission', incl. 'Report or Letter written by Baron von Stotzingen at El-Ala on or about May 5, 1916', *The Arab Bulletin*, No. 13, 1 August 1916, pp. 133–9.
21 *The Arab Bulletin*, No. 22, 19 September 1916, pp. 272. The association between von Stotzingen and Khairi Bey was assembled from Sigint, Turkish documents seized at Katia (Sinai) and the mission's captured papers. See 'Further information', 'Other Stotzingen Papers', *The Arab Bulletin*, No. 22, 19 September 1916, pp. 263–74. See also 'Stotzingen-Neufeld Mission', and 'Report or Letter', *The Arab Bulletin*, No. 13, 1 August 1916, pp. 133–9. The Arab Bureau wondered if the Turks' attempt to 'extend the front of her threat against our communications with India by one thousand miles' and employment of Neufeld suggested a project more than 'mere wireless telegraphy' – something involving submarines, for instance. 'Stotzingen–Neufeld Mission …', *The Arab Bulletin*, No. 13, 1 August 1916, pp. 135–6. See also 'Further information', *The Arab Bulletin*, No. 22, 19 September 1916, pp. 272–3. For Arab Bureau assessments of enemy designs on Allied troops at

Somaliland, Abyssinia, Eritrea, the Sudan, and Aden using German seaborne detachments from the Yemen or Hadhramaut, and their concern that the Hejaz railway 'would soon have shown the world the weakness – for us – of this long corridor of sea from Aden to Suez', see: 'Further information', *The Arab Bulletin*, No. 22, 19 September 1916, pp. 272–4; 'Feisal's Table-Talk', report by Lawrence, *The Arab Bulletin*, No. 42, 15 February 1917, pp. 78–80.

22 'Stotzingen–Neufeld Mission', *The Arab Bulletin*, No. 13, 1 August 1916, pp. 134, 138. *The Arab Bulletin*, No. 22, 19 September 1916, pp. 264, 268, 272.

23 Months later, the Arab Bureau still hoped the wireless equipment dropped at Yenbo would be found. After testimony by a Rifaa Juheinah, the British 'spent fruitless hours dragging for it in the harbour', see Lawrence, *Seven Pillars*, p. 157. See also 'Stotzingen–Neufeld Mission to Arabia' *The Arab Bulletin*, No. 22, 19 September 1916, p. 272. First draft of tel. from von Stotzingen, probably at Damascus, to Military Attaché, in Lt Grobba's notebook (Second draft sent 9 June 1916), 'Further information', *The Arab Bulletin*, No. 22, 19 September 1916, pp. 268, 271; 'Report or Letter', No. 13, 1 August 1916, pp. 137–9. Turkish documents captured at Wejh in February 1917 helped confirm these events. 'Wejh papers', *The Arab Bulletin*, No. 43, 28 February 1917, p. 103.

24 'Summary of some Points of the Stotzingen Expedition (c) Wireless', 'Other Stotzingen Papers', *The Arab Bulletin*, No. 22, 19 September 1916, p. 271.

25 'Extracts from Report by Colonel Wilson on his meeting with Sherif Feisal Bey at Yenbo, August 27 and 28, 1916', *The Arab Bulletin*, No. 20, 14 September 1916, pp. 241–2. The Anazeh were a confederation of the Rualla, Muhallaf and Wuld Ali tribes, led by the Paramount Rualla chief, Nuri Shaalan. Hogarth, 'The Anazeh Tribes and Chiefs', *The Arab Bulletin*, No. 32, 26 November 1916, p. 490.

26 fforde tried to elaborate on Cairo's different perspective to India, with a gentle reprimand regarding the latter's usual practices:

> The only point to bear in mind is that [HMG] are committed to the principles of Arab independence and local autonomy, which means, I take it, that we must not set one chief above another, if we wish to, without the consent of their subjects.
>
> fforde to Grant, 25 April 1916, 662W, item 4:
> 'The Arab Question. – Cairo Policy', R/20/A/1569 IOLR.

27 The HMS *Anne*, HMS *Suva* and SS *Surada* transported an Egyptian battery, six mountain guns and a six-gun maxim battery staffed by sixty Egyptian gunners, 3,000 rifles, munitions and foodstuffs. The need for Muslim Arab gunners was clear and McMahon had appealed to India to transfer any available Arab artillerymen amongst their PoWs to the Hejaz. McMahon to Viceroy, 17 June 1916, tel. 294, S, No. 700 W/C #87 R/20/A/1569 IOLR. See also: Intelligence Summaries, GHQ, Egyptforce, 21 June 1916, WO157/705; Cornwallis, 'Report on Jeddah', 8 July 1916, FO882/4 HRG/16/31, fos 224–6; McMahon to Murray, 20 June 1916, FO141 738/3818/11, item 4; *The Arab Bulletin*, No. 9, 9 July 1916, p. 7.

28 Al-Faruqi had persuaded the Sherif to make him his Agent in Cairo. The British declined to give him a private telegraph clerk, forcing him to transmit his communications through the British wireless operators. The Arab Bureau soon obtained the 'key' to al-Faruqi's encryptions and read all his transmissions. fforde reported to Delhi that 'there is not a word [in them] so far to arouse suspicion of duplicity of disloyalty to us. This is about as good a test as we want'. fforde to Grant, 13 July 1916, D.O. No. 187, W/C R/20/A/1569 IOLR. Rafei had been employed by the Sudan Agency in Cairo. He now declared himself the Sherif's Civil Representative in Jiddah. Cornwallis, 'Report on Jeddah', 8 July 1916, FO882/4 HRG/16/31, fos 240–1, pp. 226–40 *passim*.

29 Four mountain guns, the maxim battery and escort continued on to Rabegh. Cornwallis, 'Report on Jeddah', 8 July 1916, FO 882/4 HRG/16/31, fos 227–8.

30 Rabegh's Turcophilic chief, Sheikh Hussein Mubeirig, and a band of Turks organized the blockade with thousands of Arab sympathizers after hearing rumours that Britain's Egyptian troops would be landed 'by force'. Cornwallis, 'Report on Jeddah', 8 July 1916, FO882/4 HRG/16/31, fos 232–5.
31 Cornwallis, 'Report on Jeddah', 8 July 1916, FO882/4 HRG/16/31, fos 235–8, p. 240.
32 Ibid., fos 231–2.
33 Cornwallis also wondered whether an Arab Military Mission from Cairo might be of use to the Sherif, despite Cairo's Arab nationalists' apparently being interested only in 'an unlimited supply of gold, supplies and munitions', but this interesting proposal was never adopted. Cornwallis, 'Report on Jeddah', 8 July 1916, FO882/4 HRG/16/31, fos 243–5.
34 Al-Faruqi demanded a 'nucleus' regular army of 30,000 (echoing al-Masri's request) drawn from prisoners in Egypt, India and Basra, supplied by Britain and led by al-Masri and himself. Cornwallis, 'Report on Jeddah', 8 July 1916, FO882/4 HRG/16/31, fos 229–30.
35 Ibid., fos 242–3. fforde remarked on same to Delhi:

> We may take it that the invasion of Syria and consequent complications with the French are very far off. [The Sherif] is not wanted to go beyond the Hedjaz. At present his control over the Arabs there is not really effective, witness the Rabugh or Rabegh incident and the conditions round Yembo.
>
> fforde to Grant, 14 July 1916, No. 187, W/C R/20/A/1569 IOLR.

36 Kitchener drowned on 5 June 1916 after his ship, the HMS *Hampshire*, struck a German mine off the North Sea coast.
37 fforde to Grant, 18 June 1916 (Secret) W.C.140, Item 26, R/20/A/1569 IOLR. Gertrude Bell remarked of Kitchener: 'He knew, at any rate, that there's such a thing as the Arab question, and that's an asset.' G. Bell to Hardinge, 12 June 1916, Private letter, Hardinge Papers, #23, Vol. II, p. 94.
38 Despite Wingate's initial optimism regarding McMahon's arrival, he was soon complaining to Clayton that 'in spite of my position in Egypt & the Sudan & the number of years I have been in the country, little use has been made of my experience in this, or in other matters connected with the situation.' Wingate to Clayton, 18 February 1915: 'Very Private.' Sudan Archive, Box 469/8/40, pp. 1–2. See also: Wingate to Clayton, 14 January 1915, Sudan Archive, Box 469/8/14, p. 3; Wingate to Clayton, 27 February 1915, 'Very Private.' Sudan Archive, Box 469/8/44.
39 Operations by the Turcophilic Senussi tribes along the Libyan border had dwindled after British troops defeated their most militant leader in February 1916, and the Egyptian army had stopped an incursion in the west country by the Sultan of Darfur in May.
40 McMahon to Murray, 20 June 1916, FO141 738/3818/11, item 4.
41 Wingate to McMahon, 30 June 1916, tel. 862, FO141 738/3818/11, item 7.
42 Ibid. See also: Wingate to Hogarth, 5 July 1916, Private, Sudan Archive, W/138/3/51–54. See also: Wingate to Parker, 3 July 1916, Private letter, Sudan Archive, W/138/3/55–6:

> When one thinks of the old days with Lord Cromer and Lord Kitchener in the Agency chair, and how they would have dealt with such a matter, you can perhaps appreciate my feelings and what I have had to submit to practically ever since the war began.

43 A prescient statement on future Arab operations. McMahon to Sirdar, 26 June 1916, FO141 738/3818/11, item 6.
44 McMahon to Wingate, 2 July 1916, FO141 738/3818/11, fo. 10. Draft to C-in-C, 1 July 1916; GHQ to McMahon, 2 July 1916, FO141 738/3818/11, item 11.
45 fforde to Grant, 30 June 1916, R/20/A/1569, No. 140 W.C. #29.

46 Wingate to McMahon, 4 July 1916, FO141 738/3818/11, item 12.

47 McMahon to Wingate, 2 July 1916, FO141 738/3818/11, item 10. Draft telegraphed to C-in-C, 1 July 1916. McMahon appealed to Murray: 'The Sirdar has, I think, got an exaggerated idea of the scope of his new task' in assuming military control for the Hejaz for 'it is limited by the small extent to which unfortunately we can assist the Sherif.' McMahon to Murray, 1 July 1916, FO141 738/3818/11, item 9

48 Wingate to McMahon, 4 July 1916, FO141 738/3818/11, item 12.

49 Wingate also requested the transfer of Cornwallis (or a similarly qualified officer), a cipher officer and an interpreter to Port Sudan. Wingate to McMahon, 4 July 1916, FO141 738/3818/11, item 12. None of the proposals were implemented.

50 Wingate to McMahon, 4 July 1916, FO141 738/3818/11, item 12.

51 Wingate also wanted the Sherif's 'war material (including guns)' to be sent directly 'to Jeddah instead of retaining them at Suez'. Wingate to McMahon, 7 July 1916, FO141 738/3818/11, item 13.

52 fforde to Grant, 13 July 1916, D.O.187 W/C R/20/A/1569 IOLR.

53 Murray to Robertson, 15 June 1916, A.M.652 cipher, FO141 738/3818/11, item 2; also in WO158/625.

54 Robertson to Murray, 16 June 1916, L7939 cipher. FO141 738/3818/11, item 3.

55 Intelligence Summary, GHQ, Egyptforce, for 24 June 1916, WO157/705.

56 Murray to McMahon, 19 June 1916, FO141 738/3818/11, item 1.

57 McMahon to Murray, 20 June 1916, FO141 738/3818/11, item 4.

58 Murray to Wingate, repeating McMahon, 25 June 1916, FO141 738/3818/11, item 5. Parker to Wingate, 6 July 1916, Letter, Sudan Archive, W/138/3/69, 2.

59 fforde to Grant, 14 July 1916, R/20/A/1569 D.O. No. 187.

60 Parker to Wingate, 6 July 1916, Letter, Sudan Archive, W/138/3/69, 2–3.

61 Lawrence, *Seven Pillars*, p. 61.

62 fforde to Grant, 14 July 1916, No. 187 W/C R/20/A/1569 IOLR.

63 For more discussion on this rumour as well as the limited impression made by the Kaiser's 'embrace of Islamic faith' after so much 'Turkish misrule', see Sir L. Mallet (Brit. ambassador to Turkey), 14 October 1914. Relaying report, consul at Aleppo, FO371/2140/46756, fo. 340.

64 Clayton, 30 October 1914, in Cheetham to Grey, 30 November 1914, FO371/2140/46261, fos 180–1. Al-Faruqi would make the same claim in 1915. See Clayton, memorandum, 11 October 1915, in Ormsby-Gore, 'Summary of historical documents', 29 November 1916, FO882/5 HRG/16/65.

65 *The Arab Bulletin*, No. 12, 19 July 1916, p. 1.

66 Wilson to Wingate, 30 June 1916, tel. 522, Sudan Archive, W/137/7/120 fo. 121.

67 Cornwallis, 'Report on Jeddah', 8 July 1916, FO882/4 HRG/16/31. Al-Masri had aired similar rumours regarding some 15,000 deserters waiting at Jebel-Druse. Clayton, 30 October 1914, in Cheetham to Grey, 30 November 1914, FO371/2140/46261, fos 180–1. Al-Faruqi's erratic performance led to his dismissal by the Sherif, who soon chose to transmit to Cairo directly through Wilson, Pilgrimage Officer (Jiddah Agent). McMahon to Hardinge, 22 July 1916, Hardinge MSS, Vol. II, #23, fos 165–7.

68 Translation of letter from Sherif Hussein to McMahon; contained in McMahon to Viceroy, 18 April 1916, item #57, Enclosure #3, D.O. No. 700 W/C R/20/A/1569 IOLR. *The Arab Bulletin*, No. 9, 9 July 1916, 7. See also: fforde to Grant, 4 May 1916, item #8, Enclosure No. 1, Serial No. 8 R/20/A/1569 IOLR; Murray to Robertson, 14 July 1916, Private, CAB44/15 122.

69 It was believed that rebel activity by the Rualla and other tribes might draw the Turks back from the Sinai, and leave the railway exposed at Beersheba. Tribes nearer the Red Sea to the south might assist Egyptforce in taking the port of Aqaba. fforde to Grant, 28 July 1916, item #47, D.O. No. 187, W/C R/20/A/1569 IOLR; see also Minutes of War Committee meeting, 7 July 1916, CAB42/16/1.

70 fforde to Grant, 28 July 1916, D.O. No. 187, item #47, R/20/A/1569 IOLR. Minutes

of War Committee meeting, 7 July 1916, CAB42/16/1. See also Hardinge, FO to Grant, 3 August 1916, MSS.Eur.D.660/10. IOLR.

71 'I am surprisingly short of topographical information'. Murray to Robertson, 14 July 1916, Private, CAB44/15 122. See also: fforde to Grant, 28 July 1916, D.O. No. 187, item #47, W/C R/20/A/1569 IOLR; Minutes of Ismailia Conference, 12 September 1916, FO882/4 HRG/16/46.

72 AIR 1/1706/204/123/65, 30 July 1916, Serial [Flight] Nos 22–3; 1 August 1916, Serial No. 24; C. L'Estrange (Squadron Cmmdr, RN, HMS *Ben-my-Chree*) 7 August 1916. 'Confidential' *Raven II.*

73 Photographs include: communication trench along Glass Hills, south of Wadi Ithm, #4 and #5; main entrenchments, Wadi Munslini, NE of Aqaba fort, #6; Aqaba Gully with crisscrossing trenches, #13–15; Ma'an Road merging into Wadi Ithm, north of Aqaba fort, #22 and #23; front view of Aqaba fort and Aqaba Gully, #28. AIR1/2284/209/75/8. 'I have had careful reconnaissances made of the landing places in the Gulf, and I find that even initial operations present great difficulties.' Murray to Robertson, 18 August 1916, Private, CAB44/15, 141.

74 For more discussion on prospects of British landing at Aqaba, see: McMahon to Hardinge, 5 September 1916. Hardinge MSS, Vol. IV, #25, fos 61–2; Hardinge to McMahon, 13 September 1916, Hardinge MSS, Vol. IV, #25, fos 109–10.

75 'Information obtained from two Arab officers recently arrived in England from Kermanshah via the Caucasus, and examined by Sir M. Sykes, War Office, 25 September 1916,' 29 September 1916, FO371/2781/193557. Sent by DMI to USS for FA. See also: Statements from an agent in Aleppo in early November 1916, GHQ, Egypt to DMI, London, 4 December 1916, I.A.2704 WO33/905, No. 6252.

76 Appreciation of the Annexed Arabian Report No. XI (New Series), 9 October 1916, FO371 2781/201201. *The Arab Bulletin* reported the various speculations about the Anazeh: the pro-Turk Billi chief, Suleiman Rifada, told Parker that 'all the Anazah and tribes of the interior' were with the Turks. No. 23, 26 September 1916, 303. But the Sherif's reports claimed that the southern Anazeh including the Rualla sided with him, in spirit if not in practice. No. 24, 5 October 1916, 324.

77 Feisal asked for 15,000 more rifles to arm these now 'loyal' Northern tribes. Wilson to Arbur [Arab Bureau], Cairo, 3 November 1916, W.482 cipher, WO/603/61A.

78 *The Arab Bulletin*, No. 32, 26 November 1916, 493.

79 GHQ, Egypt to WO, London, 3 November 1916, WO33/905, No. 6064 No.A.M.1215; WO to GHQ, Egypt, 8 November 1916, WO33/905, No. 6083.

80 Murray to Wingate, 8 November 1916, A.M.1234 cipher (relaying content of A.M.1233 to CIGS), WO158/603/77A.

81 Such an enterprise would require heavy-weight-carrying aircraft, as requested, to transport the arms, personnel and fuel supplies inland. Murray to Robertson, 8 November 1916, WO33/905, No. 6089 A.M.1233. Ibid., 12 November 1916, WO33/905, No. 6125 A.M.1251. For CIGS's mention of report on Nuri's revolt to War Committee, see Minutes of War Committee, 7 November 1916, Vol. 23. CAB42/23/9. For Wingate's expression of support for this 'admirable' scheme, see: Wingate to Robertson, 9 November 1916, WO33/905, No. 6097, tel. 747.

82 Wilson to the Sherif of Mecca, 19 November 1916, FO686/55/1212, fos 1–2.

83 Murray repeated his intention to extend the railway to el Arish and Rafa, where he might then attack Beersheba. The intended aerodrome would be within seventy miles of the railway. Murray to Robertson, 10 December 1916, WO33/905, No. 6287 A.M.1380.

84 Robertson to Murray, 15 December 1916, WO33/905, No. 6232, No. 26624 cipher. See also: Murray to Robertson, 10 December 1916, WO33/905, No. 6287, A.M.1380; Robertson to Murray, 9 December 1916, WO33/905, No. 6279, No. 26174; FO to Wingate, in Robertson to Murray, 16 December 1916, WO33/905, No. 6335, No. 26663 cipher.

85 The railroad would reach el Arish by 15 January 1917 and Rafa by late February and

divert the Turks' attention from the Hejaz. Murray to Wingate, 15 December 1916, WO33/905, No. 6326, A.M.1397.

86 The Arab Bureau was certain in late November that the Druse had not yet joined the Arab Revolt, being too fearful of reprisals by Jemal. *The Arab Bulletin*, No. 32, 26 November 1916, p. 493.

87 Murray welcomed the French offer but insisted on retaining overall command over operations and communications with Nuri Shaaan, or 'matters will naturally be somewhat more complicated' (more complicated, apparently, than they already were). Murray to Robertson, 16 November 1916, WO33/905, No. 6148, A.M.1271.

88 Parker (Intelligence Department, Cairo) to Wingate, 6 July 1916, Letter, Sudan Archive, W/138/3/69, 3–4.

89 fforde to Grant, 7 July 1916, item 32, R/20/A/1569 IOLR. See also fforde to Grant, 30 June 1916, item 29, R/20/A/1569 IOLR.

90 The Arab Bureau was nevertheless certain that 'the Sherif has 90% of the (Syrian) Sheikhs firmly on his side'. *The Arab Bulletin*, No. 9, 9 July 1916, pp. 6–7.

91 'Extracts from a private letter', *The Arab Bulletin*, No. 16, 18 August 1916, p. 169.

92 *The Arab Bulletin*, No. 13, 1 August 1916, pp. 128–9. See also statement from representative, Berne, Switzerland. *The Arab Bulletin*, No. 10, 14 July 1916, p. 1.

93 Clayton also noted that the rifles 'promised him (from us) by the Sherif did not arrive', after which Nuri moved north-east 'again'. Arab Bureau (Clayton), 6 November 1916, memorandum, WO158/603/64A.

94 *The Arab Bulletin*, No. 32, 26 November 1916, p. 493.

95 Wingate to Arbur, 8 November 1916, WO158/603/85A; minute [unsigned, but by Lawrence] also in Sudan Archive, W/143/2/29. See also: Wingate to Arbur, 8 November 1916, Sudan Archive, W/143/2/28; Arbur to Wingate, 8 November 1916, A.B.175, Sudan Archive, W/143/2/30. Wilson, ever considerate of diplomatic courtesies, suggested that any proposal of co-operation for Nuri should be sent from Sherif through Feisal, who could reply to Murray 'by a trusted messenger'. Wilson to Arbur, repeat Sirdar. 9 November 1916, W.485 WO158/603.

96 'Diary of Captain Lawrence, 2–5 December 1916', FO882/6 HRG/16/73. This view was reiterated by Hogarth in an essay, 'The Anazeh Tribes and Chiefs' in *The Arab Bulletin*, No. 32, 26 November 1916, pp. 489–91: 'He will not fight openly [...] on the Sherif's side till his tribe of over 70,000 souls is secure, not only of arms, but of food; for his markets, both west and east, are still under Turkish control.' (490).

97 Antonius, *Arab Awakening*, pp. 225–7. Nuri's commitment to the Arab nationalists' agenda was always more conditional on the immediate welfare of his tribes and pragmatic with regard to Turkish power than some activists may have hoped. In May 1915, Nuri sent his son Nawaf to the presentation of the Damascus Protocol to Feisal, rather than attend personally. Four months later, Nuri turned over to Jemal Pasha's police three members of the Decentralization party who had fled to him for protection. Tauber, *Arab Movements*, pp. 62–8, 83–100.

98 Nuri was also asked to send a letter giving Royle protection, should he have to land en route. Wilson to Emir Feisal, 19 November 1916, FO686/55/1212, fos 82–3. Wilson to the Sherif of Mecca, 19 November 1916, FO686/55/1212, fos 84–5. As an alternative option, the Sherif wrote a letter for Royle to take to Nuri, declaring that the pilot expected 'neither compensation nor thanks from us but only the exaltation of the Arabs and freeing them from abasement and contemptibleness and to recover for them their glory and authority', etc. 'Translation of Sherif's letter', 20 November 1916, FO686/55/1212, fos 90–1. See also: Wilson to Nuri Shaalan, 18 November 1916, FO686/55/1212, fo. 72; Wilson to Parker, Rabegh, 19 November 1916, FO686/55/1212, fo. 81. Clayton to Wingate, 27 November 1916, Private letter, Sudan Archive, W/143/6/89.

99 Wingate to Wilson, 18 November 1916 (no tel. no.), FO686/55/1212, fo. 80. Wilson to Emir Feisal, 19 November 1916, FO686/55/1212, fo. 83. Wilson to Wingate, 21

November 1916, W.644, FO686/55/1212, fo. 96. Wingate to Wilson, 22 November 1916 (rec.23), tel. 947, FO686/55/1212, fo. 61.

100 P.C. Joyce to Wilson, 5 December 1916, No. 99, in Wilson to Wingate, 6 December 1916, W.809, Sudan Archive, W/144/1/140.

101 Lawrence (Yenbo) to Wilson, 5 January 1917, FO882/6 HRG/17/1.

102 The Government of India's office at Basra also parted company with Cairo by addressing the political demands of regional sheikhs with offers of direct payment rather than inquiries into shared political or military purpose, or, failing that, applications of military pressure. See 'Tribal Situation in Mesopotamia. Report by GHQ, Basra,' *The Arab Bulletin*, No. 26, 16 October 1916, pp. 364–8. For further examples regarding southern Mesopotamia, see: *The Arab Bulletin*, No. 12, 19 July 1916, p. 2; No. 13, 1 August 1916, pp. 122–3; No. 16, 18 August 1916, pp. 170–5; No. 20, 14 September 1916, pp. 232–5; No. 25, 7 October 1916, p. 335.

3 Arriving at a doctrine of guerrilla warfare, June–October 1916

1 McMahon to Wingate, 2 July 1916, FO141 738/3818/11, fo. 10; McMahon to Hardinge, 22 July 1916, Hardinge MSS, Vol. II, #23, fos 165–7.

2 Wingate to McMahon, 30 June 1916, tel. 862, FO141 738/3818/11, fo. 7.

3 The Egyptian batteries were now operating south of Medina. Pearson's report to the Sirdar, Jiddah, 9 July 1916, FO882/4 HRG/16/31/A, fo. 256; Cornwallis, 'Report on Jeddah', 8 July 1916, FO882/4 HRG/16/31; fforde to Grant, 21 July 1916, D.O. No. 187 W/C item #52, R/20/A/1569 IOLR.

4 fforde to Grant, 10 July 1916, No. 187, W/C item #33, R/20/A/1569 IOLR.

5 'Note', Parker, 25 June 1916, relayed in fforde to Grant, 30 June 1916, No. 140, W/C item #29, R/20/A/1569 IOLR. See also fforde to Grant, 10 July 1916, No. 187 W/C item #33, R/20/A/1569 IOLR.

6 McMahon to Wingate, 26 June 1916, FO141 738/3818/11, fo. 6.

7 fforde to Grant, 14 July 1916, D.O. No. 187, W/C item #33, R/20/A/1569 IOLR.

8 Hardinge to Sir V. Chirol, 3 August 1916, Hardinge MSS, Vol. III, #24, fo. 25255.

9 Sykes contrasted McMahon unfavourably against Kitchener whom he saw as the more proper 'link with Lord Cromer, Gordon, and the early years of energy and vitality, and the tradition of flails and scorpions for the idle or incompetent'. See 'Evidence of.… Sykes … July 6, 1916', CAB42/16/1, fos 1–5.

10 fforde to Grant, 14 July 1916, D.O. No. 187, R/20/A/1569 IOLR; see also 'Evidence of … Sykes', CAB42/16/1, fos 36–7.

11 Minutes of War Committee meeting, 7 July 1916, CAB42/16. For more on Clayton's understanding of the need to avoid 'any "side shows" which might commit us to send reinforcements from the main theatre', see Clayton to A.L. Lynden-Bell (GHQ, Ismailia), 17 August 1916, FO882/4 HR/16/1.

12 Robertson to Murray, 10 July 1916, *The Military Correspondence of Field-Marshal Sir William Robertson* (Murray–Robertson MSS, British Library, Add 52461; LHCMA, Robertson MSS, 1/32/48), Army Records Society, Vol. 5, London, 1989, p. 71. See also Robertson to Murray, 15 March 1916, Private, pp. 42–3: 'We want *men* badly. Can't get the recruits we need. Men, men'.

13 Minutes of War Committee meeting, 7 July 1916, CAB42/16; fforde to Grant, 28 July 1916, D.O. No. 187, W/C item #47, R/20/A/1569 IOLR.

14 McMahon to Wingate, 10 July 1916, FO141 738/3818/11.

15 Ibid.

16 '[I]t now looks as if Suez and not Port Sudan were to be the advanced base for supplies for Jeddah which means that the Sirdar will have less to do with operations such as they are.' fforde to Grant, 12 July 1916, D.O. No. 187 W/C R/20/A/1569 IOLR.

17 Hogarth assured the Viceroy that India had nothing to fear from an Arab victory in the Hejaz. The Sherif was a symbolic asset and would 'remain a small protected

sovereign of much religious consideration – which we ought to share', but the regional war 'will eventually be decided by the Russians at Diarbekir and perhaps, at Alexandretta, and by us at Maan'. Hogarth to Chelmsford, 2 August 1916, D.O. No. 187, W/C. Enclosure to item #51, R/20/A/1569 IOLR.

18 *The Arab Bulletin*, No. 13, 1 August 1916, pp. 130–1; No. 16, 18 August 1916, p. 177.

19 Ibid., No. 20, 14 September 1916, p. 244.

20 Ibid., No. 13, 1 August 1916, p. 130.

21 Hogarth to Chelmsford, 2 August 1916, D.O. No. 187, W/C. Enclosure to item #51, R/20/A/1569 IOLR.

22 fforde to Grant, 14 July 1916, D.O. No. 187, W/C R/20/A/1569 IOLR.

23 See Storrs' discussion of the 'Anglophobes' amongst the intelligentsia, 'the classes nationalist in sentiment and hostile to the present [i.e. British] regime', groups who supported the Turks and the Germans, favoured a restoration of the Egyptian Khedive, and who believed the Sherif was only a 'servile instrument of the English'. 'First Note – 30th June –' [1916, by R. Storrs] *The Arab Bulletin*, No. 9, 9 July 1916, pp. 2–3.

24 'The Hejaz Revolt in the Azhar', [El Azhar Mosque and University of Cairo]. Contributor unsigned but identified as T.E. Lawrence in copy, see: fforde to Grant, 7 July 1916, No. 140, W/C item #32, R/20/A/1569 IOLR. *The Arab Bulletin*, No. 9, 9 July 1916, pp. 4–6.

25 Hogarth to Chelmsford, 2 August 1916, D.O.187 W/C. Enclosure to item #51, R/20/A/1569 IOLR.

26 'Following from R[Ruhi] to R[onald] S[torrs]. From Jeddah, 17/7/1916.' 2 August 1916, FO882/4 HRG/16/36.

27 fforde to Grant, 21 July 1916, D.O. No. 187, W/C item #52, R/20/A/1569 IOLR.

28 *The Arab Bulletin*, No. 17, 30 August 1916, p. 187.

29 Sherif Hussein bin Ali belonged to the 'Awn family of Hashemites. Sherif Haidar was also a Hashemite, but of the Zayd family. See Hasan Kayali, *Arabs and Young Turks: Ottomanism, Arabism, and Islamism in the Ottoman Empire, 1908–1918*, pp. 148–9.

30 'From the "Balag" at Damascus, June 11, 1916,' *The Arab Bulletin*, No. 13, 1 August 1916, p. 130. Cairo intelligence tracked Ali Haidar's reluctant progress southward through informants in Constantinople and Smyrna, and the Syrian press: *The Arab Bulletin*, No. 13, 1 August 1916, p. 131; No. 14, 7 August 1916, p. 144; No. 17, 30 August 1916, pp. 182, 191–2; fforde to Grant, 28 July 1916, No. 961-W item #47, R/20/A/1569 IOLR. For Feisal's knowledge of Ali Haidar and the Turks' bribery of the tribes, see 'Extracts from Report by Colonel Wilson on his meeting with Sherif Feisal Bey at Yenbo, August 27 and 28, 1916,' *The Arab Bulletin*, No. 20, 14 September 1916, p. 242.

31 Grant to fforde, 2 October 1916, D.O. No. 230, W.C. (referred to later as No. 205.-W.C.) item #63, R/20/A/1569 IOLR. fforde to Grant, 5 November 1916, D.O. No. 333, W.C. item #67, R/20/A/1570 IOLR.

32 'Translation of Proclamation issued in the Hejaz by Sherif Haidar on August 9, 1916,' *The Arab Bulletin*, No. 20, 14 September 1916, pp. 237–40.

33 fforde to Grant, 26 August 1916, D.O. No. 230, W/C item #59, R/20/A/1569 IOLR.

34 *The Arab Bulletin*, No. 11, 17 July, pp. 5–6; No. 16, 18 August 1916, p. 177; No. 17, 30 August 1916, pp. 195–6; 'Wilson ... August 27 and 28, 1916', No. 20, 14 September 1916, pp. 241–3.

35 *The Arab Bulletin*, No. 13, 1 August 1916, 131; No. 17, 30 August 1916, p. 195.

36 Ibid., No. 9, 9 July 1916, p. 7; No. 11, 17 July 1916, pp. 5–6; No. 14, 7 August 1916, p. 153. 'Wilson ... August 27 and 28, 1916', No. 20, 14 September 1916, pp. 241–3.

37 Russian intelligence placed the 42nd Regiment at Medina. *The Arab Bulletin*, No. 17, 30 August 1916, pp. 195–6. British intelligence now concluded that in addition

to the 14th Division, the force at Medina was a composite of Turkish and North Syrian troops from the 41st, 43rd and 44th Divisions of the Twelfth Army Corps. *The Arab Bulletin*, No. 14, 7 August 1916, pp. 153–4. For McMahon's confidence in the original rumour that the Turks had brought Germans to Medina, see McMahon to Hardinge, 31 August 1916. Hardinge MSS, Vol. III, #24, fos 201–2. For Murray's scepticism regarding recent Sigint [a rare explicit reference to 'intercepted enemy wireless messages'] that the 60th Foot Artillery Regiment which contained German personnel was moving from el Arish to Jerusalem, possibly then by rail to the Hejaz, see Murray to Robertson, 30 September 1916, No.I.A. [?] WO33/905 No. 5846.

38 Parker, 'Extracts [...] September 10', *The Arab Bulletin*, No. 23, 26 September 1916, p. 301; No. 16, 18 August 1916, p. 177; 'Extracts from Report by Colonel Wilson on his meeting with Sherif Feisal Bey at Yanbo, August 27 and 28, 1916', No. 20, 14 September 196, p. 242.
39 *The Arab Bulletin*, No. 17, 30 August 1916, pp. 195–6.
40 Ibid., No. 13, 1 August 1916, p. 130.
41 Ibid., No. 14, 7 August 1916, pp. 153–4; No. 16, 18 August 1916, p. 177. fforde to Grant, 13 July 1916, D.O. No. 187, W/C R/20/A/1569 IOLR. fforde to Grant, 28 July 1916. No. 187 W/C item #47, R/20/A/1569 IOLR.
42 *The Arab Bulletin*, No. 17, 30 August 1916, p. 195.
43 'Wilson ... August 27 and 28, 1916', *The Arab Bulletin*, No. 20, 14 September 1916, pp. 242–3.
44 fforde to Grant, 8 September 1916, D.O. No. 230, W/C item #61, R/20/A/1569 IOLR.
45 Parker, 'Extracts ... September 10', *The Arab Bulletin*, No. 23, 26 September 1916, pp. 301–2.
46 Ibid., pp. 301–3.
47 *The Arab Bulletin*, No. 17, 30 August 1916, p. 196.
48 The Holy carpet used in ritual of *hajj*. For progress of Syrian *mahmal* and escort to Medina, see Parker, 'Extracts ... September 10', *The Arab Bulletin*, No. 23, 6 September 1916, p. 303; No. 20, 14 September 1916, pp. 243–4; No. 24, 5 October 1916, p. 325.
49 Parker, 'Extracts ... September 10', *The Arab Bulletin*, No. 23, 26 September 1916, pp. 302–3.
50 'Minutes from Interdepartmental Conference at Ismailia', 12 September 1916, FO882/4 HRG/16/46, fo. 334.
51 Ibid., fos 334, 344; Sir R. Wemyss, HMS *Eurylus* to Admiralty, 19 September 1916, ADM137/594, 5–19 September 1916. M 08706/16 SA 483, No. 721/1199.
52 Ibid., fos 346–7.
53 Murray to Robertson, 1 September 1916, Private, CAB14/15, 146.
54 'Minutes ... Conference at Ismailia', 12 September 1916, FO882/4 HRG/16/46, fos 336–7, pp. 346–7.
55 Ibid., fo. 338.
56 Ibid., fos 345–6.
57 Robertson to Murray, telegram, 19 September 1916 in Ormsby-Gore, 'Summary of historical documents', 29 November 1916, FO882/5 HRG/16/65, fo. 266. Murray privately assured the CIGS that even if the Sherif were overrun, it would have no more effect on Muslim populations than had the evacuation of Kut or Gallipoli, but in any case 'the necessity has not yet arisen to send either black or white troops to Rabegh'. Murray to Robertson, 29 September 1916, No. A.M.1088 WO33/905, No. 5873. See also Clayton, 'Note', dated '?30' September 1916, but likely earlier. 'Sent H.E.' FO882/4 HRG/16/47, fos 349–50.
58 Robertson to Wingate, 26 September 1916, WO33/905, No. 5816. Murray to Robertson, 26 September 1916, No. A.M.1074 WO33/905, No. 5820. Robertson to Murray, 27 September 1916, No. 23255 cipher, WO33/905, No. 5823. Wingate to

Robertson, 27 September 1916, No. 352, WO33/905, No. 5825. Murray to Robertson, 29 September 1916, No. A.M.1088 WO33/905, No. 5837.

59 Fifteen British sailors and twenty-five Arabs composed the party. *The Arab Bulletin*, No. 23, 26 September 1916, p. 305.

60 Wemyss to Admiralty, 19 September 1916, ADM137/594, 5–10 September 1916, M08706/16 SA 483, No. 721/1199. For McMahon on the unwanted option of a French brigade for Rabegh, see 'Minutes … Conference at Ismailia', 12 September 1916, FO882/4 HRG/16/46, fo. 348.

61 *The Arab Bulletin*, No. 23, 26 September 1916, p. 303; No. 24, 5 October 1916, p. 323; see also No. 30, 15 November 1916, pp. 438–9.

62 Feisal's army included four Egyptian quick-firing (QF) mountain guns and four maxims. The princes gave Wilson the results of their meeting at Rabegh. See: Arab Bureau to DMI, 25 September 1916, No. I.G.1509 WO33/905, No. 5815; *The Arab Bulletin*, No. 23, 26 September 1916, pp. 303–5; No. 24, 5 October 1916, pp. 323–4. It was also claimed that 600 men from Abdul Aziz bin Saud's territory had joined Ali. *The Arab Bulletin*, No. 24, 5 October 1916, p. 323.

63 Arab Bureau to DMI, London, 25 September 1916, No. I.G.1509 WO33/905, No. 5815. Arab Bureau to DMI, London, 26 September 1916, No. 1522, WO33/905, No. 5821. *The Arab Bulletin*, No. 23, 26 September 1916, pp. 304–5.

64 Clayton, 'Note,' dated '?30' September 1916, but likely earlier, FO882/4 HRG/16/47, fo. 349.

65 Unsigned remark on Grant to fforde, 2 October 1916, l D.O. No. 230 W.C. item #63, R/20/A/1569.

66 Hardinge to McMahon, 4 October 1916, Hardinge MSS, Vol. V, #26, fos 182–4.

67 Hardinge to Grant, 4 October 1916, MSS.Eur.D.660/11 IOLR. Grant apologized for having 'conveyed the false impression that we should regard with complacency the Sherif's collapse. This is not so.' Grant to Hardinge, 12 October 1916, Hardinge MSS, Vol. V, #26, fos 65–6.

68 'Information obtained from two Arab officers recently arrived in England from Kermanshah via the Caucasus, and examined by Sir M. Sykes. War Office, 25 September 1916', 29 September 1916, FO371/2781/193557.

69 Clayton, 'Note', dated '?30' September 1916, but likely earlier, FO882/4 HRG/16/47, item 119, p. 349.

70 Flight 'C' of Squadron No. 14, RFC, originally with four planes, disembarked at Rabegh on 16 November 1916, Arbur to Wingate, 5 November 1916, A.B.160, Sudan Archive, W/143/1/165. One plane crashed in Wadi Hamdh, leaving three planes listed in the RFC's report of the Flight's transfer to Wejh in March 1917. 'Report on work done by 'C' Flight […] winter of 1916–17'. [Major Ross] Headquarters, Middle East Brigade, RFC to Wilson, 26 April 1917, FO686/6, Part II, fos 39–42.

71 Parker, 'Note', 25 June 1916, in fforde to Grant, 30 June 1916, No. 140 W/C item #29, R/20/A/1569 IOLR.

72 fforde to Grant, 21 August 1916, item #60, D.O. No. 230, W/C R/20/A/1569 IOLR.

73 Arbur to Wilson, 23 August 1916, I.G.1237 FO882/4 HR/16/2.

74 *The Arab Bulletin* No. 23, 26 September 1916, p. 305. For more on bin Rifada, see *The Arab Bulletin*, No. 14, 7 August, 154; No. 19, 9 September 1916, p. 227; No. 20, 14 September 1916, p. 244; Arab Bureau to DMI, 25 September 1916, I.G. 1509 WO33/905, No. 5815. Parker was also trying to negotiate with northern tribes from Wejh, in anticipation of Murray's advance. 'Minutes … Conference at Ismailia', 12 September 1916, FO882/4 HRG/16/46, fo. 341.

75 Parker (aboard HMS *Dufferin*) to Arab Bureau, 8 October 1916, FO882/5 HRG/16/49.

76 Contained in Wilson to Arbur, 10 October 1916, tel. 279, FO882/5 HRG/16/50.

77 McMahon admitted to Hardinge that the 'changeability of Arab demands, and the

indecision, natural enough perhaps under their conditions, of my local British Advisers with the Arabs' was at times frustrating. McMahon to Hardinge, 6 October 1916, Hardinge MSS, Vol. V, #26, fos 104–5.

78 Note by the Arab Bureau on Wilson, tel. 279, 10 October 1916, FO882/5 HRG/16/51.

79 Feisal's intelligence identified the Turkish force as the 130th Regiment, the 42nd Regiment, a mixed infantry regiment with two artillery battalions, a mixed camelry and cavalry regiment, and three (apparently grounded) aeroplanes. *The Arab Bulletin*, No. 26, 16 October 1916, p. 371; No. 27, 26 October 1916, p. 392.

80 For reports on the *hajj*, see: *The Arab Bulletin*, No. 24, 5 October 1916, p. 325; No. 25, 7 October 1916, pp. 346–8; No. 28, 1 November 1916, pp. 398–401. Storrs, Wilson and Wemyss were in Jiddah when the Egyptian *mahmal* arrived. Wemyss was invited to lead the *mahmal*'s procession through Jiddah, but gratefully declined. Wemyss to Admiralty, 19 September 1916, ADM137/594 5–10 September 1916, M 08706/16 SA 483, No. 721/1199.

81 McMahon to Hardinge, 13 October 1916. Hardinge MSS, Vol. V, # 26, fos 107–8. By contrast, '[t]he Arab Revolt proceeds on its obscure and anaemic course', insisted India. Grant to Hardinge, 12 October 1916, Hardinge MSS, Vol. V, #26, fo. 65.

82 Wemyss to Admiralty, 17 October 1916, ADM137/594, 7–17 October 1916, M 09776/1917 SA 503, No. 843/1139.

83 Foreign Office, London to McMahon, 3 October 1916, FO141 738/3818/1. See also Hardinge to McMahon, 10 October 1916, Hardinge MSS, Vol. V, #26, fos 185–9. Wingate requested 'carte blanche' from McMahon. See Wingate to McMahon, 13 October 1916, No. 418, FO141 738/3818/12. McMahon agreed with respect to 'local political matters concerning the Hedjaz only and [...] not [...] affairs outside Hedjaz or [...] general policy of Arab movement'. McMahon to Wingate, 20 October 1916, No. 918, FO141 738/3818/15.

84 McMahon to FO, London, 4 October 1916, FO141 738/3818/2.

85 Robertson to Murray, 5 October 1916, No. 23572, cipher, WO33/905, No. 5863.

86 'To conduct political control from Cairo and Military control from Sirdar appears to me to be unworkable', said Murray. Murray to Robertson, repeated McMahon. 5 October 1916, FO141 738/3818/4. See also: FO to McMahon, 3 October 1916, No. 787, FO141 738/3818/1; CIGS to Murray, 4 October 1916, No. 23507, cipher, WO33/905, No. 5859; Murray to CIGS, 5 October 1916, No. I.A.2451 WO33/905, No. 5871; Murray to CIGS, 6 October 1916, No. I.A.2455 WO33/905, No. 5875.

87 McMahon to FO, London, 10 October 1916, tel. 871, in Wingate to Robertson, 24 October 1916, No. 527, WO33/905, No. 5989. The French Military Mission at Rabegh was headed by Colonel Brémond.

88 Wingate also asked London if a French Algerian brigade, soon to arrive at Suez, might be sent if British troops were unavailable. Wingate to McMahon, 13 October 1916, No. 418, FO141 738/3818/12. Murray agreed to one company of British troops 'as a camp guard' for the Flight. Murray to Robertson, 12 October 1916, No. A.M.1136 WO33/905, No. 5909, containing Wingate to Murray, 12 October 1916, No. 412, cipher.

89 McMahon to Hardinge, 13 October 1916. Hardinge MSS, Vol. V, #26, fos 107–8.

90 Wemyss added that even if the Turks did manage to take the port, their occupation could be 'made untenable by ship's guns'. Wemyss to Admiralty, 6 October 1916, ADM137/594, 20 September–6 October 1916, M 09120/16 SA 494, No. 778/1139.

91 Robertson to Murray, 19 October 1916, No. 24024, cipher, WO33/905, No. 5953. For more on the French proposal to hold aside two French batteries with machine gun sections for Jiddah, under mixed Christian and Muslim officers, see Murray to

Robertson, 19 October 1916, No. A.M.1159 WO33/905, No. 5956. For more on the Sudanese mountain battery, see Robertson to Murray, 5 October 1916, No. 23572, cipher, WO33/905, No. 5863.

92 'My sole object is to win the war and we shall not do that in the Hedjaz nor in the Sudan. It makes one despair to see the shortsighted views held by the Sirdar.' Robertson to Murray, 16 October 1916, *Military Correspondence* [...] *Robertson*, p. 96.

93 Wingate to Robertson, London, 21 October 1916, No. 493, WO33/905, No. 5967. See also Murray to Robertson, 18 October 1916, No. I.A.2506 WO33/905, No. 5946; Wemyss to Admiralty, 17 October 1916. ADM137/594, 7–17 October 1916, M09776/1917 SA 503, No. 843/1139.

94 The War Committee was prepared to approve Europeans for aircraft maintenance and specific technical services only when Muslim personnel were not available. Robertson to Wingate, 23 October 1916, No. 2414, cipher, WO33/905, No. 5981. For Wingate's views on the French offer of Muslim troops, see Wingate to Robertson, London, 21 October 1916, No. 493, WO33/905 No. 5967; Wingate to Robertson, London, 24 October 1916, No. 527, WO33/905, No. 5989.

95 Wemyss to Admiralty, 17 October 1916, ADM137/594, 7–17 October 1916, M09776/1917 SA 503, No. 843/1139.

96 Lawrence, 16 October 1916.

97 Grant to Hardinge, 7 November 1916, Hardinge Papers, Vol. VI, # 27, fos 35–6.

98 Hardinge to McMahon, 25 October 1916, Hardinge Papers, Vol. V, #26, fos 309–11. Grey 'gathered that there was no great confidence in Sir Henry McMahon.' Minutes, War Committee meeting, 7 November 1916, CAB42/23/9, Vol. 23, fo. 7.

99 McMahon to Hardinge, 10 November 1916, Hardinge MSS, Vol. VI, #27, fo. 58.

100 For more on local personal opposition to McMahon, see Ronald Graham (FO adviser to Egyptian government's Ministry of the Interior) to Hardinge, 9 September 1916, Hardinge MSS, Vol. IV, #25, fos 46–7. McMahon to Hardinge, 22 September 1916, Hardinge MSS, Vol. IV, #25, fos 218–21.

101 Lawrence, *Seven Pillars* (O) 42. Lawrence also suggested that Graham had sacrificed McMahon as a scapegoat for his own ministry's failings. Ibid., pp. 41–2.

102 Ibid., p. 8.

103 See fforde to Grant, 14 July 1916 and 7 August 1916, D.O. No. 187, W/C item #48, R/20/A/1569 IOLR.

104 fforde to Grant, 14 July 1916, D.O. No. 187, W/C R/20/A/1569 IOLR.

105 Lawrence to his mother, 18 November 1916. Brown (ed.), *Letters*, pp. 90–1. Lawrence had earlier despaired of his MI colleagues: 'There ought to be intelligence enough in the bunch to down Turkey – but unfortunately half of them are only doorposts and window-frames – ' Lawrence to his mother, 10 October 1916. Brown (ed.), *Letters*, p. 86.

106 Clayton was replaced at MI, GS by Lt Colonel G.W.V. Holdich.

107 Wingate to Arbur, 13 October 1916, No. 419, FO141 738/3818/13A, fo. 2.

108 McMahon to Wingate, 16 October 1916, No. 44, FO141 738/3818/13A, fo. 1. See also Wingate to McMahon, 17 October 1916, No. 456, FO141 738/3818/14a; McMahon to Wingate, 18 October 1916, No. 915, FO141 738/3818/14c; Wingate to McMahon, 20 October 1916, No. 484, FO141 738/3818/14d.

109 McMahon to Wingate and to FO, London, 20 October 1916, No. 918, FO141 738/3818/15. McMahon to Wingate, 20 October 1916, No. 919, FO141 738/3818/16.

110 Sykes, 'Appreciation of attached Arabian Report No. XIV', 20 October 1916, FO371/2781/210071.

111 Hardinge to Bell, 18 October 1916. Hardinge MSS, Vol. V, #26, fos 271–4.

112 The PID would have liaison officers with MI in London and issue joint weekly military and political reports for the H.C. and the GOC-in-C. DMI, London to USS for

Foreign Affairs, FO, 7 December 1916, M.I. 1/688/N.E. 0143/1076. P5205 #99 R/20/A/1569 IOLR.

113

> This [PID proposal] is another step in the direction of creating an Egyptian Foreign Office. It is not, however, inspired by any such motive, but merely designed to get rid of friction which has been engendered between Brig. Genl Clayton and G.O.C. Egypt.

So noted Arthur Hirtzel, Secretary of the Political Department of the IO, referring to Clayton's recent removal from MI, GHQ. Hirtzel, minute, 11 December 1916, #97, to DMI to USS for FA, FO, 7 December 1916. M.I. L/688/N.E. 0143/1076 P5205 #99 R/20/A/1569 IOLR.

114 Wingate, H.C. to FO, London, 1 January 1917, No. 3, P23/1917 #95 R/20/A/1569 IOLR.

115 Wemyss to Admiralty, 31 October 1916, ADM137/594, 18–31 October 1916, M010256/16 SA 493, No. 892/1139.

116 Arbur to Wilson, 23 August 1916, I.G.1237 FO882/4 HR/16/2.

117 Lawrence, *Seven Pillars*, p. 62.

118 Feisal concluded that composite sections from the 55th Regiment faced him. A Turkish draft had restored the 130th and 42nd regiments to full strength. Humint from PoWs suggested that part of the 3rd Division had reinforced Maan in anticipation of British attacks 'on or from Akaba'. *The Arab Bulletin*, No. 27, 26 October 1916, pp. 392–3.

119 *The Arab Bulletin*, No. 27, 26 October 1916, p. 393.

120 Arab Bureau Report, 31 October 1916, FO371/2781. Lawrence reported to Clayton from Jiddah that he agreed with the rejection of the brigade, despite Abdullah's disappointment, but believed the counter-order against the Flight was ill-judged. Lawrence to Clayton, 18 October 1916, Brown (ed.), *Letters*, p. 88.

121 Arab Bureau to DMI, relaying telegram from Lawrence at Jiddah, 19 October 1916, A.B.34 WO33/905, No. 5958.

122 Lawrence, *Seven Pillars*, pp. 69–71.

123 Parker to Clayton, 24 October 1916, in H.V.F. Winstone (ed.), *The Diaries of Parker Pasha*, p. 158.

124 McMahon to Hardinge, 21 November 1916, Hardinge MSS, Vol. VI, #27, fos 236–7.

125 Lawrence, 'Notes', 17 November 1916, FO882/5 HRG/16/6626–54A. See also: Lawrence, *Seven Pillars*, p. 113; Brémond to A. Defrance (head of French diplomatic mission in Cairo), 16 October 1916, Service Historique de l'Armee, Box 17 N.498, file 2, in M. J-M Lares: *T.E. Lawrence, La France et Les Francais*, p. 156.

126 'Report by Captain Lawrence, of Intelligence Staff, Cairo [Sent by G.O.C.-in-C., Egypt, to DMI, and dated November 17, 1916 (I.A.2629)]', WO33/905, No. 6156, in Murray to Robertson, 17 November 1916, A.M.1272 WO33/905, No. 6151.

127 Murray warned London: 'the French are not in the least desirous of affording us cordial support in the Hedjaz but have sent their troops to secure political advantages'. Murray to Robertson, 28 November 1916, CAB44/15, fos 169–70. See also McMahon to Hardinge, 21 November 1916 Hardinge MSS, Vol. VI, #27, fos 236–7; Hardinge to McMahon, 30 November 1916, Hardinge MSS, Vol. VI, #27, fos 295–6; Sykes, 'Appreciation attached to Arabian Report No. XVIII', 23 November 1916, FO371/2781/236383; Wingate to Wilson, 23 November 1916, Sudan Archive, W/143/6/54–55; 'Proceedings of a Conference held at Cairo on the 29 November 1916', [actually 28 November] FO882/5 HRG/16/68, fos 316–18; McMahon to Hardinge, 13 December 1916, Hardinge MSS, Vol. VII, #28, fo. 121;

> What France knows is that an increase of Moslem influence in Syria involves a decrease in French influence and an exaggeration of British influence, and it is

> [...] this knowledge of the weakness of her position vis-à-vis the Syrian Moslems which governs that attitude of the French towards the Arab movement in the Hejas.
>
> G.A. Lloyd, Jiddah to Lynden-Bell, 'Political', Report on the Hejaz. 22 December 1916, GLLD 9/8.

128 Lawrence to Clayton, 18 October 1916, Brown (ed.), *Letters*, p. 89, emphasis in original.
129 Ibid.
130 Arab Bureau to DMI, relaying telegram from Lawrence at Jiddah, 19 October 1916, A.B.34 WO33/905, No. 5958.
131 Lawrence to his mother, 18 November 1916, Brown (ed.), *Letters*, p. 90. Wemyss noted that it was Lawrence who requested the Khartoum meeting. Wemyss, Jiddah to Wingate, 4 November 1916, tel. 1345, Sudan Archive, W/143/1/146.
132 Lawrence, 'Feisul's Operations', 30 October 1916, FO882/5 HRG/16/57-#2.
133 Arab Bureau to Wingate, 30 October 1916, Summarizing reports from Lawrence (21 October 1916) and Parker (24 October 1916), A.B.109 WO33/905, No. 6024. See also N.N.E. Bray, *Shifting Sands*, London: Unicorn Press, 1934, p. 100. Captain (later Major) Bray of the Indian Army visited the Jeddah and Rabegh, before transferring to Jiddah as a new intelligence officer under Wilson.
134 Arab Bureau to Wingate, 30 October 1916, A.B.109 WO33/905, No. 6024. Robertson to Wingate, 10 November 1916, No. 24887, cipher, WO33/905, No. 6103. Wingate to Robertson, 12 November 1916, No. 777, WO33/905, No. 6121. Bray informed the War Committee that the Turks seemed to have 'a large number of camels, and to be buying and requisitioning more'. 'Report on the Situation in the Hejaz by Captain N.N.E. Bray, 18th King George's Own Lancers', 8 November 1916, Arabian Report, No. XVII, FO371/2781.
135 Lawrence, 'Military Notes', 3 November 1916, FO882/5 HRG/16/57-#4.
136 The enemy force was two-thirds Turk (infantry, camel corps and some cavalry). The remaining third was Arab: 400 Syrian Arabs in the 1,400-strong 130th Regiment, 200 Arabs with the 900-strong Mohafis, 500 Ageyl camelmen from Medina (who apparently did 'not do much fighting'), and 300 Shammar from Nejd. Lawrence, 'Military Notes', 3 November 1916, FO882/5 HRG/16/57-#4. Lawrence, 'Feisul's Operations', 30 October 1916, FO882/5 HRG/16/57-#2. Bray also speculated that the Turks might, through bribes or coercion, induce local Arabs to ride as well-armed mobile units against the Sherif's armies. Bray, 'Report', 8 November 1916, Arabian Report, No. XVII, FO371/2781.
137 Lawrence, 'Feisul's Operations', 30 October 1916, FO882/5 HRG/16/57-#2. Lawrence, 'Military Notes', 3 November 1916, FO882/5 HRG/16/57-#4.
138 Ibid., 'Notes', 17 November 1916, FO882/5 HRG/16/6626–54A; also in GOC-in-C to DMI, 17 November 1916, I.A.2629 WO33/905, No. 6156.
139 Ibid., 'Military Notes', 3 November 1916, FO882/5 HRG/16/57-#4. Lawrence, 'Feisul's Operations', 30 October 1916, FO882/5 HRG/16/57-#2.
140 Ibid., 'Feisul's Operations', 30 October 1916, FO882/5 HRG/16/57-#2. Lawrence, 'Military Notes', 3 November 1916, FO882/5 HRG/16/57-#4.
141 Ibid., 'Feisul's Operations', 30 October 1916, FO882/5 HRG/16/57-#2, fo. 44.
142 As Callwell well understood: '[F]or while the organized forces are dependent upon communications which their antagonists may attack and even cut, they cannot retaliate. And as operations directed against an opponent's communications present the most effective weapon in the armoury of strategy, the regular army is clearly at a disadvantage.' Callwell, *Small Wars*, pp. 86–7.
143 Lawrence, 'Military Notes', 3 November 1916, FO882/5 HRG/16/57-#4.
144 Ibid., 'Feisul's Operations', 30 October 1916, FO882/5 HRG/16/57-#2.
145 Ibid., 'Military Notes', 3 November 1916, FO882/5 HRG/16/57-#4.
146 Ibid., 'Notes', 17 November 1916, FO882/5 HRG/16/6626–54A. Also in GOC-in-C to DMI, 17 November 1916, I.A.2629 WO33/905, No. 6156. Joyce also reported on

the state of 'entire mistrust' between the Egyptian troops and the Arabs, advising that 'very careful consideration' should be given to extending their joint activities. Joyce to Wilson, 19 November 1916, FO882/5 HRG/16/62.

147 Ibid., 'Feisul's Operations', 30 October 1916, FO882/5 HRG/16/57-#2.

148 Ibid., 'Hejaz Administration', 3 November 1916, FO882/5 HRG/16/57-#3. Feisal paid rewards for Turkish prisoners and live transport, as well as £1 for each Turkish rifle – which he then returned to the bearer. Lawrence, 'Feisul's Operations', 30 October 1916, FO882/5 HRG/16/57-#2.

149 Ibid., 'Military Notes', 3 November 1916, FO882/5 HRG/16/57-#4.

150 'The money question is going, I think, to be decisive', Lawrence wrote presciently to Clayton in a private letter. 'The old man [Sherif Hussein] is frightfully jealous of his purse-strings [...] I think both Abdullah and Feisal should have allowances.' Lawrence to Clayton, 18 October 1916, Garnett (ed.), *The Selected Letters of T.E. Lawrence*, London: Jonathan Cape, 1938, p. 89. The total cost of maintaining the Hashemite family, their armies, and the Emirate of Mecca amounted to £130,000 per month, of which Britain had to pay about £125,000. Feisal and Abdullah received £30,000 allowances from the Sherif. Lawrence believed that, in addition to command expenses, Feisal made payments to the Billi, Fakir and Rualla representatives in camp during his visit. Ali had to ask his father for funds, around £25,000–35,000 per month. Lawrence, 'Hejaz Administration', 3 November 1916, FO882/5 HRG/16/57-#3.

151 Bray later recalled:

> The Sherif wished to decide every question which arose, whether with regard to policy or military action. He trusted no one, not even his own sons, of whom he was as suspicious as of all with whom he had to deal. Every petty detail of supply, finance or administration was dealt with by him personally.
>
> Bray, *Shifting Sands*, pp. 75–6.

152 Arab Bureau to Sirdar, 30 October 1916, A.B.109 WO33/905, No. 6024, summarizing reports from Lawrence (21 October 1916), and Parker (24 October 1916).

153 Lawrence, 'Military Notes', 3 November 1916, FO882/5 HRG/16/57-#4.

154 Ibid., 'Military Notes', 3 November 1916, FO882/5 HRG/16/57-#4. Unlike Lawrence, Bray assumed the Turks would move 'self-contained [...] in the greatest possible strength at the greatest possible speed straight for Mecca', without leaving posts in communication. Once at Mecca, 'by wholesale hangings and terrorism they will try to subdue the movement by fear and terrible punishments to any opposition'. Bray, 'Report', 8 November 1916, Arabian Report, No. XVII, FO371/2781.

155 Ibid., 'The Sherifs', 27 October 1916, FO882/5 HRG/16/57.

156 Ibid., 'Feisul's Operations', 30 October 1916, FO882/5 HRG/16/57-#2.

157 Ibid., 'Feisul's Operations', 30 October 1916, FO882/5 HRG/16/57-#2.

4 Intelligence on trial: the Rabegh crisis, November 1916–January 1917

1 Wireless message from Abdullah, relayed in Wilson to Wingate, 1 November 1916, W.461, Sudan Archive, W/142/1/43. The Turks had advanced to Bir ibn al Hassani. Arab Bureau to DMI, 1 November 1916, A.B.126 WO33/905, No. 6036. Repeated to Sirdar, to Naval C-in-C, and to GOC-in-C, Egypt. *The Arab Bulletin*, No. 29, 8 November 1916, p. 417. Parker, assisting al-Masri with regular army training at Rabegh, clarified the party's identity. Arbur to Wingate, 2 November 1916, A.B.140, Sudan Archive, W/143/1/93. Arab Bureau to DMI, London, 3 November 1916, A.B.144 WO33/905, No. 6060.

2 Murray to Robertson, 3 November 1916, A.M.1216 WO33/905, No. 6065. Murray to Robertson, 5 November 1916, A.M.1225 WO33/905, No. 6073. *The Arab Bulletin*, No. 29, 8 November 1916, p. 417. Murray was also preoccupied with moving

Egyptforce's headquarters from Ismailia to Cairo. The transfer was a loss in Wemyss's view, for he had found his 'daily intercourse' with Murray and the exchange of information useful. Wemyss to Admiralty, 31 October 1916, 18–31 October 1916, ADM137/594 M 010256/16 SA 493, No. 892/1139.

3 Robertson to Murray, 2 November 1916, No. 24574, cipher, WO33/905, No. 6047. A valued Arab source (Ottoman deserter) recalled the monitor's 'very destructive' power. 'Information respecting Turkey. Information obtained from two Arab officers [. . .]', 29 September 1916, FO371/2781/193557.

4 Arab Bureau to DMI, London, 3 November 1916, A.B.144 WO33/905, No. 6060. See also Wemyss to Admiralty, 21 November 1916, 1–21 November 1916, ADM137/594 M 010595/16 SA 493, No. 933/1139. Murray to Robertson, 3 November 1916, A.M.1216 WO33/905 No. 6065, *The Arab Bulletin*, No. 29, 8 November 1916, p. 417.

5 Arab Bureau to DMI, London, 3 November 1916, A.B.144 WO33/905, No. 6060.

6 Arbur to Sir Wingate, 13 November 1916, A.B.205, Sudan Archive, W/143/2/190–192.

7 Bray, *Shifting Sands*, p. 70. Unlike most of his intelligence colleagues, and despite his impressive pre-war investigations into Arab nationalist parties in Syria, Bray later seemed strangely determined to reject a link between the military and political requirements of the Arab campaign. He refused to connect the tribes' autonomy as irregulars in the field with their larger political autonomy, a disinclination that eventually crippled his relationship with the Arab leaders.

8 See Bray, *Shifting Sands*, pp. 65, 70, 101–13.

9 'Report on the Situation in the Hejaz by Captain N.N.E. Bray, 18th King George's Own Lancers', 8 November 1916, printed in the Arabian Report, No. XVIII, 23 November 1916, FO371/2781/236383, fos 5–8.

10 Robertson to Wingate, 11 November 1916, No. 24923, cipher, WO33/905, No. 6108.

11 McMahon to FO, London, 10 October 1916, tel. 871 in Wingate to Robertson, 11 November 1916, No. 763, WO33/905, No. 6110.

12 Wingate to Robertson, 11 November 1916, No. 763, WO33/905, No. 6110, referring to announcement through FO telegram #9, 9 November 1916; Sirdar's earlier request, 24 October 1916, No. 527, WO33/905, No. 5989; McMahon's original request to FO, 10 October 1916, tel. 871. Wingate to Robertson, 12 November 1916, No. 777, WO33/905, No. 6121. Wingate to Robertson, 27 November 1916, No. 017, WO33/905, No. 6211.

13 Wingate to Robertson, 12 November 1916, No. 777, WO33/905, No. 6121.

14 See Joyce, Jiddah to Wilson, (copy to Arbur) 2 December 1916, FO882/6 HRG16/70.

15 Wingate to Clayton, 2 November 1916, tel. 623, cipher, Sudan Archive, W/143/1/38. Wingate to Arbur, 2 November 1916, tel. 627, Sudan Archive, W/143/1/49. For more on dispatch of the Flight, see Murray to Robertson, 12 October 1916, A.M.1136 WO33/905, No. 5909. Robertson to Murray, 29 October 1916, tel. 24411, cipher, WO158/603/1A; GHQ, Egypt to Middle East Brigade, RFC, 1 November 1916, O.A.188, cipher, WO158/603/5A; 'Special Instructions for the Office Commanding R.F.C. Flight'. 8 November 1916, WO158/606/73B ('utmost care' must be taken 'to avoid friction with the natives of the country').

16 Lawrence described Garland as 'a most excellent man, [he] has won over everybody here. The very man for the place'. Lawrence to Director, Arab Bureau (Major K. Cornwallis), 2 December 1916, Brown (ed.), *Letters*, p. 91.

17 Wingate to Robertson, 12 November 1916, No. 777, WO33/905, No. 6121.

18 Wingate to Arbur, 7 November 1916, tel. 9, 2/58/1, WO158/603/79A.

19 Wingate to Robertson, 12 November 1916, No. 777, WO33/905, No. 6121.

Lawrence later claimed that Wingate's motivation was to augment his 'nominal expeditionary force, the Hejaz Force, which in reality comprised a few liaison officers and a handful of storemen and instructors' into 'a genuine brigade of mixed British and French troops', with all the accompanying prestige and responsibility. Lawrence, *Seven Pillars*, p. 113.

20 See Wingate to Robertson, 22 November 1916, No. 935, WO33/905, No. 6183.

21 Wingate to Wilson, 12 November 1916. I could not find this letter amongst Wingate's papers. The date would place it in file W/143/2 (November 1916, Part II, Sudan Archive). J.M. Wilson cites its location as file W/143/1 but it was in neither place at the time of this research. Wilson, *Lawrence*, p. 323.

22 Arbur to Wingate, 13 November 1916, A.B.205, Sudan Archive, W/143/2/190–192. Lawrence, due to leave for Yenbo on 25 November, had been about to undertake the comparatively neglected propaganda function as a full commitment, taking over from Philip Graves. Arab Bureau Report for October 1916. 31 October 1916, FO371/2781/233121. Tasks already included counter-propaganda, coordinating items with the pro-Sherif newspaper at Mecca and activists in Egypt, and producing pamphlets for air-drops over the enemy in the Sinai, Russia and Anatolia. For examples of Turkish propaganda, see '*El Sharq*, November 1, 1916', in 'Extracts from Syrian Newspapers', *The Arab Bulletin*, No. 35, 20 December 1916, pp. 538–40.

23 Wingate to Clayton, 14 November 1916, tel. 812, Sudan Archive, W/143/2/193, fos 1–3. Wingate informed Robertson that Lawrence 'must return to Cairo as soon as he can be released for work with the Arab Bureau'. Wingate to Robertson, 22 November 1916, No. 935, WO33/905, No. 6183.

24 Wingate to Clayton, 14 November 1916, Sudan Archive, W/143/2/193, fos 1–3. Clayton accepted. Arbur to Wingate, 15 November 1916, A.B.217, Sudan Archive, W/143/2/248.

25 Murray to Robertson, 12 November 1916, A.M.1251 WO33/905, No. 6125. The defence of Egypt became critical within the week when Suez was bombed again, on 17 November 1916. Murray to Robertson, 17 November 1916, A.M.1277 WO33/905, No. 6154.

26 Robertson to Murray, 16 November 1916, No. 25108, WO33/905, No. 6143.

27 Clayton, 'Precis', to Lawrence, 'Notes', 17 November 1916, '?Nov./16' FO882/5 HRG/16/6626–54. See also Lawence, *Seven Pillars*, p. 114.

28 Lawrence's summary encapsulated the futility of a brigade in three points: the real defence of Rabegh depended on the perimeter hill-tribes, not a resident force at the port; the Arabs thoroughly distrusted European intentions, so if a brigade were to land, 'they would, I am convinced, say "We are betrayed" and scatter to their tents'; fresh intelligence on the roads and inland water supplies suggested that the Turks could 'advance along any of the central or eastern roads to Mecca, leaving the Franco-British force a disconsolate monument on the dusty beach at Rabegh'. 'Report by Captain Lawrence, of Intelligence Staff, Cairo, [Sent by GOC-in-C, Egypt, to D.M.I., and dated November 17, 1916 (I.A.2629)]', WO33/905, No. 6156, in Murray to Robertson, 17 November 1916, A.M.1272 WO33/905, No. 6151. See also: Arabian Report XVIII, 23 November 1916, FO371/2781/236383, fos 8–9. Original report as Lawrence, 'Notes', 17 November 1916, FO882/5 HRG/16/6626–54A.

29 Lawrence disagreed with Parker's view that the Flight required a brigade-size escort for its European support crew. 'Report by Captain Lawrence … November 17, 1916', WO33/905, No. 6156. This report was circulated to the War Cabinet: see 'Report from Captain Lawrence, of Intelligence Staff, Cairo, dated 17 November 1916.' Appendix to War Committee Meeting No. 133, 'Secret', 16 November 1916, CAB42/24/1 01/54/177. Telegram from Murray and Lawrence forwarded by Robertson, 19 November 1916, Appendix 133/A, fo. 4.

30 'Report by Captain Lawrence ... November 17, 1916', WO33/905, No. 6156. See also Arabian Report XVIII, 23 November 1916, FO371/2781/236383, fos 8–9.
31 'Captain Lawrence's Report', Arabian Report, No. XIX, 29 November 1916, FO371/2781/244263 (filed 4 December 1916), fo. 3.
32 Wingate to Wilson, 6 November 1916, tel. 167, Sudan Archive, W/144/1/231–233.
33 The Arab consultant was Said Ali el Mirghani. 'The Sherif of Mecca: Sir R. Wingate on the Situation', 'Captain Lawrence's Report', Arabian Report, No. XIX, 29 November 1916, FO371/2781/244263 (filed 4 December 1916), fos 1–4.
34 In addition to the British or French brigade earmarked at Suez, Wingate also wanted Brémond's French artillery units brought to Suez and their mobile artillery sent on to the Hejaz. 'The Sherif of Mecca ...', Arabian Report, No. XIX, 29 November 1916, FO371/2781/244263 (filed 4 December 1916), fos 1–3, referring to Wingate, tel. 29, 22 November 1916; tel. 32, 23 November 1916; and quoting letter from Parker, 8 November 1916:

> [T]he presence of one singular regular brigade at Rabegh would absolutely safeguard the situation at that place and the Arab cause; but if the Arabs are to be left to hold it unaided against a serious advance, should this come about, the risks would be very grave.

Joyce, in charge of Egyptian escort for Flight, agreed. See Joyce to Wilson, 19 November 1916, FO882/5 HRG/16/62. For Brémond's offer, 24 November, see 'French Guns for the Sherif', Arabian Report, No. XIX, 29 November 1916, FO371/2781/244263 (filed 4 December 1916), fo. 4, referring to Wingate, 24 November 1916, tel. 35, and Grey, 27 November 1916, tel. 2738. Asked by the Committee to comment on Lawrence and McMahon's warnings regarding the French, Wingate did concede that, unlike the British, the French would regard an Arab capture of Medina 'with some alarm':

> [I]n view of their future Syrian policy, the great increase of strength which the Sherif's cause would immediately obtain by the active support of all Arab tribes in the Syrian hinterland, they having sworn to rise in aid of the Sherif directly he obtains possession of Medina.

A rather significant discrepancy in aims. 'The Sherif of Mecca ...', Arabian Report, No. XIX, 29 November 1916, FO 371/2781/244263 (filed 4 December 1916), fo. 2.
35 Hardinge to McMahon, 22 November 1916., Hardinge MSS, Vol. VI, #26, fos 292–4.
36 McMahon to Hardinge, 21 November 1916, Hardinge MSS, Vol. VI, #27, fos 236–7.
37 Robertson to Murray, 22 November 1916, No. 25371, cipher, WO33/905, No. 6179.
38 Wingate to Wilson, 23 November 1916, Sudan Archive, W/143/6/52–56. Clayton admitted that he had agreed 'in the main with Lawrence's conclusions', but assured Wingate that Hejaz affairs were entirely in the latter's hands and he should only be 'amused' at the confusion. Clayton to Wingate, 23 November 1916, 'Strictly Private', Sudan Archive, W/143/6/44–46.
39 'Absolutely reliable' as a code-name for Sigint apparently originated with the signals intelligence section of the Mesopotamian Expeditionary Force (MEF). Special Service Officer (SSO) Gerard Clauson, a code-breaker with the MEF since July 1916, noted that a colleague, Crocker, had coined the term, and their intelligence section was code-named 'A.R.' as a result. Clauson was disgusted with GHQ, Egypt's comparative laxness in signals security:

> We do not send written reports out at all. Apart from wires to the WO nothing leaves the section in recognizable form and nothing is put in our Intelligence Summaries, but the information is of course used to check and co-ordinate

other information [...] it makes one absolutely cat to see how Egypt splash it about in printed summaries and things, but that I think is stopped now thank God.

G. Clauson, Baghdad, to Crocker, 9 October 1917, 'personal and secret', Clauson papers, Box 2, 80/47/2 item 6. IWM.

For the DMI's warnings to GHQ, Egypt on signals security see: DMI (G.M.W. Macdonogh) to GHQ, 1 January 1917, No. 27362, cipher, WO33/905, No. 6428; GOC-in-C to DMI, 2 January 1917, I.A.2827 WO33/905, No. 6434; DMI to Lynden-Bell, 20 January 1917, No. 28211, cipher, WO33/905, No. 6552; Lynden-Bell to DMI, 21 January 1917, I.D.263 WO33/905, No. 6562.

40 Murray to MacDonogh (DMI), London, 22 November 1916, I.A.2648 WO33/905, No. 6180. 'Turkish Force in Hejaz,' Arabian Report, No. XIX, 29 November 1916, FO371/2781/244263 (filed 4 December 1916), fo. 4.

41 McMahon to Hardinge, 21 November 1916, Hardinge MSS, Vol. VI, #27, fos 236–7.

42 Lawrence, 'The Turkish Hejaz Forces and their Reinforcement. [Compiled from information in possession of G.H.Q. (E.E.F.).]', *The Arab Bulletin*, No. 32, 26 November 1916, pp. 487–9.

43 *The Arab Bulletin*, No. 33, 4 December 1916, p. 505. Aaron Aaronsohn (1876–1919) and his sister, Sarah, founded the Nili espionage network in Palestine, which Allenby later credited with organizing most of his Field Intelligence behind Turkish lines in 1917, until their capture in October. A. Engle, *The Nili Spies*, London: Hogarth Press, 1959, pp. 45–6 *passim*, 201. R. Bidwell, *The Arab Bulletin*, Vol. I, p. 009.

44 Murray to MacDonogh (DMI), London, 21 November 1916, I.A.2645 WO33/905, No. 6175. This figure was less than the 16,000 men with twelve guns discussed by the War Committee weeks before. Nevertheless it raised the bar high for a British detachment as any reinforcements 'must be of sufficient strength and mobility to defeat a force of strength equal to that mentioned', Robertson to Wingate, 10 November 1916, No. 24887, cipher, WO33/905, No. 6103. See also Robertson to Murray, 11 November 1916, No. 24903, cipher, WO33/905, No. 6106. The question of 'sufficient force' had already been raised by the French authorities to support the launch of a full regular campaign; and by Murray during the Ismailia conference to desist from the same.

45 The other option would be to hand over the responsibility to the French. Hardinge to McMahon, 22 November 1916, Hardinge MSS, Vol. VI, #26, fos 292–4.

46 Murray told Brémond in late November in Cairo that 'action in Syria is decisive while the Hedjaz theatre was merely subordinate', and Brémond agreed. 'Proceedings of a Conference held at Cairo on the 29 November 1916', [actually 28 November] FO882/5 HRG/16/68, fos 316–18. Brémond was returning to Jiddah 'to watch matters for his Government but his troops do not leave Suez'. Murray to Robertson, 28 November 1916, CAB44/15.

47 Feisal's raids, carried out on 24 and 28 November 1916, captured twenty Turkish prisoners and sixty camels. *The Arab Bulletin*, No. 31, 18 November 1916, p. 453; No. 33, 4 December 1916, pp. 498–9; No. 34, 11 December 1916, p. 517. Arab Bureau to DMI, London, 18 November 1916, A.B.229 WO33/905, No. 6163.

48 *The Arab Bulletin*, No. 33, 4 December 1916, p. 499.

49 Ibid., No. 29, 8 November 1916, p. 417; No. 31, 18 November 1916, p. 453. Murray to Robertson, 25 November 1916, A.M.1316 WO33/905, No. 6203. 'Hejaz Railway', Arabian Report, No. XIX, 29 November 1916, FO371/2781/244263 (filed 4 December 1916), fo. 4. *The Arab Bulletin*, No. 33, 4 December 1916, p. 499. Also of note were reports on the repercussions of a Turkish massacre at the small village of Awali outside Medina. The outraged Harb, Beni Salim, Fahdah and Masruh tribes 'joined forces and became one' in revenge, raided the Turks' lines of communica-

tion and declared loyalty to the Sherif. *The Arab Bulletin*, No. 28, 1 November 1916, p. 402.

50 Wingate to Wilson, 23 November 1916, Sudan Archive, W/143/6/56. Ormsby-Gore, now assigned to the Arab Bureau, also misread the strategic advantage of al-Masri's move, suggesting that he should transfer south to Jiddah instead. The British Military Mission could assist with the army training and his troops would buttress the bulwark around Mecca. Another Arab Bureau member (perhaps Clayton) noted on Ormsby-Gore's report that this was 'merely an expression of opinion and [?] unofficial'. 'Note on the military situation in the Hejaz by Ormsby Gore. Nov? 1916', FO 882/5 HRG/16/67.

51 Clayton to Wingate, 20 November 1916, Sudan Archive, W/143/6/2–3, emphasis added.

52 *The Arab Bulletin*, No. 31, 18 November 1916, p. 453. 'The Advance on Wejh', *The Arab Bulletin*, No. 41, 6 February 1917, p. 60. Feisal could not rely exclusively on the Juheinah because of jealousy within its ibn Bedawi family over ultimate influence. Lawrence to Director, Arab Bureau, 5 December 1916, FO882/6 HRG/16/71B.

53 Clayton to Wingate, 20 November 1916, Sudan Archive, W/143/6/3. See Lawrence, 'Feisul's Operations', 30 October 1916, FO882/5 HRG/16/57, p. 44.

54 Lawrence believed that only a segment of Medina townspeople and the 300 Shammar lent from Ibn Rashid were actively fighting on the side of the Turks. Lawrence, 'Extracts from a Report on Feisal's Operations', 30 October 1916, *The Arab Bulletin*, No. 31, 18 November 1916, p. 462.

55 Lawrence, 'Extracts ... Feisal's Operations', 30 October 1916, *The Arab Bulletin*, No. 31, p. 18, November 1916, pp. 462–4. Arab Bureau to DMI, London, 4 December 1916. A.B.337 WO33/905, No. 6254. *The Arab Bulletin*, No. 34, 11 December 1916, p. 517. Lawrence, *Seven Pillars*, p. 119.

56 Arab Bureau to DMI, London, 18 November 1916, A.B.229 WO33/905, No. 6163.

57 Wingate to Clayton, 2 November 1916, tel. 623, cipher, Sudan Archive, W/143/1/38.

58 Parker received his orders to return to Egyptforce on 1 December 1916. Joyce greatly regretted his departure. Joyce to Wilson (copy to Arab Bureau), 2 December 1916, FO882/6 HRG/16/70.

59 Supplies and twenty maxim guns had now reached Rabegh. Ali had taken four guns, augmenting his four maxim guns, two field guns, two howitzers and a gun battery left by the Egyptian artillery unit. Joyce to Wilson (copy to Arab Bureau), 2 December 1916, FO882/6 HRG/16/70. The CIGS wrote Murray that 'Rabegh has been a perfect nuisance during the last few weeks', in part due to French pressure but also to lobbying by 'one or two of your so-called local authorities who look at matters from a very narrow point of view and not very intelligently at that', apparently referring to Parker and Joyce. Robertson to Murray, 1 December 1916, *Military Correspondence* [...] *Robertson*, p. 118.

60 Lloyd, Yenbo to Clayton, 2 December 1916, Personal letter, GLLD 9/8. Lawrence praised Lloyd's grasp of the situation, as well, telling Cairo that Lloyd had come to the heart of the matter and his report would be worth reading. Lawrence to Director (Cornwallis), Arab Bureau, 2 December 1916, FO882/6 HRG16/71A.

61 Lloyd also urged that British officials posted to the Hejaz should speak Arabic and have experience working in Arab countries. Lloyd, Yenbo to J. Murray, 2 December 1916, GLLD 9/8.

62 Lloyd, Yenbo to Clayton, 2 December 1916, Personal letter, GLLD 9/8.

63 Abd el Kerim Bedawi, a Juheinah notable who left Feisal's camp on 30 November, was the Arab Bureau's source for this event. Lawrence, *Seven Pillars*, p. 119. *The Arab Bulletin*, No. 34, 11 December 1916, p. 517.

64 Wilson to Arbur, 7 December 1916 (rec. 8 December), No. 1455, W.838, FO882/6 HRG/16/75 [Message sent through S.N.O. at Yenbo]. Arab Bureau to DMI, 12

December 1916, A.B.404 WO33/905, No. 6306. *The Arab Bulletin*, No. 34, 11 December 1916, p. 517. Arab Bureau to DMI, 3 January 1917, A.B.524 WO33/905, No. 6443. Lawrence, 'The Advance from Wejh,' *The Arab Bulletin*, No. 41, 6 February 1917, p. 61.

65 H. Garland, Yenbo to Arab Bureau, 3 December 1916, in Arab Bureau to DMI, 7 December 1916. A.B.364 WO33/905, No. 6268.

66 Feisal's message relayed via Garland, in Wilson to Wingate, 5 December 1916, W.795, Sudan Archive, W/144/1/113. 'Report from Senior Naval Officer, Red Sea patrol, 4 December, from Yanbo', Arab Bureau to DMI, 5 December 1916, A.B.350 WO33/905, No. 6259. See also SNO, Red Sea Patrol, Rabegh, to Naval C-in-C, 3 December 1916, in Arbur to Wingate, 5 December 1916, A.B.348, Sudan Archive, W/144/1/111. Wemyss found Zeid's performance 'distinctly disappointing' and believed it contributed to Feisal's forced retreat from Wadi Yenbo. Wemyss to Admiralty, 21 December 1916, ADM137/594 7–21 December 1916, M 073/17 SA 554, No. 1043/1139. Parker, recently returned to Egypt, also complained about the tribesmen's 'desultory' efforts, warning again that they would never face down Turkish artillery. 'The Situation in Hejaz', in Arabian Report N.S. No. XXI, 13 December 1916, FO371/2781/253852 (15 December 1916), fo. 2, relaying Wingate [to FO] 9 December 1916, tel. 68. Ali's weakened condition after troop and gun transfers to Feisal and Zeid was also a concern. See the *The Arab Bulletin*, No. 34, 11 December 1916, p. 518.

67 DMI to Arab Bureau, 6 December 1916, No. 26005, cipher, WO33/905, No. 6260.

68 Arab Bureau to DMI, 7 December 1916, A.B.364 WO33/905, No. 6268.

69 Lawrence to Wilson, 6 December 1916, in Garnett (ed.), *Letters*, pp. 96–7.

70 Lawrence to Director (Cornwallis), Arab Bureau, 5 December 1916, FO882/6 HRG/16/71B. Lawrence left Yenbo for Nakhl Mubarak on 2 December 1916 with Abd el Kerim as escort. Lawrence, 'Diary of Captain Lawrence', 2–5 December 1916, FO882/6 HRG/16/73.

71 Wilson to Arbur, 7 December 1916 (rec. 8 December), No. 1455, W.838, FO882/6 HRG/16/75.

72 See Lawrence to Wilson, 6 December 1916, in Garnett (ed.), *Letters*, p. 96.

73 Lawrence asked Cornwallis to refrain from publishing his letter in *The Arab Bulletin* 'or elsewhere, it is not just – because I am done up'. Lawrence to Director (Cornwallis), Arab Bureau, 5 December 1916, FO882/6 HRG/16/71B. Lawrence later qualified the collapse as partly due to Zeid: 'If Zeid had not been so slack, things would never have got to this pass. The Arabs outside their hills are worthless.' Lawrence (en route from Yenbo to Rabegh on HMS *Suva*) to Director, Arab Bureau, 11 December 16, FO882/6 HRG/16/95. See also Lawrence, *Seven Pillars*, p. 122.

74 Wilson to Wingate, 5 December 1916, W.787, Sudan Archive, W/144/1/106.

75 Britannia to Wingate, 8 December 1916, Sudan Archive, W/144/1/183. Arab Bureau to DMI, 12 December 1916, A.B.404 WO33/905, No. 6306. See also Wemyss to Admiralty, 21 December 1916, ADM137/594, No. 1043/1139, 7–21 December 1916, M 073/17 SA 554.

76 Lawrence to Director (Cornwallis), Arab Bureau, 5 December 1916, FO882/6 HRG/16/71B.

77 Wilson to Arbur, 7 December 1916 (rec. 8 December), No. 1455, W.838, FO882/6 HRG/16/75. See also Lawrence 'Diary of Captain Lawrence', 2–5 December 1916, FO882/6 HR/16/73; Lawrence, 'Diary of a Second Journey', *The Arab Bulletin*, No. 36, 26 December 1916, p. 550.

78 Lawrence to Wilson, 6 December 1916, in Garnett (ed.), *Letters*, p. 96.

79 *The Arab Bulletin*, No. 34, 11 December 1916, pp. 517–18.

80 Lawrence to Wilson, 6 December 1916, in Garnett (ed.), *Letters*, p. 96. Lawrence's extensive topographical experience with the Geographical Section made him ideal for this task. Boyle instructed one of the seaplanes from the carrier *Raven* to fly a bombing mission over Turkish positions in Wadi Yenbo, with a map drawn on the spot by Lawrence. Wilson, *Lawrence*, p. 338. No source given.

81 Wilson to Wingate, 5 December 1916, W.787, Sudan Archive, W/144/1/106–7.
82 Wilson hoped the Sinai offensive would begin 'in earnest' and give relief to the Hejaz. Wilson to Arbur, 7 December 1916. Addressed to Sirdar, repeat Arbur. W.625 cipher, conveying L.28 [Message from Lawrence, with Feisal's communication to C-in-C, Egyptforce] FO882/6 HRG/16/74. Wilson to Wingate, 7 December 1916, relaying L.28 (Lawrence). 'Urgent.' W.825, Sudan Archive, W/144/1/162.
83 The Arab Bureau confirmed that Feisal was facing the 130th Regiment, 55th Regiment (5,000 strong), a camel regiment, a mule-mounted battalion and a mountain artillery battalion. The 42nd Regiment was still at Bir el Mashi, guarding the left flank. Arab Bureau to DMI, London, 4 December 1916, A.B.337 WO33/905, No. 6254.
84 Feisal had also warned the Sherif of Turkish reinforcements arriving from the Sinai, but Wingate assured the FO that these claims were unconfirmed. 'The Sherif …', Arabian Report N.S. No. XXI, 13 December 1916, FO371/2781/253852 (15 December 1916), relaying Wingate [to FO] 7 December 1916, tel. 65. See also Sykes, 'Appreciation of Attached Arabian Report No. XXI', 'Secret', [13 December 1916] FO371/2781/253852, fo. 1. Lloyd guessed that a full Turkish advance had been projected from the evidence of a few 'Turkish reconnoitring parties […] along the various roads', as earlier, based on unreliable Humint. Lloyd, Jiddah to Clayton, 6 December 1916, Private letter, GLLD 9/8. For rumours that Enver Pasha and Jemal Pasha had also arrived at Medina, see 'The Situation in Hejaz', Arabian Report N.S. No. XXI, 13 December 1916, FO371/2781/253852 (15 December 1916), fo. 2, relaying Wingate [to FO], 8 December 1916, tel. 66; Appreciation of Attached Arabian Report, No. XXI, 'Secret', [13 December 1916] FO371/2781/253852, fo. 1; DMI, London to GHQ, Egypt, 15 December 1916, No. 26629, WO33/905, No. 6324; Murray to DMI, London, 16 December 1916, I.A.2755 WO33/905, No. 6343.
85 'The Situation in Hejaz', Arabian Report N.S. No. XXI, 13 December 1916, FO371/2781/253852 (15 December 1916), fos 1–2, relaying Wingate [to FO], 7 December 1916, tel. 65.
86 *The Arab Bulletin*, No. 35, 20 December 1916, p. 535. 'The Situation in Hejaz', Arabian Report N.S. No. XXI, 13 December 1916, FO371/2781/253852 (15 December 1916), fos 2–3, relaying Wingate [to FO], 10 December 1916, tel. 70. Arab Bureau to DMI, London, 12 December 1916, A.B.404 WO33/905, No. 6306. Arab Bureau to DMI, London, 18 December 1916, A.B.438 WO33/905, No. 6354. Lawrence, 'The Arab Advance on Wejh', *The Arab Bulletin*, No. 41, 6 February 1917, p. 61. Lawrence, *Seven Pillars*, pp. 131–3.
87 'The Situation in Hejaz', Arabian Report N.S. No. XXI, 13 December 1916, FO371/2781/253852 (15 December 1916), fo. 2, relaying Wingate [to FO], 8 December 1916, tel. 66.
88 Ibid., fo. 3, relaying Wingate [to FO], 11 December 1916, tel. 72.
89 *The Arab Bulletin*, No. 34, 11 December 1916, p. 518. Arab Bureau to DMI, London, 12 December 1916, A.B.404 WO33/905, No. 6306. *The Arab Bulletin*, No. 35, 20 December 1916, pp. 536–7. Lawrence, 'The Arab Advance on Wejh', *The Arab Bulletin*, No. 41, 6 February 1917, p. 61. Lawrence, *Seven Pillars*, p. 136. For further remarks on the princes' movements, see Wemyss to Admiralty, 21 December 1916, ADM137/594, 7–21 December 1916, M 073/17 SA 554, No. 1043/1139. Arab Bureau to DMI, London, 12 December 1916, A.B.404 WO33/905, No. 6306.
90 Wilson to Arbur, 11 December 1916, relaying L.41 from Lawrence, W.873, FO882/6 HRG/16/78.
91 'The Situation in Hejaz', Arabian Report N.S. No. XXI, 13 December 1916, FO371/2781/253852 (15 December 1916), fo. 2, relaying Wingate [to FO], 8 December 1916, tel. 66 [referring to Wilson to Arbur, W.625 cipher. FO882/6 HRG/16/74, and Wilson to Arbur, W.838 FO882/6 HRG/16/75].
92 Robertson to Murray, 9 December 1916, No. 26173, cipher, WO33/905, No. 6278.
93 'The situation in Hejaz', Arabian Report N.S. No. XXI, 13 December 1916, FO371/

2781/253852 (15 December 1916), fo. 2, relaying FO to Wingate, 8 December 1916, tel. 34, and Wingate to FO, 10 December 1916, tel. 69.

94 Wemyss to Admiralty, 21 December 1916, ADM137/594, 7–21 December 1916, M 073/17 SA 554, No. 1043/1139. 'The Situation in Hejaz', Arabian Report N.S. No. XXI, 13 December 1916, FO371/2781/253852 (15 December 1916), fo. 3, relaying Wingate to FO, 11 December 1916, tel. 72.

95 'The Situation in Hejaz', Arabian Report N.S. No. XXI, 13 December 1916, FO371/2781/253852 (15 December 1916), fo. 2, relaying Wingate [to FO], 9 December 1916, tel. 68.

96 Ibid., fo. 3, relaying Wingate [to FO], 10 December 1916, p. 70.

97 Lloyd, 'Shereef's Visit to Jidda', *c.*12–14 December 1916, GLLD 9/8. See also Report by Wilson, 16 December 1916, contained in Wilson to Wingate, 19 December 1916, No. 17, FO882/6 HRG/16/83.

98 Lloyd, 'Shereef's Visit to Jidda', *c.*12–14 December 1916, GLLD 9/8. Wilson to Arbur, 11 December 1916, relaying L.41, W.873, FO882/6 HRG/16/78. See also Wilson to Arbur, W.869.

99 'The Situation in Hejaz', Arabian Report N.S. No. XXI, 13 December 1916, FO371/2781/253852 (15 December 1916), fo. 3, relaying Wingate [to FO], 11 December 1916, tel. 72 and tel. 74; fo. 4, relaying Wingate [to FO], 13 December 1916, tel. 77. Wilson to Wingate, 19 December 1916, No. 17 FO882/6 HRG/16/83, containing his 'Report on Sherif's visit to Jeddah, 10–15 December 1916', dated 16 December 1916. See also Wemyss to Admiralty, 21 December 1916, ADM137/594, 7–21 December 1916 M 073/17 SA 554, No. 1043/1139.

100 *The Arab Bulletin*, No. 34, 11 December 1916, p. 518.

101 'The Situation in Hejaz', Arabian Report N.S. No. XXI, 13 December 1916, FO371/2781/253852 (15 December 1916), fo. 3, relaying Wingate [to FO], 11 December 1916, tel. 72 [two days after interview with Boyle]. Arab Bureau to DMI, London, 12 December 1916, A.B.404 WO33/905, No. 6306. *The Arab Bulletin*, No. 35, 20 December 1916, p. 535.

102 *The Arab Bulletin*, No. 35, 20 December 1916, p. 535.

103 'The Situation in Hejaz', Arabian Report N.S. No. XXI, 13 December 1916, FO371/2781/253852 (15 December 1916), fo. 4, relaying Wingate [to FO], 12 December 1916, tel. 76. Humint from an Arab NCO deserter at Yenbo suggested that the British planes' bombing raids forced Fakhri Pasha to withdraw from Nakhl Mubarak to Bir Said. *The Arab Bulletin*, No. 37, 4 January 1917, p. 4.

104 Lawrence also wanted to relieve the overworked seaplanes which had been 'doing yeoman work these last two days', dropping bombs on Bruka [just south of Nakhl Mubarak] and scouting the enemy. Lawrence (en route from Yenbo to Rabegh on HMS *Suva*) to Director, Arab Bureau, 11 December 1916, FO882/6 HRG/16/95.

105 'The Situation in Hejaz', Arabian Report N.S. No. XXI, 13 December 1916, FO371/2781/253852 (15 December 1916), fo. 3, relaying Wingate [to FO], 11 December 1916, tel. 72 [two days after interview with Capt. Boyle].

106 Wilson to Arbur, 11 December 1916, relaying L.41, W.873, FO882/6 HRG/16/78. See also 'The Situation in Hejaz', Arabian Report N.S. No. XXI, 13 December 1916, FO371/2781/253852 (15 December 1916), fo. 4, relaying Wingate [to FO], 11 December 1916, tel. 77 on Lawrence's telegram.

107 Lawrence to Director, Arab Bureau, 11 December 1916 (en route from Yenbo to Rabegh on HMS *Suva*), FO882/6 HRG/16/95.

108 Lloyd, 'Employment of Christian Troops in the Hejas' and 'Political', in 'Report on the Hejas', Lloyd, Jiddah to Lynden-Bell, 22 December 1916, GLLD 9/8.

109 Wemyss to Admiralty, 21 December 1916, ADM137/594, 7–21 December 1916, M 073/17 SA 554, No. 1043/1139.

110 Wilson to Arbur, 11 December 1916, relaying L.41, W.873, FO882/6 HRG/16/78. Wilson was particularly worried by Fuad el Khatib's remarks that the Sherif only

agreed (temporarily) to Christian troops because 'he thinks we wish it', knowing nevertheless that the landing would destroy 'his cause [...] in the eyes of the Arabs'. Wilson to Wingate, 15 December 1916, W 615, FO882/6 HRG/16/81 (copies to Lawrence and Joyce). See also 'Report/Diary on the Sherif's visit to Jeddah'. Wilson to Wingate, 19 December 1916, No. 17, FO882/6 HRG/16/83 (copies to Sirdar (Lee O. Stack), Arab Bureau, Joyce, Lawrence). fforde repeated Fuad's interpretation to India. fforde to Grant, 2 January 1917, Item #3, D.O. No. 71, W/C R/20/A/1570 IOLR.

111 'The Situation in Hejaz', Arabian Report N.S. No. XXI, 13 December 1916, FO371/2781/253852 (15 December 1916), fo. 3, relaying FO to Lord Bertie, 11 December 1916, tel. 2947; fo. 5, relaying Lord Bertie to FO, London, 10 December 1916, tel. 1312, fo. 5, relaying Lord Bertie to FO, London, 12 December 1916, tel. 1327. The French Senegalese units comprised technical detachments, two artillery batteries, a mountain battery, eight machine-gun sections, a company of Engineers and various French and native officers, non-coms and experts. 'The Situation in Hejaz', fo. 4, relaying Lord Bertie to FO, London, 9 December 1916, tel. 1306, enclosing memorandum from French Minister for War. Clayton was relieved at France's withdrawal, believing they had 'had their chance when those Senegalise battalions were asked for, but thank heavens they don't seem to have taken it'. Clayton to Lloyd, 28 December 1916, Private, GLLD 9/8.

112 Ibid., relaying FO to Wingate, 11 December 1916, tel. 36. See also Robertson to Murray, 9 December 1916, No. 26173, cipher, WO33/905 No. 6278; Murray to Robertson, 10 December 1916 A.M.1382 WO33/905, No. 6290.

113 Murray to Robertson, 12 December 1916, A.M.1391 WO33/905, No. 6305.

114 Wingate to Wilson, 13 December 1916, tel. 272, FO686/55/1212, fo. 2. 'The Situation in Hejaz', Arabian Report N.S. No. XXI, 13 December 1916, FO371/2781/253852 (15 December 1916), fo. 4, relaying Wingate [to FO], 13 December 1916, tel. 77.

115 The two extra battalions of British infantry had been urged by Brémond, who had also convinced Wingate that the Sherif would respond to 'a little pressure'. Wingate to FO, London, 14 December 1916, tel. 83, WO158/604, contained in GLLD 9/8, emphasis added.

116 Wingate to Wilson, 14 December 1916 (rec. 15 December), W289 FO882/6 HRG/16/80 (copies to Lawrence and Joyce).

117 Wingate to FO, London, 16 December 1916, tel. 86, WO158/604/215A.

118 FO, London to Wingate, relayed in Robertson to Murray, 16 December 1916, No. 26663, cipher, WO33/905, No. 6335.

119 Wilson to Wingate, 15 December 1916, W 615 FO882/6 HRG/16/81.

120 Wilson quoted advice delivered by the Governor of Jiddah, Sherif Mohsen bin Mansur, and a respected representative of the Sherif, Sheikh Mohammed bin Oreifan. Wilson to Wingate, 19 December 1916, No. 17, FO882/6 HRG/16/83 (copies to Sirdar (L. Stack), Arab Bureau, Joyce, Lawrence).

121 Emphasis added. Lloyd also noted:

> Familiarity is apt to breed if not contempt at all events an attitude of scepticism, but it is probable that a couple of years ago we should never have questioned the views of the Grand Shereef of Mecca on a Moslem question of this kind.
>
> 'Report on the Hejaz.' Lloyd, Jiddah to Lynden-Bell, 22 December 1916, GLLD 9/8.

122 By chance, the ship's wireless transmission of Feisal's direct request was delayed for at least a day due to bad weather and naval backlog, giving the Imint returns time to be reviewed. Lawrence's relay of Feisal's message reached Wilson's Jiddah office on 11 or 12 December. Wilson wired the message to Wingate, who wired the FO on 13 December. 'The Situation in Hejaz', Arabian Report N.S. No. XXI, 13 December

1916, FO371/2781/253852 (15 December 1916), fo. 4, relaying Wingate [to FO], 13 December 1916, tel. 77.

123 *The Arab Bulletin*, No. 35. 20 December 1916, p. 535. The Turks' Arab guide, Dakhil Allah, described the retreat to Lawrence who concluded, 'that night, I believe, the Turks lost their war' [Lawrence was already onboard the HSM *Suva* during the stand-off, en route to Rabegh. See Lawrence, *Seven Pillars*, p. 134]. For more on Rabegh defences, see: Lawrence to Director, Arab Bureau, 2 December 1916, FO882/6 HRG/16/71A; Lawrence, 'Diary of Captain Lawrence', 2–5 December 1916, FO882/6 HRG/16/73; Storrs, 'Extract from Diary: Visit to Grand Sherif', entry for 13 December 1916, FO882/6 HRG/16/79.

124 'The Situation in Hejaz', Arabian Report N.S. No. XXI, 13 December 1916, FO371/2781/253852 (15 December 1916), fo. 4, relaying Wingate [to FO], 12 December 1916, tel. 76.

125 Arab Bureau to DMI, London, 18 December 1916, A.B.438 WO33/905, No. 6354, Arab Bureau to DMI, London, 23 December 1916, A.B.473 WO33/905, No. 6390A. *The Arab Bulletin*, No. 35, 20 December 1916, p. 537. Imint in late December suggested that the Ghayir district was evacuated. 'Fresh tracks' to the south may have been Turk or Arab. *The Arab Bureau*, No. 36, 26 December 1916, p. 547. By early January 1917, intelligence, most likely Sigint, superseded the aerial observations with evidence that the Turks were still at Ghayir and trying to obtain supplies from central Arabia. Ibid., No. 37, 4 January 1917, p. 4.

126 'Report on work done by "C" Flight, 14 Squadron, RFC in the Hejaz during winter of 1916–1917.' Ross, Headquarters, Middle East Brigade, RFC to Wilson, 26 April 1917, FO686/6, Part. II, 2 (fo. 41).

127 *The Arab Bulletin*, No. 36, 26 December 1916, p. 547.

128 Lloyd to Clayton, 6 December 1916, GLLD 9/8.

129 Arab Bureau to DMI, London, 23 December 1916, A.B.473 WO33/905, No. 6390A.

130 *The Arab Bulletin*, No. 36, 26 December 1916, p. 547. See also Arab Bureau to DMI, London. 12 December 1916, A.B.404 WO33/905, No. 6306; *The Arab Bulletin*, No. 35, 20 December 1916, p. 535.

131 Wemyss to Admiralty, 21 December 1916, ADM137/594, 7–21 December 1916, M 073/17 SA 554, No. 1043/1139.

132 The report is dated 16 December 1916. The covering letter is dated 19 December 1916. Wilson to Wingate, 19 December 1916, FO882/6 HRG/16/83 (copies to Sirdar (L.O. Stack), Arab Bureau, Joyce, Lawrence).

133 McMahon to Hardinge, 13 December 1916, Hardinge MSS, Vol. VII, #28, fo. 121.

134 Lloyd to Lynden-Bell, 'Private', 22 December 1916, GLLD 9/8.

135 'Shereef's answer of December 25th to Sirdar's [Wingate's] message asking him if his refusal to allow Xtian troops to land was final & throwing all responsibility on the Shereef for his refusal.' GLLD 9/8.

136 Report by Bray, attached to Wilson, Yenbo to Wingate, 28 December 1916, FO882/6 HRG/16/93.

137 Wilson, Yenbo to Wingate, 28 December 1916, FO882/6 HRG/16/93.

138 Ibid., emphasis added. *The Arab Bulletin*, No. 37, 4 January 1917, p. 3.

139 Brémond confessed to Pearson that 'it was scarcely his intention that his troops would be immobile, and he surmised that we would find similar impossibility'. H. Pearson, Jiddah to Wingate, Cairo, c/o Arbur, 28 December 1916, W.006 FO882/6 HRG/16/92. See also 26 December (W.4); 2 January 1917; 3 January (W.99); 4 January 1917 (tel. 535).

140 Lloyd to Wingate, 1 January 1917, Private, GLLD 9/9.

141 Wingate, Cairo to Wilson [Pearson], Jiddah, 28 December 1916, A.B.486, FO882/6 HRG/16/91.

142 Murray to Robertson, 5 January 1917, relaying telegram 1225 from the Sherif to Wingate, A.M.1475 WO33/905, No. 6452. Pearson may not have interpreted the message correctly, but fforde did, and described the Sherif's 'final refusal to allow

British Christian troops to be landed in the Hedjaz' as 'wise'. fforde to Grant, 2 January 1917, D.O. 71 W.C. item 3, R/20/A/1570 IOLR.

143 Pearson to Arbur for Wingate, tel. W099, 4 January 1917, WO158/627.
144 Murray to Wingate, 5 January 1917, WO158/627.
145 Clayton, Cairo to Lloyd, Private letter, 7 January 1916, GLLD 9/8.
146 Wilson to Pearson, Jiddah, relayed in Pearson to Arab Bureau, tel. 9003, contained in GOC-in-C to CIGS, 8 January 1917, A.M.1485 WO33/905, No. 6472. See also Wilson, Jiddah to Arab Bureau, 7 January, W.142, relayed in GHQ, Egypt to DMI, London, 10 January 1917, I.A.2865 WO33/905, No. 6493.
147 Wilson, W.118, 6 January 1917, contained in Murray to Robertson, 7 January 1917, A.M.1482 WO33/905, No. 6466. Wilson warned Wingate again the next day that a telephonic message from the Sherif could not be considered an official request for troops. Wilson to Arab Bureau, 7 January 1917, W.142, relayed in GHQ, Egypt to DMI, 10 January 1917, I.A.2865 WO33/905, No. 6493.
148 Wilson to Arab Bureau, 7 January 1917, W.142, relayed in GHQ, Egypt to DMI, 10 January 1917, I.A.2865 WO33/905, No. 6493.
149 E. Brémond, *Le Hedjaz dans la Guerre Mondiale*, Paris: Payot, 1931, p. 109.
150 *The Arab Bulletin*, No. 37, 4 January 1917, pp. 3, 5.
151 Ibid., No. 36, 26 December 1916, p. 547; No. 37, 4 January 1917, pp. 3, 5. Robertson to Murray, 9 January 1917, No. 27661, cipher, WO33/905, No. 6479.
152 Robertson to Murray, 6 January 1917. tel. 27542, WO33/905, No. 6455.
153 Murray to Robertson, 7 January 1917, A.M.1481 WO33/905, No. 6465.
154 Ibid., 10 January 1917, A.M.1492 WO33/905, No. 6490.
155 Robertson to Murray, 9 January 1917, No. 27661, cipher, WO33/905, No. 6479.
156 Informants said the Turkish planes might have carried maxims but were without wireless capability. 'Rabugh Intelligence', *The Arab Bulletin*, No. 42, 15 February 1917, p. 81. The intelligence was compiled from PoWs captured at Wadi Hamra on 4 January 1917. 'Turkish Situation', *The Arab Bulletin*, No. 39, 19 January 1917, p. 27.
157 David Lloyd George became Prime Minister on 7 December 1916. On 9 December, a new War Cabinet was assembled, supported by the Secretariat of the CID under Sir Maurice Hankey. '*Quite as bad as the old lot*', complained Robertson to General Haig, 10 December 1916, in *Military Correspondence* [...] *Robertson*, p. 129, emphasis in text.
158 Robertson to Murray, 8 January 1917, No. 27639, cipher, WO33/905, No. 6473. Lloyd later conveyed the opinion of the DMO that apparently 'the Government decision not to send Christian troops to the Hejaz was due to General Robertson's views and to those of the staff of the War Office and the DMO cordially approved of our attitude in regard to *that* question'. Lloyd to Lynden-Bell, 28 February 1917, GLLD 9/9.
159 Robertson to Murray, 9 January 1917, No. 27661, cipher, WO33/905, No. 6479. By 22 January 1917, Robertson confirmed finally that Murray could release from standby the brigade earmarked for Rabegh. Robertson to Murray, 22 January 1917, WO33/905, No. 6566, No. 28297, cipher.
160 Wilson to Clayton, 20 September 1917, Sudan Archives. Box 470/7/14.

5 Reorientation: the Arab Revolt shifts north, January–April 1917

1 Keegan, *First World War*, p. 323.
2 *The Arab Bulletin*, No. 35, 20 December 1916, pp. 536–7.
3 Ibid., No. 35, 20 December 1916, p. 542; No. 36, 26 December 1916, pp. 557–8. Wemyss to Admiralty, 21 December 1916, ADM137/594, 7–21 December 1916, M 073/17 SA 554, No. 1043/1139.
4 *The Arab Bulletin*, No. 37, 4 January 1917, p. 4.
5 Lloyd to Wingate, 1 January 1917, 'Private', GLLD 9/9.
6 Wemyss to Admiralty, 21 December 1916, ADM137/594, 7–21 December 1916, M 073/17 SA 554, No. 1043/1139. See also Joyce to Wilson, 19 November 1916,

FO882/5 HRG/16/62, and 2 December 1916, FO882/6 HRG/16/70. Joyce blamed Ali's weak personality and poor military skills for the dishevelled state of Rabegh's defence: 'He is getting no moves on at all. He can't organise and won't let anybody else even try and the days pass by and the time wasted makes me mad.' Joyce to Wilson, 26 November 1916, Akaba Archive I/3 H13, King's College, London. Aziz el-Masri, arriving at Rabegh on 23 December, also 'expressed great disappointment and dissatisfaction with the state of affairs in Sherif Ali[']s forces'. *The Arab Bulletin*, No. 36, 26 December 1916, p. 547. Clayton, 'Memorandum', 20 December 1916, FO882/5 HRG/16/84.

7 'Sidi Ali', *The Arab Bulletin*, No. 39, 19 January 1917, p. 29.

8 Lawrence, Yenbo to Wilson, Jiddah, 25 December 1916, FO882/6 HRG/16/87. '[T]he difficulty is to find any troops capable of holding trenches, even with the support of ships' fire.' *The Arab Bulletin*, No. 36, 26 December 1916, p. 547. Lawrence 'The Arab Advance on Wejh', *The Arab Bulletin*, No. 41, 6 February 1917, p. 61. Lawrence, *Seven Pillars*, p. 137. For Bray's reassurance to Cairo that 'Feisal does not believe in their disaffection', see Bray, 'Report' attached to Wilson, Yenbo to Wingate, 28 December 1916, FO882/6 HRG/16/93. For explanation of Subh's alleged defection, see: Lawrence, 'Arab Advance on Wejh', *The Arab Bulletin*, No. 41, 6 February 1917, p. 61; No. 37, 4 January 1917, p. 3.

9 Lawrence estimated that Feisal's total force at Yenbo numbered 6,000. Lawrence to Wilson, 25 December 1916, FO882/6 HRG/16/87.

10 For Lloyd's observations on Turks' elaborate methods of concealment and deception on the road 'to mislead the aeroplanes' in the Sinai, see Lloyd, Jiddah to Wingate, 1 January 1917, Private letter, GLLD 9/9.

11 Lawrence, 'Arab Advance on Wejh', *The Arab Bulletin*, No. 41, 6 February 1917, pp. 60–1. Wilson to Wingate, 28 December 1916, FO882/6 HRG/16/93. Lawrence, *Seven Pillars*, p. 138.

12 Wilson, Yenbo to Wingate, 28 December 1916, FO882/6 HRG/16/93.

13 Wemyss to Admiralty, 21 December 1916, ADM137/594, 7–21 December 1916, M 073/17 SA 554, No. 1043/1139. On 19 December, British seaplanes dropped bombs on the Turkish fort at Wejh and spotted forty soldiers there, as well as 400 camelmen holding the first ridge outside the town. Arab Bureau to DMI, London, 23 December 1916, A.B.473 WO33/905, No. 6390A.

14 Ibid., 22 December 1916–10 January 1917, M0972/17 SA 553, 10 January 1917, ADM137/594, No. 26/1139.

15 Hogarth referred to recent intelligence from a Turkish officer 'whose notes have reached us', that confirmed Sir Richard Burton's notes on an Eastern Road (Darb esh-Sharqi), lying east of the Fura and Gaha roads, travelled by pilgrims and populated with villages, wells and forage. Hogarth believed it 'could probably be traversed by a mobile column in from fifteen to twenty days marching'. Hogarth, memorandum on 'The Rabugh Question', for the Arab Bureau, 10 January 1917, fos 2–4, GLLD 9/9. For Humint from deserting Arab Ottoman Army NCO on Medina's waning forage supply, see *The Arab Bulletin*, No. 37, 4 January 1917, p. 4.

16 Wilson added in the margin: 'I agree with this view.' Wilson, Yenbo to Wingate, 28 December 1916, FO882/6 HRG/16/93.

17 Bray, 'Report' attached to Wilson to Wingate, 28 December 1916, FO882/6 HRG/16/93. For more on advantages of pursuing a dynamic campaign, see 'Excerpts from a Report made by Captain T.E. Lawrence to Lt Colonel Wilson on January 8, 1917', *The Arab Bulletin*, No. 42, 15 February 1917, p. 77.

18 Arab Bureau to DMI, London, 3 January 1917, A.B.524 WO33/905, No. 6443. *The Arab Bulletin*, No. 41, 6 February 1917, p. 55.

19 Ibid., No. 37, 4 January 1917, p. 4.

20 Ibid.

21 Lawrence, 'Route Notes', from 'Excerpts', *The Arab Bulletin*, No. 42, 15 February

1917, pp. 75–6. Arab Bureau to DMI, London, 9 January 1917, A.B.566 WO33/905, No. 6484.

22 Lawrence, 'Route Notes', from 'Excerpts', *The Arab Bulletin*, No. 42, 15 February 1917, pp. 75–6.

23 'Turkish Situation', *The Arab Bulletin*, No. 39, 19 January 1917, p. 27. 'Rabugh Intelligence', *The Arab Bulletin*, No. 42, 15 February 1917, p. 80.

24 'Rabugh Intelligence', *The Arab Bulletin*, No. 42, 15 February 1917, pp. 80–1.

25 'Turkish Situation', *The Arab Bulletin*, No. 39, 19 January 1917, p. 27.

26 'Rabugh Intelligence', *The Arab Bulletin*, No. 42, 15 February 1917, p. 81.

27 The Arab Bureau also wondered whether any Turkish agents, the Sheikh of Subh for example, might have been tempted to distort their information to suggest conditions 'not very encouraging to [the Turks] and rather flattering to the Sherif's forces', in order to keep the Turks, a regular employer, from moving away. *The Arab Bulletin*, No. 39, 19 January 1917, p. 27.

28 'Rabugh Intelligence', *The Arab Bulletin*, No. 42, 15 February 1917, pp. 80–1. See also 'Turkish Situation', *The Arab Bulletin*, No. 39, 19 January 1917, p. 27; No. 38, 12 January 1917, p. 13; Arab Bureau to DMI, London, 9 January 1917, A.B.566 WO33/905, No. 6484.

29 Intelligence from PoW statements put the first [half-battalion] and second Battalion of the 55th Regiment at Hamra with mountain guns and two field-guns, extending to Bir ibn Hassani; the 3/55th at Bir Derwish; and the 4/55th at Bir Abbas. Part of the 129th Regiment camped at Bir Raha, the 42nd Regiment remained around Ghayir, and a Camel Corps Regiment stayed south of Hamra. *The Arab Bulletin*, No. 38, 12 January 1917, p. 13; Lawrence, 'Route Notes', from 'Excerpts', *The Arab Bulletin*, No. 42, 15 February 1917, pp. 75–6. Note, a possible misstatement of 4/55th at Bir Derwish see Arab Bureau to DMI, London, 9 January 1917, A.B.566 WO33/905, No. 6484.

30 *The Arab Bulletin*, No. 37, 4 January 1917, p. 3.

31 Lawrence, 'With the Northern Army', 'Excerpts', *The Arab Bulletin*, No. 42, 15 February 1917, p. 75.

32 'The Political Situation', *The Arab Bulletin*, No. 41, 6 February 1916, p. 55.

33 This statement was reported by an 'apparently reliable' deserter. Arab Bureau to DMI, London, 3 January 1917, A.B.524 WO33/905, No. 6443.

34 Arab Bureau to DMI, London, 17 January 1917, A.B.621 WO33/905, No. 6538. For Sigint on enemy sick rate [from an 'absolutely reliable source'] see GHQ, Egypt to DMI, London, 5 January 1917, I.A.2844 WO33/905, No. 6454. See also the *The Arab Bulletin*, No. 38, 12 January 1917, p. 13. Another source, probably Sigint, located a battalion of the 131st Regiment at Medina in mid-December 1916, previously in Syria but now supporting communication between Bir Ali and Kheif, while the 55th and 130th Regiments advanced from Bir Abbas or Bir Derwish to Kheif [Turkish Jedeida]. *The Arab Bulletin*, No. 35, 20 December 1916, p. 536. By late January 1917, intelligence, probably Sigint, placed two, possibly three battalions of the 131st at Medina. *The Arab Bulletin*, No. 40, 29 January 1917, p. 41.

35 Lawrence, 'Advance on Wejh', *The Arab Bulletin*, No. 41, 6 February 1917, p. 62.

36 'Sherif Abdullah's occupation of Wadi Ais rendered possible Feisal's move north to Wejh, and Abdullah's occupation was indirectly secured by the operations at el Arish and Rafah.' Lawrence, 'Arab Advance on Wejh', *The Arab Bulletin*, No. 41, 6 February 1917, p. 62.

37 Murray to Robertson, 21 December 1916, A.M.1418 WO33/905, No. 6376. Murray to Robertson, 10 January 1917, A.M.1494 WO33/905, No. 6491. Murray was determined to launch 'serious operations in Palestine' by the end of February, and was pushing forward with construction of the Sinai railway. Murray to Robertson, 7 January 1917, A.M.1481 WO33/905, No. 6465.

38 Feisal's departure ran ten days over schedule. He arrived at Wejh on 25 January, five days later than agreed. Abdullah's progress ran nearly thirteen days late. He arrived

at Wadi Ais on 17 January 1917. Wilson, Yenbo to Wingate, 28 December 1916, FO882/6 HRG/16/93. Lawrence, 'Arab Advance on Wejh', *The Arab Bulletin*, No. 41, 6 February 1917, p. 62; No. 38, 12 January 1917, p. 13.

39 Lawrence, 'The Sherifial Northern Army', *The Arab Bulletin*, No. 41, 6 February 1917, p. 63. Arab Bureau to DMI, London, 17 January 1917, A.B.621 WO33/905, No. 6538. The resulting sum of 8,138 tribesmen is certainly higher than the 3,000 anticipated by the Arab Bureau before departure (artillery estimates also vary slightly: see 'Feisal's Movements', *The Arab Bulletin*, No. 39, 19 January 1917, p. 28) or the 4,500 that Bray estimated would be available for wider operations a few weeks earlier. Bray had also been more pessimistic in estimating that 2,000 of the Southern Juheinah tribesmen who dispersed after the December occupation of Nakhl Mubarak 'till Feisal rode in alone among them and pulled them together', would decline to move north, being 'tired of the present state of affairs and [reluctant to] leave this district'. Bray, 'Report' attached to Wilson to Wingate, 28 December 1916, FO882/6 HRG/16/93. For more on Maulud el Mukhlus of Tekrit and his mule-riders who became 'prodigies in the Arab ranks [...] the value of so tough a unit for reconnaissance was obvious', see Lawrence, *Seven Pillars*, pp. 141, 93–4, 122.

40 'Feisal's Movements', *The Arab Bulletin*, No. 39, 19 January 1917, p. 28.

41 Lawrence, 'Advance on Wejh', *The Arab Bulletin*, No. 41, 6 February 1917, p. 62.

42 *The Arab Bulletin*, No. 38, 12 January 1917, p. 13. 'Feisal's Movements', *The Arab Bulletin*, No. 39, 19 January 1917, pp. 28–9.

43 'Sidi Ali', *The Arab Bulletin*, No. 39, 19 January 1917, p. 29.

44 Ibid. Arab Bureau to DMI, 9 January 1917, A.B.566 WO33/905, No. 6484. Arab Bureau to DMI, London, 17 January 1917, A.B.621 WO33/905, No. 6538. *The Arab Bulletin*, No. 38, 12 January 1917, p. 13.

45 Lawrence, 'The Sherifial Northern Army', *The Arab Bulletin*, No. 41, 6 February 1917, p. 63. Bray had earlier reported that the Northern Juheinah were 'in the mood for action' and 'ready to co-operate' in the move against Wejh. Wilson to Wingate, 28 December 1916, FO882/6 HRG/16/93.

46 Lawrence, Um Lejj to Newcombe, 17 January 1917, Private letter. Brown (ed.), *Letters*, p. 102. Lawrence did still advise Feisal's deputy at Yenbo, Sherif Sharraf, to embark all munitions, explosives, petrol and foodstuffs onto the HMS *Hardinge* in case the Turks attacked before Wejh was taken. Lawrence, 'Advance on Wejh', *The Arab Bulletin*, No. 41, 6 February 1917, p. 62. Lawrence wanted Boyle to land north of the town, and work southward. Lawrence, Um Lejj to Newcombe, 17 January 1917, Private letter, Brown (ed.), *Letters*, p. 102. Feisal left Tewfik Bey, a Syrian officer, at Bir Said with 450 men and artillery to guard the ordnance stores. Bray, 'Report' attached to Wilson, Yenbo to Wingate, 28 December 1916, FO882/6 HRG/16/93. Lawrence, *Seven Pillars*, p. 146. Abd el Kader (civilian) soon clashed with Tewfik Bey (military). Lawrence sent word to Feisal, who sent Sherif Sharraf and 500 Harb to Yenbo to settle the matter. The episode was significant for Lawrence in that it demonstrated again the transcendent power of the ashraf, even over non-Bedouin subjects. Lawrence, 'The Sherifial Northern Army', *The Arab Bulletin*, No. 41, 6 February 1917, pp. 63–4. 'Feisal's Movements', *The Arab Bulletin*, No. 39, 19 January 1917, p. 28. Lawrence, *Seven Pillars*, p. 146. See also Arab Bureau to DMI, 17 January 1917, A.B.621 WO33/905, No. 6538. Lawrence rode with Feisal out of Yenbo but was soon recalled to the port, to assist there. Afterwards he sailed with the HMS *Suva* to Um Lejj and rejoined Feisal's army for the final stage to Wejh. Lawrence, *Seven Pillars*, pp. 145–8.

47 Wemyss to Admiralty, 30 January 1917, ADM137/594, 11–30 January 1917, M 01746/17 SA 563, No. 132/1139. 'The Capture of Wejh', 'Precis and Extracts from a Report by Captain A.N.E. [*sic*] Bray', *The Arab Bulletin*, No. 41, 6 February 1917, p. 67.

48 Lawrence, 'Feisal's Order of March', *The Arab Bulletin*, No. 41, 6 February 1917,

p. 65. Arab Bureau to DMI, London, 17 January 1917, A.B.621 WO33/905, No. 6538. The HMS *Anne* kept track of Feisal's advance.

49 Drought had inflated the price of forage. Many of Feisal's camels starved to death on the march, and surviving animals could not carry their full burden. The only compensation in Lawrence's view was that the Arab fighters' material needs remained far below a regular army's requirements. Feisal's force numbered roughly 4,000 camel corps, 4,000 infantry, mule-mounted infantry, mountain-guns and machine-guns, and required just 380 baggage camels for eight days' supply of food, thirty-six days' supply of water and ammunition for all arms. Another contrast: Feisal's previous mountain-battery, manned by its Egyptian escort, had required 360 camels for transport, while Feisal's current battery, carrying the same quantity of ammunition but manned by Arabs, needed only thirty-two camels for a two-day march, and eighty for the fourteen-day march to Wejh. Lawrence, 'Feisal's Order of March', *The Arab Bulletin*, No. 41, 6 February 1917, pp. 65–6.

50 Typically, Lawrence avoided criticizing the Arab leaders or tribesmen in his reports; he emphasized that the food and water shortages did not affect 'the spirits of the men' nor 'their speed or energy'. 'Feisal's Order of March', Lawrence, *The Arab Bulletin*, No. 41, 6 February 1917, pp. 65–6.

51 Lawrence, *Seven Pillars*, p. 155.

52 'The Capture of Wejh', 'Precis [...] A.N.E. [*sic*] Bray', *The Arab Bulletin*, No. 41, 6 February 1917, pp. 66–7. *The Arab Bulletin*, No. 42, 15 February 1917, p. 82. The Arab Bureau's watched Suleiman Rufida closely; see *The Arab Bulletin*, No. 20, 241; No. 14, 154; No. 22, 264, 277; No. 23, 305; No. 28, 403; No. 31, 464; No. 33, 511. The most important arrival was twenty-seven year old Sherif Nasir of Medina, whom Feisal named as his second-in-command. The younger brother of the Emir of Medina, Nasir was already an experienced commander and would play a central role in the Arab campaign's future. Lawrence described him as 'the opener of roads, the forerunner of Feisal's movement', and maintained that 'from beginning to end all that could be told of him was good'. His family were Shias descending from the younger child of Ali, and second only to the Emir of Mecca in lineage. Lawrence, *Seven Pillars*, pp. 164–5.

53 'The Capture of Wejh', 'Precis ... Bray', *The Arab Bulletin*, No. 41, 6 February 1917, p. 67.

54 Lawrence, 'Advance on Wejh', Lawrence, *The Arab Bulletin*, No. 41, 6 February 1917, p. 62. Lawrence, *Seven Pillars*, p. 166. For Wemyss' decision that the Arabs could not wait longer aboard ship, see Wemyss to Admiralty, 30 January 1917, ADM137/594, 11–30 January 1917, M 01746/17 SA 563, No. 132/1139. Lawrence, *Seven Pillars*, pp. 145–8. 'Capture of Wejh', 'Precis ... Bray', *The Arab Bulletin*, No. 41, 6 February 1917, p. 67.

55 'Capture of Wejh', 'Precis ... Bray', *The Arab Bulletin*, No. 41, 6 February 1917, p. 67.

56 Ibid., pp. 68–9; No. 40, 29 January 1917, p. 42. The plane's observer was killed by enemy fire during one of these flights. The only other British casualty during the two-day engagement was a wounded seaman.

57 'Capture of Wejh', 'Precis ... Bray', *The Arab Bulletin*, No. 41, 6 February 1917, pp. 68–9. The HMS *Fox* reported fewer Turkish casualties than Bray: fifty-five Turks captured and twelve killed. Arab Bureau to DMI, 25 January 1917, A.B.657 WO33/905, No. 6598. Newcombe later reported that only seventy of the Turkish garrison who fled Wejh on 24 January 1917 reached el Ula; the remainder were killed by Arabs. Arab Bureau to DMI, 7 February 1917, A.B.707 WO33/905, No. 6678.

58 Wemyss to Admiralty, 30 January 1917, ADM137/594, 11–30 January 1917, M 01746/17 SA 563, No. 132/1139.

59 *The Arab Bulletin*, No. 42, 15 February 1917, pp. 81–2.

60 'Report from T.E.L. dated Wejh 11.2.1917', FO882/6 HRG/1710. Ahmed Teqeiqah needed more camels to fully mobilize. *The Arab Bulletin*, No. 45, 23 March 1917, p. 134.

61 Wemyss to Admiralty, 22 February 1917, ADM137/594. 31 January–22 February 1917, M 02732/17 SA 562, No. 242/1139.
62 *The Arab Bulletin*, No. 45, 23 March 1917, p. 134.
63 Ibid., No. 43, 28 February 1917, p. 103.
64 See *El Ikbar*, 15 January 1917, contained in 'Extracts from Newspapers', *The Arab Bulletin*, No. 42, 15 February 1917, pp. 83–4.
65 This article appeared in *El Sharq* on 8 February 1917. *The Arab Bulletin*, No. 45, 23 March 1917, pp. 134–5.
66 The Arab Bureau noted the contrast between the Turks' 'Germanized army' and the leaner, mobile Arab armies: 'the administrative developments of modern scientific war seem to have clogged [the Turks'] mobility and destroyed their dash'. *The Arab Bulletin*, No. 39, 19 January 1917, pp. 27–8. See also Arab Bureau to DMI, London, 17 January 1917, A.B.621 WO33/905, No. 6538.
67 *The Arab Bulletin*, No. 39, 19 January 1917, pp. 29–30. Mecca's latest intelligence on the German officers was from a 'reliable source', probably an informant, but was unconfirmed by other sources. Arab Bureau to DMI, London, 17 January 1917, A.B.621 WO33/905, No. 6538. The Arab Bureau had already noted rumours that Baron von Oppenheim was in Medina, hoping to negotiate peace terms with the Sherif on the CUP's behalf. *The Arab Bulletin*, No. 37, 4 January 1917, p. 4.
68 *The Arab Bulletin*, No. 40, 29 January 1917, p. 42.
69 A possible exception was the Zobeid section of the Harb, influenced by the Turcophile chief Hussein bin Mubeirig. 'The Political Situation', *The Arab Bulletin*, No. 41, 6 February 1917, pp. 56–7.
70 Ibid., p. 57.
71

> One thing, of which the tribes are convinced, is that they have made an Arab Government, and consequently that each of them is it [...] the tribes know they are independent, and mean to enjoy their independence. This will not entail anarchy, since the family tie and the system of tribal responsibility will be tightened, but it entails the practical disappearance or negation of central power in internal affairs.
>
> 'Nationalism among Tribesmen', Lawrence, *The Arab Bulletin*, No. 32, 26 November 1916, p. 483.

72 'The Political Situation', *The Arab Bulletin*, No. 41, 6 February 1917, p. 57.
73 Wingate requested a rank of General Staff Officer, first grade, for each member of the Military Mission. Wingate to WO, London, 7 January 1917, A.B.551 WO33/905, No. 6467. See also Clayton to Lloyd, Jiddah, 28 December 1916, Private, GLLD 9/8.
74 Wilson said the Mission should communicate with chiefs such as Nuri Shaalan only in the name of the Sherif and after consultation with Feisal and Abdullah, remembering their subordinate position under the Sherif at all times. Wilson to Newcombe, 15 January 1917, FO882/6 HRG/17/6.
75 Lawrence to Newcombe, 17 January 1917. Um Lejj, en route to Wejh. Brown (ed.), *Letters*, pp. 102–3.
76 'Memorandum on the General Situation in Arabia (Hedjaz) and the Policy and Organization of the British Mission to Grand Sherif', C. Vickery, Wejh, 2 February 1917, FO882/6 HRG/17/8.
77 Wilson to Arbur, 25 January 1917, W.300, FO141/736/2475.
78 'Memorandum', Vickery, 2 February 1917, FO882/6 HRG/17/8. Wilson told Newcombe to send urgent communications simultaneously to the Arab Bureau and himself to save time, although Wilson maintained that he held final authority over the Mission itself and questions of supply. Wilson to Newcombe, 15 January 1917, FO882/6 HRG/17/6.

79 'Memorandum', Vickery, Wejh, 2 February 1917, FO882/6 HRG/17/8.
80 Newcombe also wanted the base for supply to be Suez in view of the campaign's reorientation northwards, replacing Cairo, Port Sudan and Rabegh. Newcombe to Wilson, 4 February 1917, fos 2–3, GLLD 9/9.
81 'Memorandum', Vickery, Wejh, 2 February 1917, FO882/6 HRG/17/8.
82 Ibid.
83 Ibid.
84 Garland rode out to Jeida on 2 February 1917. 'Report from T.E.L. dated Wejh 11.2.1917', FO882/6 HRG/17/10.
85 Newcombe to Wilson, 4 February 1917, fos 3, 6–7, GLLD.
86 Vickery expressed exasperation with the Syrian officers' performance in the field and blamed it on their conflicted political agenda.

> 'It is difficult to conceive the military value of a body of Syrians who one day were taking part – not a very active one it is true – in the defence of a town against Sherif Faisal's army and two days later appeared on parade at a review of the aforementioned army and gained mention for being the only body of men who kept in step when going past.' Perhaps only when confronting the Turks' railway garrisons, 'will these Syrians be able to justify their inclusion in an army or armies which might have been of much more value if they had consisted entirely of Arabs and been officered by their own leaders'.
> 'Memorandum', Vickery, Wejh, 2 February 1917, FO882/6 HRG/17/8.

87 Arab Bureau to DMI, London 22 January 1917, A.B.639 WO33/905, No. 6469. *The Arab Bulletin*, No. 40, 29 January 1917, p. 41; see also No. 42, 15 February 1917, p. 74. Eshref had participated in the Turkish attacks on the Suez Canal in January/February 1915. He had also delivered Constantinople's appeal to Ibn Rashid to attack the British – in other words, 'an unredeemed ruffian'. *The Arab Bulletin*, No. 26, 16 October 1916, pp. 361–2.
88 *The Arab Bulletin*, No. 40, 29 January 1917, p. 41; No. 43, 12 March 1917, p. 122.
89 Ibid., No. 26, 16 October 1916, p. 361.
90 Lawrence, *Seven Pillars*, pp. 159–60.
91 *The Arab Bulletin*, No. 40, 29 January 1917, p. 41; No. 43, 12 March 1917, p. 122
92 *The Arab Bulletin*, No. 39, 19 January 1917, p. 30. Arab Bureau to DMI, London, 17 January 1917, A.B.621 WO33/905, No. 6538.
93 GHQ, Egypt to DMI, London, 23 January 1917, I.A.2908 WO33/905, No. 6582. *The Arab Bulletin*, No. 40, 29 January 1917, p. 40. Arab Bureau to DMI, London, 7 February 1917, A.B.707 WO33/905, No. 6678. Hafah had been Divisional Headquarters for Fakhri Pasha. 'Rabugh Intelligence', *The Arab Bulletin*, No. 42, 15 February 1917, p. 80.
94 *The Arab Bulletin*, No. 40, 29 January 1917, p. 41.
95 'Report from T.E.L. dated Wejh 11.2.1917', FO882/6 HRG/17/10.
96 *The Arab Bulletin*, No. 42, 15 February 1917, p. 81.
97 Ibid., No. 43, 28 February 1917, p. 97. Wemyss to Admiralty, 22 February 1917, ADM137/594, 31 January–22 February 1917, M 02732/17 SA 562, No. 242/1139.
98 Some small parties of Beni Atiyeh from the triangle between Muweilah and Aqaba had joined Feisal's camp after Wejh, but in the main they waited to see whether the Arab armies would reduce Tebuk. *The Arab Bulletin*, No. 42, 15 February 1917, pp. 81–2.
99 Ibn Saud supplied this information to the CPO, Basra, Sir Percy Cox. 'Euphrates Intelligence, December 5–6, 1916', *The Arab Bulletin*, No. 38, 12 January 1917, p. 22.
100 Saud es-Subhan was also an important ally of another of Ibn Rashid's rivals, the Aslam Shammar of north-central Arabia. *The Arab Bulletin*, No. 38, 12 January 1917, p. 13. Arab Bureau to DMI, 9 January 1917 A.M.566 WO33/905, No. 6484.

'Saud es-Subhan' [probably written for the Arab Bureau by Gertrude Bell]. *The Arab Bulletin*, No. 38, 12 January 1917, p. 21.

101 In March 1917, the Arab Bureau was still noting that 'nothing gets through unplundered'; the caravans from Nejd had started aiming for Mecca instead of Medina, 'to avoid the danger zone'. *The Arab Bulletin*, No. 43, 12 March 1917, p. 122.

102 The force comprised several clans, all valuable fighters. *The Arab Bulletin*, No. 39, 19 January 1917, p. 30.

103 *The Arab Bulletin*, No. 40, 29 January 1917, p. 41.

104 Arab Bureau to DMI, 9 January 1917, A.B.566 WO33/905, No. 6484. Arab Bureau to DMI, London, 17 January 1917, A.B.621 WO33/905, No. 6538. *The Arab Bulletin*, No. 40, 29 January 1917, pp. 41–2.

105 Arab Bureau to DMI, 7 February 1917, A.B.707 WO33/905, No. 6678. *The Arab Bulletin*, No. 40, 29 January 1917, p. 42; No. 43, 28 February 1917, p. 97.

106 Murray to Robertson, 17 February 1917 WO33/905, No. 6755. *The Arab Bulletin*, No. 42, 15 February 1917, p. 73. Arab Bureau to DMI, 7 February 1917, A.B.707 WO33/905, No. 6678.

107 Wingate to Robertson, 23 February 1917, A.B.820 WO33/905, No. 6796.

108 Aziz al-Masri, the Minister of War, left the Hejaz at this time due to irreconcilable differences with the Sherif. He was replaced by Captain Mahmud el-Kaisuni, the former Egyptian commandant of the Mecca garrison. *The Arab Bulletin*, No. 44, 12 March 1917, p. 115.

109 Imint from Major Ross on 5 March 1917 showed Jebel Ohod to be 'strongly fortified'. *The Arab Bulletin*, No. 44, 12 March 1917, p. 115. For vacillating reports on the occupancy of Jebel Ohod, see *The Arab Bulletin*, No. 45, 23 March 1917, p. 125; No. 47, 11 April 1917, p. 162; No. 54, 22 June 1917, p. 277. For proposals to form 106th Squadron comprising the Flight at Rabegh, the Flight being composed at Aden and at Abyssinia, see GOC, Middle East Brigade, RFC to WO, 17 February 1917, T.1072 WO33/905, No. 6751, and T.1073 WO33/905, No. 6572.

110 *The Arab Bulletin*, No. 44, 12 March 1917, p. 115.

111 Arab Bureau to DMI, London, 13 February 1917, A.B.745 WO33/905, No. 6716. See also *The Arab Bulletin*, No. 43, 28 February 1917, p. 96.

112 The Sherif's spies who visited the Medina in February 1917 reported that the people were 'deeply disaffected towards the Turks, and ready to turn on them at the first opportunity.' *The Arab Bulletin*, No. 44, 12 March 1917, p. 115. A French Muslim officer with Abdullah reported that five Turkish battalions had left Medina earlier in the month as escort for women and children travelling north. Report dated 17 February 1917. Arab Bureau to DMI, 3 March 1917, A.B.872 WO33/905, No. 6862.

113 Intelligence from various sources stated that the 1/163rd joined the main concentration of Turkish troops at Medain Salih, the 3/163rd reinforced el-Ula, and the 2/163rd and 4/163rd were en route north. *The Arab Bulletin*, No. 43, 28 February 1917, p. 97.

114 Lawrence, *Seven Pillars*, p. 139.

115 The influx of northern fighters released many of the southern tribes from duty, e.g. the Juheinah, who were said to be 'getting tired of being in Billi country, and are being (for the most part), sent home'. *The Arab Bulletin*, No. 43, 28 February 1917, p. 97.

116 See WO to Wingate, 13 February 1917, No. 29423, cipher, WO33/905, No. 6712. Wingate's correspondence with the WO contained regular pleas for more munitions:

> I fear the Arabs' present campaign will break down [...] Unless arms and ammunition in sufficient numbers are forthcoming tribesmen will not move [...] For this failure we should inevitably incur a measure of responsibility in

the eyes of the Shereef and his military leaders [...] They attach probably exaggerated importance to the possession of mountain guns of the latest type which will not be outranged by Turkish artillery.

Wingate to WO, 17 February 1917, A.B.782 WO33/905, No. 6756.

See also: WO to Wingate, 21 February 1917, WO33/905, No. 6776 & 6778; *The Arab Bulletin*, No. 47, 11 April 1917, pp. 162–3.

117 Report from French Muslim Officer with Abdullah, Wadi Ais, dated 17 February 1917. Arab Bureau to DMI, 3 March 1917, A.B.872 WO33/905, No. 6862.

118 Lawrence, Yenbo to Wilson, 5 January 1917, FO882/6 HRG/17/1. This letter was sent to Clayton and the précis to Wilson; see FO882/6 HRG/16/95.

119 See 'Diary of Captain Lawrence', 2–5 December 1916, FO882/6 HRG/16/73.

120 Lawrence, Yenbo to Wilson, 5 January 1917, FO882/6 HRG/17/1. The Arab Bureau noted, 'this opens up possible difficulties with Ibn Saud, who undoubtedly regards the elimination of Ibn Rashid as his particular job'. 'Feisal's Movements', *The Arab Bulletin*, No. 39, 19 January 1917, p. 29.

121 Lawrence, Yenbo to Wilson, 5 January 1917, FO882/6 HRG/17/1. 'Feisal's Movements', *The Arab Bulletin*, No. 39, 19 January 1917, p. 29.

122 Lawrence, Yenbo to Wilson, 5 January 1917, FO882/6 HRG/17/1; see also Lloyd, Jiddah to Wingate, Cairo, 1 January 1917, Private letter, GLLD 9/9; Wilson, Yenbo to Wingate, 28 December 1916, FO882/6 HRG/16/93 (Bray's comments attached).

123 Arab Bureau to DMI, London, 17 January 1917, A.B.621 WO33/905, No. 6538.

124 Lloyd, Jiddah to Wingate, Cairo, 1 January 1917, Private letter, GLLD 9/9. See also McMahon to Hardinge, 10 November 1916, Hardinge MSS, Vol. VI, #27, fos 56–7; 'The Sherif's 'Coronation', *The Arab Bulletin*, No. 33, 4 December 1916, p. 508.

125 Lloyd, Jiddah to Wingate, Cairo, 1 January 1917, Private letter, GLLD 9/9.

126 Lloyd to Clayton, 7 February 1917, Private letter, GLLD 9/9.

127 Lloyd, Jiddah to Wingate, Cairo, 1 January 1917, Private letter, GLLD 9/9.

128 As far as the provisions of the Sykes–Picot Agreement enforced this division of Ottoman assets, British indulgence of a French Syria would ensure the establishment of a British bank – and leave Great Britain 'the predominant political influence in the Hejaz'. Lloyd to Clayton, 7 February 1917, Private, GLLD 9/9. See also FO, London to Wingate, 10 March 1917, GLLD 9/9; Wingate to FO, 21 March 1917, GLLD 9/9.

129 See below, Lloyd to Lynden-Bell, 7 March 1917, GLLD 9/9.

130 Imperial pragmatism could still not remedy the awkwardness for British representatives on the ground when challenged on conflicting promises for the peace. Lawrence recalled a meeting with Nuri Shaalan, most likely in June 1917. Nuri held up a file of correspondence from the British offering terms for an alliance, 'asking in puzzlement which of them all he might believe', to which Lawrence could only reply, 'The last in date'. Lawrence, *Seven Pillars*, pp. 572–3.

131 Robertson to Murray, 2 March 1917, No. 30326, cipher, WO33/905, No. 6847.

132 See also Report, Vickery to Arab Bureau, 1 March 1917, FO686/6, Part I, fos 47–8.

133 Memorandum, Clayton, 8 March 1917, FO686/6, Part I, fo. 46. Copies to Wingate, Wilson and (now Captain) Lawrence, who probably saw his copy after returning to Wejh in mid-April.

134 The War Cabinet and Egyptforce were gauging their ability to resist French interference; for discussions on how they might limit French demands for military authority in Gaza and Palestine, see Robertson to Murray, 12 April 1917, No. 32531, cipher, WO33/905, No. 7121; Murray to Robertson, 13 April 1917, A.M.1799 WO33/905, No. 7135. Sykes contributed, as well; see Murray to Robertson, 14 April 1917, A.M.1813 WO33/905, No. 7149.

135 'Minute by Brigadier Clayton', 'Plans of Emir Feisal', Clayton, 29 May 1917, FO882/6 HRG17/44, fo. 388, in response to Wilson, 'Note on the proposed Military Plan of Operations of the Arab Armies', 1 May 1917, FO882/6 HRG/17/36, fos

351–2, and 'Note by S.F. Newcombe, D.S.O.', 24 May 1917, GLLD 9/9. Clayton also framed Aqaba in terms of Egypt's security in a private letter to Lloyd in late December 1916:

> Key hope is that, even now, Akaba may be seized upon by both sides as a compromise which will save their respective dignities and that, thus, the real key may be inserted and the lock turned./Twist 'Alexandretta' [Cairo's earlier strategy] and turn 'Akaba'. These two names will be engraved on my heart.
>
> Clayton to Lloyd, 28 December 1916, GLLD 9/8.

136 Murray to Robertson, 14 February 1917, WO33/905, No. 6726. Murray to Robertson, 15 February 1917, WO33/905, No. 6735.
137 Murray to Robertson, 6 March 1917, A.M.1668 WO33/905. Wingate saw Murray's telegram to the CIGS and concurred. Wingate to Robertson, 6 March 1917, A.B.896 WO33/905, No. 6884.
138 'It was an unprecedented manoeuvre, and if we [Abdullah's force at Wadi Ais] gained ten days to get in place, and they then attempted anything so silly, we should have a chance of destroying them all.' See Lawrence, *Seven Pillars*, pp. 182–3.
139 Lawrence, *Seven Pillars*, p. 182. Lawrence may also have emphasized the wisdom of winning Murray's gratitude at this stage, for the latter was now in a position to help or hinder the Arab forces' intentions in Syria. The British authorities in Egypt had decided on 21 February 1917 that Murray's eventual advance into Palestine would require his exercising full control over any operations by Arab fighters acting on his right flank, i.e. from Aqaba and Maan northwards, and the Syrian interior; such as these operations could be envisioned by Egyptforce. Wingate's Hejaz sphere was now officially capped at the territory surrounding Tebuk. See Wilson, *Lawrence*, pp. 373, 379.
140 'Visit to Sherif Abdullah', 'Report by Captain Lawrence', Lawrence, Wejh to Wilson, 16 April 1917, FO882/6 HRG/17/29.
141 Wingate to Robertson, 21 March 1917, A.B.065 WO33/905, No. 6976.
142 Wingate to GOC, Force 'D', Basra, 20 March 1917, A.B.050 WO33/905, No. 6968.
143 Wingate to Robertson, 21 March 1917, A.B.065 WO33/905, No. 6976.
144 Ibid., 12 March 1917, A.M.1862 WO33/905, No. 6921 Wemyss, confident of the Arab armies' momentum at this stage, was organizing water supply for the Flight and future operations in the north from a distilling ship outside Wejh. He reported that if Medina fell, 'as seems probable', the impact on the tribes in eastern Syria would be immediate, thus 'arrangements are being made to gain their support and to supply them through Wej [*sic*] so that serious pressure may be put on the Turks behind their positions in Palestine'. Wemyss to Admiralty, 16 March 1917, ADM137/594 M03969/17 SA 561. For more on the naval support of Wejh, see Wemyss to Admiralty, 27 April 1917, ADM137/594 M05745/17 SA 555, No. 538/1139.
145 The strength of the Turkish force in the Hejaz was now calculated to be the following: for infantry: the 42nd, 55th and 130th Regiments with three battalions each, and the 129th and the 131st Regiments with one battalion each, totalling 7,000 rifles; for camelry: two regular and three irregular corps, totalling 700 rifles; station companies at Tebuk and Medain Salih, totalling 500 rifles; the Mohafzia (L. of C.), totalling 1,500 rifles; three field companies of engineers, totalling 600 rifles; resulting in 10,300 enemy rifles in all. There were also five mountain-gun batteries numbering twenty guns, two field guns and twenty machine guns. Turkish air power consisted of six to eight planes, of which only half were probably functioning. There was also a wireless telegraph detachment. *The Arab Bulletin*, No. 46, 30 March 1917, pp. 144–5.
146 For more on the commander at Tebuk and other intelligence returns regarding on large horse cavalry unit there. *The Arab Bulletin*, No. 46, 30 March 1917, 145; No. 48, 21 April 1917, p. 178.
147 *The Arab Bulletin*, No. 45, 23 March 1917, p. 125.

148 Ibid., No. 48, 21 April 1917, pp. 177–8.
149 Bir Aar, five miles south of Bir Derwish, was reported evacuated around 14 March 1917, probably on the basis of Imint which was active in the area. Wingate to CIGS, 15 March 1917, A.B.997 WO33/905, No. 6941.
150 Wingate to CIGS, 20 March 1917, A.B.052 WO33/905, No. 6969. Wingate to CIGS, 21 March 1917, A.B.065 WO33/905, No. 6976. Zeid's force now numbered 4,000 men, armed with three guns and six maxims manned by Syrian gunners. *The Arab Bulletin*, No. 45, 23 March 1917, p. 125.
151 Ibid., 23 March 1917, A.B.086 WO33/905, No. 6984. *The Arab Bulletin*, No. 46, 30 March 1917, p. 153; No. 47, 11 April 1917, p. 162.
152 *The Arab Bulletin*, No. 46, 30 March 1917, p. 153.
153 Ibid., No. 47, 11 April 1917, p. 162.
154 DMI, London to GHQ, Egypt, 23 April 1917, No. 33276, cipher, WO33/905, No. 7209.
155 *The Arab Bulletin*, No. 49, 30 April 1917, p. 193. On the basis of this intelligence, Wemyss informed the Admiralty that the Turkish garrison was running out of food and ammunition, and barring a new source of supply he 'is likely to surrender'. Wemyss to Admiralty, 27 April 1917, ADM137/594 M05745/17 SA 555, No. 538/1139.

6 An unauthorized policy triumph: intelligence and Aqaba, February–July 1917

1 Wingate to WO, London, 5 February 1917 [tel. no. missing], WO33/905, No. 6666A.
2 Newcombe to Wilson, 4 February 1917, in Wilson to Hogarth, Director, Arab Bureau, 8 February 1917, GLLD 9/9. Brémond met with Feisal and Newcombe on 30 January 1917.
3 Murray to Robertson, 5 February 1917, A.M.1571 WO33/905, No. 6666B. George Lloyd and the DMO in London admired Murray's imperturbability with Brémond. See Lloyd [to Lynden-Bell,] 28 February 1917, GLLD 9/9.
4 Lawrence, *Seven Pillars*, p. 173.
5 Ibid., p. 233.
6 For more on Lawrence's discussions with Feisal, and friction with Brémond, see Lawrence, *Seven Pillars*, pp. 173, 332, 572, 681.
7 Ibid., p. 179.
8 'Situation in Wedj', Joyce to Wilson, 1 April 1917, FO882/6 HRG/17/22, fo. 227.
9 *The Arab Bulletin*, No. 47, 11 April 1917, pp. 162–3. Wingate to Robertson, 12 April 1917 A.B.278 WO33/905, No. 7123.
10 'Note on Information received from Col. Newcombe dated 5th April [1917]', WO158/606/9A.
11 'Situation in Wedj', Joyce to Wilson, 1 April 1917, FO882/6 HRG/17/22, fo. 227.
12 Eight hundred Rualla tribesmen arrived at Wejh on 3 April. A personal representative of Nuri Shaalan was already present. A few sections of the Billi and Beni Atiyeh remained independent. 'Situation at Wedj', Joyce to Wilson, 1 April 1917, FO882/6 HRG/17/22, fo. 227. Joyce to Director, Arab Bureau, 9 April 1917, FO686/6, Part.I, fo. 161. Wilson to Arbur, 6 April 1917, W.797 WO158/606/6A. *The Arab Bulletin*, No. 47, 11 April 1917, p. 162; No. 148, p. 21 April 1917, p. 178. Arbur to Dirmilint, London, 9 April 1917, A.B.2522 WO158/606/7A. Leading Shammar sheikhs had also pledged loyalty to Abdullah. Wilson to Arbur, 4 April 1917, W.777 WO158/606/3A.
13 Wingate to Robertson, 11 April 1917, A.B.269 WO33/905, No. 7116. Lloyd had praised the Druse to Wingate in early 1917 as being by 'far the best fighters in these areas' who, 'if encouraged with money and help[,] might be of value to operate above Nuri Shalaan [*sic*], and thus complete the chain to the north'. Significantly, he

noted at the time that he was 'not aware that we have had communications with them yet on this subject [...] but in view of our traditional protection of their interests and their devotion to England a good deal might possibl[y] be done'. Lloyd to Wingate, 1 January 1917, 'Private' GLLD 9/9.

14 Wingate to Robertson, 11 April 1917, A.B.269 WO33/905, No. 7116.

15

> I am waiting for your coming because I want to see you very much because I have many things to tell you. The destruction of the Railway [at Wadi Ais] is easy. Major Garland has arrived and we can send him for this purpose [i.e., in Lawrence's place].
>
> Prince Feisal to Lawrence, *c.*30 March 1917, FO686/6, Part.II, fo. 150.

16 Wingate to CIGS, 11 April 1917, A.B.269 WO33/905, No. 7116.

17 *The Arab Bulletin*, No. 48, 21 April 1917, pp. 177–8; Wilson to Arbur, 9 April 1917 (rec. 10 April), W.814 WO158/606/8A. For more on Ali's 'frequent and urgent appeals' for air support of his Medina operations, see Joyce to Wilson, 7 May 1917, WO158/606/27. Activity against the Turks was equally lacklustre around Wadi Ais, although Abdullah reported that he was cutting the railway there every night. *The Arab Bulletin*, No. 49, 30 April 1917, p. 194. Newcombe had complained two months earlier that Abdullah was doing nothing against the railway and did not even know that Feisal had taken Wejh: '[he] is apparently waiting for Feisal to do something before he will begin operations himself'. Newcombe to Wilson, 4 February 1917, GLLD 9/9.

18 Rail track and telegraph lines were destroyed near Dar el-Hamra, and prisoners taken. Wingate to Robertson, 3 April 1917, A.B.193 WO33/905, No. 7054. Abu Na'am station and its train were severely damaged, and forty Turks killed. Wingate to Robertson, 4 April 1917, A.B.205 WO33/905, No. 7065. Track north of Medain Salih and a culvert at Abu Taka were demolished. Wingate to Robertson, 1 April 1917, A.B.266 WO33/905, No. 7115. A bridge near Wadi Hamdh was destroyed, and a large-scale attack undertaken against the Muadhdham-Dar el-Hamra section of railway, in part to impress the local Fuqara tribe. The attack failed to shift the 200 Turks at Muadhdham station. Intelligence from PoWs suggested that two-thirds of the 300 infantry at Medain Salih were Syrians. El Ula was apparently held by five hundred Turks and Syrians, camel and cavalry units. Tebuk's entire composite force numbered around 5,000 soldiers. Wingate to Robertson, 12 April 1917, A.B.278 WO33/905, No. 7123. *The Arab Bulletin*, No. 47, 11 April 1917, pp. 161–2; No. 48, 21 April 1917, p. 178; No. 49, 30 April 1917, pp. 193–4.

19 *The Arab Bulletin*, No. 56, 9 July 1917, pp. 302–3. Extra track for a possible rail extension was also at Tebuk. See *The Arab Bulletin*, No. 49, 30 April 1917, p. 195.

20 Ibid., No. 49, 30 April 1917, pp. 193–4.

21 Precise details on the demolitions such as the number of hours taken to repair each of the breaks were obtained through a 'sure source', which was almost certainly Sigint. A Turkish relief train from the north managed to reach Muadhdham, demonstrating the raids' failure. *The Arab Bulletin*, No. 49, 30 April 1917, pp. 193–4. Wingate to CIGS, 15 April 1917 A.B.291 WO33/905, No. 7158. Arab Bureau to DMI, 16 April 1917, A.B.295 WO33/905, No. 7171. Wingate to Robertson, 20 April 1917, A.B.325 WO33/905, No. 7189. Wingate to Robertson, 28 April 1917, A.B.376 WO33/905, No. 7253.

22 *The Arab Bulletin*, No. 51, 23 May 1917, p. 242. Newcombe remained with his Bedouin party until late May when he travelled to Jiddah and Cairo. *The Arab Bulletin*, No. 52, 31 May 1917, p. 251.

23 Newcombe was also annoyed at being 'asked to be patient with the Bedouin, and not to punish or be severe with Bisha or Hadtheil, but merely give more "buchshish"'. Report, Newcombe, 4 May 1917, FO686/6 Part II, fos 80–1.

24 *The Arab Bulletin*, No. 52, 31 May 1917, pp. 253–4.
25 Ibid., No. 53, 14 June 1917, pp. 266–7.
26 Lawrence, *Seven Pillars*, pp. 186–7.
27 Ibid., p. 232.
28 See Clayton to Wingate, 20 November 1916, Private letter, Sudan Archive, W/143/6/3.
29 For Bray's strong objections to abandoning the strategic priority of taking Medina and his continuing resentment after the war of Lawrence's influence in promoting a northern campaign, see Bray, *Shifting Sands*, pp. 138–49.
30 Lawrence, *Seven Pillars*, p. 232.
31 Lawrence, 'Wejh to Wadi Ais and back', *The Arab Bulletin*, No. 51, 23 May 1917, p. 40. See also pp. 232–42, and *The Arab Bulletin*, No. 52, 31 May 1917, p. 260. These reports foreshadowed Lawrence's 'Twenty-Seven Articles', a crystallization of 'commandments' for British officers working with the Bedouin which the Arab Bureau published three months later in their Bulletin. Lawrence's central argument was that the British could wield greater influence in Arab circles by practising cultural respect, tolerance and subtlety instead of arrogantly expecting obedience – and resorting to punitive measures when these failed. Lawrence, 'Twenty-Seven Articles', *The Arab Bulletin*, No. 60, 20 August 1917, pp. 347–53. Lawrence also submitted a detailed topographical report on his journey to Abu Markha that confirmed information from Major Ross's (RFC) sketches from the air, and contributed to revisions of the Survey of Egypt map of Wejh. See *The Arab Bulletin*, No. 52, 31 May 1917, p. 260.
32 *The Arab Bulletin*, No. 51, 23 May 1917, p. 242.
33 Lawrence, *Seven Pillars*, pp. 228–33.
34 Wemyss to Admiralty, 27 April 1917, ADM137/594 M05745/17 SA 555, No. 538/1139. *The Arab Bulletin*, No. 49, 30 April 1917, p. 193. Murray to Robertson, 28 April 1917, A.M.1852 WO33/905, No. 7249.
35 Lawrence interviewed nine prisoners, and found that one Turkish regiment was rumoured to be at Ma'an. Intelligence Note by Lawrence, in Wilson to Director, Arab Bureau, 29 April 1917, FO686/6 Part II, fos 88–9.
36 Lawrence, *Seven Pillars*, p. 233.
37 'Wilson, Proposed Military Plan of Operations of the Arab Armies', 1 May 1917, FO882/6 HRG/17/36, fo. 351. See also 'Note by Colonel Newcombe, DSO', 24 May 1917, Sudan Archive, W/145/7/37.
38 The diplomatic party originally included two British and two French Assistant Political Officers, a 'representative' of 'the King of the Hejaz', nine Arab liaison officers, ten interpreters, and four or five similarly nominal Arab delegates. Robertson to Murray, 2 March 1917, No. 30326, cipher, WO33/905, No. 6847. See also Lloyd to Wingate, 28 February 1917, GLLD 9/9. Sykes suggested that Lloyd might also attend as liaison officer from Intelligence, GHQ, Egypt. Macdonogh to Lynden-Bell, 26 March 1917, No. 31664, cipher, WO33/905, No. 7001.
39 Lloyd to Lynden-Bell, 28 February 1917, GLLD 9/9.
40 Lloyd, London to Lynden-Bell, 7 March 1917, GLLD 9/9.
41 fforde to Grant, 28 March 1917, Item #9, D.O. No. 71, W/C R/20/A/1570 IOLR. Egyptforce and the War Committee privately intended to curb all French interference once British troops crossed into Palestine. See Robertson to Murray, 12 April 1917, No. 32531, cipher, WO33/905, No. 7121. Murray to Robertson, 14 April 1917, A.M.1813 WO33/905, No. 7149. Murray to Robertson, 13 April 1917, A.M.1799 WO33/905, No. 7135.
42 Wilson also agreed with the view that 'the class of Indian Moslem whose opinion was of importance' would only accept the Sherif's action against Turkey if he replaced the Turkish Caliphate with an Arab one and became 'Protector of Islam'. Wilson to Clayton, 'Secret', 21 March 1917, FO882/12 KH/17/8, fos 197–9.

43 Egyptforce had only recently been encouraged by Sigint (26 March 1917) suggesting that the 53rd Turkish Division's defence was flagging: 'Enemy blew up his wireless station and reported to Von Kress that he must surrender.' Murray to Robertson, 1 April 1917, A.M.1751 WO33/905, No. 7040.
44 Sykes, Jiddah to Foreign Office, London, 6 May 1917, in FO to Wingate, 8 May 1917, No. 496, Sudan Archive, Box 145/7/95.
45 Sykes wrote these remarks after meeting three Arab delegates in Cairo who had formed a committee of investigation regarding Arab and Syrian desiderata. Sykes to FO, London, 30 April 1917, tel. 21, FO882/16 SP/17/23, fo. 90.
46 Wilson to Clayton, 24 May 1917, Letter, GLLD 9/9, p. 7. Some British were prepared to see Picot as representing at least a less aggressively imperial French foreign policy than Brémond, and thus more likely to accommodate Britain's policy position for Arabia and Syria. Lloyd, London, to Lyden-Bell, 28 February 1917, GLLD 9/9.
47 Wilson to Clayton, 24 May 1917, Letter, GLLD 9/9, pp. 1–2.
48 Feisal had told Wilson that once he appeared 'on the railway near Hama, a general revolt will break out'. Wilson, 'Proposed Military Plan', 1 May 1917, FO882/6 HRG/17/36, fos 350–2.
49 'Note of a Meeting at the Residency, Cairo, on 12th May 1917', Sudan Archive, W/145/6/61–63. Lloyd to CGS [Lynden-Bell], 12 May 1917, GLLD 9/9.
50 As Newcombe reported, Sykes and Picot made no verbatim record of any of these exchanges. Wilson, Newcombe, Fuad, Sykes and Picot submitted recollections afterwards. Note by Newcombe, in Wilson to Clayton, 24 May 1917, Letter, GLLD 9/9.
51 Wilson expanded on the two points' irreconcilability with other statements made to the Arabs. Wilson to Clayton, 24 May 1917, Letter, GLLD 9/9.
52 'Secret. Note by Sheikh Fuad el Khatib taken down by Lt Col Newcombe', in Wilson to Clayton, 24 May 1917, Letter, GLLD 9/9.
53 Neither Fuad nor Wilson questioned the existence of McMahon's alleged letter to the Sherif. Wilson to Clayton, 24 May 1917, Letter, GLLD 9/9, p. 6.
54 Wilson to Clayton, 24 May 1917, Letter, GLLD 9/9, pp. 7–8.
55 Lawrence, Wejh to Wilson, 16 April 1917, in Brown (ed.), *Letters*, 108. Lawrence later testified to Wilson's personal integrity by recalling Abdullah's view that 'he knew we [the British] were sincere, since otherwise we would not be represented at Jeddah by Colonel Wilson'. In contrast to Lawrence's own willingness under pressure to

> fall back on artifice [...] Wilson never told even a half-truth. If instructed to inform the [Sherif] diplomatically that the subsidy of the month could not at present be increased, he would ring up Mecca and say, 'Lord, Lord, there is no more money'.
> Lawrence, *Seven Pillars*, p. 221.

56 Wilson to Clayton, 24 May 1917, Letter, GLLD 9/9, p. 11
57 'Secret. Note by Sheikh Fuad el Khatib', in Wilson to Clayton, 24 May 1917, Letter, GLLD 9/9.
58 The passages marked by Newcombe as his own ideas are italicized. Note by Newcombe, in Wilson to Clayton, 24 May 1917, Letter, GLLD 9/9.
59 Note by Newcombe, in Wilson to Clayton, 24 May 1917, Letter, GLLD 9/9.
60 Murray to Robertson, 5 June 1917, I.B.1727 WO33/935, No. 7527 (includes reference to telegram from Wingate to FO, London, M.583).
61 In late July, the Sherif was still boasting to Lawrence that he had felt 'pleased to have trapped M. Picot' into only a temporary military occupation of the country. He believed the French had renounced all ideas 'of annexation, permanent occupation, or suzerainty of any part of Syria', and declared:

> I will neither take them myself nor permit anyone else to take them [...] the Hedjaz and Syria are like the palm and fingers of one hand, and I could not

have consented to the amputation of any finger or part of a finger without leaving myself a cripple.

Lawrence, Jiddah to Wilson, 30 July 1917, in Brown (ed.), *Letters*, p. 112.

Despite the Sherif's famous political shrewdness, no contemporary suggestion is made that his position was a ruse intended to tie British interests to his own inveiglement.

62 *The Arab Bulletin*, No. 52, 31 May 1917, pp. 251–3. PoWs, probably from Newcombe's recent expedition, claimed that food shortages were fuelling Arab and Turkish desertions. *The Arab Bulletin*, No. 51, 23 May 1917, p. 243. Wilson reviewed 'all recent information' and agreed that Fakhri Pasha was the moving force. See Report, Wilson to Clayton, 20–25 May 1917, 'Secret', GLLD 9/9, p. 3. *The Arab Bulletin*, No. 53, 14 June 1917, p. 266.
63 *The Arab Bulletin*, No. 52, 31 May 1917, pp. 251–3.
64 PoWs reported an aerodrome at Medain Salih, but not planes or artillery. *The Arab Bulletin*, No. 49, 30 April 1917, p. 195. PoWs stated that many train engines on the Medina section were damaged. *The Arab Bulletin*, No. 50, 11 May 1917, p. 226.
65 *The Arab Bulletin*, No. 56, 9 July 1917, pp. 302–3.
66 Hogarth, 'A Year of Revolt', *The Arab Bulletin*, No. 52, 31 May 1917, pp. 249–50.
67 For the rejection of a proposal to return the RFC Flight to Yenbo with an advance base at Bir Abbas and landing ground near Bir el-Mashi, to stiffen Ali's army, see Joyce to Wilson, 7 May 1917, WO158/606/27. (Brigadier-General) W. Salmond, Commanding Middle East Brigade, RFC, 26 May 1917, WO158/606/35A. Wilson to Clayton, 20–25 May 1917, 'Secret', GLLD 9/9. *The Arab Bulletin*, No. 52, 31 May 1917, p. 251; No. 53, 14 June 1917, p. 265. Lawrence, *Seven Pillars*, p. 350.
68 The Egyptian detachment still had to camp one and half miles away, but was otherwise 'all in good order'. *The Arab Bulletin*, No. 54, 22 June 1917, pp. 275–6. See also No. 53, 14 June 1917, p. 266. Ironically, in July 1918, Joyce would object to Lawrence's suggestion to bring a British camel corps contingent to assist the Arabs' operations against Deraa, because to 'introduce foreigners would unman the Arabs'. Lawrence, *Seven Pillars*, p. 556.
69 *The Arab Bulletin*, No. 52, 31 May 1917, p. 251.
70 Ibid., No. 50, 13 May 1917, p. 207; No. 51, 23 May 1917, p. 231; No. 52, 31 May 1917, p. 251.
71 Ibid., No. 53, 14 June 1917, p. 265.
72 Ibid., No. 54, 22 June 1917, pp. 277–8.
73 Several testimonies from a range of human sources were analysed to assess this raid. See Wingate to Robertson, 13 June 1917, A.B.707 WO33/935, No. 7583. Wingate to Robertson, 26 June 1917, A.B.808 WO33/935, No. 7651. Wingate to Robertson, 29 June 1917. A.B.831 WO33/935, No. 7670. See also *The Arab Bulletin*, No. 53, 14 June 1917, p. 269; No. 54, 22 June 1917, p. 285; No. 55, 28 June 1917, p. 291; No. 56, 9 July 1917, p. 299; No. 57, 24 July 1917, p. 316. Ibn Rashid's involvement was confirmed in July by captured correspondence from a Turkish mail delivery, in which Sherif Haidar and Enver Pasha offered him their congratulations. *The Arab Bulletin*, No. 56, 9 July 1917, p. 302. Wingate to Robertson, 15 June 1917, A.B.724 WO33/935, No. 7589. Wingate to Robertson, 26 June 1917, A.B.808 WO33/935, No. 7651. Wingate to Robertson, 29 June 1917, A.B.831 WO33/935, No. 7670.
74 The Arab Bureau confirmed the Abdah's new allegiance after reading (under unexplained conditions) a letter from Abdullah to his father. *The Arab Bulletin*, No. 51, 23 May 1917, p. 231; No. 56, 9 July 1917, p. 303; No. 57, 24 July 1917, p. 313.
75 Ibid., No. 51, 23 May 1917, p. 231.
76 Ibid., No. 52, 31 May 1917, p. 251.
77 Ibid., pp. 252–3.
78 Ibid., No. 50, 11 May 1917, p. 226.
79 Ibid., No. 52, 31 May 1917, p. 253. An earlier report suggested that the Huweitat

were already demonstrating their sympathies by fighting against two sections of the Beni Atiyah who had not yet joined the Sherif. *The Arab Bulletin*, No. 50, 11 May 1917, p. 207.

80 Intelligence supplied on 22 May 1917. Macdonogh to Murray, 27 May 1917, 35219, cipher, WO33/935, No. 7477.

81 Newcombe, 'Note', 24 May 1917, in Wilson to Clayton, 20–25 May 1917, 'Secret', GLLD 9/9.

82 Raising another gust into this fog of cross-purposes, Brémond's continuing but unsuccessful attempts to dominate Feisal gave rise to more rumours that the French were on the brink of landing troops (60,000) in Syria. 'Note on Information received from Col. Newcombe dated 5 April [1917]', WO 158/606/9A, fo. 2.

83 Antonius, *Arab Awakening*, pp. 225–6.

84 Clayton also pointed out that Feisal's force numbers for Aqaba did not provide adequate protection against counter-attack. Minute by Clayton, attached to 'Plans of Emir Feisal', to Wingate, 29 May 1917, FO882/6 HRG/17/44, fo. 388. Clayton told Wilson the proposal was 'impracticable' because it would be impossible to establish a line communication between Aqaba and el Arish via Auja and Tafileh, as was suggested. There were also 'grave disadvantages' to taking Aqaba itself. He suggested that Newcombe accompany a small Arab party to Jebel Druse instead to study the situation instead, noting that 'if they did not want him, they would merely send him away'. Tellingly, Clayton advised Wilson that in his communications with London, 'it is essential to keep the despatch on purely military, and very general lines. No politics should be touched upon as they are a matter for the Foreign Office'. Clayton to Wilson, 29 May 1917, FO882/6 HRG/17/73, fos 380–4.

85 *The Arab Bulletin*, No. 54, 22 June 1917, p. 278

86 These Huweitat sections were either Ibn Jazi or Dhumaniyah. *The Arab Bulletin*, No. 53, 14 June 1917, p. 271. See also W.T. Massey, *The Desert Campaigns*, London: Constable & Co., 1918, p. 17.

87 *The Arab Bulletin*, No. 55, 28 June 1917, pp. 290–1. Wemyss to Admiralty, 26 June 1917, ADM137/594 M08368/17 SA 548, No. 855/1139.

88 Lawrence, *Seven Pillars*, p. 281.

89 'Secret ... Lawrence's journey'. Sudan Archive, Box 694/5/26–7. *The Arab Bulletin*, No. 59, 12 August 1917, pp. 336–7. Lawrence, *Seven Pillars*, p. 270.

90 *The Arab Bulletin*, No. 59, 12 August 1917, pp. 336–7. Lawrence, *Seven Pillars*, pp. 235, 241, 280–2. Clayton's notes after Lawrence's debriefing mentioned only that Nesib was 'volatile and shortsighted', that he had departed north 'with the instructions attached', that he would not carry these out 'exactly – but no other agent was available'. 'Secret ... Lawrence's journey'. Sudan Archive, Box 694/5/27.

91 'Secret ... Lawrence's journey'. Sudan Archive, Box 694/5/27. For more on the activities of al-Rikabi, see Tauber, *Arab Movements*, p. 116 *passim*.

92 This report begins: 'Attention is called to the necessity of keeping secret the names of the persons with whom Captain Lawrence had interviews.' 'Secret ... Lawrence's journey'. Sudan Archive, Box 694/5/26–7. Lawrence later gave the date of return as 16 June 1917. Lawrence, *Seven Pillars*, pp. 281–4. Although some historians have questioned the plausibility of this journey (see S. Mousa, 'Arab Sources on Lawrence of Arabia: New Evidence', *Army Quarterly and Defence Journal*, 136 (April 1986) 159), it could be argued that in its sheer audacity it is the more credible, reflecting Lawrence's increasing desperation that the larger expedition, lacking official sanction, was possibly doomed to failure. Lawrence's superiors considered the intelligence accumulated during this reconnaissance journey to be premium information, vital to future action in Syria, and therefore designated 'very secret' with regard to France. See Arab Bureau (Wingate) to Chief, London, 13 July 1917, A.B.959 FO141/668/4332/23. Robertson to Sir E.H.H. Allenby, 9 October 1917, No. 42857, WO33/935, No. 8348. Allenby to Robertson, 13 October 1917, I.A.4191

WO33/935, No. 8366). After Egyptforce failed to take Gaza, the War Cabinet replaced Murray as GOC-in-C, Egyptforce with General Sir Edmund Allenby in mid-June 1916. Secretary of State for War to Murray, 11 June 1917, A.B.C.1 WO33/935, No. 7561.

93 Herman, *Intelligence Power*, p. 170.

94 Lawrence, *Seven Pillars*, p. 292.

95 Their targets were Atwi (eighty miles north of Ma'an) and Minifir (140 miles north of Ma'an). 'Secret ... Lawrence's journey'. Sudan Archives, Box 694/5/27–8. Lawrence practised a two-phase demolition strategy during these raids: he used gelignite charges to blow up the rarer curved rails; when the repair locomotive arrived from the north, he blew it up too – using a Garland mine deploying three simultaneous charges. *The Arab Bulletin*, No. 57, 24 July 1917, p. 307; No. 59, 12 August 1917, pp. 336, 342–3 (later successes). Lawrence, *Seven Pillars*, pp. 290–302.

96 Lawrence, *Seven Pillars*, pp. 292, 302. Lawrence may have assumed the theft was a ruse when in fact it was genuine. Newcombe was in fact caught in a skirmish with Turkish patrols on the railway at Qaleat al Zumarrad. A Turkish officer, Ismet Karadoyan Bey, returned the papers to Newcombe after the war and the two men corresponded. See M. Brown (ed.), *Letters*, p. 102. In his report in late May 1917, Newcombe had named Tadmor as a good base for Feisal's operations against Homs and Hama. See Newcombe, 'Note', 24 May 1917, in Wilson to Clayton, 20–25 May 1917, GLLD 9/9. It is possible that this theft inspired Newcombe's colleague Richard Meinertzhagen's similar and more famous deception of 'the lost rucksack' with Egyptforce during the Palestine Campaign. British intelligence buttressed Meinertzhagen's phony documents with false, easily intercepted British wireless messages.

97 Lawrence's report, initially naming Nawaf, helped to rehabilitate the latter in Cairo's view. *The Arab Bulletin*, No. 59, 12 August 1917, pp. 336–7. A possible lag in information led 'Nawaf' to be corrected later to 'Trad', Nuri's nephew. See Lawrence, *Seven Pillars*, p. 302.

98 *The Arab Bulletin*, No. 56, 9 July 1917, p. 303.

99 Lawrence, *Seven Pillars*, pp. 295, 300.

100 'Secret ... Lawrence's journey'. Sudan Archive, Box 694/5/28. *The Arab Bulletin*, No. 57, 24 July 1917, pp. 307–8; No. 59, 12 August 1917, p. 336. Lawrence, *Seven Pillars*, pp. 304–5.

101 'Secret ... Lawrence's journey'. Sudan Archive, Box 694/5/28. *The Arab Bulletin*, No. 57, 24 July 1917, pp. 307–8; No. 59, 12 August 1917, p. 337. Lawrence, *Seven Pillars*, pp. 305, 313.

102 *The Arab Bulletin*, No. 59, 12 August 1917, p. 337. Wingate to Robertson, 10 July 1917, A.B.942 WO33/935, No. 7726. Lawrence, *Seven Pillars*, pp. 306–7, 313.

103 'Secret ... Lawrence's journey'. Sudan Archive, Box 694/5/28. *The Arab Bulletin*, No. 57, 24 July 1917, pp. 307–8; No. 59, 12 August 1917, pp. 337–8 (on the Huweitat's vengeance for Turks' execution of rebel leader from Kerak). Lawrence, *Seven Pillars*, pp. 312, 317.

104 'Secret ... Lawrence's journey'. Sudan Archive, Box 694/5/28. *The Arab Bulletin*, No. 57, 24 July 1917, p. 308; No. 59, 12 August 1917, p. 338. Lawrence, *Seven Pillars*, p. 313.

105 *The Arab Bulletin*, No. 56, 9 July 1917, p. 304.

106 Ibid., No. 57, 24 July 1917, p. 308; No. 59, 12 August 1917, pp. 338–9. Lawrence, *Seven Pillars*, pp. 313–16.

107 Wingate to Robertson, 10 July 1917, A.B.942 WO33/935, No. 7726. 'Secret ... Lawrence's journey'. Sudan Archive, Box 694/5/28. Wemyss to Admiralty, 19 July 1917, ADM137/594 M09657/17 SA 549, No. 980/1139. *The Arab Bulletin*, No. 57, 24 July 1917, p. 308; No. 59, 12 August 1917, pp. 338–9, 342.

108 Details such as the Turkish commander's name who was killed at Mreigha suggest a Sigint source. 'Intelligence', *The Arab Bulletin*, No. 56, 9 July 1917, pp. 298–9.

109 Feisal was preparing to attack el Ula within weeks. But recent intelligence, probably Sigint, suggested it was 'more than likely' that the Turks knew of these plans and were reinforcing el Ula. 'Intelligence', *The Arab Bulletin*, No. 56, 9 July 1917, p. 298. On 6 July, Feisal's force made a preliminary two-pronged attack against the railway, destroying 150 rails and over twenty telegraph poles. The RFC flew over el Ula on 12 July and bombed the station and water tanks, observing just under a thousand men and 200 mules at the base. *The Arab Bulletin*, No. 57, 24 July 1917, p. 307.

110 'The Northward Move', *The Arab Bulletin*, No. 56, 9 July 1917, p. 300. For intelligence on Turkish sabotage of wells along the northern Hejaz line, as well, see 'Lieut.-Colonel Newcombe's Report', *The Arab Bulletin*, No. 56, 9 July 1917, p. 300.

111 'The Northward Move', *The Arab Bulletin*, No. 56, 9 July 1917, p. 300.

112 'Intelligence', *The Arab Bulletin*, No. 57, 24 July 1917, p. 307. 'The Occupation of Aqaba', *The Arab Bulletin*, No. 59, 12 August 1917, p. 336. Arbur to Wilson and Bassett, Wejh, 12 July 1917, A.B.94B FO141/668/4332/22 (14 July 1917), item 3. Wingate to FO, London, 13 July 1917, 773. FO141/668/4332/22 (14 July 1917), item 1. Wingate described Lawrence's actions as a 'magnificent achievement – in my opinion one of the finest done during the whole war'. Wingate to Wilson, 15 July 1917, Sudan Archive, W/146/1/15. Only three weeks earlier, Wingate's report to the WO on the Hejaz operations' progress did not mention Lawrence. Wingate to WO, London, 25 June 1917, FO141/668/4332/20, fos 1–11.

113 Wingate to Robertson, 14 July 1917, WO33/935, No. 7746. Robertson had asked Wingate whether he recommended Lawrence for a reward. Robertson to Wingate, 12 July 1917, No. 37633, cipher, M.O. WO33/935, No. 7738. See also Arab Bureau (Wingate) to Dirmilint, London (?13 July 1917), A.B.943. Lawrence was not eligible for the Victoria Cross because no British officer witnessed his actions in northern Syria or at Aqaba. After Aqaba, Lawrence was promoted to major and recommended for the Companion of the Bath, which he refused to accept. In November 1917, he was awarded the *Croix de Guerre avec palme et citation à l'ordre de l'Armée* by the French Government, which he accepted, apparently as an ironic gesture, given his opposition to a French presence in Syria. In early 1918 Lawrence was recommended for the Distinguished Service Order for his role in the battle at Siel el Hesa outside Tafileh, but refused to accept it. In late 1918 he was awarded a knighthood in a private investiture with the King, but again refused – this time to the King's face. According to the king's private secretary, Lawrence said 'that he had pledged his word to Feisal, and that now the British Government were about to let down the Arabs under the Sykes–Picot Agreement. He was an Emir among the Arabs and intended to stick with them through thick and thin and, if necessary, fight against the French for the recovery of Syria. Colonel Lawrence said that he did not know that he had been gazetted or what the etiquette was in such matters, but he hoped that the King would forgive any want of courtesy on his part in not taking these decorations.' The King, by all accounts, did. See Wilson, *Lawrence*, p. 577, quoting from Sir A.J. Stamfordham to Lawrence, 17 January 1928, in *Letters to T.E. Lawrence*, p. 186. See also Wilson, *Lawrence*, pp. 424–5, 492, 1057–8, 1075.

114 Robertson to Allenby, 2 July 1917, No. 37086, cipher, M.O. WO33/935, No. 7687. Allenby to Robertson, 4 July 1917, E.A.24 WO33/935, No. 7702. Allenby to Robertson, 16 July 1917, E.A.61 WO33/935, No. 7767. For other communications deferring to Lawrence's judgement regarding the field, see: Wingate, memorandum, 20 July 1917, 14W, FO141/668/4332/24; Baghdad to Chief, London, 23 July 1917, X.2930, cipher, FO141/668/4332/25.

115 See Arab Bureau (Wingate) to Robertson, A.B.959, 13 July 1917, FO141/668/4332/23. Wingate to Wilson 15 July 1917, Sudan Archive, W/146/1/15. By January 1918, Lawrence was graded as Special Service officer, second grade, and by March 1918 he was promoted to the rank of lieutenant-colonel and upgraded

to Special Service officer, first grade. Until March 1918, Lawrence was subordinate to Leiutenant Colonel Joyce, Special Service officer, first grade, who was posted to Aqaba as commander of all British troops in the area of southern Syria, and de facto director of Arab operations in the field in tandem with Jaafer Pasha. Allenby to WO, tel. GS1001, 9 March 1918, WO95/4415.

116 Allenby to Robertson, 13 October 1917, I.A.4191 WO33/935, No. 8366, emphasis added.
117 Ibid., E.A.405 WO33/935, No. 8371, emphasis added.
118 Antonius, *Arab Awakening*, p. 225.
119 Lawrence, *Seven Pillars*, p. 60.
120 Allenby to Robertson, 9 October 1917, E.A.391 WO33/935, No. 3850.
121 The Arab forces in Syria would incorporate several British advisers and artillery officers, and at times work in conjunction with Allied forces such as Australian cavalry (under General Sir Henry G. Chauvel) and French artillery units (under Captain Pisani). Perhaps the single departure from the Arabs' irregular method of operations occurred in January 1918 when Lawrence, Zeid, Auda and other Arab leaders plotted an engagement at Tafileh which, while unfolding as an extended ambush, also followed conventional lines. For more on Lawrence's ambivalence regarding the battle at Tafileh, see Lawrence, *Seven Pillars*, pp. 485–92. For an excellent intelligence studies history on the Palestine Campaign, see Yigal Sheffy, *British Military Intelligence in the Palestine Campaign, 1914–1918*.
122 'Now an army may be likened to water, for just as flowing water avoids the heights and hastens to the lowlands, so an army avoids strength and strikes weakness.' Sun Tzu, *The Art of War*, p. 101.

Conclusion

1 'Irregular war is far more intellectual than a bayonet charge.' Lawrence, 'The Evolution of a Revolt', *Army Quarterly*, No. 1 (October 1920), in *Oriental Assembly*, A.W. Lawrence (ed.), Imperial War Museum (London, 1991; 1939), p. 131.
2 Lawrence, 'The Evolution of a Revolt', p. 117.
3 Herman, *Intelligence Power*, p. 147. Italics in text.
4 Statement by Parker, in Wingate to Clayton, 4 December 1915, tel. 863, FO882/2 AP/15/12.
5 Because pre-war intelligence services acted mainly as military planning staffs, they failed to anticipate 'large questions, such as [...] how new technology might change the character of the war,' as Ernest May has remarked; 'pre-1914 intelligence bureaus got little things right but big things wrong'. E.R. May, *Knowing One's Enemies: Intelligence Assessment before the Two World Wars*, pp. 504–5. Emphasis added.
6 Hogarth to the Viceroy (Chelmsford), 2 August 1916, D.O. No. 187 W/C Enclosure to item #51. R/20/A/1569 IOLR.
7 This phrase was used to describe a later variation on this model, the Clandestine Service of the CIA. *The 9/11 Commission Report: Final Report of the National Commission on Terrorist Attacks Upon the United States*, p. 90.
8 Lawrence, *Seven Pillars* (O), p. 5.
9 Ibid., 'The Evolution of a Revolt', p. 132.
10 '[I]t is critical that the intelligence community not advocate policy, especially not openly. If it does, it loses the most important basis for its credibility and its claims to objectivity. When the intelligence analysts critique one another's work, they use the phrase "policy prescriptive" as a pejorative, and rightly so'. Paul Pillar, 'Intelligence, Policy, and the War in Iraq'. Reprinted by permission of FOREIGN AFFAIRS, Vol. 85 (March/April 2006), p. 17. Copyright (2006) by the Council on Foreign Relations, Inc.
11 See discussion in Abram N. Shulsky, *Silent Warfare, Understanding the World of Intelligence*, New York: 1991, p. 137.

Bibliography

Archival sources

Public Record Office, London

Records of the Air Ministry

AIR 1/2284/209/75/8	Historical Branch Records: Series I, 1862–59
/2285/209/75/13	
/1706/204/123/64–5	

Records of the Admiralty

ADM 137/594	War of 1914–15: Historical Section Papers

Records of the Cabinet Office

CAB 14	Records of the Committee of Imperial Defence, 1904–39
CAB 17/7	Committee of Imperial Defence: Correspondence and Miscellaneous, 1902–18
CAB 27/1	War Cabinet and Cabinet: Misc. Committees; Records (General Series) to 1939 (British desiderata in Turkey in Asia, de Bunsen Committee)
CAB 41	Cabinet Office Memoranda
CAB 42/1	Papers and Minutes of the War Council, Dardanelles Committee and the War Committee
/2	
/16	
/23	
/24	
CAB 44/15	Historical Section Compilations: Committee of Imperial Defence, Historical Branch and Cabinet Office, Historical Section.

Records of the Foreign Office

FO 141/668	Embassy and Consular Archives, Egypt
/736	
/738	
/739	
FO 371/1812	General Correspondence, Political
/2139	
/2140	
/2468	
/2479	
/2482	
/2486	
/2681	
/2767	
/2768	
/2781	
FO 686/6	Embassy and Consular Archives, War of 1914–18.
/55	Jedda Agency, papers
FO 800/381	Private Collections, Ministers and Officials. Papers of Sir Arthur Nicolson
FO 882	War of 1914–18: Arab Bureau Papers
/2 ARB/15	Arab Bureau
/16	
AP/15	Arabian Policy
AP/16	
/3 HM/16	Hedjaz (Miscellaneous)
/3 HRG/16	Hedjaz Rising
/4 HRG/16	
/5 HRG/16	
/17	
/6 HRG/17	
/12 IND/16	India
/12 KH/17	King Hussein
/13 MES/15	Mesopotamia
/13 MES/16	
/15 PNA/15	Pan-Arabism
/16	
/16 SP/17	Sykes–Picot Mission
/18 TU/12	Turkey

Records of the War Office

WO 33/747	Reports and Miscellaneous Papers
/905	
/935	(European War: 'Egypt' Secret Telegrams)
WO 95/4415	War of 1914–18: War Diaries
WO157/694	War of 1914–18: Intelligence Summaries

/705	
/711	
WO 158/603	War of 1914–18: Papers of Military Headquarters
/604	
/606	
/616	
/627	
WO 159	Creedy Papers (Box 2, Misc.)

Imperial War Museum, London

Papers of Gerard I.M. Clauson

80/47/1

/2

India Office Library and Records, London (Oriental and India Office Library)

L/P&S/10/576	Political and Secret Department. File 4744/1915, Part I: The war; Arabia, the Arab Bureau at Cairo, 1915–18
R/20/A/1569	Correspondence and Papers on the formation and work of the Arab Bureau in Cairo, 1916–17
MSS Eur E389	Papers of Charles Hardinge, 1st Baron of Penshurst (1858–1944)

Sudan Archive, Middle East Centre, University of Durham

Private and official correspondence of General Sir Francis Reginald Wingate

W/135/4

/6

W/137/7

W/138/3

W/143/1

W/143/2

/6

W/144/1

W/145/6

/7

W/146/1

Private and official correspondence of Brigadier General Sir Gilbert Falkingham Clayton

Box 693/12

Box 694/4

/5

Box 469/8
Box 470/6
/7
Box 473/2

Churchill Archives Centre, Churchill College, Cambridge

Papers of Charles Hardinge, 1st Baron of Penshurst
vols II–VII
Papers of Lord Lloyd of Dolobran
GLLD 9/1
9/8
9/9

Liddle Hart Centre for Military Archives, King's College London

Akaba Archive
1/3 H13 Akaba Papers of Pierce Joyce, miscellaneous papers on the Arabian war.

Published sources

Published primary sources

Bidwell, R. (ed.), *The Arab Bulletin*, vols I–III, Oxford: 1986.
Bourne, K. and Cameron Watt, D. (eds), *British Documents on Foreign Affairs: Reports and Papers from the Foreign Office Confidential Print, Series H, The First World War, 1914–1918. The Allied and Neutral Powers: Diplomacy and War Aims*, vols I–II, University Publications of America: 1989.
—— *Source Records of the Great War*, vols I–IV, USA: National Alumni, 1923.
Lawrence, T.E., *Military Report on the Sinai Peninsula*, Fordingbridge: 1990 (first published for restricted circulation by the War Office General Staff, Geographical Section, in 1914).
Lawrence, T.E. and Woolley, C.L., *The Wilderness of Zin*, Palestine Exploration Fund Annual, No. 3, 1914–15, Palestine Exploration Fund, London: 1914 (1936 reprint).
—— *Correspondence between Sir Henry McMahon ... and the Sherif of Mecca*, London: HMSO, 1939.
—— *Report of the Commission appointed by Act of Parliament to enquire into the Operations of War in Mesopotamia*, Cmd.8610, London: HMSO, 1916.
—— *The Military Correspondence of Field-Marshal Sir William Robertson* (Murray-Robertson Mss, British Library, Add 52461; LHCMA, Robertson Mss, 1/32/48) Army Records Society, vol. 5, London, 1989.
—— *The 9/11 Commission Report: Final Report of the National Commission on Terrorist Attacks Upon the United States*, New York: W.W. Norton & Company, 2004.

Secondary sources

Andrew, C., *Her Majesty's Secret Service: The Making of the British Intelligence Community*, New York: Viking Press, 1987.

Andrew, C. and Dilks, D. (eds), *The Missing Dimension: Government and Intelligence Communities in the Twentieth Century*, Illinois: University of Illinois Press, 1984.

Andrew, C. and Kanya-Forstner, *France Overseas: The Great War and the Climax of French Imperial Expansion*, London: Thames and Hudson, 1981.

Antonius, G., *Arab Awakening*, Beirut: Khayats, 1938.

Bray, N.N.E., *Shifting Sands*, London: Unicorn Press, 1934.

Brémond, E., *Le Hedjaz dans la Guerre Mondiale*, Paris: Payot, 1931.

Brown, M. (ed.), *The Letters of T.E. Lawrence*, New York: Oxford University Press, 1988.

Callwell, C.E., *Small Wars: A Tactical Textbook for Imperial Soldiers*, London: Presidio Press, 1990 (1st edn, 1896).

Davis, Paul K., *Ends and Means: The British Mesopotamian Campaign and Commission*, London: Associated University Presses, 1994.

Engle, A., *The Nili Spies*, London: Hogarth Press, 1959.

Ferris, J., *British Army and signals intelligence during the First World War*, London: Army Records Society, 1992.

Foot, M.R.D., *SOE: an outline history of the Special Operations Executive 1940–1946*, London: British Broadcasting Corporation, 1984.

Fromkin, D., *A Peace to End All Peace: Creating the Modern Middle East*, New York: Henry Holt & Co., 1989.

Garnett, D. (ed.), *The Selected Letters of T.E. Lawrence*, London: Jonathan Cape, 1938.

Gilbert, Martin, *First World War*, London: Weidenfeld and Nicolson, 1994.

Glubb, Sir J., *A Short History of the Arab Peoples*, New York: Dorset Press, 1969.

Handel, M., *War, Strategy and Intelligence*, London: Frank Cass, 1989.

Herman, M., *Intelligence Power in Peace and War*, Cambridge: Cambridge University Press, 1996.

Hitti, P., *The Near East in History: A 5000 year story*, New Jersey: D. Van Nostrand Co. Inc., 1961.

Kayali, H., *Arabs and Young Turks: Ottomanism, Arabism, and Islamism in the Ottoman Empire, 1908–1918*, Berkeley: University of California Press, 1997.

Kedourie, E., *England and the Middle East: The Destruction of the Ottoman Empire, 1914–1921*, Sussex: Harvester Press, 1978.

—— *In the Anglo-Arab Labyrinthe: The McMahon-Husayn Correspondence and its Interpretations*, London: Frank Cass, 2000.

Keegan, J., *The First World War*, London: Pimlico, 1999.

Kent, S., *Strategic Intelligence for American World Policy*, Connecticut: Archon, 1965.

Lares, J.-M., *T.E. Lawrence, La France et Les Francais*, Paris: Publications de la Sorbonne, Imprimerie nationale, 1980.

Lawrence, T.E., *Seven Pillars of Wisdom*, New York: Penguin, 1981.

—— *Seven Pillars of Wisdom* (1922 'Oxford text' version), London: J. and N. Wilson, 2004.

Liddell Hart, B.H., *Lawrence of Arabia*, New York: Da Capo, 1989 (reprint of original 1934 edition, *Colonel Lawrence: The Man Behind the Legend*, New York: Dodd, Mead & Co).

—— *'T.E. Lawrence' in Arabia and After*, London: Jonathan Cape, 1934.

Lieshout, R.H., *Without Making Elaborate Calculations for the Future: Great Britain and the Arab Question 1914–1916*, Netherlands: 1984 (published PhD dissertation).

MacLeod, R. (ed.), *Government and Expertise: Specialists, Administrators and Professionals, 1860–1919*, Cambridge: Cambridge University Press, 1996.

Massey, W.T., *The Desert Campaigns*, London: Constable & Co., 1918.

May, E.R. (ed.), *Knowing One's Enemies: Intelligence Assessment Before the Two World Wars*, Princeton: Princeton University Press, 1986

Monroe, E., *Britain's Moment in the Middle East, 1914–1956*, London: Chatto and Windus, 1964.

Mousa, S., 'Arab Sources on Lawrence of Arabia: New Evidence', *Army Quarterly and Defence Journal*, 136 (April, 1986).

Nevakivi, J., 'Lord Kitchener and the Partition of the Ottoman Empire, 1915–1916', in Bourne, K. and Watt, D.C. (eds), *Studies in International History*, London: 1967.

—— *Britain, France and the Arab Middle East*, London: Athlone Press, 1969.

Presland, J. (pseud., Gladys Skelton), *Deedes Bey*, London: Macmillan, 1942.

Popplewell, R., *Intelligence and imperial defence: British intelligence and the defence of the Indian Empire, 1904–192*, London: Frank Cass, 1995.

Richards, T., *The Imperial Archive: Knowledge and the Fantasy of Empire*, London: Verso, 1993.

Rothwell, V.H., *British war aims and peace diplomacy, 1914–1918*, Oxford: Clarendon Press, 1971.

Robertson, W.R., *Soldiers and Statesmen*, London: Cassell and Co., 1926.

Sheffy, Y., *British Military Intelligence in the Palestine Campaign, 1914–1918*, London: Frank Cass, 1998.

Shulsky, Abram N., *Silent Warfare, Understanding the World of Intelligence*, New York: Brassey's, 1991.

Steiner, Z., *Britain and the Origins of the First World War*, London: Macmillan, 1977.

Storrs, R.H.A., *Orientations*, London: Nicholson & Watson Ltd, 1945.

Tauber, E., *The Emergence of the Arab Movements*, London: Frank Cass, 1993.

—— *The Arab Movements in World War I*, London: Frank Cass, 1993.

Tzu, S., *The Art of War*, Oxford: Oxford University Press, 1963.

Trumpener, U., *Germany and the Ottoman Empire, 1914–1918*, Princeton: Princeton University Press, 1968.

Weldon, L.B., *'Hard Lying': Eastern Mediterranean, 1914–1919*, London: Herbert Jenkins, 1925.

Westrate, B., *The Arab Bureau: British Policy in the Middle East, 1916–1920*, University Park, Pennsylvania: Pennsylvania University Press, 1992.

Wilson, J.M.W., *Lawrence of Arabia*, New York: Atheneum, 1990.

Winstone, H.V.F. (ed.), *The Diaries of Parker Pasha: war in the desert 1914–18 told from the secret diaries of Colonel Alfred Chevallier Parker, nephew of Lord Kitchener and governor of Sinai*, London: Quartet, 1983.

Winstone, H.V.F., *The Illicit Adventure: the story of political and military intelligence in the Middle East from 1898 to 1926*, London: Jonathan Cape, 1982.

Articles

Lawrence, T.E., 'The Evolution of a Revolt', *Army Quarterly*, No. 1 (October 1920), contained in *Oriental Assembly*, Lawrence, A.W. (ed.), Imperial War Museum, London, 1991 (original print 1939).

Pillar, P.R., 'Intelligence, Policy, and the War In Iraq', *Foreign Affairs*, vol. 85, March/April 2006.

Unpublished theses

Scoville, S.A., 'British Logistical Support to the Hashemites of Hejaz: Ta'if to Ma'an 1916–1918', PhD dissertation, Los Angeles: University of California, 1982 (ref. DDJ82–12874).

Index

Lightning Source UK Ltd.
Milton Keynes UK
25 October 2009

145368UK00002B/2/P